Maria Jane (DE-601)345609085 MacIntosh

Two pictures

What we think of ourselves, and what the world thinks of us.

Maria Jane (DE-601)345609085 MacIntosh

Two pictures

What we think of ourselves, and what the world thinks of us.

ISBN/EAN: 9783741172779

Manufactured in Europe, USA, Canada, Australia, Japa

Cover: Foto ©Andreas Hilbeck / pixelio.de

Manufactured and distributed by brebook publishing software (www.brebook.com)

Maria Jane (DE-601)345609085 MacIntosh

Two pictures

TWO PICTURES;

OR,

WHAT WE THINK OF OURSELVES, AND WHAT THE WORLD THINKS OF US.

BY

M. J. McINTOSH,

AUTHOR OF "TWO LIVES; OR, TO SEEM AND TO BE;" "CHARMS AND COUNTER CHARMS," ETC., ETC.

"There is some soul of goodness in things evil,
Would men observingly distil it out."—SHAKSPEARE, *Hen. V.*

NEW YORK:
D. APPLETON AND COMPANY,
443 & 445 BROADWAY.
LONDON: 16 LITTLE BRITAIN.
1863.

Entered, according to Act of Congress, in the year 1862, by
D. APPLETON AND COMPANY,
In the Clerk's Office of the District Court of the United States for the Southern District of New York.

PREFACE.

THERE are some, it may be, to whom this book will be more a memory than an imagination—some, who may recognize in the child-hearted Commodore Moray—in his wisdom, free from one taint of guile, in his generous consideration for others, in his sensitiveness to every touch of honor, in his more than womanly tenderness, and his more than manly courage,—a feeble portraiture of one of whom it may indeed be said,

"None knew *him* but to love *him.*"

It has been suggested to the author that the discovery of one portrait may lead to the search for others; that in the *official* personages, at least, and more especially in those connected with the historical incident of the landing of our troops on the Mexican coast, the sketches, however imperfect, may be supposed to be sketches from life. Such a supposition would be unjust to all concerned, and, most of all, unjust to the author, who has simply availed herself of the *vraisemblance* communicated to a story by the working in of a historical fact, and who selected the fact in question mainly because the time of its occurrence, and the incident of the officer who first commanded the squadron having been withdrawn and another appointed in his stead before the landing was effected, harmonized with her plan.

The *incidents*, and with the one exception to which allusion has been made, the *characters* of the book are purely imaginary,—its *principles*, she trusts, will be recognized as universally and eternally true. It may, perhaps, be as well to say that the scheme of Hugh Moray, for the gradual elevation of those committed to his care, was suggested by her acquaintance with various experiments made by conscientious Southern masters, for the advantage of their slaves. The work was not only planned, but nearly completed, while there was peace in the land, and nothing seemed likely to interfere with the execution of designs so truly Christian. The delay in its publication has been the result of circumstances of no interest to any but the author.

NEW YORK, *March 25th*, 1863.

TWO PICTURES;

OR,

HOW WE SEE OURSELVES, AND HOW THE WORLD SEES US.

CHAPTER I.

> "Where'er we roam,
> Our first, best country ever is at home."—GOLDSMITH.

Home! Home! I have had many resting places in my not very long life—this is my nineteenth birthday,—but I have had, and can have but one home. For eight years, I have not seen it with the bodily eye, and yet, how vividly it stands before me at this moment! A month ago, I determined to make a picture of it. The picture, to which I have given all my leisure hours, is done;—here, in this record of thought and feeling, meant only for myself, I may say what I truly think, that it is well-done;—yet I am not satisfied.

There is the very beach on which I gathered shells with my faithful nurse,—my kind, devoted Charity. To the eastward, the blue waves are lifting their white foam-crests to the sun. Inland, I can distinguish amid the mass of verdure which marked the almost tropical luxuriance of St. Mary's Isle, the glistening leaves of the orange trees half concealing their snowy flowers and golden fruit, and the darker green of the old oaks, "the king of forests all," from whose giant boughs the long pendent moss suspends its floating drapery of silvery gray. Within the circle of those oaks, rises the home which sheltered my orphan childhood;—a building of wood, two stories in height, surrounded by a piazza, whose pillars, wreathed with roses, honeysuckles and woodbine, gave something of airy lightness to what would otherwise have been without ornament or grace.

So far, pencil and brush have done their part truly. The gnarled, misshapen trunk of that old oak, those great arms that seem to me now to be thrown out as in a grand despair,—they looked not thus in my childhood,—all, all are perfect. The very stains and streaks upon the weather-beaten walls of the house, have been faithfully retained in my memory and rendered here; but ah! I could not give the shimmer and the sheen as the sunlight flashed from the waves, and the leaves were stirred by the soft breath of heaven. And the sky!—I have spent hours on it in vain. Where could I find a blue so soft? What brush could give a touch so light as those white, gauzy clouds that floated along its surface?

One day I shall give this a companion picture. It shall be St. Mary's Isle as it appeared to me when the demon of the storm was abroad. Then, I could neither ramble through the woods, or over the flowery savannas, gay with pink anemones, crimson coral-plants, purple violets, and the yellow spires of the golden rod; nor could I stand upon the beach, while Charity gathered for me the smoothest and brightest of shells, musing with a child's simple wonder on the mysteries of that great and deep sea, with its ever-sounding voice. The voice I still heard on stormy days, as standing on a window seat in my uncle's library,

I looked out upon its wildly tossing waves; but its usual, deep-toned murmur became, then, a roar at which I trembled. I was called a fearless child, because at six years old I would ride my uncle's hunting horse whenever I was permitted, sitting in his large saddle as if it were a chair of state; or, I would lay my hand upon our great St. Bernard dog, regardless of his thunderous growl; but he would scarce have thought me brave, who had touched my cold hands, or felt my wild heart-beats, when the storm dashed the ocean spray against the window by which I stood, tossed the fruit and flowers from the orange trees, and catching the outstretched arms of the giant oaks, made them shiver in its grasp, or bowed their lofty heads to the earth.

I have heard that my uncle had been a gay man in his youth, and that afterward he had devoted himself to politics for a time, with extraordinary zeal. Long before my birth, both these phases of his life had passed away. I remember him first as a lonely man, rarely leaving his island home except on business connected with the sale of his crops, or the purchase of articles demanded by his large plantation. There was no doubt a history appended to this change,—a history which might account for the tinge of moroseness that marked his character as I knew him; but it remains an untold tale; at least, I never heard it.

There was nothing of the miser about my uncle. He had inherited a large property, which had been yearly increased by his judicious management. Whatever he did, was done with a free, he would have said, "with a *gentlemanly* spirit." The negro laborers on his plantation were as well, perhaps a little better, fed and clothed than others of the same class. St. Mary's was famed for its numerous deer, and scarcely less so for its master's hospitality to those who sought it for the pleasure of the chase, or for the enjoyment of its ocean breezes. Public and private charities found in him a generous contributor. But his principal outlay was for books. Few private libraries in our country, I have heard it said, could equal, in the number or value of their books, that plain, unadorned room, which was known by the name of "the study" in my Southern home. Yet, with all this expenditure, my uncle grew richer and richer, till Hugh Moray, of St. Mary's Isle, was talked of as one of the wealthiest men south of the Potomac.

Much that I have here said of my uncle I have recalled by an effort of memory, desiring to record for my own satisfaction those varied traits which make up the picture of the man. Children are more impressed by externals, and what occurs to me spontaneously when I think or speak of this guardian of my early life, is a man of medium height, with a vigorous, athletic form, curling hair of a dark brown mingled with gray, a forehead broad, straight, and somewhat low, eyes unusually grave and thoughtful, but flashing with a quick gleam of passion at slight provocation, a straight nose, and lips whose firm pressure seemed rigid as marble. Most vividly do I recall him, clad in a hunting suit of dark green cloth, the legs and thighs protected by leathern galligaskins,—as I think they were called,—a light cap upon his head, a powder flask, shot pouch, and small horn slung across his breast, mounting his horse amid the barkings and yelpings of his joyous hounds, to ride forth to the hunt; or sitting at dinner with his guests, shaming younger men by the neatness and good taste of his dress; or, as was more frequent still, spending nearly the whole day in his study, seated in a hard, straight-backed chair, completely absorbed in the book before him.

Uncle Hugh's only associate on the island was an old clergyman, Mr. Mortimer, who had been his tutor in his college days. Mr. Mortimer, having outlived his wife, and the children who had probably inherited her consumptive tendencies, had been persuaded, in his lonely old age, to occupy a cottage which his former pupil had caused to be built for him, at the distance of little more than a mile from his own home. Here he employed the last years of a well-spent life, in giving the instructions of a Christian pastor to the negroes on the plantation, and to the occasional visitors on the island. In the midst of one of the clumps of oak dotting the level green of the savanna, rose the plain, unpainted, barn-like building, which was the scene of these instructions. My uncle made a point of attending them every Sabbath morning, whether from respect to Mr. Mortimer, or interest in his sacred theme, I know not. How unlike any thing to be seen elsewhere were these Sabbath scenes at St. Mary's! On that day was brought out a heavy old family coach, which Charity assured me had been very handsome when my uncle purchased it on my father's marriage. Before I knew it, however, the *silver* ornaments showed too much of their copper base, and the paint was dull and scratched. It was still *the* coach, the only coach ever seen at St. Mary's, and I felt no little increase of dignity when, seated in it beside my uncle, I was drawn to church by two shaggy ponies, natives of the island, like myself. My uncle would have thought his beautiful saddle horses ruined by being put into harness.

A few benches in the church—I cannot call them pews—were reserved for us and our guests, seldom numbering more than eight or ten, and the rest of the building was filled, crowded with negroes. It was a gay sight—I think I was dimly conscious of its picturesque character even in my childhood—to see the negroes in their bright-colored holiday dresses, wending their way to the church, along the road and over the savanna, where the view was broken only here and there, at considerable intervals, by clumps of trees. The women especially added to the brightness of the picture, by the gay handkerchiefs wound around their heads, somewhat in the fashion of a turban. Mr. Mortimer, I am convinced, thought as much of these negroes, in his teachings, as of those among his hearers whose skin was colored like his own; perhaps he thought even more of them; yet my childish heart was often touched by his earnest, fervent prayers, and simple, tender lessons, as it has never been touched in richly ornamented churches, where the most artistic music pealed " through long drawn aisles and fretted vaults," and all the graces of popular oratory lent their charm to the ministrations of the pulpit.

The strongest passion of my Uncle Hugh's passionate nature—I have good reason to know it—was pride of family. I verily believe he would have rejected the largest estate, or the noblest place that could have been offered him, had it been necessary to its acceptance that he should cease to be a Moray, or as he would have said, *the* Moray; for he never himself forgot, and did not like others to forget, that though the name might be borne in other lands by some who had won proud titles to prefix to it, he was still *the* Moray—the eldest son of the eldest branch—the head of the house.

Whatever had been the disappointments or disgusts which had driven him at once from the social enjoyments and the political contests of life, they had probably prevented his marrying, and I think there could have been no greater proof of their power. I am convinced, for reasons which will appear in this narrative, that when Uncle Hugh's brow grew suddenly dark, when he checked my childish glee and sent me from the room in which he sat, he was goaded by the thought that the place which he had hoped would become the seat of a new dynasty of Morays, must descend to a girl, and would probably pass eventually, by her death or marriage, into some other family, and so lose all connection with the name he desired to perpetuate. Uncle Hugh would not probably have fondled any child very much; but to me he rarely spoke, except to blame or silence me. My birth had disappointed his most cherished desire. My father was his nephew, the son of his only brother, and he had adopted and educated him as his heir. With his ready consent, this highly prized heir married an orphan girl of good family, but without fortune. In little more than a year after this marriage, the war of 1812 with England began. The captain of a volunteer corps of cavalry, my father could not resign his position, because he foresaw that what had been hitherto a mere holiday show, was about to become a reality, full of danger to himself, and of heart-sickening dread to those who loved him. His company was called into action, and he died at its head. I was but a few days old when intelligence of his death was brought to his home. It was impossible to conceal it long from the poor young wife, whose senses had been quickened by anxiety. She suffered but one pang, sinking immediately into unconsciousness, and passing in that state from this world, to one in which there is neither parting nor death.

And so my life began—the life of a lonely orphan, left to the guardianship of one to whom its birth had brought only disappointment. Father! Mother! What sweet names! Even their lifeless miniatures—love tokens, not to their child, but to each other—look to me as no other faces have ever done. And yet, I was not all uncared for. Charity, the negress assigned to me as my nurse, took me to her warm heart, and taught me all my childhood knew of love. Mr. Mortimer had always a kind word for the orphan, and my uncle took care that my physical wants were supplied. He was careful that my dress should be such as became Miss Moray of St. Mary's, and that I was kept from associations which might communicate a tinge of vulgarity to the manners of his supposed heiress. And so, for several years, I had nature for my teacher, and Charity for her interpreter. And no bad interpreter she proved. I learned from her to believe that there was a soul in all things. When the night winds swept around the room in which I lay, she heard the soft footfalls of my father and mother, or felt the touch of their cloud garments, as they glided by her low couch, to stand beside the crib in which their baby slept. She caught their whispers in the soughing of the wind through the pine forest, and according to her, they breathed into my childish ears, through the convolutions of the sea shell, some faint echo of the angels' song, which, if they could succeed in giving it full expression, would draw my spirit upward to them in heaven.

It may be thought that these were unhealthy influences, and would have made a child of sickly fancies: they only made me more than ordinarily sensitive to all the aspects of nature, soothed and gladdened by her gentleness, awed, till, as I have already said, my hands grew cold and my heart beat tumultuously when she spoke in wrath. Of anything else but this mute, irresistible power, I had never experienced a sensation approaching to fear; for, though my uncle had chided or passed me coldly by, he had never punished, or even threatened me; and to all others Charity had taught me to think myself superior. Of my fearlessness of animals I gave an early proof.

"Put me up," I said, at six years old, to Gib, my uncle's somewhat elderly attendant, as he stood beside Black Prince, the hunting horse from which his master had just descended.

"I can't, missis; I 'feared for you," the old man answered, with a good-natured smile at my ambition.

"Put me up!" I repeated, stamping my foot in childish wrath.

"I 'feared, Miss 'Gusty," he replied again, glancing at his master, who had stopped in the piazza on hearing my tone of authority, and who was looking on with some appearance of interest.

"Put her on," he said to Gib, "and hold her in the saddle."

Gib obeyed.

"Let me go," I cried, struggling violently to release my dress from his grasp, regardless of his exhortations to be quiet, lest I should frighten the horse. At a sign from his master, he let the dress go, and only walked beside the well-trained horse, accustomed to obey his voice. I think I rose considerably that day in my uncle's estimation. Doubtless he sighed heavily, that one exhibiting so much of the genuine Moray character should be only a girl. Still, he began to entertain the idea that she deserved some culture, and that with proper training, she would reflect no disgrace upon her name.

I do not remember how my consent was won, but I soon found myself, for a part of every morning, the companion of Mr. Mortimer instead of Charity. My vanity may perhaps have been flattered at first by the exchange; but very soon, all personal considerations were lost in the excited curiosity, which made me willing to give much more time to my books than was demanded by my indulgent teacher. This new element of my life, important as it was, exercised no immediate influence on character. I remained what nature and my first teacher, Charity, had made me—shy, yet fearless to my equals or superiors, haughty to my inferiors, or to those whom I considered such, yet not ungenerous, if they submitted to my claims. Such I was when new threads began to weare themselves into the web of my destiny, giving to it at once a richer and a darker coloring.

But my pulses must throb less wildly before I can write of these; besides, I shall be wanted soon in the drawing room, to preside at the tea table, or to play polkas and waltzes, till my weary fingers sympathize with my aching head and heart. Either employment would need steadier nerves than such a retrospect would give me. So, farewell to the pictures conjured by memory! dim shadows of the past, farewell till another hour of freedom shall restore me to myself and to you. Alone! alone!—so distant and yet so near! Would that the wide world divided me from all I once loved! *Once* loved? Ah me!

CHAPTER II.

*"O Life! how pleasant is thy morning,
Young Fancy's rays the hills adorning!
Cold, pausing Caution's lessons scorning,
We frisk away."*—BURNS.

ONCE more I am alone. Enchantress! by whose power the past and the distant stand again visibly before us, wave thy wand, and transform this chill, bare room, and the brick-walled street on which it looks, into the leafy bowers, the open sky, the blue waters of my home; bid me lay aside the burdened heart and bitter consciousness of the woman, for the careless glee of the child; let me sit again on the floor of the dining room at St. Mary's, weaving chaplets of the orange flowers and jessamines gathered in my morning walk, while my uncle sits longer than usual over his wine, in compliment to a stranger guest. I was a curious child, listening, with an air that did not seem to listen, to conversations which would scarcely have been supposed to interest me, and puzzling over their meaning or no meaning, till I could win an explanation, sometimes from Charity, sometimes from time.

The gentleman who was dining with my uncle on the day to which I allude, was from Scotland. He had brought a letter of introduction from a friend of Mr. Moray, then in Europe. So far I had learned from Mr. Mortimer, who had shown me Scotland on the map, and had traced the course by which the visitor had reached St. Mary's Isle.

It may be that to after conversations with good Mr. Mortimer, who was present, I am indebted for engraving on my memory the very words and tones which, though they awakened my attention at the time, could scarcely have conveyed their full meaning to my childish apprehension. However this may be, my remembrance of the scene seems to me, at this moment, life-like. Again I stand within the pleasant, shaded dining room; before me is the table with its old-fashioned, tall wine glasses and decanters, finely cut and gilded,—the high-backed, dark mahogany chairs,—the stranger with his smiling face and *dégagé* manner, picking his nuts, and dropping them into his wine as he spoke,—my uncle, grave and earnest, kindling occasionally into warmer feeling.

"And so, Mr. Moray," said the stranger, "you are the only one of your name in America?"

"By no means; at least, there are hundreds of Murrays here, and it may be that the name was originally the same; but, so far as I know, I am the only one of the Scottish Morays in this country."

"It is a pity you lost the Scottish estate; it is a noble one."

"It was lost in a good cause; better lost than preserved at the expense of truth and loyalty. My birthright no man can take from me. Kings can do much, but even they cannot make another the Moray of Moray."

"And you will found here a new dynasty of Morays?"

"A short-lived dynasty—it ends with me; that child," pointing to me as I sat on the floor, busy with my flowers, "that *girl* is the only one left to bear my name, and take my place when I am gone."

"What! that little girl! You must marry her to a Moray."

"A thing more easily said than done; I must first find the Moray."

"Oh! there is no difficulty in that. Import one from Scotland. Such an estate as you have here, would make a nice provision for a younger son——"

"Of a younger son—doubtless; but I should like to go nearer the root in looking for an heir."

"Ah! I see you have a grudge against the family at home."

"It is not easy to forget that they came into possession through disloyalty to their king, and treachery to their chief; traits which I should not care to perpetuate or reward."

"And you are sure that no members of the family, except your grandfather, came here after the rising in '45?"

"My grandfather had a younger brother who, like him, came here with General Oglethorpe; but when the rumor of the last abortive attempt of Charles Edward reached this country, he returned home. It was useless to hope anything for a cause already dead; at least, so my grandfather thought. The brothers parted in coldness, and though the elder, when time had healed all irritation, sought again to open communication with the younger, the effort was unsuccessful, and we have heard nothing of him to this time."

"He may have had children and children's children," said the stranger, smiling.

"He may; but I have no means of ascertaining it," my uncle replied.

"Perhaps I may be in the way of making some discoveries for you. I shall travel pretty extensively through the United States, and having letters to the descendants of Scottish families in most of your large cities, it may be that

I shall hear of a Moray among them. I shall certainly inform you if I do. Come, little lady! what will you give me for a husband? I will not charge high—only a kiss paid in advance."

He held out his hand as he spoke, but I drew myself out of his reach, and looked, I dare say, haughty enough.

"Proud as a Moray! She proves her lineage, sir," said the stranger.

"Perhaps," suggested kind Mr. Mortimer, thinking even then of the future to which I, poor, unconscious child, was so blind, "Perhaps she has no desire to relinquish her place to an heir."

"Oh! it will only be to share her dignities—to take a king-consort," and the stranger lightly laughed.

And so one whose very name I should have forgotten, but that I still preserve a letter found among my uncle's papers to which it is subscribed, one who came from a distant land to my remote Island home, in the gossip of an idle hour, changed the whole color of my destiny, and, having done his work, passed on, and we saw him no more.

Strange it is to find the threads of our being thus crossed by other threads that have come so far to meet them!

I know not how it was with my uncle, but I had quite forgotten the stranger when the letter was received from him, which, as I have said, I still preserve. No foreboding had troubled my childish life. Mr. Mortimer was my teacher, and a most indulgent one. I had become, at eleven, an omnivorous reader; not of the little books intended for children, for of these I had none. But I did not need them, for I had the glorious dream of Bunyan, Defoe's weird tale of the shipwrecked solitary, and before I had wearied of these, I became almost equally enchanted by Herodotus, with his quaint stories of a strange old world, half human, half divine, and Froissart, with his vivid pictures of knightly times. Of any existing world beyond St. Mary's, I neither knew nor thought. Its groves of orange and clumps of oak, its flowery savannas, its sparkling sea, and shell-strewn beach, were the whole visible, tangible universe to me.

I love to linger over those untroubled years in which my life was so peacefully unfolding; but the letter came, and all was changed.

This letter told of two families of the name of Moray, living in Elizabethtown, in the State of New Jersey. These were both descendants of my great-grandfather's long-forgotten brother. In each of these families there was a son; in one, the only son—the only child of his mother, and she was a widow. In the other, there were two daughters, both younger than the son, and the father and mother were living, the former being an officer in the United States Navy. Mr. Home, my uncle's correspondent, seemed really interested in the success of the scheme he had suggested, and took some pains to introduce the heirs expectant, favorably. He narrated his visit to both families in a manner not uninteresting. There was even something dramatic in his introduction to them, which may be presented thus:

Act I, *Scene* 1:—The playground of a large school—boys playing ball—one immediately attracts the stranger's observation by the beauty of his person and the activity and grace of his movements. This is Charles Moray—the widow's son—the leader of the school, both in sport and study. The stranger accosts him, is met with gentlemanly courtesy, and conducted to his mother's house. *Scene* 2. —The mother, a graceful woman, fashionably and somewhat gaily attired, receives him graciously, laments that she can give him no information respecting her husband's family, as he had lived but a short time after their marriage. She directs him, however, to her brother-in-law's, Captain Moray's. Captain Moray is absent, she adds, but his wife and Hugh will be able to tell him all he wishes to know of a family in whom he professes a warm interest. Charles Moray offers to be his guide to the house of his uncle, and so Mr. Home goes to—*scene 3d:* a small house, the door of which is opened by a young girl, whom Charles Moray accosts as cousin Jane. She invites the visitors into a parlor, neatly, but plainly furnished, and having seen them seated, goes to call her mother. The mother enters—a beautiful woman, with the dark of her hair broken by a few silvery lines, with a somewhat careworn expression of face, and a style of dress whose Quaker-like plainness presents a singular contrast to that of Mrs. Charles Moray. Charlie Moray, having introduced the stranger, asks for Hugh, and is told that he will find him in his "den,"—a term explained to the stranger, as "a name we have given to the room appropriated to my son for his studies and sports." The mother, with somewhat of a mother's pride, bringing a sudden color into her pale cheeks, adds to this explanation: "He is just now absorbed in the wonders of a telescope which he has lately purchased for himself."

"Purchased for himself!" exclaims the blunt Mr. Home, with a sufficiently significant glance at the plain furniture of the room in which he sits. The answer shows that the glance was understood.

"It has been purchased with the savings of eight years, made from the sum allotted by his father for his clothing, schooling, and all his expenditures. He begged to manage this himself, and we made no objections, for we felt that the habit of self-denial which he was forming, would be more valuable to him than even his coveted telescope."

"You say he was eight years in collecting the necessary sum—may I ask how old he is now?"

"Eighteen," was the answer.

"Then he began his savings at ten."

"Yes, at ten; the last year or two, he has added to them by some copying done in his leisure hours for a friendly lawyer."

Mr. Home proposes a visit to the den, and Mrs. Moray accompanies him to *scene*—but, no—I must drop everything that savors of the theatrical, when speaking of one who is truth and simplicity itself.

Mr. Home ascended, under the guidance of Mrs. Moray, to the attic, and was ushered into a room having one window that looked toward the west. He glanced around the room for some evidence of the owner's tastes. Pictures in water colors, without frames, decorated the walls. A terrier greeted the strangers with a sharp bark; on being silenced, he retreated to a corner, whither Mr. Home's eyes following him, rested upon a strangely shaped, large tin vessel. Mrs. Moray led the way to it, saying, "Some of my son's pets," and looking in, Mr. Home saw that the vessel was filled half with water and half with earth, making an appropriate abode for two alligators about a foot long. But at this moment, Hugh, who had been arranging something about his telescope, turns and perceives the stranger, who, to use his own words,—they are before me—"finds him a sickly looking, sallow faced lad, a head taller than Charlie, who is only fifteen, but wanting his easy, graceful, and even polished manner." Still, Mr. Home concludes, after some conversation with him, that he has unusual talent, and may be a credit to his name, of which he is evidently very proud; but he thinks "he is better fitted to acquire distinction in one of the learned professions, than to play the part of a gentleman of large, landed estate, to whom great social influence must necessarily pertain."

How strangely this letter stirred the quiet current of our lives at St. Mary's! My uncle could speak of little else, and for me, my sleeping as well as my waking dreams were filled with the sayings and doings of these newly found cousins, who were to combine all the accomplishments of all my favorite heroes. A correspondence was at once opened between my uncle and the Morays of Elizabethtown, which resulted in the promise that the two boys should pass the ensuing winter at St. Mary's, whither they would be accompanied by Mrs. Charles Moray.

Let me try to recall what I was then, eight years ago—almost half my lifetime. I will try to write of myself as I might of another, and an indifferent person. I had some gifts usually accounted good. I have no vanity to gratify in naming them, even were this paper intended for other eyes than mine, for they have proved themselves in my case, of little value—they have won for me no love that I desired—they have shielded me from no evil that I dreaded.

In the dining room at St. Mary's, hung a few family portraits. Among them was one of a remote ancestress of my uncle. This picture went by the name of the Moray beauty, and had always been greatly valued as presenting the highest type of the physical features of the family. It was probably for this reason that my great-grandfather had, at much inconvenience to himself, as I have often heard my uncle tell, brought it over with him from Scotland, when compelled to leave his paternal estate. It was a face of the purest Caucasian lineaments—a perfect oval—the forehead broad, the eyebrows delicately arched, the eyes large, of a brownish gray, and fringed by lashes of unusual length, the nose straight and finely cut, the mouth exquisitely formed, and expressive of tenderness and sensibility. It was the common remark of visitors at St. Mary's, that this, allowing for the difference of age—the portrait represented a young woman of twenty or thereabouts—might have been taken for me. An artist who came to St. Mary's to take a likeness of my uncle, said, "It is very like, certainly, but there are decided points of difference. Already the pale chestnut of the hair and eyebrows in the portrait, has deepened in the child into a darker brown; the position of the head is different, and see, if you please, how that slight change affects the expression. In the picture, the head inclines a little to one side, and the expression is that of innocence and gentleness. In the child, it is set farther back, and held remarkably upright; it does not bend even now, though the color rises, and the eyes are cast down with girlish shame—and pride is its predominant character."

Dear Mr. Mortimer! to you, at least, I gave satisfaction; from you I never heard the accents of blame. But Mr. Mortimer, kind and judicious as he was, could not supply to the poor orphan a mother's vigilant and tender training. Charity might have done more for me in the cultivation of the heart, but my poor Charity thought all I did, was " wisest, virtuousest, discreetest, best." My temper was —ah! I fear I should say, *is*—unsubdued, my impulses uncontrolled. I had great faults of which I thought little, while I prided myself on my truthfulness, and on the absence from my character of what was mean or selfish. Wild as an untamed colt, my association with a punctilious gentleman, such as my uncle, could not fail to awake in me some perception of the proprieties, and even of the courtesies of life. My movements were perfectly untutored. I walked or ran, talked or was silent, sat on the floor or the window sill, was gentle or brusque, according to the humor of the hour. Mrs. Charles Moray, I remember, pronounced me "a little savage,"—but that is anticipating. Back, Memory, to the day and the hour! bring up from the grave of the past, that morning, big with so much of woe, yet rising "so calm, so still, so bright," like George Herbert's "bridal of the earth and sky!" My uncle had gone to Savannah to meet his stranger kindred. Mr. Mortimer had received a letter from him the evening before, announcing their arrival, and requesting to have a boat sent to a point on the mainland, eight miles distant, to meet them this day, on the arrival of the stage coach. I stood with Charity, in the early morning, under the great oak whose boughs overhung the landing place, as the men pushed off the boat and rowed away, the wind being too light for a sail. What a pretty picture, the whole scene, as I remember it, would make—I will paint it some day—the great overhanging oak with its trailing moss, the child with her unshadowed face, full at that moment of gay fancies and but half defined hopes, the old nurse at her side with her shining black face, surmounted by a handkerchief of gay colors, wound in turban fashion around her head, and the black boatmen with their red flannel shirts, and pantaloons made of a coarse dark blue cloth, called by the planters, negro cloth.

I stood on the same spot in the evening, with Mr. Mortimer, to receive the expected guests. I had been pleasantly excited during the day, for I had been helping Charity to prepare their rooms. When I afterward saw Mrs. Charles Moray's room at her own house, with its rosewood and canopied bedstead, its lace curtains, its velvet carpet, and brocade covered couch and lounging chairs, I remembered with a smile, that prepared for her at St. Mary's—the bedstead with tall posts and faded chintz curtains, the chintz curtained windows, the ingrain carpet, the pattern of which was blurred with frequent darns, and the old inlaid bureau with its mirror, from both of which the once rich gilding had been well-nigh effaced. Even Mrs. Moray, however, I remember, admired the antique china vases on the mantlepiece, and the fragrant flowers that filled them.

In the room appropriated to her son and nephew, there was not even an attempt at ornament, nothing to redeem its rudeness and bareness, except perfect cleanliness, the finest and whitest of bed linen and napkins—the last supplied with an abundance which I have often had occasion to remember regretfully, in more ostentatious homes.

Such as the preparations were, they had occupied Charity and me through the whole day. The floors had been made white as a curd, the small panes of glass were clear from spot, and the dark mahogany furniture glistened with wax and hard rubbing. It was five o'clock, and the season being now late in November, the sun was near its setting, when Mr. Mortimer came for me. He considered it an act of respect due to my uncle's guests, to meet them on their landing, and the boat was now in sight.

"But you are not dressed, my child," he said.

"Must I dress, sir?" I asked as, my thoughts thus directed to myself, I felt, for the first time in my life, something like timidity stealing over me, and the question "How will they like me?" arose in my mind. The feeling thus excited was not allayed by Mr. Mortimer's answer.

"Oh, yes! you must be dressed, my dear. You do not know the importance of first impressions—I wonder Charity did not think of it before."

"Charity was not to blame," I answered, quickly; "she wanted me to dress, but I was so busy."

Mr. Mortimer's face relaxed into a smile as he repeated, "On hospitable thought intent; but go quickly, my child, you have no time to spare—you must go down with me."

My toilette was easily made. I had no *embarras des richesses* in the way of dresses. To smooth the abundant ringlets that fell nearly to my waist, to exchange the blue merino dress I wore for a crimson of the same material, made by Charity precisely after the same pattern as those

worn by the little negroes on the plantation—a straight
tight waist, low in the neck, and with short sleeves—to add
to this a coat or pelisse of dark red cloth—grown somewhat short in the waist and sleeves, since the previous winter—and to take my Sunday straw bonnet in my hand,
dangling it by its long ribbon strings, and solemnly promising Charity to put it on before I should meet the strangers
—this was all my preparation.

Mr. Mortimer and I stood where Charity and I had
stood in the morning, watching the approaching boat. I
remember he looked down on me and said, " What is the
matter that you look so pale and breathe so quick? Are
you frightened?"

I did not like the word "frightened," and answered
stoutly, " No," making a great effort at the same time to
control or conceal the agitation which I did not understand.

Till Mr. Mortimer's evident anxiety respecting the
first impression I should make upon my cousins, had aroused
a doubt of my acceptance with them, I did not know how confidently I rested on their affection, or what joyous anticipations were connected with it. The calm, gentle regard of
Mr. Mortimer, the devotion of Charity, these were all I had
known of love. I had never seen another white child. I
had loved my flowers and my pets, my old nurse and my
tutor, the last perhaps more than he had loved me. I
would have loved my uncle—oh, how dearly!—if he had
not repulsed me so often, but I knew even then, that there
was love very different from all those—love which I was
ready to bestow—love which I thirsted to receive. The
poor, simple, child-heart, how full it had been of imaginings
since the discovery of these stranger cousins! How often
in fancy I had played with the gay Charlie, or stood by the
graver Hugh, while he arranged his telescope and permitted
me to take a peep through it at the starry heavens, and

with a tender feeling—a feeling that made the tears start to my eyes, I knew not why—had rested in the arms, and laid my head upon the bosom of the lady, whom I pictured to myself as having Charity's heart, within a form of beauty and grace! And now they were coming, and the thought had suddenly been awakened, that I might not please them; that all this wealth of love and joy would be brought near me, would touch my very lip, but that, Tantalus-like, I must not drink of it. It was no wonder that my breath came quick, that my color varied, that I trembled.

But the boat approached the wharf, the boys sprang on shore, and Mr. Mortimer led me forward. My uncle handed Mrs. Moray from the boat, and after he had shaken hands with Mr. Mortimer, who seemed to divine that I had some thought of running away, and consequently held me fast, he presented me to the lady and to her young companions as his niece, Augusta Moray.

"Augusta Moray! what a noble name, and what a noble looking creature she is—positively beautiful!" and the lady kissed me, saying, as she lifted her graceful head again, "Charles! here is your cousin Augusta—come, speak to her—Hugh!"

Charlie came forward easily, held out his hand with a smile, and greeted me in a pleasant, frank way, as if he had known me all his life, or, at least, all mine. Hugh turned at his aunt's call, but nothing further being said, he only bowed to me, and stood waiting for further directions. Will it be believed this grave, reserved youth pleased me better than the graceful, suave lady, or the ready Charlie? A genuine, inartificial child stands ever in the palace of Truth. I am convinced that at the age to which I now refer, I knew instinctively the truth or falsehood of those who approached me; not that I recognized those as the qualities which depressed and chilled me with some, or gave me, with others, a pleasant feeling of satisfaction and repose. Now, I almost shrank from the touch of Mrs. Charles Moray's lips—I drew my head proudly up as Charles spoke to me—but as my eyes met Hugh's, they softened, and, had he given me the least encouragement, I should have gone up to him, taken his hand, and walked to the house with him. But he did not encourage me, and Mrs. Charles Moray drawing me to her, made me walk with her, and called Charlie to my other side. My uncle busied himself with seeing to the safety of the baggage, and sending it up, and Hugh and Mr. Mortimer walked on a little before us. We were followed by Mrs. Moray's maid. As I had never seen one of my own color occupying a menial station, I did not at all understand the position of this very respectable looking young woman, and was painfully embarrassed at the remembrance that not a word of welcome had been addressed to her. Mrs. Moray, at length, noticed my backward glances.

"Do you want your uncle, my dear?" she asked.

"No ma'am—but—if you please—no one has spoken to the lady."

I spoke with hesitation, directing the last epithet by a glance to the girl. Looking back too quickly, I caught the exchange of glances between Charles and his mother, and the smiles which had not yet quite died from their lips.

"Do not disturb yourself about her, my dear," said Mrs. Moray; "it is only my maid."

My uncle came up and addressed some observations to Mrs. Moray. She was immediately all attention to him, and slipping my hand out of hers, I went quickly up to Mr. Mortimer, placed my hand in his, and walked along on the opposite side from Hugh. They were speaking of his home.

"Did you bring your telescope?" I ventured to ask, with a beating heart.

He looked at me for a moment, his face, sombre hitherto in its expression, was lit up by a bright, cordial smile, as he answered, "No!—I could not bring it; but how did you hear of my telescope?"

"Oh! Mr. Home wrote my uncle about it. I am so sorry you did not bring it."

"Why are you sorry?"

"I wanted to see it, and I thought, may be, you would let me look at the stars through it, and then Mr. Mortimer said I should learn something about astronomy."

"Then indeed I am very sorry, for I should have liked to learn too from Mr. Mortimer, if he would have permitted me."

"Oh! you would, sir—wouldn't you?" I cried, eagerly, to Mr. Mortimer. My heart was on my lips, for I felt that here was a small portion of the rich feast which imagination had presented to me, that might indeed be mine, and I longed to secure it.

"Certainly, my dear," said Mr. Mortimer, with a smile at my earnestness. "It would give me great pleasure—and perhaps the telescope may be supplied—I cannot promise, but I think it may."

I clapped my hands with delight.

"What pleases you so much, *ma cousine!*" asked Charlie, coming up to us. He had a habit, as I afterward found, of using French words and phrases. His voice sobered me instantly, and I left Mr. Mortimer to explain the source of my pleasure.

"Will you join us, Charlie?" asked Hugh.

Charlie laughed gaily, and shook his head as he said, "I hope neither Mr. Mortimer nor my *petite cousine* here will think very badly of me, if I acknowledge that I should like a little holiday first;" then, turning to Mr. Mortimer, he added, "I cannot be such a very good boy as

Hugh, sir; my mother says my motto should be, 'Vive la bagatelle!'"

Mr. Mortimer, ever gentle to the young, did not answer Charlie by lecturing. "The bagatelle will not always charm," he said gently; "when you grow tired of it, we shall be glad to have you."

"Thank you, sir; you are very kind," said Charlie, and Hugh added, "Charlie has had more opportunity to study than I have had, sir—that will account for his liking play better."

And I liked Charlie better in this conversation. I felt he had been true.

If Mrs. Charles Moray missed the elegancies of her home, we were, happily, too ignorant to dream of such a feeling, and she was too courteous to manifest it; but the poor girl who had come as her attendant to a land in which the laboring class is separated from all others by natural distinctions: holding herself superior to the one caste, and held inferior to the other, led a life so lonely and so divorced from sympathy, that it touched the compassionate heart of my kind Charity.

"Poor ting! poor ting!" I heard her say one day, with a sad shake of her head, as Alice passed the window.

"Why do you call her so, Charity?" I asked. "What makes you say 'poor thing?'"

"'Cause you see, Miss 'Gusty, him is poor, an' I tink poor buckra is worse off an' we."

"But why, Charity? Alice is a lady's maid; her work is not hard; you work harder than she does."

"I know, Miss 'Gusty; but den you see we was make for work; it comes sort o' nat'ral, an' people doesn't look down on we; we jist as much respected, you know, as ef we didn't work, an' more; nobody tinks much o' a lazy person o' color; but tain't so wid a poor buckra, more

pertickler where there ain't no other poor buckra to keep
company with 'em—for we don't like to 'mean ourselves to
'sociate with 'em, nohow; an' so, the poor tings ain't got
no companion; but don't you tink, Miss 'Gusty, may be de
obershay an' he wife would like Miss Alice?"

Upon this hint I acted. That very afternoon I obtained
permission from Mrs. Moray, on the plea that Charity was
busy, for Alice to accompany me in a walk, and, going to
the overseer's house, I had the pleasure of seeing her quite
at home before the visit was over.

In the meantime, my acquaintance with my new relations progressed pleasantly enough. To Mrs. Moray I was
a darling, a beauty, a sweet pet,—and yet, strange to say, the
lady did not win my favor. I liked her flattery; under its
warm rays, some traits of character which I had not yet
exhibited, were rapidly developed; and yet, I did not like
her. Why was this, I wonder. I think there was something in the very sound of her voice, that did not ring true
to my ear. But some of her conversations with me may
suggest a better explanation of the mystery. Let me try
to recall one:

"My darling beauty! how they have neglected you!
Just see, Alice, that dress is really made of very pretty
Thibet, fine, and a good color, though I should not choose
so deep a crimson for her, myself; but only see how it is
made! a straight jacket for the waist, and the skirt dangling
to her heels. I wonder how she ever learned to walk so
freely and gracefully. Positively, Alice, you must set to
work, and remodel all her dresses. Good woman," to
Charity, who was with me as usual, "just give Alice all
Miss Augusta's dresses, and let her see what can be done
with them."

"Yes, ma'am," Charity answered, and was turning away
to obey the command, but I had heard the quiver in her

voice, and seen the moisture in her eye, and I flew to her, and casting to the winds all the compliments to my beauty and my grace, cried almost fiercely, "I don't care what you think about my clothes, I want them just as Charity made them. I won't have them altered—Alice shall not touch them."

I caught the slight shrug of Mrs. Moray's pretty shoulders, and the arch of her brows as she turned to leave the room, without a word. Had she answered me, I might have remained firm; but this silence, this waving me aside from her path, as it were, made me feel at once the distance between the accomplished lady and the untutored child. She had seemed to mean me a kindness—her words had been very gracious, and I had met them with rudeness,—I blushed and hung my head, while hot tears, half of passion and half of shame, wet my cheeks. Yet I could not ask her pardon. I felt shame for my own want of self-control, not regret for having offended her. Her contempt crushed my pride, but wounded no affection. Charity saw my trouble, and hastened to say for me what I could not or would not say for myself. Mrs. Moray had not advanced two steps, when she arrested her, placing herself in her path, courtesying humbly, and saying deprecatingly, " Please, ma'am, don't go. You see, ma'am, the poor chile a'n't used to strangers—'specially to great ladies, like you, ma'am—" Charity understood the uses of flattery—"An' she didn't mean nothing, ma'am, please—she jist was a thinking o' poor Charity, an' she was afeard, ma'am, I might feel bad, 'cause I made the dresses, ma'am, an' so she forgot who she was talkin' to; but please, ma'am, I'll be so glad ef you an' Miss Alice will only show me how to make the frocks, ma'am."

Mrs. Moray—let me do her justice—has a placable temper. She was quite mollified before Charity had reached the conclusion of her appeal. Drawing me to her side, she touched my still wet and burning cheek with her cool lips, saying, "Poor little beauty! did she think I was disrespectful to Charity? Why, I think Charity the best mammy in the world, and so, worth a dozen French dressmakers; but now Alice and I will set to work on your wardrobe, and you shall see what a metamorphosis will ensue—you will scarcely know yourself."

She did not promise more than she performed.

I was a little awkward in my new trappings at first, especially after hearing Mr. Mortimer exclaim, "The butterfly has burst from the chrysalis;" but my uncle was delighted at the change, and I soon caught somewhat of his satisfaction.

When Alice had finished the first suit—and it was complete, from the frilled pantalets, to the dress with its flounced skirt and low neck and short sleeves, exposing the white shoulders and rounded arms—Mrs. Morny dressed me herself, brushing my curls back from my forehead, and so giving a new character to the childish face beneath them; then she led me into the library to my uncle. If there was any one in the world of whose admiration I was covetous, it was he. As the natural result of this desire, I entered, blushing, and looking foolish and awkward enough, I doubt not. Yet my uncle was pleased, and looking at me with a gentler smile than his face ordinarily wore to me, he said, "She certainly is like that old portrait; I never saw the likeness so strongly before; but why do you blush so, child? If you had the pride that becomes your name, dress would not discompose you."

"So I think, sir," said Mrs. Morny, catching his tone in an instant. "Miss Moray should be always well dressed, but if by any accident she is otherwise—what then? She is still Miss Moray."

"Very true, madam," said my uncle, gravely; "you have expressed my thought better than I could have done myself."

And so the best cure that my uncle knew for the vanity that was shadowing the child's unconscious grace, was pride! This was setting one disease to drive out another—one demon to overthrow another; and it was successful. I no longer simpered, and if I could not altogether refrain from blushing, I felt provoked with myself for it, considering it a weakness unworthy of Miss Morny. Perhaps I recovered my equanimity the sooner, from finding that my dress did not recommend me to every one. Charlie, on first seeing me in my butterfly state, exclaimed, "Why, Miss 'Gusty!"—he delighted to tease me by using the name adopted by the blacks, for the high sounding Augusta—"How improved you are! *Ma cousine, vous êtes tout-à-fait belle.*"

"Charlie, how ridiculous you make yourself with your parade of French!" cried Hugh, in a testy tone.

"Well! it's true, if it is French," replied Charlie.

"It is not true," returned Hugh, with increasing discomposure. "I don't believe any one was ever perfectly beautiful—I don't even think she is improved; for my part, I like to see a little girl look like a little girl."

We were standing near the library door. The boys had just come in from a hunt with my uncle, and were going to their rooms to dress for dinner, when they were arrested by my appearance. They now passed on, and I shrank into the library, mortified and depressed. Twenty minutes after, Hugh, whose *toilette* was always quickly made, came in to look for a book. He found me resting my head upon a table, and sobbing violently. Seating himself beside me, he lifted my tear-stained face, and insisted on knowing what was the matter.

"Let me alone!" I exclaimed, struggling in vain to escape from him; "let me alone! you know you don't care a bit for me."

"I don't care for you! You don't know anything about it; I love you as if you were my own little sister."

"But you told Charlie I wasn't beautiful," I sobbed out.

"Oh! that's it, is it? You are crying because you are not thought perfectly beautiful."

I felt the arm with which Hugh was clasping me to his side, slackening its grasp.

"I don't care whether I am beautiful or not," I answered, quickly, and a little hypocritically, I fear; "but I do care to be loved, and when we love people, we think they are beautiful."

"*We* do?—well, I don't," said Hugh, with a smile in his voice. "I love both my sisters, and one of them is not in the least beautiful."

"But your mother. Is beautiful—I heard you say so," I rejoined.

"And you want me to love you as I love my mother?"

Hugh laughed, and so quickly are the tears of childhood dried, that I laughed with him.

"I cannot promise to do that," he continued, playfully, "but I love you quite as much as you can wish me to do, as my own darling little cousin, whom I would not exchange for any other, though the other were twice as beautiful," and Hugh bent down and kissed me very tenderly. My cheek did not burn then to receive his kiss, as it does now to remember it. It was his first kiss—the first kiss, except Charity's, that had ever seemed to me to have love in it.

I was very happy. I longed to do something for Hugh, and I whispered, softly, "Hugh, if you would like me better in my old frocks, I won't have any more altered, and I'll take off this, and put on one they have not touched."

Again Hugh lifted my downcast face and kissed me.

"My dear little cousin," he said, "your dresses do not make the least difference in my love. I dare say I shall like this dress best when I have become accustomed to it. The truth is, I believe I was a little cross when I said what distressed you."

As he said this, Hugh's face was very grave, though full of interest and affection.

"What made you cross, Hugh?" I asked.

"Because I was afraid," he said, "that they were going to spoil my simple-hearted little cousin, and to make her like some of the foolish, vain girls I have seen at my Aunt Moray's, who think more of their sashes and curls than of anything else in the world."

"But I won't do that, Hugh, because my uncle says dress cannot make any difference to Miss Moray."

"So—so—" said Hugh, softly, "call in pride to kill vanity. Well—it is the more respectable of the two; but, Augusta," here Hugh turned again to me, the first part of his sentence having been in soliloquy, "do you ever read the Bible?"

"Sometimes," I answered, "with Mr. Mortimer, and on Sundays."

"There are two verses in it, which I want you to learn for me; will you do it?"

"Oh yes, Hugh!"

I was glad he had asked me to do something for him. He turned over the leaves of a large Bible on the table, till he found the First Epistle of Peter, third chapter, and third and fourth verses, and read: "Whose adorning, let it not be that outward adorning of plaiting the hair, and of wearing of gold, or of putting on of apparel; but, let it be the hidden man of the heart in that which is not corruptible, even the ornament of a meek and quiet spirit, which is in the sight of God of great price."

Having read it over with me, and made me read it myself to him, he was leaving me to learn it, but the tender conscience of the child was touched, and drawing him back, I asked, " Hugh, is it wrong to wear this ?" showing, as I spoke, a small cameo pin which Mrs. Moray had stuck in my dress.

" No, dear—not wrong to wear them, but wrong to make them your adornments—the things for which you value yourself."

Hugh left me very happy. I learned the verses, and when I recited them to him that evening, he made me promise that I would repeat them whenever I was dressed. I keep the promise even to this hour. Sweet memories! Ah! who would not be a child again?

As the hours of that winter pass before me, there are few salient points on which memory may rest, few prominent traits to sketch into my picture; yet how surely was my life acquiring new tone and coloring. My sky was becoming more picturesque, its blue expanse being shadowed now and then by floating clouds, and far away, in the distant horizon, a far seeing eye might have espied one rising, no bigger than a man's hand, yet inspiring fear by the depth of its hue, and its steady, though not rapid approach.

My uncle had purchased a telescope at the request of Mr. Mortimer, who spent many a clear evening upon the balcony with Hugh and Charlie and me, pointing out the different constellations, and giving names to those " bright particular stars," which most attracted our admiration. To Hugh, this was the most delightful relaxation after intense study, for he soon drew Mr. Mortimer far beyond what he had originally intended, by his offer of instruction in astronomical science. The mere elements of astronomy were all that I could understand, all that Charlie cared for; but Hugh plunged at once into a deep sea, which we had no line to sound, and where even Mr. Mortimer, I sometimes thought, was upheld by the buoyancy of his companion.

Looking into the library one morning, and finding both Mr. Mortimer and Hugh absorbed in the calculation of some abstruse mathematical problem, my uncle exclaimed, "Come, come, Hugh! All work and no play makes Jack a dull boy. The old Morays were soldiers, not bookworms. Your horse is at the door, and this is just the morning for a hunt."

I knew that Hugh loved a canter over the breezy savannas, and that the excitement of a deer hunt to him, who had known little of the free joyousness of youth till he came to St. Mary's, was a source of the keenest delight. I lifted my eyes from the book I was studying in the corner, and fixed them on his face. His usually sallow cheek was glowing, the eyes he raised to my uncle's face were sparkling with pleasure, as he half rose from his chair; but he seated himself again, the sparkle died out, the color faded, and he said, "I believe, sir, it will be more in the spirit of the old Morays to stay till I have conquered this dragon of a problem. They never left a foe but half subdued—did they, sir?"

My uncle smiled as he answered, "No! I think not;" then added, "but, Hugh, this visit to the South was intended for a holiday. Charlie is enjoying it thoroughly, while you are sitting in a confined room, and studying as if you were at school. Are you so dull always? Do you not like such manly sports as riding and hunting?"

"Oh dearly, sir!—dearly! and I am not dull; but Charlie can go to school again when he goes home, and I—I—"

Hugh had spoken with fluency and animation, but at this point, he stopped suddenly, and his eyes fell.

"Well!" cried my uncle, after waiting some seconds in vain for the continuance of his explanation, "you—"

"I do not expect to go to school again," Hugh concluded, in an indifferent, matter of fact way, very unlike the impulsive, animated manner in which he had commenced.

"And why will you not go to school again?"

Again Hugh reddened, but even I, child as I was, could see that the color came from a different feeling from that which had lately flushed his cheek, and sparkled in his eye. After a moment's pause, he answered, simply, "For several reasons, sir."

My uncle looked hard at him, but left the room without another word. The next minute, he and Charlie rode by in a brisk canter, with the hounds barking in a glad chorus around them. Hugh followed them for one moment with his eyes, and then I heard a suppressed sigh, as he turned again to his calculations. I slipped from my chair, and approached to offer such consolation as I could give, but before I reached his side, he was evidently so absorbed in his problem, that I could not venture to disturb him.

Sometimes, when Hugh had conquered some great difficulty in his course, he would bound up from the chair to which his resolute will had chained him, fling aside his books, rush out to the stables for his horse, take his gun, if he knew that my uncle was hunting, and gallop off with an exuberance of enjoyment manifest in his face and movements, such as even Charlie rarely showed. Though he had seldom mounted a horse before his visit to St. Mary's, he had soon become, under my uncle's instruction, a fearless and graceful rider, and a very fair shot. Charlie was an adept in every manly accomplishment that ministers to pleasure. His gay, *insouciant* nature never denied itself a gratification. It was said of him by some one, that he seemed to be perpetually singing in his heart, "Begone dull care;" but for my part, I think care never came sufficiently near him to be sent away. He spoke truly when he said that the motto of his life was "Vive la bagatelle."

Everybody was charmed with the graceful, handsome boy. Even Mr. Mortimer's face kept its brightest smile for Charlie. My uncle's eye rested on him with equal pride and pleasure, and the very negroes, while they bowed or courtesied respectfully to both the youths, kept their brightest glances and merriest words for Charlie. I was the only exception to this, and I grew jealous for Hugh. Charlie's brightness seemed to throw him into shadow, and I did not like it. This feeling doubtless made me unjust at times. Hugh was the first to show me this.

It was a rainy morning, and no outdoor amusement could be thought of. Charlie threw himself on the sofa in the library, with an old novel which he had obtained by climbing to the highest shelf in the room. I was doing little better than he, giving only half my attention to the book I held in my hand, while with the other half I was watching the rain drops as they fell from a drooping bough, and trickled, bright and clear, down the panes of glass beside me. I was startled from my dreamy mood by Charlie's springing to his feet, throwing down his book, and crying, "Come, Hugh! Put down those everlasting books, and let us do something to keep us alive."

"Thank you; I do not feel my life in any present danger," said Hugh, with a quiet smile.

"Come, 'Gusty! you have not read a page of your history this half hour, you little make-believe. Now come and play a game of battledore in the long room."

He snatched at my book as he spoke, but I clung to it

exclaiming, "I don't want to play battledore—I don't like battledore."

"You liked it yesterday, when Hugh called you to play with him."

"I like to play with Hugh," I said, sulkily.

"Which means that you don't like to play with me—an avowal somewhat more frank than polite, Miss Morny; but *chacun à son goût.*"

I was not mollified by Charlie's French, for, as I could not understand it, I always believed that he made it the vehicle of a sarcasm. He now left the room with a heightened complexion. I looked toward Hugh, and met his eyes fixed upon me, with an expression of grave rebuke. I hung my head.

"What made you so cross to Charlie?" he asked.

"I did not want to play with him," I answered, evasively.

Hugh bent forward, stretched out his hand, and drew me to him.

"Why did you not want to play with Charlie? Would you not play with me if I should ask you?"

He was answered by a smile, though I still declined to meet his eye.

"Charlie is always pleasant to you—he is pleasant to every one."

I spoke suddenly, quickly, angrily, I suppose. "I wish Charlie had never come. I am tired of hearing people say 'Charlie's pleasant.'—as if it was so hard to be pleasant."

"I should think you had proof in yourself, that it was sometimes hard to be so. Do you remember, the other day, how angry you were with the Athenian who voted for the exile of Aristides, because he was so weary of hearing him called the just. I am afraid you have no better reason for wishing Charlie away."

"Well, it was reason enough, if the Athenian knew some one more just than Aristides, who never got any praise, while every one was talking of him."

"And so you are jealous of Charlie's reputation, are you?"

"I am not jealous—I don't want people to think me pleasant," I said, hotly.

"No! but you want that they should think me so," and Hugh stooped and pressed his lips to my flushed brow; then, taking my hand in his, he added in that gentle, yet earnest tone which always thrilled my very heart, and made me willing to attempt anything he could propose: "My little cousin's love is very dear to me. I would rather have that love, than know that a thousand people for whom I do not care a great deal, said, how pleasant I was; but then her love to me must not make her unjust, or spoil her temper. Charlie is pleasant—pleasanter than I am."

"I don't think so," I exclaimed.

"That is because you love me; but strangers will always find such a gay, sunny temper as Charlie's, agreeable, while they must wait awhile, and know what is behind my grave face, before they can like me."

"I did not wait—I liked you best at the very first, Hugh."

"I think you did, but I have never understood how that came about. Can you tell me why you liked me best?"

"Because,"—I stopped; I found reasons not so plenty as blackberries,—"because I liked you best—I mean, because you suited me—I don't know, Hugh—somehow I felt comfortable with you."

Hugh laughed, and rising from his chair, said, "And you suit me, and I am very comfortable with you; but now we will be generous, and find poor Charlie, and try to make him comfortable too."

Charlie had already forgotten his little pique against
me, for I must do him the justice to say, that he is, and
always has been very good tempered. I really think I
should in time have forgiven him the little conceited ways
that annoyed me, and have liked him heartily in the main,
though we might still have quarrelled occasionally, had not
his mother so often wounded my self-love, and irritated my
quick temper. I do not yet understand how it was that
Mrs. Charles Moray, never appearing to be discomposed
herself, could yet work my nature into a tempest; how,
petting me as I had never been petted before, she could yet
infuse into my heart suspicion, never felt before, of the
truth and the kindness of all around me, herself included.
There was a falsetto tone in her voice that roused me to
opposition, as the trumpet stirs a war horse. And yet
others thought it was "*so sweet.*" How intensely unamiable
I must have appeared to the onlookers in these scenes!

I know not how soon after Mrs. Moray's arrival it was
that I became conscious of a change in my feelings to my
uncle. I have said that while sheltering me in his home,
and providing liberally for my wants, he had never manifested to me anything like love,—had never caressed me
in my infancy, or taken pleasure in my society as I grew
older. But my uncle was liberal to all, and a paper of
candies, or a new toy, made an epoch in the life of a child
so lonely, and the giver was sure to be remembered with
pleasure. There was more than this in my feeling to my
uncle. I was proud of him, as I have already said, proud
to belong to one who seemed to my childish fancy so
great a man. Does he love me? was a question I had
never asked myself, till Mrs. Charles Moray both suggested
and answered it.

It is probable that I did not immediately notice the pa-
thetic intonation of voice and the glance of the eye, by which

she gave deeper significance to the "Poor darling!" her usual name for me when we were alone. But I was not long permitted to retain this happy unconsciousness. It was not long before I found myself watching my uncle's words and manner, as I had never watched them before, and feeling something of resentment take the place of admiration and gratitude. The serpent had entered my Eden. I was no longer satisfied to accept, with glad, untroubled heart, the good gifts showered upon me. I had entered the path through which every earnest life must pass to glory, or to shame—to the joy of success, the diviner joy of self-ronunciation, or the unmixed bitterness of disappointment. I coveted the unattainable. I would *know* both the evil and the good.

It was cruel to disturb so early my beautiful dream of life. All I have since experienced might have come, but it would have come gradually, and I should have been stronger to bear it. Our visitors had come in the autumn, and when spring had covered our savannas with its more delicate flowers, I had already begun to feel that I had no more right to call St. Mary's mine—my home—than they had. And this was very bitter, for my life seemed a part of that beautiful nature, with which and in which I had lived so long. Oh the desolateness of heart with which I first admitted the thought, that there was no natural bond between it and me! The hour and the scene rise before me, in which I was made to stand face to face with that idea, already perhaps dimly imagined, but then first endowed with life and power.

My uncle and Hugh and Charlie were all away. They had gone to a little town on the mainland—my uncle on business, my cousins for the enjoyment of boating—on a bright, warm, spring day. The house was dull without them, and as soon as my lessons were over, I had wandered off, in my old fashion, with Charity. Coming back laden with flowers, I sat down upon the upper step of the piazza to weave them into chaplets, with which I thought to astonish Mrs. Moray. They were not yet ready for exhibition, when she came out from the house, and putting her hand caressingly on my bowed head, said in her usual soft falsetto, " My poor darling! have you come back ?"

She had often given me this pitying title, and I had borne it quietly. I know not why it was, that on this especial day I could not bear it. I answered quickly, " What makes you call me poor, Mrs. Moray ? I don't like to be called so—I am not poor."

"Are you not, dear child ? I feel as if every one was poor who was left an orphan, with no one to love them very dearly."

"I have my uncle to love me, and——" I was going to add Hugh, but a feeling which I did not understand, restrained me. Mrs. Moray finished the sentence for me.

"And Mr. Mortimer," she said. "You are right—I believe he feels as kindly to you as any one in the world, poor dear!"

"But I am *not* poor, Mrs. Moray," I repeated, pertinaciously. "My uncle is rich."

"True—he is. This is a very valuable place, and you love it dearly, Augusta, do you not ?"

Love! I had never asked myself the question; it would have been as natural to ask if I loved light, or air, or any of those blessed things which are so essential to our life, that they seem but a part of it, and we forget to be thankful for them as for separate gifts.

"You would not like to go away, and never see St. Mary's again, would you ?" Mrs. Moray again questioned, as I sat mutely gazing upon the waving boughs and gleaming waters of my beautiful home.

"Never see St. Mary's again!" I repeated, slowly. What infinite sadness there was in the words!

"Why, you know, my dear child, it might be so." Mrs. Moray seated herself beside me on the step, and continued very gently, "You must remember you are not Mr. Moray's child, and should he die, as every one, you know, is liable to do at any time, he might leave it to some other person—to some person whom you would not like to live with, or who would not care to have you here. Indeed, even during Mr. Moray's life, if you displease him, he may send you away; so you see now, darling, why I called you poor. And now, my pet, I have told you these things, not to make you unhappy, but because I think you will be more careful not to offend your uncle, after you understand them. I know it is not easy always to please him, but you must try—you must not be so independent, and you are so cold in your manner to him; you must be more affectionate; you must caress him; take his hand, and lean on him, and talk to him as you do to Mr. Mortimer, sometimes. You see, dear child, I am thinking only of your good."

Was this true? Did she seek my good? If so, she was a poorer judge of character than I think. I doubt if any more certain way of estranging my uncle could have been chosen than the fawning, forced caresses thus advised. But there was no danger of these. She might have seen that there was not, by the burning cheek and sullen brow that met her eyes when she strove to read, in my face, the answer my tongue refused to utter; by the cold withdrawal of the hand she would have taken; by the passion with which, at last, as she began another of her soft sentences, I sprang down the steps, and rushed from her presence—the vain, impotent passion of a child, which soon dissolves in tears. As soon as I was fairly out of sight of the house, I threw myself down at the foot of an old oak tree, and resting my head against its trunk, wept bitterly. When the fit of weeping was over, I went down to the beach, and sat for what seemed to me a very long time, throwing pebbles into the water, and trying to picture to myself some other child living in my home, enjoying my few simple pleasures —my uncle's niece, Mr. Mortimer's pupil, Hugh's cousin— and I, separated from all these, a poor castaway, it might be, begging my daily bread—for a childish imagination, once excited, is a wonderful exaggerator.

At length I heard Charity's voice calling me. I did not wish to meet her—I would have been glad to meet no one that day; for, though the passion of my grief had abated, it had left me cross—dissatisfied with myself, and yet more dissatisfied with others. I returned home, avoiding the direction from which Charity seemed to be approaching. When I reached the house, I found that my uncle had arrived, that dinner had been served, and that all the family were seated at table. The two greatest faults I could commit, in my uncle's estimation, as I had long since learned, were want of punctuality at meals, and want of neatness. That day I was reckless, and I walked into the dining room, fifteen minutes or more after the rest had been seated, with my hair and dress in disorder, my face stained with tears, and my hands soiled with the flowers I had gathered in my walk, and the pebbles I had since handled. Without a word of apology for my tardiness, or of greeting to those whom I had not seen since the day before, I walked to my place, and was about to take the vacant chair that stood there. My uncle looked up, and said, not angrily, "You are late, Augusta."

I turned my face toward him without speaking. His brow grew stern. He bade me come to him, and when I obeyed, he looked with coldly investigating eyes upon my disordered hair and dress, and my soiled face and hands. I

did not shrink from the examination. I think I was in the
mood to be rather pleased with the prospect of a combat.
If so, the desire did not seem likely to be gratified, for my
uncle only ordered a waiter to call Charity, and when she
appeared, desired her to take me to my room, and arrange
my dress, before she suffered me to come to table
again. My heart swelled high with pride and anger; I
shook off the light touch which Charity had laid upon my
arm, and turned to leave the room. I had to pass Mrs.
Moray's chair, and as I did so, she stretched out her round,
white arm, covered with bracelets, and drew me, spite of
my resistance, to her side.

"My darling child," she whispered in my unwilling
ear, "remember what I said to you to-day—speak gently
to your uncle—ask his pardon for being so careless of his
wishes;" then, still holding me fast, she turned to my
uncle and said, aloud, "Mr. Moray, you must forgive our
little pet; I am sure you would, if you knew how anxious
she was to please you."

Every word she had said, had been as fuel to the fire of
my passion, and it was no longer to be controlled. Tearing my hand from her clasp, and showing, I doubt not, in
looks and gesture, the fury that had mastered me, I cried,
in a voice that sounds even now in my memory, sharp and
high, "I wish you'd let me alone; I am not your darling
child, and you know you're telling a story when you say
that I'm anxious to please Uncle Hugh; I don't care to
please him—I won't ask his pardon—I don't care for him—
I don't care for anybody."

My uncle had not attempted to interrupt me. As I
began, he put down, untasted, the glass of wine he had raised
to his lips, and looked at me coldly, calmly, as at a strange
study. When I accused Mrs. Moray of untruth, his face
flushed, and he rose from his chair; but he did not advance

to me until I had finished my speech, then, two steps placed him at my side. He laid his hand heavily on my shoulder, and pushed me toward Mrs. Moray.

"You have insulted a lady—a guest at my table—ask her pardon," he said, in a low, determined voice. Even then, child as I was, his stillness awed me more than angry words could have done; but at that moment, not even this could bow me to make any amends to Mrs. Moray. I was sullenly silent.

"Ask her pardon on your knees," and my uncle attempted to press me down. I offered only passive resistance. I would not kneel. I did not speak, but I did not attempt to escape his pressure; I did not lift my eyes to his. Perhaps if I had, the stern, unbending purpose I should have seen there, would have overpowered my will; but I know not, it was very strong. My only contests hitherto had been with Charity, and I had always conquered her. During this scene, there was perfect silence in the room. Mrs. Moray had indeed begun an expostulation, but my uncle stopped her with a look, and then all were still, and waited—a minute or an hour—I know not; but it seemed to me very long, before my uncle lifted his hand from my shoulder, and said, "Go to your room—you will not leave it again until you are ready to obey me, and I request that no one in my house will hold any communication with you till then."

I walked out of the room with a firm step, carrying my head somewhat more proudly erect than usual, went to my room, and locking my door against Charity, who was following me, I threw myself on the floor, and wept as only a child can weep. There was no healing in such tears—they left me as they found me, hard, proud, and resentful. One word of kindness would have melted me. Could I but have seen Hugh!

The long hours wore on, and no one came except Charity, whom I sent angrily away. At length, there was another step, a knock—it might be Hugh. I sprang up, I opened the door; I saw the waving of a white dress, closed it instantly, and locked it. My visitor was Mrs. Moray.

"Open the door!" she cried, in guarded tones, as if afraid of being overheard, "I have come to see you, while your uncle is lying down in the library. I have brought you some candy that Charlie got for you this morning. Let me in, and we will make friends, and I will tell your uncle you have asked my pardon, and all will be right again."

The candy might have softened me, but the offer to tell an untruth for me, made me despise her more than ever; no, I could not ask her pardon, I could not be friendly with her.

"If you will not let me in, I must go," she said, at last. I did not speak—I did not move.

"Well, good by," the last word lingeringly pronounced, as if to give me time for repentance, and then she was gone. As her steps died away, I wept again. I wished, perhaps, that I had yielded, for I was hungry, having eaten no dinner. The evening came on cold and dark. Will they leave me here all night alone, I asked myself; and then I thought of some of Charity's stories of ghostly visitants. My father and mother—would they visit me tonight? For the first time, the thought brought a shudder with it. My spirit was not in accord with angel visitants.

Suddenly a light shone under the door, and Charity's voice called to me to open it. With more pleasure than I would have liked to confess, I admitted her, and with her came light and fire and food.

"Did Uncle Hugh tell you to bring me my tea?" I questioned Charity, after I had emptied the well-filled plate of buttered toast, and drank every drop of milk from the bowl she brought me.

"No, Miss 'Gusty! you think I wait for as 'im? You think I let strange people come here and starve my chile?"

Charity's resentment was as strong and keen as mine, and evidently pointed in the same direction.

"Charity, did you see Hugh?" The question cost me no little effort.

"I has not seen Master Hugh since he's went to Mr. Mortimer's, Miss 'Gusty," said Charity, in reply.

"How do you know that it was to Mr. Mortimer's he went?"

"Well, I hearn him tell Master Charles so, and he telled him too as how he thought Mr. Mortimer ud be the best peacemaker."

My heart sprang up, and threw off the heaviest part of the load that had been oppressing it. Hugh was not indifferent to me. Though he had not disobeyed my uncle by coming to me, he was thinking of me, and trying to bring me help. I was long silent and thoughtful; then came another question, spoken hesitatingly, and with low and faltering tones, for I was not quite sure that it was right thus to interrogate a servant, even though the servant was Charity.

"Charity, did you go back to the dining room after I came away?"

Charity turned her face away, and pretended to be too busy at the fire to look up, as she answered, "Yes, Miss 'Gusty, I went back and stayed round awhile, 'cause I wanted to hear."

I waited with the hope that she would tell me, unasked, all I wished to know; but she remained silent, and I was obliged again to question.

"What did they say, Charity?"

"Oh! Misses Moray say she's bery sorry; she wish master ud let you come back.; you is only a chile, and she don't care for you to beg pardon; but master, he say—well, —I don't know a'cisely, but he warn't goin' to send for you."

"But Hugh—did Hugh say nothing?"

"No, Miss 'Gusty! but he looked bery sorry, and he excused hisself, an' has went, as I telled you, to Mr. Mortimer's."

I was very weary that evening, and fell asleep more than once in my chair; but the house was all still before Charity could persuade me to go to bed, so strong was my hope that either Hugh or Mr. Mortimer would visit me.

The next morning, Charity wanted me to remain in bed, saying that I had been feverish, and talked all sorts of nonsense in the night—with me, a common effect, as I have since found, of any very great excitement. But I was wilful as usual, and rising early, dressed myself, saw Charity put my room in order, and then sat waiting and listening. The morning was warm, and Charity had raised one of the sashes in my room. Oh how lovely it was! I can smell even now the sweetbrier, which sent its delicate sprays, all gemmed with morning dews, across my window. The dew lay upon the grassy lawn, and its pendent drops were like a thousand mimic suns suspended from every bush and tree. The majestic oaks and their gray drapery looked gay in that morning light, and the mocking birds seemed to feel it, as they fluttered from bough to bough, and poured forth their rich melody. And I, as free in general as they, must be shut up in this room, catching only glimpses of the beauties of sky and sea and land, which I had till lately felt were all my own, to be enjoyed at will. My spirit passed into a rebellious mood. "It is too hard," I said to myself; "besides, as Mrs. Moray said, I am not Uncle Hugh's child, and so I am not bound to obey him. And what more can he do than send me back, and shut me up here, if he meets me? At any rate, I will have one good run." My hand was on the sill of the window, my foot on a chair, from which I intended to spring out, when Charity opened the door, and entered with a waiter filled with all I best liked. She had nearly let the waiter fall as she saw what I was about.

"Why, what is the chile a doing! Here, your uncle's been an' sent you' breakfast, an' you is agoin' out when he is say, 'Stay in!'"

Charity spoke with evident alarm. Such an act of antagonism to my uncle's will seemed fearful to her.

Her fears infected me, and I drew back from the window, cowed and yet more depressed. I had no appetite for the breakfast which, sent by my uncle, seemed another mark of my bondage. Poor Charity's eyes filled with tears, as she saw me push aside the dainties she had prepared so carefully, and, crossing my arms on the table, drop my head upon them, and weep bitterly. I could have borne punishment in the shape of pain, sharp and quick, or privation of some definite pleasure; I could have stood my ground against angry words, or even against hard blows; but this stern quietude, this leaving me to myself, this shutting me out from all the sweet influences of nature and books and friends, this pressure of a power that did not even expose itself to the contact of rude words from me, which cared not for my sorrow, and would release me only on submission—it crushed me—it ground me down beneath its heel, but it did not subdue my spirit; it did not hush the voice of passion—it increased the virulence of the hatred, for the expression of which I was suffering; but it made me, at the same time, feel that I was powerless—it reduced me to despair.

I know not how long it was after this—for I had no

means of measuring time but my own weary sensations, and what seemed many hours may have been only one— when Mr. Mortimer turned the latch of my door, and asked if he might enter. My heart beat so as almost to stifle my voice as I strove to answer, "Yes." He came in, and I rose from my chair; but there was something in my heart which prevented my springing to meet him as I was accustomed to do. I stood before him with my sullen face bent downward, and my arms hanging lifelessly at my side, but not for long. The good man placed himself in the chair from which I had risen, and passing his arm around me, rested his other hand gently on my head, saying, softly, "Poor child! poor child!"

At once the hardness seemed to melt from my heart, and my head dropped upon his shoulder, as if I had found there a resting place and shelter. He looked at me kindly, lovingly, for a moment, and then asked, "Have you asked God to bless you, this morning, Augusta?"

I did not answer, for, in truth, I had not dared that day to repeat the prayer which asks to be forgiven as we forgive.

"Let us do it now," said Mr. Mortimer, and without any change of position, he asked God's blessing and guidance for us through the day, and not for us only, but for all; for our friends—for our enemies; interweaving with this petition an acknowledgment of guilt, and a prayer that we might be enabled to show that mercy to others which we sought for ourselves. There was about this good man a simplicity, a vivid truthfulness of manner, that seemed to bring the Being he addressed so near, to make his intercession so thorough a reality, that the impression was almost overpowering to the sensitive mind of a child. Thus Mr. Mortimer had made me feel that it was a duty to put away resentment from my heart—nay, he had, as it were, introduced me into a presence in which I feared to show angry feeling, before he began to speak on the subject which had brought him to me. We were both silent for a while after his prayer; then raising my head from his shoulder, and placing me where he could look full into my face, he said: "And now come, tell me what troubles you. Why should you stay shut up in this room—you who love liberty so well—when you have only to say you are sorry for your rudeness to Mrs. Moray, and walk out of it? Come, tell me, what is your reason?"

"Because I won't tell a story, and I am not sorry," I answered immediately.

"Of course you cannot tell an untruth; but did you say you were not sorry for being rude to a lady who is your uncle's guest, at his own table? besides, she was your guest, too."

"I only said what was true; she did tell a story; she said I was so anxious to please Uncle Hugh."

"And are you not anxious to please Uncle Hugh—Uncle Hugh who loved your dear father as if he were his own son, and who has always taken care of you? For shame, Augusta; can you be so ungrateful?"

My cheek flushed, I hung my head and answered, almost in a whisper: "I did not care to please him then."

"And why not?"

"Because Mrs. Moray said that Uncle Hugh did not love me much, and that if I did not take great pains to please him, he would send me away from St. Mary's and never let me come back; and then she told Uncle Hugh I was so anxious to please him—just as if I was afraid of him, and was making believe."

"All this, Augusta, only shows that Mrs. Moray did not understand either you or your uncle very well; it may have been all kindly meant, and she may have believed all she said. At any rate, if she had done wrong, it did not become a little girl to tell her so, and in her own home, too."

"But she said it was not my home."

"She could not mean that it was not your home; but, even suppose it had not been, do you think it was proper for a little girl like you, to speak as you did to a lady like Mrs. Moray? Answer me, Augusta; I know you will answer truthfully."

I answered "No!"

"Then surely, my truthful little friend, you will not refuse to obey your uncle, and tell Mrs. Moray what you have told me."

"But they ought not to treat me so—she ought not to tell me such things."

"The question is not what *they* ought to do, or what *she* ought *not* to do, but what you, Augusta Moray, ought to do—always the most important question in the world for you, my child."

How could I resist such a teacher! Oh that he were beside me now! Then he conquered all my opposition, and led me out, if not prepared with a very ample apology, willing, at least, to assent to his assurances that I saw I had acted very improperly, and regretted having given way to angry feeling. I was received by Mrs. Moray with the utmost apparent cordiality; her tenderness during the day was wellnigh overpowering—to my temper, at least; but with the help of Charlie's candies and an outpouring of my full heart to Hugh, I managed to endure it.

This was by no means the only occasion on which Mrs. Moray aroused my combativeness, or insinuated, in her gentle tones and tender manner, doubts of my uncle's kindness to me. I can recall now the change which passed over my feelings and manner, and I can remember, too, how his indifference grew into irritability, and, as I verily believe, for a time into positive dislike. Had Hugh remained at St. Mary's, he might have helped me to resist the evil in my own heart; but he was gone, and under Mrs. Moray's influences, I went from bad to worse, till even Charity exclaimed that "she did not know what had come to her chile."

My uncle seemed, at first, equally pleased with the two boys. He liked Charlie's gay, adventurous spirit, and he was gratified by Mr. Mortimer's report of Hugh's talents. Perhaps he may sometimes have feared that a bookworm, as he was disposed to consider Hugh, must lack the qualities on which the old Morays had built their fame. If he had such a doubt, it did not long exist.

My uncle and Charlie went out as usual one morning on a hunt, and left Hugh, as usual too, at his studies. The hunters had not returned at one o'clock, when Mr. Mortimer was going home to his early dinner. Hugh and I walked home with him. Ah! how spicy the woods were on that warm, winter's day. Hugh and I were sauntering slowly back again, stopping now to listen to the song of a bird, and now to watch a squirrel jumping from tree to tree, or a rabbit scampering off among the bushes, frightened by the sound of our tread upon the dry leaves in our path, when we were startled by hearing a woman's scream. Hugh, bidding me remain where I was, sprang off in the direction of the scream, or screams, for they were repeated several times. A little frightened at finding myself alone, I followed, and was soon in presence of a scene which by no means tended to calm my terrors.

A schooner was then lying near the Island, taking in my uncle's cotton for market. The sailors from this schooner had been guilty of some disorderly conduct, which had caused my uncle to forbid their coming on shore,

except at the point at which the cotton was to be delivered;
yet here was one of them,—a thickset, powerful man, with
a knife by his side, just sufficiently intoxicated to make him
insolent, and opposite to him, defending himself by a stick
he had caught from the ground as he ran, was Hugh, a
mere stripling. How noble he looked, his sallow cheeks
flushing, his dark eyes gleaming, his graceful form swaying
hither and thither, to evade the blows which his brutal
antagonist showered thickly on the air. Behind Hugh was
a young negress, who had been pursued by the sailor, and
whose screams had drawn us there. And now I resorted to
the same feminine weapon. Again and again I uttered that
sharp cry which terror prompts. Fortunately, my uncle
and Charlie were at no great distance from us, on their
return homeward. They heard me, and arrived just as the
wretch, who had drawn his knife, had succeeded in giving
Hugh a pretty severe cut upon the head. Of course the
battle was at an end as soon as the horsemen appeared.
The man took to flight, and, though punished afterward by
confinement on board the schooner, escaped then with only
a blow from my uncle's whip in passing, for all attention
was engrossed by Hugh, down whose face the blood was
flowing in a stream. A Southern planter is not unaccustomed to act as a surgeon on a sudden emergency, and
in a few minutes my uncle had closed the wound on Hugh's
head, fastened the edges together with adhesive plaster,
which he always carried in his pocketbook, washed the
blood away with Hugh's handkerchief, which he dipped in
the water of a neighboring ditch, and tied his own around
Hugh's head. While he was doing this, he complimented
him warmly on the prowess he had displayed, and even I
was not dissatisfied with the manner in which he told the
story the next day to Mr. Mortimer. I was less pleased
with Mrs. Charles Morsy's remarks upon it. It is true her

words were even more flattering than my uncle's. She talked of Hugh's heroism, called him a "preux chevalier"— "un heros de roman;" for, like Charlie, she was accustomed to use many French phrases.

I did not quite understand all this. So far as it was intelligible to me, I thought it just and true; but there was a tone in Mrs. Moray's voice, a sparkle in her eye, which made me doubt whether she meant what she said; and this doubt was strengthened by observing that her speeches vexed Hugh, and that even Charlie was sometimes annoyed by them, and answered impatiently. These little scenes, be it observed, did not occur in my uncle's presence.

One afternoon, Hugh and Charlie were amusing themselves with pitching quoits, on a level spot about a hundred yards from the house. I was not with them, not from any idea on my part that the game was unfeminine, but because I was absorbed in a book brought me that morning by Mr. Mortimer. I sat just within the library door; my uncle, Mr. Mortimer, and Mrs. Moray were on the piazza near the same door, which was open. They were watching the play of the young men, with occasional observations on the vigor and grace of their movements.

"How we shall miss them when they leave us!" said Mr. Mortimer.

"They will be often with us, I hope," my uncle answered.

Then came the soft voice of Mrs. Moray, which always had a disagreeable sort of fascination for me, and I laid down my book to listen.

"I am sure, sir, nothing would give Charlie greater pleasure," she said; "but then, what shall we do about his school? Northern schools give their long vacation in the summer, when it is scarcely safe to come from a northern climate to your beautiful home."

My uncle did not reply immediately to this. The mention of schools seemed to have sent his thoughts off in another direction.

"Hugh told me the other day that he did not expect to go to school again. Does he not intend to enter college?"

"I believe not," Mrs. Moray answered; "I have heard that Mrs. James Moray intended her son to go into her brother's counting house or office—I hardly know how they style it; he is in some sort of money making business."

"And so Hugh Moray is to go into trade?"

I knew by my uncle's tone, how his eyes were flashing.

"I believe so," said Mrs. Moray, who, I have observed, seldom commits herself positively to a statement of facts.

"You surprise me, madam," exclaimed my uncle. "I cannot understand how Captain Moray, himself holding an honorable position in the military service of the United States, can consent to such a thing."

"Captain Moray seldom withholds his consent from anything proposed by his wife. He is an easy, good-natured man, who has no great partiality for the military service to which his father devoted him."

"No partiality!" my uncle repeated, impatiently; "a military man and not love his profession! strange indeed!"

Mrs. Moray laughed—a low, merry, musical laugh—yet it heated me as I sat listening, and made me angry for Hugh's father.

"My dear Mr. Moray, what would you have? Men love that pursuit in which they distinguish themselves. Captain Moray says the Department is unjust to him—he never obtains any place of distinction."

Now, every word of this statement was true, but the tone! the tone! that said the Department was not unjust;

that it was wise to give Captain Moray no very responsible position.

I heard my uncle push back his chair, and pace the piazza with the quick step that marked, with him, a ruffled spirit. But a peacemaker was near.

"Hugh is a fine lad, with uncommon abilities, and a brave and enterprising fellow withal," said Mr. Mortimer, after allowing a little time for my uncle's irritability to calm itself.

"So he is," said uncle Hugh, with decision, "and he shall not go into trade."

The next morning, before Mr. Mortimer came, Hugh was helping me with a Latin sentence which I found somewhat beyond my reach, when my uncle entered the library, so quietly that we were both, for a moment, unconscious of his presence. Hugh was not quite unprepared for what followed, for I had communicated to him Mrs. Charles Moray's statements of the evening before, and the effect they had produced on my uncle. The communication had been made in the way of questions, beginning, "Does not your father like?" and "does your father say?"

I had hoped to obtain a prompt denial of Mrs. Moray's facts, but to my surprise and chagrin, Hugh's answers confirmed them all, and when I said, at length, "Mrs. Moray said so, but I did not believe her," he answered, "It is all true, Augusta, though it may be that Mrs. Moray has drawn some incorrect conclusions from them. I hope Mr. Moray will know my father one day, and then he will see how much reason I have to be proud of him."

"Well, uncle Hugh says you shan't go into trade. What does that mean, Hugh? Is it anything bad?"

Hugh smiled as he answered, "It means a great deal more than you can understand at present; but it is nothing bad."

So Hugh was prepared for my uncle's visit. Seating himself in Mr. Mortimer's chair, my uncle said: "Hugh! how old are you?"

"Eighteen, sir."

"Why, my dear boy, you ought to have been in college two years ago; if you enter now, you will be of age sometime before you can graduate."

Hugh's face flushed; he lowered his eyes and was silent.

"Are you not prepared to enter?" asked my uncle, showing by the question what interpretation he put upon Hugh's embarrassment.

"Yes, sir! my teachers thought that I might enter the Sophomore class, at Columbia College, a year ago, and I do not think that I have lost anything since."

"And why did you not enter when you were so well prepared?"

Hugh's brow became of a yet deeper crimson. I pitied the embarrassment, which I did not understand, and drawing near to him, laid my hand on his. He clasped it closely, and as if the contact with one who loved him gave him strength: he answered: "I have no hope of a collegiate course, Mr. Moray. My father has done all he could for me. I have sisters to be provided for. My father has given me a very good academical course, and I cannot ask for more. I ought now to be doing something for myself and for them too."

"And what have you thought of doing, Hugh? I should think from what I saw yesterday, that you would have no objection to your father's profession; or, would you like the army better?"

"Oh, yes, sir! the army—West Point—a West Point education I should prefer to any other; but—" here Hugh's uplifted head drooped again—"I must not think of it.

There is but one thing my father is obstinate about—he will never consent to a military life for me."

"And why not, Hugh? I have little doubt that I could procure a cadet's appointment to West Point for you. I think it strange your father should object to it."

"Ah! Mr. Moray, you would not think it strange if you had had my father's experience. He says I may be a ship carpenter if I will, but he never wishes to see me command a ship in the United States' service, or enter its military service in any way; he could not bear to see me wear away life, as he has done, in the sickness of hope deferred."

"But I do not see that you need do that, Hugh; you are brave and active, you would, I hope, soon distinguish yourself by promptitude and daring."

"It is hard to do that in a time of peace, Mr. Moray; but as far as it could be done, my father has done it; he has never been under arrest; he has the highest testimonials from every officer under whom he has served; he has seen more sea service than many officers who have worn the uniform of the country longer than he, and he has volunteered for every enterprise of difficulty or danger that has been undertaken in his time."

"How old is your father, Hugh?"

"Fifty, Mr. Moray; he entered the navy at sixteen."

"Well, he is now Post-Captain—we have no higher rank."

"He is not Post-Captain, sir; he is only a Commander."

"What salary does that give him?"

"Twenty-five hundred dollars when on duty either on sea or shore, and fifteen hundred when waiting orders."

"Is it possible that this is all he has won by the devotion of over thirty years of his life? I had no idea our naval officers were so ill paid. Of course, your father must keep constantly employed at sea or on shore, for it would be impossible to support a family, as an officer of his rank would be expected to do, on an income of fifteen hundred dollars."

"He would be very glad to be always employed; but he cannot often obtain service on shore; such favors are reserved for those who, having independent fortunes, can afford to live at Washington, and make themselves agreeable in society there, or for those who can command great political influence."

My uncle was long silent; at length, he said: "This seems a hard case, Hugh."

"No harder than many others, sir."

Hugh strove to speak cheerfully, but it would not do; tears rushed to his eyes, he bit his lip, his chest heaved against the passionate emotion he would fain have suppressed, and he covered his face to hide his agitation. I wept with him, and kneeling at his side, kissed again and again the hand which still clasped mine, wetting it with my tears as I did so. My uncle himself twinkled away some unusual moisture from his eyes as he said, "Don't—don't, Hugh! Calm yourself, my dear boy, and hear me; I have something to propose to you."

Hugh had already mastered himself, though his moist eyes and flushed face showed with what difficulty.

"I wish to take charge of your education in future, Hugh; if your father will consent to West Point, I think I have interest enough to procure an appointment there."

"I am sure he will not consent, sir."

"He may—he may, Hugh—I will write myself; but if he should not, select your profession, and I will be answerable for all your expenses while preparing for it."

"Oh, Mr. Moray! you overpower me with kindness. How shall I thank you?"

How I loved my uncle at that moment, as I looked at Hugh's happy, beaming face!

"You owe me no thanks, Hugh," said my uncle; "I only perform a duty that devolves on me as the head of our house, in making this proposition; but if you think yourself indebted to me, you can repay me a thousand fold, by making the name of Moray as distinguished in America as it was in Scotland. Do for it, Hugh, what I have failed to do, and you will make me your debtor—but we will speak of this another time; write now to your father—we have no time to lose."

"My father is cruising on the coast of Africa; but I will write to my mother. She will know exactly how he feels, and whether I may hope for West Point."

"And if you may not hope for West Point, what will be your next choice?"

"I can scarcely say, sir. I have never hoped for a profession, the preparation was so expensive."

"Well! think of it now. How would the law suit you?"

"I should like it very much, sir; better than anything except West Point, I think."

"You had better write without delay to your mother. I will give you a note to enclose to her—" my uncle took out his watch while speaking, and having glanced at it, added, "It is but ten o'clock—if you write immediately, I will send a boat up with the letter, and it will be quite in time for the weekly mail which leaves Sunbury to-morrow."

A little more than a fortnight later it must have been, I think, that as we were seated at the breakfast table, the weekly mail was brought in, and my uncle having examined its contents, handed a letter to Hugh. There was another addressed in the same handwriting to himself. Both were from Mrs. Captain Moray, as we afterward learned.

Hugh glanced at his letter, turned very pale, and rising from table, hurried from the room and from the house. When he came back, about an hour afterward, I was sitting on the upper step of the piazza waiting for him, while my uncle stood but a little removed from me, taking some observation of the weather, which threatened rain. Hugh seemed to see no one but my uncle; he walked directly to him, and said: "My mother tells me she has written to you, Mr. Moray. She has thanked you, I feel sure, better than I can do; but I will try to fulfil your wishes, and I desire to be guided in all things by your advice."

"That is enough, Hugh;"—my uncle grasped for a moment the hand that Hugh held out to him—"never speak to me of thanks. My life promised much which it has not fulfilled, Hugh—let it not be so with yours; exert your great talents—rise to distinction in your chosen career—help to redeem some of my failures by the honor you reflect on the name we both bear, and it is I who shall be the debtor."

My uncle spoke with an emotion which I had never seen him show before. This rivetted my attention, and impressed on my memory words which I did not fully understand. I was surprised and somewhat impatient that Hugh did not answer; but I suspect the glow on his cheek, and the light in his eye, were a better answer in my uncle's opinion, than any words could have been. They walked side by side once across the piazza in silence. Then my uncle spoke again.

"And so we must relinquish West Point. Were you much disappointed at that, Hugh?"

"More than I expected to be, sir. I hoped to the last that my mother might find some way of reconciling my father to what I wished so much; but I am sure she is right, and I am quite reconciled now."

But I found it much more difficult to be reconciled, when I knew that the result of all this would be to take Hugh away nearly a month earlier than had been originally intended. My uncle, indeed, seemed impatient of every day's delay. He had thrown himself into the question of Hugh's success with all the ardor of his nature.

Hugh left us the last of April. My parting with him was a great sorrow. How well I remember every incident connected with it! I helped him pack his trunk, and make the little arrangements necessary for his journey to Savannah and his voyage thence. He had a parting present for me—it was Campbell's "Pleasures of Hope."

"To-morrow you will know all about them, Augusta," he said, with a smile, "for as soon as we part, you must begin to hope that we are to meet again under the happiest circumstances."

"And never to part again—Hugh, may I hope that? When you come back, will you stay always?"

"Stay here, at St. Mary's, always! Why, Augusta, what should I do with my law-learning here? No—my dear child, I have no prospect of staying in any place half so pleasant—I must live in a great, bustling city."

"And will you send for me, Hugh? When you are done with college, will you send for me, and let me live with you?"

"Would you come to me if I sent? Would you live with me?"

Hugh looked into my eyes with such an earnest expression that it brought the hot blood into my cheek—innocent child as I was—but I answered, decidedly, nevertheless, "To be sure I will," and laid my little hand in his for confirmation of the promise.

"Would you leave your beautiful home here, and all your friends for me?"

"I love St. Mary's," I answered, with a childish simplicity, "but it can't love me back—you will love me back, won't you, Hugh?"

I was very much in earnest, and I doubt not both eye and voice expressed it. Hugh's was the only hand, except Charity's, from which I had ever tasted that sweet draught of love which makes all other draughts insipid. He knew this well, and the knowledge doubtless touched him to a tenderer feeling. He threw his arm around me as I stood before him, and drawing me close—close to him, kissed my forehead, and said gravely and impressively, "I will, dear child—I will love you truly, so long as I live."

As he raised his head, I saw him color, and at the same time, I heard Mrs. Charles Moray's low laugh, and then followed words, uttered in a taunting tone.

"And so—I have been present at the betrothal! Really, Hugh, you seem to be hurrying rapidly to the goal; you are determined to secure yourself at all points; but I hardly thought you would be so dishonorable as to bind a child like that by promises."

Mrs. Moray's color rose, and her breathing quickened as she spoke. Hugh rose from his seat, still holding my hand, and meeting her angry eyes with a firm, manly look, he said, "I will not pretend to misunderstand you, Mrs. Moray, but I entreat you to spare the innocence and simplicity of this child. As for me, I am willing to repeat to Mr. Moray every word of our conversation."

"Oh! I dare say; but that is quite unnecessary as far as I am concerned,—quite,—of course I was only jesting—just as I am when I remind you, Hugh, that .

"'There's many a slip,
Between the cup and the lip.'"

She turned and left the room. I suppose I looked a

little frightened as well as puzzled, for Hugh smiled cheerfully on me and said, "Don't be alarmed—there is no harm done. I have promised to love you always, and I will keep my word. Be sure you keep yours, and we can both rejoice in the pleasures of hope."

Some time after Hugh had gone away, Mrs. Charles Moray told my uncle what she had heard him say to me in that interview. She did not know I was near her, yet she spoke very gently of Hugh. She said he was a very fine young man, but too young to know all the consequences of his words; she was sure he had no wrong meaning; but Miss Moray was such an heiress,—men were so selfish,—one could not be too careful—she had felt it her duty to tell Mr. Moray, though at first she had hesitated for Hugh's sake. My uncle heard her with a smile; he was much obliged to her for her care; but the young man had told him of this the evening before he left St. Mary's.

There was enough in all this to have completely turned my little head, and it would doubtless have done so had I understood Mrs. Moray then as I do now,—had there been near me any one who would have instructed me in the world and the world's ways. But my only *confidante* was Charity, and when I asked her for an explanation of Mrs. Moray's meaning, she said: "Mrs. Moray was cross, and she was sure it was right for cousins, like Hugh and me, to love one another—adding, "I only wish to goodness, Miss 'Gusty, Master Hugh had been your brother!"

And did not I, wish it too! What a sweet word "brother" seemed to me! I long called Hugh so in my heart, and sometimes in the answers that I sent to the little notes that came to me through my uncle, with whom Hugh corresponded regularly, though not frequently. His letters I never saw, but I have since heard all of his life at this time, which they could have told, from lips which reported more partially of Hugh, than Hugh would have reported of himself. Desirous to complete his course of study as rapidly as possible, both that he might lessen his pecuniary debt to my uncle, and that he might hasten the time, when, by the practice of his profession, he should not only win independence for himself, but contribute also to the comfort of those he loved, he pursued his preparatory studies with untiring ardor. My words seem cold, as I remember how his sister Esther's eyes grew moist and her lips trembled, as she told me how the color our Southern sun had burned into his cheeks paled away, and the fire of his eye grew dim, and his movements languid, as if he were giving his life in exchange for the knowledge which was to be power —the power of benefitting others.

Amid all the degradation, all the squalid misery of this our earth, it is a pleasant thought that the pure eyes of angels turned hitherward see some unwritten epics, more glorious than any that the poet's genius has commemorated; some unconscious martyrdoms, whose silent suffering has in it as much of true sublimity as has ever poured its glory around the fagot and the stake.

Mrs. Moray and Charlie left us two months after Hugh, and one month later still, my uncle and I followed them. Oh, that parting from my home! How I lingered on the beach that last evening! how I kissed the very turf in my favorite walk under the orange trees! Some of that turf, so green and soft, I brought away with me. It is all withered and dried up long since, yet as I press my lips to it even now, my heart throbs, and my eyes grow dim with the memory of what it was that day. And how I sobbed myself to sleep that night in the arms of my poor Charity, whose tears dropped upon my cheek, I doubt not, long after I slept, for we too were to part. "Oh Times! Times!" I stretch out my arms across that long, weary interval between then and now, and my heart aches with the longing to draw back all I lost that day—my home—Mr. Mortimer—Charity.

Yet I was not all sorrowful at that departure, for if I was going from St. Mary's, I was going to Hugh, and I was to see his home, and his beautiful mother and his sisters, and like him, I was to be a student, for four years, my uncle aid, and I was to learn to paint glorious pictures, of which I sometimes dreamed; and in my dreams, there was the softly blue southern sky, and the white beach, on which dashed the great, foam-crested waves, and under the sky, and on the beach, and sometimes borne toward me on those great waves, was ever one form, one earnest, kind face—and the form and the face were Hugh's.

This record, originally intended only as a picture of my early home, in all its aspects, varied as no pencil could vary it—giving all its changes from storm to calm, from fragrant morn to dewy eve, from the stern and almost gloomy constraint within, to the brightness and the freedom without,—this record should close here with my parting from St. Mary's Isle; but in the dearth of human companionship, I have learned to love the employment in which I can pour out my soul, though it be but to these lifeless pages. It is not the first time that I have confided the gladness or the sorrow of my soul to inanimate objects; but then, the sea seemed to give me back my exulting shout—the winds to answer with their wail to my wild cry, and I could cheat myself into the belief of sympathy, even from these "mute ministries of nature." Here all is lifeless; and yet, as I turn to the dead past, it looks not at me with such a fixed and stony gaze from these pages, as from the grave in which I strive in vain to bury it.

Hugh met us in New York, and went with us to Elizabethtown. My uncle drove to a hotel, left our baggage there, and then we called, under Hugh's guidance, at Mrs. Charles Moray's. Here the unusual luxury dazzled my childish eyes, and yet there was no vulgar glare. The coloring was rich, yet subdued, the forms chaste and elegant; still, it had not to me a home-like look. Very different was that home to which Hugh and Charlie next accompanied us. The house might once have been a farm house, so rudely simple was its style of architecture. It stood now as it had stood within its surrounding fields in former times. The fields had become a part of the city. There were brick pavements now where once there had been grassy meadows, and rows of houses where once the clover had scented the air, or the harvests of yellow grain had waved. But still the great elms stretched their protecting arms above the old house, which stood back from the street, with its little plot of flowers in front, its porch covered with climbing roses, now all in bloom, and the parlor windows draped with honeysuckles. We entered the parlor, and I think we both felt at once it was a *home*, simple and sweet. I cannot describe it, familiar as its aspect afterward became to me—there was nothing to describe. I only know that it seemed like rest and peace. Cool and shaded it was, with no bright thing in it except the flowers in old-fashioned china vases, which decked the mantle shelf. We were not expected, for my uncle had not permitted Hugh to announce our arrival, and as the front door was open, we entered the hall, and caught a glimpse of the tableau in the room on our right, before we were perceived.

What a picture it was—the stately lady, with her beautiful, Madonna face, the hair yet black and glossy as in youth, the dress so simple, yet so marked with refinement. And the young sisters, one a year or two older than Hugh—how very old she seemed to me then—I thought of her

as her mother's sister. The other was about my own age.
The elder, Esther, was not beautiful—indeed, she would
probably be considered plain—but for the plainness of her
features she atoned by a countenance of thoughtful intelligence, and by a neatness of dress which satisfied the most
fastidious eye. On a footstool at her mother's feet, sat the
bright-eyed, curly-headed pet of the family, Lily, reading
aloud. It was but a moment's glimpse we had. Hugh
stepped quickly forward, saying, "Mamma, Mr. Moray, of
St. Mary's."

Mrs. Captain Moray, raising her graceful head, perceived us, and coming forward, welcomed the strangers
with a union of quiet dignity and genial kindness that I
know now, as I remember it, must have charmed my uncle.
I am surprised to find how vividly these pictures have
impressed themselves upon my memory. Perhaps it is
because no single trait in all our future intercourse ever
seemed incongruous with the impressions of that hour.
There are no cross lines blurring their clear, distinct outlines.

How grateful I was to my uncle for consenting to Mrs.
Moray's request, that he would leave me in that sweet home!
How dear is the memory of those bright summer weeks!
Hugh and Charlie were both gone with my uncle, and by
his invitation, to travel through the Northern and Eastern
States, and into Canada. And I scarcely missed them, living
in Hugh's home, with Hugh's sisters and mother. Mother!
There I learned all the dignity and all the tenderness
of that name. When Mrs. Moray's hand rested, as it
sometimes did, caressingly on my head, I felt as if I had
indeed found a mother, and but for a strange diffidence with
which she had inspired me, I would have thrown myself in
her arms and told her so. I loved Lily, and venerated
Esther almost as much as I did her mother. And she

deserved it, for the perfect propriety of her manners, her unvarying neatness, her conscientious perseverance in whatever she esteemed a duty, and her ready surrender of her own pleasures for the gratification of others. I have seen her plain features lit by the glow of feeling, till they became almost beautiful, as she pleaded for permission to take her mother's place in the performance of some necessary task at home, that the dear mother herself might be free to accept some proffered recreation. There was much that was new to me in this family life, so regular, so self-governed, so harmonious.

"Remember that this is your Northern home," said Mrs. Moray, on the day I left her to enter the school chosen for me in New York.

I did remember it, and my holidays were all spent there. Bright and pleasant were these holidays. Their very memory brings a flush of pleasure to my cheeks, as I recall the bounding of my heart, when I was told that Hugh was waiting for me in the parlor; then came the walk with him to the boat, the sail up the Hackensack, the drive through the woods, the loving greetings from the dear ones at home—each of which, singly, was enough to make the happiness of a day to the lonely child, thirsting for love and for freedom. Ah me! Two homes lost!

I shall say nothing of my school life. It was, on the whole, happy, but it was not picturesque; it had its lights and its shadows, doubtless; but in the glow and the tempest which succeeded, they were obliterated. It was in the second year of my school life, when I was about fourteen, that dear Captain Moray returned from his cruise on the African coast. At first, his presence threw a shadow on the brightness of my days at Elizabethtown. He was himself very grave and silent, and others became grave and silent in his presence; but, child as I was, I soon saw and loved, as all capable of one generous emotion must have loved the nature at once so child-like and so manly, the quick, generous sympathies, the open truthfulness, incapable of disguise, and never suspecting it in another, the more than womanly tenderness and delicacy, the more than manly courage and sense, which formed the rare, if not unique combination of qualities in his character. Dear old friend! father as he would have had me call him! My cold, dead heart throbs still with a little life as I name him. *He* was never cold to me! He was very unlike his son in appearance,—indeed, Esther was the only one of his children who at all resembled him in features. Hugh towered above him in height full half a head, though part of that was lost to Captain Moray by a habit of stooping. His hair was gray, yet it still retained the curl I had admired in the brown locks which Esther had shown me, as having been cut from his head some years before. I have said that he was grave and silent, yet when he laughed, it was with an entire abandonment to the pleasurable sensation, such as we rarely hear after childhood, and when his sympathies were aroused by another's sorrow, or his heart touched by a noble or a tender trait, tears, which his manhood often strove to hide, rushed to his eyes as quickly as to a woman's.

And mine are flowing as I write. My pictures are growing sad—sad even as my present; they bring me no relief—I will have done with them. Even Charlie's merry face comes back to me, shadowed with the gloom which it wore under the constraints of West Point, where, after much opposition on his part, my uncle had placed him, and whither I once accompanied his mother, during my summer vacation, to see him, or with a deeper shadow still upon his face and life.

I have welcomed these glowing pictures of the past, as

the one excitement of my life. In my few hours of leisure, I have locked my door upon the outer world, and said to them, "Come!" though each as it passes, plants a barbed sting within my heart—"come! better the keen pang that tells of life, than this 'waveless calm'—this torpor allied to death." But I overestimated my strength; there are some things I dare not face—some, from whose shadowy forms, half revealed, half shrouded in the dark veil of mystery, I shrink. No! I will write no more. Here I leave these pages; I will not destroy them, but I will place them under a seal which shall not be removed till the hand that traces these characters moulders in dust—unless the future shall withdraw the veil from the past. The future! what future is there when hope is dead? The past! It is lost to me, since I dare not awaken its memories. Henceforth, my life moves on under leaden clouds, and through dreary mists which close around it, narrowing its horizon to that space on which it stands at each succeeding moment. "Live in your duties, my dear," said Miss Drayton, when I said to her that I had neither hope nor memory left to me.

Duties! a cold life, indeed! Well, there is such a thing as freezing to death. But I must go further from Elizabethtown. My poor, weak heart still throbs, tears still start to my eyes when I think of the kind old Commodore. How tender was our last parting!

And now they tell me he is wounded;—if—if—but, no—he will get well again. The honors he craved, not for himself, but for his loved ones, are his, and he will be happier. He will forget me—and better so—I should only trouble him now. Forget him I never shall! Thank God! I can remember him without a pang. Into that wellspring no bitterness has been infused. I know he loves me. I think he will sorrow for me, but he will be comforted.

CHAPTER III.

*"I could not love thee, dear, so much,
Loved I not honor more."—LOVELACE.*

THE manuscript, withdrawn from the oblivion to which it had been thus determinately consigned, in a manner to be hereafter made known to the reader, has acquainted us with the childhood of Augusta Moray. How the proud, passionate nature, springing to meet the lightest touch of tenderness, recoiling with scorn from the approach of falsehood however veiled, turning from the hopes which had faded as a dream, only to pour the glowing light of a free, strong spirit upon hopes that might prove as unsubstantial as they,—how this nature could have sunk into the "waveless calm" described in the last page, it shall be our task to unfold.

Six years of a school girl's busy life had passed happily over Augusta. Her inquiring mind had found delight in exploring the varied paths through God's wondrous universe which lay open before her. Yet true to that quality in woman, from which springs at once her weakness and her strength, her mind drew half its power from her heart. She passed the last Saturday and Sunday of every month, as well as the weeks of her summer vacation, at Elizabethtown, and she well knew the pleased smile with which Hugh would greet every new acquisition she made.

And what had these years brought to Hugh? He had graduated, studied law, been admitted to the bar, and now life was at a standstill with him. The full tide of action which had swept him so far on toward the fulfilment of his hopes, was suddenly checked. Well! he had expected this; he must "bide his time." Waiting was as much a preparation for life as action was. So hopeful, so strong of spirit he was, and none ever knew that he was otherwise. Months—a year passed—the slow passing weeks grew into months again, and the receipts from Hugh's practice at law, had scarcely done more than clothe him. He grew more quiet—though quiet he had always been in manner—more concentrated in thought. It was such a change as might come over a man, who, having entered upon a conflict, finds the strength of his antagonist greater than he had supposed. He does not yield, he does not even doubt, but he watches more warily, addresses himself to his task with more entireness of purpose and with more force of will. It was at some time in this second year of Hugh's independent life, that Augusta Moray began to feel or fancy some difference in his manner toward her. With all the frankness of a child, and the confidence of one who never doubted his interest in her, she asked at once, "What is the matter, Hugh? Have I done or said anything to hurt you?"

Hugh colored as he answered with a quick disclaimer, "Not at all; what could make you ask such a question?"

"Because something is the matter with you, and it is not at all like you to deny it."

"I did not deny it, Augusta; my reply was addressed to the latter part of your question, whether you had said or done anything to hurt me."

"Then somebody has vexed you—I knew it."

"You mistake—nobody has vexed me."

"Then what is it, Hugh? I shall think you very unkind if you do not tell me," Augusta added, after a moment's pause, during which Hugh remained silent.

"There is nothing to tell, my child," he said, gently, looking into the clear brown eyes that were fixed upon his face; "nothing but the old story—as old as man himself—of manhood awakening from the dreams of the boy, and sorrowing to see his beautiful bubbles breaking."

Hugh's last words were spoken with a sort of bitterness, in which an experienced ear might have recognized the tone of one who scorned himself, either for his past credulity, or for his present sorrow.

"What bubble is it, Hugh? Can we not do as the children do—blow another bubble in its place?"

"Of course; that is the approved mode, and we shall do as others do; but no bubble will ever take the place of that, Augusta."

"I don't know; how can I know when you will not tell me what it was; I dare say, if I only knew, I could blow you up one twice as handsome."

"Do you think so? What if this carried away with it my hope of early independence—of honorable standing among my fellow men, and of that home—that simple yet beautiful home, for so I had pictured it—to which you had promised to come when it was ready for you!"

A flush suffused Augusta's face, and her eyes drooped beneath Hugh's earnest look. He remembered well the clear, frank, childish face that had been turned calmly to his when the promise to which he had referred was given, and his heart beat more quickly, and more passionate feeling made his voice unsteady, as he said, "You do not answer me. You cannot promise to replace such a bubble."

The flush grew deeper on her cheeks, but she lifted her eyes—he saw it was with an effort—and said, speaking rapidly, "I do not care for bubble houses. I want nothing more beautiful than my home at St. Mary's, or—or yours at Elizabethtown."

Hugh made no rejoinder, and neither he nor Augusta ever recurred to the subject. From this time, she felt, with a pained feeling, to which she dared not give a name or assign a cause, that a change had passed over their relations to each other. Always kind to her, manifesting sometimes when she least expected it, watchfulness of her comfort, Hugh no longer showed a desire to appropriate her in any degree to himself. He was always too much engaged to come for her—often prevented by important business from seeing her for more than an hour during her monthly visits to his home. Twice he absented himself altogether, sending her, in a note to his mother, an apology for his seeming rudeness. The second time that this was done, Augusta had felt so sure of seeing him, so sure that he would be as kind as of old, or even kinder, after so long a separation, that the disappointment was too great to be borne with perfect quietude. She had some reason to fear that Captain Moray at least read an emotion which pride and girlish shame urged her to conceal, for as she tried in vain to twinkle away the tears that would come, and to steady the lips that quivered with an unuttered cry, she felt his hand laid caressingly on her head, and when she bade him "good night," she felt or fancied that there was peculiar tenderness in the fatherly kiss which he pressed upon her forehead.

As she was going toward her room that night her candle was extinguished, and she returned to the parlor to relight it. She had left no one but Captain and Mrs. Moray there, and as she drew near the door, she caught their tones in conversation, with something of earnestness in their expression which made her pause with the fear that her entrance might be an inopportune interruption. As she hesitated, these words reached her ear from Captain Moray: "Poor child! I cannot bear to see her suffer; but Hugh is right—quite right; he could not, with honor, act otherwise."

With that quick intuition which in matters of feeling supplies the place of reason, and that with a precision which reason never knew, she at once appropriated to herself the "poor child!" which would just as well have suited Lily, or some other. But neither then, nor ever, had she a doubt that she was meant, and turning, with rapid yet cautious steps, she threaded the halls, ascended the stairs, and locking herself into her darkened room, threw herself, dressed as she was, upon the bed, and wept through many hours of the long night. Those were tears rather of shame than grief, or if grief there were in them, it was for a present disappointment. A lasting estrangement from Hugh was too large a sorrow to find entrance yet into her child heart. It would have burst with the effort to entertain it.

Captain Moray had said that Hugh was right! "Of course he was—when was he wrong?" that he had acted honorably—"how could he act otherwise? but it was very provoking, nevertheless, to be treated so, and Hugh should be as sorry for it as she was before she made it up with him."

Such was the somewhat contradictory tenor of her thoughts, and then she fell asleep with tears still upon her cheeks, and dreamed that Hugh came and kissed them off as he had done when she was a little child, and laying her head upon his bosom, soothed her into deeper slumbers. Poor *child*, indeed!

Charlie Moray, somewhat earlier than this, had prevailed upon his mother to sanction his withdrawal from West Point, which he had entered with great reluctance. Its discipline had been intolerable to his self-indulgent nature, so fretting and wearing it, that his thin frame and pale cheeks made an irresistible appeal to the sympathies of his mother and Augusta, on his return home. Captain Moray, it is true, looked gravely upon him, and said it was a pity to have wasted two such important years; but Charlie cared little for his disapprobation. Only one thing seemed to trouble him—what would Mr. Moray of St. Mary's say? He evinced such anxiety on this subject, that Augusta offered to exert such influence as she might have in his favor. It was a generous offer, for it cost her no slight effort to depart from the stereotyped form of monthly letter, in which she informed her uncle of her health, her progress in study, &c., and to rise to such an interchange of feeling and thought with him as might really be termed a correspondence. She awaited his answer with many doubts. Would he think her too bold?—if he did, what would he say?—or would the penalty of her audacity be to suffer the mortification of being unanswered? Her doubts did not continue long. In a shorter time than usual the answer came. She opened it not without fear. It was unusually kind. There was something in it, which really looked like a desire to relieve her solicitude respecting Charlie's health. As to Charlie's fear of having displeased him, he said: "Tell your cousin Charles that I cannot be angry with one whose actions I have no right, and he must excuse me if I add, after the vacillation he has shown, no *inclination* to control. He is a pleasant boy, and I shall always be glad to give him a hunt at St. Mary's; but advise him from me, to study Jacob's sentence on his son Reuben: "'Unstable as water, thou shalt not excel.'"

This correspondence had really brought Mr. Moray and

his niece nearer together, than anything which immediately concerned either of them could have done. We have seen that the admiration with which she regarded him in her childhood seemed to herself nearly akin to affection, and we cannot believe that he was really without a warm, even a loving interest, for the orphan girl whom he had reared, though the coldness and reserve of his manner had been deepened to her by her association with the disappointment of his cherished hopes in respect to the perpetuation of his name in the country of his adoption. His slight unbending in the letter to which we have alluded, aroused a new interest in Augusta's heart. She could not venture on the expression of this interest to Mr. Moray himself, but she said in a letter to Mr. Mortimer, with whom her correspondence was far more intimate and more full: "Do tell me something of my uncle; is he as young—in appearance I mean, of course—as handsome, as active, as when I left him? When do you think he will let me come back to St. Mary's? I think that, without being troublesome, I could do many things now which would make home pleasanter to him. For one thing, he loves music, and I do not play badly."

Whether Mr. Mortimer showed these sentences to his friend, we know not; but very soon afterward Mr. Moray began to speak of coming North the next summer, and of having Augusta return with him in the autumn. The time was past when Augusta would have sought an opportunity of communicating this to Hugh alone, before she spake of it to others. Yet she was no less anxious to know how it would affect him, and obtaining permission from her kind instructress, she went to Elizabethtown under the care of a faithful servant, on a Saturday when she was not expected. It must not be supposed that Augusta had frankly acknowledged her motive for this, even to herself. Oh no! she was very desirous to consult her friend, Mrs. Moray, on the best course of study during the remaining months of her school life, or on her reply to her uncle, or some other very proper and young lady like reason; but she was none the less pleased, none the less conscious that the chief object of her visit was accomplished, when about eight o'clock in the evening, Hugh, little suspecting whom he should meet there, entered the room. She had time to notice that his face was pale and his movements languid, before his glance rested on her, and the pale face flushed, and he hurried eagerly forward with joy dancing in his eyes. Hugh had forgotten himself, but Augusta, who had dreamed only of this moment all day, who had in thought rehearsed her part again and again, though her very heart quivered with the long untasted joy of his presence, was able to assume her intended air of nonchalance, and even to utter the words of surprise at meeting him, which she had conned for the occasion. But oh! the unsteady, tremulous voice in which they came. She fancied it was her cold manner which sent him away to his own room that evening, to study, as he said, some difficult case. Poor *child* again! She dreamed not that those tremulous tones, that quivering hand had sent him away with a fire in his heart, which he feared would make him unable to preserve in her presence the tranquillity of manner he had prescribed to himself.

The following evening, Sunday, Charlie came in after tea. He was always welcome; but his fine tenor voice made him a great acquisition on Sunday evening, when Captain Moray always asked for sacred music. Augusta played, and added her rich contralto to the pure soprano of Mrs. Moray, the deep bass of Hugh, and the full, soft tenor of Charlie. The afternoon had been cloudy and blustering, and toward evening, a little snow had fallen, probably the last of the winter, as it was now late in April, and spring rains had already softened the frosty earth. As Augusta rose from the piano, she approached a window, expecting to see the same gloomy sky with which the day had closed in; instead of this, the moon had risen, and at that moment was pouring a flood of light through the rifts of a cloud, whose jagged edges gleamed golden in her rays. As she looked up admiringly, Charlie followed her, and exclaimed, "The moon is shining, and the snow is done! no hope for a sleigh ride to-morrow, Lily."

"Oh! I am so sorry," cried Lily, coming up, and sending her bright glances out into the night.

"You insatiable snowbird!" said Charlie; "did you ever have sleighing enough, Lily?"

"Often," she replied, trying to look dignified—a difficult, if not impossible achievement, with her *petite* form and lovely baby face. "I was not thinking of myself at all; I wanted Augusta to have all the sleighing she could this winter, as it will be her last."

"Her last! What do you mean by such a tragical announcement?"

"I do not see anything tragical in saying that one is not likely to have any more sleighing," said Lily, a little tartly, for she thought Charlie was laughing at her, and she was at the age most susceptible to the horrors of such a suspicion.

"So—it was the last sleighing, and not the last winter you were predicting for Augusta; but why should she not have sleighing another winter?"

"Because her uncle is to take her home next fall, and she is not likely, I think, to have sleighing at St. Mary's."

"You are going home!" cried Charlie, turning with animation to Augusta; "how I wish I were going with you!"

"Well! why should you not? You know my uncle said he would be glad to have you take a hunt with him—

that is equivalent to an invitation, for he never hunts except at St. Mary's."

"Come, Hugh! cut the law next winter, and let us go to St. Mary's, ride rough ponies, and shoot fat, lazy deer— what do you say? Will you come?"

"There are two objections to my doing so," said Hugh, speaking so quietly that he did not even raise his eyes from the book he seemed to be reading; "I have no time and no invitation."

Augusta, determined to appear indifferent to what she desired most earnestly to hear, had moved toward the door while he was speaking, and either her distance from him, or the slight rustling of her dress as she moved, made his words indistinct, and she mistook "no invitation" for "no inclination." Stung by what in her present mood of feeling, she was ready to believe a rudeness especially aimed at her, she opened the door, and, forgetful of everything but her desire to escape from his presence, she stepped out upon the piazza. In an instant, Hugh had sprung from the table where he sat, taken a large blanket shawl to the piazza, and thrown it over her, saying as he did so, "I do not think you are quite prudent to be here at all, Augusta; it is very cold."

"Do not mind him, Augusta; stay, and have a walk with me," said Charlie, who had followed Hugh, drawing her arm through his as he spoke.

Hugh stopped a moment and looked in Augusta's face, as if waiting some rejoinder. Inconsistent as passion ever is, the power he had conscientiously determined to make no effort to retain, he yet could not refrain from testing with the hope that he should prove it undiminished.

There was something almost defiant in the curl of Augusta's haughty lip, as, meeting his glance fully, she passed her arm yet farther through that of Charlie, and

commenced her walk. Without a word, Hugh stepped
back into the parlor. All was very quiet there. Esther
sat at the table in the centre of the room, reading by a
shaded lamp, Mrs. Moray had gone to her room, Captain
Moray sat in his large arm chair dozing, and Lily still stood
at the window, looking out at the bright moonlight, and
the broken promise of snow. Hugh, stepping lightly, not
to arouse his father, paced the little parlor to and fro.
He was taking himself to task for his departure from a
decision adopted upon principle. He had just found an
excuse for himself, in the fact that Augusta had lately had a
very troublesome cough, and that her delicacy of form
might well make her friends anxious to guard her from
exposure to anything that might cause its recurrence, when
Lily exclaimed, "Where *are* Charlie and Augusta going?"
and looking over her shoulder, Hugh saw them with uncovered heads running through the light, inch deep snow, across
the yard. "And Augusta has nothing but kid slippers on,"
said Lily.

Could Hugh have surmised that the desire to test her
power over his self command had, however slightly, entered
into the inducements to this imprudence, he would, perhaps,
have remained where he was, whatever had been the consequent suffering to both of them. As it was, Lily had
scarcely spoken, when she saw Hugh crossing the yard to
a spot somewhat in shadow, where Charlie and Augusta
were now standing still. Charlie occasionally stooped for a
moment, then rose to give vent to his amusement in bursts
of laughter, that were heard even in the parlor. He was
laughing when Hugh reached them. It was this probably
that so stirred his anger, for he exclaimed, violently, "I can
see no cause for laughter in such absurdity—such worse than
absurdity. I presume, having done enough to show your

disregard of life, Augusta, you will now be persuaded to return to the house."

Augusta did not move, and Charlie, with another laugh, exclaimed, "Hugh! my dear fellow! don't you see she can't move an inch? She's another Lot's wife, or Daphne, rooted to the soil."

It was indeed so. This shaded spot was always wet. The light snow of the evening had covered it, but through that, Augusta's slippered feet had come in contact with the tenacious clay, and every attempt to remove them was vain, except at the expense of leaving the slippers behind her. Vexed at Charlie's laughter, and scarcely less vexed at Hugh's observation of her difficulty, she determined at any cost to escape from them, and crying, "I shall leave you to take your walk alone, Charlie," with a desperate effort, she freed her feet from both shoes and mud, and would have run into the house and up to her own room, hoping by the quickness of her movements to escape observation; but she had to do with one quick to perceive and to act, and scarcely had the light glanced on her white stockings before she found Hugh's arm encircling her, and before she had power to remonstrate or withdraw from it, she was lifted from the ground, borne through the yard and piazza, and set down at the parlor door, with the quiet words, "I would advise you to go to your room and dry your feet."

It may be supposed that she needed no persuasion to adopt this advice. The next morning, when she was summoned to breakfast, Hugh had already gone to his office in New York, and she was obliged herself to return to the city in a few hours.

Augusta had been deeply wounded in her pride, if not in a purer feeling, by the results of this visit, and she vowed a vow within herself, that Hugh should come for her

himself, and entreat her very earnestly before she would go
again. Six weeks passed by, and though she had a letter
from Esther, urging her usual visit at one time, and at
another, Captain Moray himself came for her; she kept her
vow, finding at each time a civil and not untrue excuse.
One day she was called to the parlor to receive a visitor,
and found Hugh, not the cold, quiet Hugh from whom she
had parted last, but Hugh with more vivacity of manner,
more *abandon* to the feeling of the hour, than she had ever
known in him, even in his boyhood. All the conditions of
her vow were fulfilled, and with the permission of her
teacher she returned with him to Elizabethtown. Her
sympathy with his joy was in no small degree abated by
learning its cause. He was in a few days to sail for Europe
on a commission which might detain him there for months
or even for years, but whose successful termination could
scarcely fail to place wealth and professional honors within
his grasp. And Hugh had not a doubt of success. He had
studied his case thoroughly, and he was assured of the
justice of his cause, and fully convinced that somewhere
there still existed proofs of the right, recoverable by a
patience that *would* not be exhausted, and an assiduity that
would not be wearied. Hugh had faith in himself as well
as in his cause.

Two days more only were left to Hugh in his home.
His preparations were completed, with the exception of a
few of those little works which mother and sisters delight
to perform for the loved ones. In these, Augusta had
sought to share, and she now sat, on a warm June afternoon, at an open window through which floated the mingled
odors of rose and mignonette, embroidering the initials H.
M. on some fine cambric handkerchiefs.

On the other side of the low window, leaning on its sill,
stood Hugh, watching the taper fingers that moved so deftly

in his service. As Augusta laid aside a handkerchief, Hugh lifted it, looked at the letters, and said, "I shall bring these back with me, whatever else I lose, and however long I stay."

"You have not told me yet how long that will probably be."

"The law's delays, you know, are proverbial—I go for six months, I may not return for two years."

"Two years! Oh, Hugh! And you can be so glad!"

He bent down till the soft ringlets of her hair touched his cheek, and said, in those low, deep tones that bear a heart throb in every word, "Shall I tell you why I am glad?"

No answer came; but he saw the lids that drooped over the half closed eyes quiver, he saw the crimson flush that mounted even to the white temples, and he added, "Because I hope to be ten years nearer that home of which I have talked so often, and which you have promised to share. Will you not repeat that promise, now that I am going so far away? What! not a word! only say, 'Hugh, your home shall be mine.'"

The trembling lips moved, but the words which had once been uttered so easily, would not come. That sweet silence, more eloquent than speech, was broken by another voice, and they both started and looked up, to see Captain Moray standing before them.

"Let me answer for you, my child," he said, very gently, to Augusta. Her glance at him had shown her that even while speaking to her, he was looking at Hugh with an expression which she did not understand. She too turned to Hugh. He was still more unintelligible. Having risen from the careless attitude in which he had been leaning over her, he stood erect, drawn up to his full six feet of height, with his arms folded across his chest, while a smile, good-humored, yet with something defiant in it too, parted his lips, and shone in his eyes. The smile died away, however, as Captain Moray continued: "Tell Hugh he cannot expect that the woman should keep the promise made by the child, and that a beauty and an heiress would scarcely find her appropriate place in the home of a poor barrister."

It was not Hugh, but Augusta who answered him, vehemently, as if a feeling akin to indignation had restored the voice which excitement of another kind had taken from her.

"I am neither a beauty nor an heiress," she said, "and I never made a promise to Hugh that I do not mean to keep."

She was ready to die with shame the moment these words were spoken, so bold they seemed to her. Unable to meet the looks of either father or son, she hastened from the parlor to her own room, locked her door, and gave vent to her mingled emotions in a burst of tears which had more of gladness than of sorrow in them. Hugh would have escaped too, but as he would have turned away, Captain Moray said, "Do not go away, Hugh; it is necessary that we should understand each other on this subject."

"I have no desire for any concealments from you, sir," said Hugh, overcoming his natural reluctance. He sprang in the window as he spoke, and placed himself at his father's side. For a moment they looked steadfastly and silently each in the other's face. In Hugh's was the strong resolution of unbroken, vigorous manhood, and the hope, which long repressed, had just burst into life—a life fuller and more tenacious for the difficulties it had conquered. On Captain Moray's was the weariness of a long struggle which hope had ceased to cheer. In this very expression which might have seemed significant of defeat, lay his power over

Hugh, and not over Hugh only, but over every one of tender and generous heart that knew him. It would not have been so, had not all seen that the weariness was accompanied by no weakness; that there was power unsubdued to struggle on, even though he felt that the struggle must end in defeat. Defeat is a wrong word, for such struggles know no defeat—they conquer even in death. Those who have ceased to strike for success, whom hope has ceased to animate, are inspired by the nobler principle of duty, and crowns of victory which shall be immortal await the followers of this "stern daughter of the voice of God."

As he looked on Hugh, the habitual depression of Captain Moray's countenance deepened, and he turned aside with a heavy sigh. That sigh seemed to have wafted tons of weight to Hugh's heart. It sank like lead. He laid his hand on his father's shoulder and said, "What would you have me do, father?"

"Wait till I am gone, my son. It will not be long," was the despondent reply.

"Father, I have waited till every demand of honor seemed satisfied; surely when I can offer her an independent home, there can be no reason why I should wait longer. She is now eighteen—no longer a child."

"It is not years that make us old, Hugh. You are older than your twenty-four years, and she—she is a mere child—what does she know—what has she seen of life? And her uncle, Hugh! You have told me he was a proud man; what plans for his beautiful heiress—for the increase of his family wealth and influence through her, may you not be disappointing. Oh Hugh! my son! my son!"— his voice broke—a deep sob heaved his bosom, and rising hastily, he turned away to hide the emotion which he could not subdue. Brave old veteran! His heart was ever tender as a woman's to another's woe, but never had

Hugh seen him thus moved by any personal consideration. He looked toward him as he stood by another window, with his gray hairs, silvered less by age than sorrow, streaming on the breeze. Every hair seemed to Hugh to plead against him. He approached, stood beside him and said again, "Father! only tell me what you wish. All that depends on me shall be done."

"Only wait till I am gone, Hugh, and then do as your own ripened judgment shall dictate. I have nothing, Hugh, but honor. My life has been a failure in all else, but my honor I hoped to carry to my grave, unsullied by a suspicion. Let not Mr. Moray have it in his power to say, that after all he has done for us—for us I say, Hugh, for what was done for you was done for us all—let him not think that we have solicited him to let his niece make this her home while she was at the North, only that you might have a better opportunity of winning the heiress of his fortunes."

'Father! Mr. Moray will not think so; he is a just and generous man."

"The more careful should we be not to deal with him ungenerously, Hugh."

Hugh turned away, and paced the room with slow, measured steps. The sacrifice was too great; besides, was he not already committed to Augusta? He came back to the window and said: "Father, is it not too late? My own disappointment might be borne, but have I not already gone too far? Remember her own words; after such an avowal, is not my honor irrevocably bound?"

"Hugh, she is but a child; it would be most ungenerous to her to fetter her by promises before she has seen enough of the world to know her own mind: wait, Hugh, you are both young enough; wait till she has the power to compare you with others; wait till you have shown what you are; then, Hugh, perhaps you may win her uncle's consent as well as hers, and I—I will not then stand in your way, if indeed I shall not before that have left a world to which I have been but a burden."

"Oh, father! use not such words; I cannot bear them. I repeat, I will do just what you say. Shall I tell her what you have just said, and release her from her promise till I have a better right to claim it?"

"No, Hugh; that would but be to bind her by a yet stronger bond; no, you must say nothing, not so much as by looks, that shall show you are mindful of this hour. It may be that she will forget it, or that she will learn to think she gave a deeper significance to your words than you intended she should."

"And can I leave her to such a doubt? How base I shall seem in her eyes!"

"Better *seem* than *be* base," said Captain Moray, with emphasis.

Hugh flushed and turned away again from his father; when he returned, it was to say, "I cannot trust myself. I must wait a calmer moment to decide this question; now it is impossible. The conversation of this afternoon is the first step in our intercourse not already confided to Mr. Moray and sanctioned by him; but on a point of honor, no opinion could weigh with me as yours, sir—only that I would think—but it is needless to speak of that. How I am to meet her with such confusion in my mind, I know not. I must hasten my departure; I will go to-morrow, and this evening, I will spend abroad. I have some papers at the office that I intended to send for; I will go instead."

Accordingly, when Augusta that evening entered the parlor where stood the tea table, the timid, furtive glance she cast around her, told her that Hugh was not there, and while she still hesitated whether to consider his absence as a relief or a disappointment, the information came, like two galvanic shocks, rapidly succeeding each other, that he would not return till very late that evening, and that he must leave Elizabethtown for Boston at an early hour the next day.

Excess marks one phase of man's weakness. To keep the unerring line, neither approaching too near that central truth that has arrested, and is, for the time, controlling us, nor to fly off beyond its influence—this seems impossible. Most move around it in a zigzag course, delivering themselves to the force of counter attractions, till, startled by the distance to which they have been led, fear drives them back as far in the other direction, the passive slaves of impulse. A few strong spirits take their observation, mark their course and walk in it, though every step be planted on sharp thorns or burning coals. But even these rarely find the true mean. The calculations of selfishness, the generous determination to tread every selfish desire in the dust, alike mislead. To such natures as Hugh Moray's, the danger lay in the last direction. He feared the decisions which were in accordance with his wishes. This last night at home was a sleepless one to him. He reviewed every step of his intercourse with Augusta Moray. In the promise he had asked and obtained as a boy, no passion had entered; it was dictated by the calm, yet earnest affection of a brother. He saw the loneliness of soul which, as she grew older, would weigh more heavily upon her in the home of her childhood. He knew, of course, that she could not share his home alone; but, had the question of propriety been suggested to him, he would probably have answered, " Of course, when I have a home to myself, I shall either marry, or Esther will keep it for me. In either case, Augusta will be happier there, with society suited to her age, than she can be here, shut out from all the world except her uncle

and his friends. I have no doubt Mr. Moray would readily
consent to give her to us."

Mrs. Moray's sarcastic suggestions first aroused other
thoughts in his mind. They made his communication to
Mr. Moray of what had passed, more difficult, but more
essential. His stammering tongue and blushing face, certainly conveyed to Mr. Moray more than his words expressed; yet he received the confession kindly, praised the
honorable feeling which had prompted it, said he had no
doubt Hugh, if he were diligent, would achieve an early
independence, and as little doubt that he would use it honorably, and there he left the subject. And Hugh, as his
own feelings grew more deep and passionate, remembering
that their germs had been already quickening in his heart
when he had that conversation with Mr. Moray, overlooked
the fact that they had not been expressed, and felt as if Mr.
Moray's silence had given them his sanction, ever bearing in
mind, nevertheless, that the sanction depended upon his success. When he began to doubt that success would come
to him, he had withdrawn from Augusta, that he might not
be tempted to seek that which he felt was forbidden to him
except on that condition. And when fortune had again
dawned on him, the feeling to which he had refused indulgence, sprang into fuller life and more decided manifestation, for its temporary repression. Now, his father's suggestions pressed painfully upon him. Had a stain indeed
fallen upon his honor? Had he indeed given occasion to
Mr. Moray to suspect him of ingratitude—to brand him,
even in his thoughts, as a fortune hunter? Again and again
he travelled over the past, to find an answer to these questions. The result was a decided negative up to that afternoon; but there a doubt intruded. The *attainment*, not the
hope of success—that was the condition, and then the consent was only *implied* by Mr. Moray, or *inferred* by him-

self; ought he not to have waited till he could have asked a confirmation of his inference from that gentleman himself, before he sought to create a deeper interest, or to win for himself a more assured hope? He was afraid he had done wrong—afraid that in the glow of his new-born happiness, he had become blind to all that opposed him. To fear—to doubt—was with Hugh Moray, even at this period of his life, only the precursor to a sterner resolve. He had not forgotten—after those words whose remembered tone thrilled him even now he could not ignore—that the burden of silence he imposed upon his own heart, might weigh heavily upon another. That was the heaviest part of his trial, but at least she knew his wishes—he would do nothing to remind her of them, but he could not unsay them, and if she had faith in him, all might yet be well, and hope would again have painted an enchanting vision; but he turned away from it—" he would not unsay them" —so Hugh resolved, yet with the tendency to excess which we have before noted as an attendant of human weakness, the looks, the tones from which he had intended to banish passion only, leaving to them the warmth and light of friendship, became cold as death. The strong hand with which he constrained himself, if it did not altogether still the movements of his heart, at least so fettered them that they were not perceptible, and before the breakfast of that last day at home was over, each one of the little party at Captain Moray's, the captain himself excepted, was asking, "What can be the matter with Hugh that he is so distant to Augusta?" and Augusta herself, with a cheek now paling with sorrow, now burning with a proud anger, was accusing herself of having disgusted him by unwomanly unreserve. The moments hastened on and brought the parting. Under any circumstances, how bitter parting is! but how is its bitterness increased, when at that moment the shadow of an unsatisfied doubt rises between us and the friend who is about to pass beyond our vision, and our speech—a moment more and the question which is now throbbing at our heart, bursting from our lips, must remain unbroken till—till when?—it may be till the grave shall give up its dead. With some such thoughts as these swelling in her heart, burning in her cheek, and glittering like a fevered agony in her eye, Augusta stood waiting for that last clasp of the hand, that last word, that last look which should tell her all, or leave it untold forever. Hugh would not look toward her, yet he not only felt that she was there, but he believed that in some strange abnormal way, he saw every change of her color, every turn of her inquiring eye. With an almost mechanical movement, he approached his mother and received her parting embrace—then in turn Esther and Lily threw themselves into his arms, and were held for a moment to his heart—what he most dreaded could no longer be delayed—he turned to Augusta, and held out silently, not venturing even to look upon her face, a hand which did not shake, though it was cold as marble. She touched it with fingers as cold and more tremulous than his —he could not forbear lifting his eyes for one moment to those which were striving to pierce through the lids that so obstinately veiled his own. Their glances met, and revealed to each, for one flashing moment, the unuttered agony in the other's heart. Her pride gave way—one sob struggled up from her heaving bosom—the next moment he had caught her in his arms—pressed her with passionate force to his throbbing heart—touched her forehead with quivering lips— then releasing, as suddenly as he had embraced her, rushed from the room, leaving his father to follow at a more leisurely pace with the hat and gloves which he had left behind him.

CHAPTER IV.

"If to her share some female errors fall,
Look on her face, and you'll forget them all."
Rape of the Lock.

"Damn with faint praise, assent with civil leer,
And without sneering teach the rest to sneer."
Pope's Satires.

"MAN walketh in a vain show," saith the inspired teacher, and who has not proof of the saying's truth in himself? How, peaceful and calm to the outward vision is the life, when deep down below the surface, storms are raging and volcanic fires are pouring out their scorching, searing lava! Especially is it thus when the storms are raised, and the fires lighted by elements, whose existence we would gladly conceal even from ourselves. It has been said that shame entered our world as the companion of sin. It is true, and so did contrition, and both are the protest of what remains of the divine in the soul of man, against that loathsome enemy. Sometimes, indeed, that protest is made most vehemently when the transgression has not been against God's laws, but against those enactments of society which vary with varying latitudes. Of such, according to some, are those emotions which wither the self-respect and cast gloom over the life of the young, and pure, and delicate woman, who suspects herself, or fears that she is suspected by others, of having given her heart unsought. But not so does it seem to us. We believe the instinct to be true which feels the natural, eternal propriety of the Paradisaical order; that man should feel it is "not good to be alone"— that he should desire and seek his "helpmeet," ere she be given to him. Those who teach otherwise, would denude young life of its most bewitching charm, and make it hard, and cold, and loveless, even when they do not make it foul and loathsome. Thank God for those instincts adverse to such teaching, which He has Himself implanted in the soul of woman; thanks be to Him that they are so strong;— yea—thanks even for the warning agony which defends them from too rude a touch! Yet we deny not that earth-born emotion, the offspring of pride and passion, often infuses a bitterer element into this agony, and drives its iron deeper into the soul.

Pure, delicate and sensitive Augusta Moray suffered that instinctive pang; proud and passionate, her life was steeped in that greater bitterness. Exaggerated, certainly, was that suffering, for it is the characteristic of passion to exaggerate; but she was conscious of causes for it which may not have been manifest in our narration. Her words had been few and simple, such as friendship and sisterly affection might dictate; but she knew well what feeling, awakened by Hugh's tenderness, resisting Captain Moray's effort to repress it, had burned on her cheek, flashed from her eye, quivered on her lip, and given its thrilling intonation to her voice, and she believed that her throbbing heart had been at that moment laid bare before both father and son, and had been met by the one with a coldness intended to repulse, and by the other with a compassion which humiliated. Hugh's strange distance on the last morning he was at home, had planted a doubt, a fear, in her heart; but, ere it grew to more, the agitated, impassioned tenderness of his parting plucked it out. Again, however, it had taken root and sprung up, and strengthened till the doubt had become conviction, and the fear, despair. Hugh was an excellent correspondent. Every steamer brought to his mother or to Esther, his most frequent correspondents, some expression of his tender memories of home. At first Augusta watched for these letters as one weary of the night watches for the dawning. "Surely," she said to herself, "he will send me some little word to assure me that 'I too am remembered;" but nothing came, unless she could consider herself as one of "that dear circle of home," to which his loving remembrance was ever sent. As month after month passed away, and letter after letter arrived, kindling hope but to quench it, all the fire of Augusta's nature retreated to her heart, and left her manners cold and proud where Hugh or Hugh's family were concerned.

"Augusta, come write a postscript to my letter to Hugh; I hate to send him blank paper across the sea, and I cannot fill my sheet."

It was Lily who spoke.

"Excuse me—I have nothing to say to him," was the careless answer, as Augusta lifted her eyes for a moment from the book she held in her hand.

"Nothing to say to Hugh! and you have not seen him for six months!" cried the wondering Lily. "Well! I must tell him that."

"Do so, and you will find his only wonder to be that you should imagine I could have," and Augusta rose and left the room as if to escape a disagreeable subject.

Mr. Moray did not come north till late in the autumn. When the summer vacation in her school began, Augusta, according to a promise given soon after Hugh's departure, went to Captain Moray's to await her uncle's coming. Slowly and heavily the month of July passed away, and early in August she gladly embraced, with her uncle's consent, a proposition made by Mrs. Charles Moray, to accompany her to Saratoga. Charlie went with them. He was very popular and his mother scarcely less so. As for Augusta, her beauty created quite a sensation. Gentlemen gathered in the hall to see her pass in to dinner, waylaid her in her walks around the grounds, and contended for the honor of her hand in the ball room. And all this scarcely raised the color on her cheek, and certainly never caused her heart to beat more quickly. She was not only an acknowledged beauty, but also a reported heiress, and a word, or even a glance of encouragement, would have brought more than one captive to her feet; but neither glance nor word ever came, and "Beautiful, but cold as ice," or "Beautiful, but proud as the devil," were the verdicts pronounced on her. At length, the ice seemed to thaw, the pride to bend, and the world wondered more as they saw to whom.

Among Charlie's intimates at Saratoga was a young naval officer—a midshipman, of course. One afternoon, as Charlie and Augusta were riding, he joined them. Soon afterward they saw him take off his hat and make one of his lowest bows to a slender, pale faced pedestrian.

"Why, Sutton! who is that to whom you do such reverential homage?"

"Don't you know him?" asked Sutton, laughing and coloring.

"No! I should have thought him a Commodore, but that he is too young: is he your chief—the Secretary?"

"Oh, no!" and Sutton laughed again as if half ashamed of what he had to say, "he is my chief's chief—the Secretary's secretary."

"I cannot see his claims to such a very low bow yet," said Charlie.

"That is because you do not write yourself U. S. N.—

Uncle Sam's Nigger; that gentleman's good word will do more for me than the Secretary's."

"How is that, Mr. Sutton?" asked Augusta, as if the subject interested her.

"Why, you know, Miss Moray, our Secretaries are changed with every new administration; it is scarcely possible for them to master the details of the Department in four years, so they retain, as a matter of necessity, the under-secretary of the previous administration, and also, as a matter of necessity, commit themselves wholly to his guidance in all minor matters. The President and Secretary may plan expeditions, but what ships shall be sent, who shall command them, and how they shall be officered, are questions decided by Mr. Saville; and as these are the matters that influence our fortunes, he is the man to whom we pay our court. Ah, Miss Moray! A few smiles from you, if you would deign to give them, would be as good as a squadron to any captain in the navy that you wanted particularly to recommend."

"Mr. Saville can be won by lady's smiles, then?" inquired Charlie.

"When, like Miss Moray's, they can confer social distinction—otherwise, I am afraid a box of cigars would be a safer investment."

"I must ask you to introduce him to me," said Augusta.

"Thank you, Miss Moray, for the permission to do so—such an introduction will be a trump card to me."

"So you are going to intrigue for a squadron for Uncle James," and Charlie laughed at the transparency of her motives.

"Captain Moray should not need any one 'to intrigue' for him—pray excuse me, Miss Moray, for using Mr. Moray's word—intrigue. There is not a better officer in the service or one more beloved."

Charlie looked at him with surprise. He had been so accustomed to hear his mother speak in a depreciating tone of his uncle, that the ardor of young Sutton struck him strangely, especially as he saw his cheek glow and his eyes glisten. Augusta saw it too.

"You speak warmly, Mr. Sutton," she said, "do you know Captain Moray?"

"Know him! I have sailed with him, Miss Moray. I cannot tell you all I owe to him, but this I will say, if every young officer had found as kind a friend, there would be fewer shipwrecked characters to disgrace our profession."

That evening Mr. Saville was introduced to Miss Moray, and received in her most gracious manner, very much to the astonishment of Mrs. Charles Moray, who had not been present at the conversation we have just narrated.

"Who is your friend, my dear?" she asked, when Mr. Saville had left them, "he must have some extraordinary claims to your attention."

"Don't believe it," said Charlie, "she expects to be paid for all her condescension."

"Of course, in some coin or other, we all expect to be paid," retorted Augusta, gaily.

"Admitted—my question then is, in what coin do you expect payment?"

Augusta colored, laughed, and looked to Charlie for help.

"In coin stamped with a squadron, and lettered with Captain James Moray," said Charlie.

"Are you sure it would be the best thing for him to place him in such a responsible and conspicuous position, my dear?" asked Mrs. Moray, in her softest voice, and with a smile of peculiar meaning flitting across her face.

Augusta's face grew hot and her eyes flashed.

"I am sure there is no position to which he would not do honor," she exclaimed.

"I dare say Hugh will be pleased, if you succeed," and Mrs. Moray smiled again as she raised her eyes quickly to Augusta's face.

"I know and care nothing about Hugh's pleasure," she exclaimed, warmly, with yet deepening color; "if Hugh were out of the world as he is out of the question, it would not lessen my love for Captain Moray, or my desire to serve him."

"Indeed!"—it is a simple word—"indeed"—but its meanings are numberless. As spoken now by Mrs. Moray, and interpreted by a look, it forced Augusta to turn away, abashed, indignant, and scarcely able to repress her tears.

Charlie did not understand his mother—he seldom did —but he saw that Augusta was displeased, or distressed. Either was an uncomfortable feeling, and Charlie did not like uncomfortable feelings for others or himself, so he came forward in her defence.

"Augusta is quite right, and you would think so, if you could hear how Sutton speaks of my uncle—and you can hear him, for he is just coming this way. Here, Sutton!" he caught the young midshipman by the arm as he was passing, and drew him toward his mother, adding, "come and tell my mother what you told my cousin and me about Captain Moray."

Sutton told her not only this but more. He seated himself beside Mrs. Moray, and with an eloquence which sprang from feeling, he told of the trials of a midshipman's life, of the mad longing to break away from the restraint and confinement of a ship, of the tempters which lie in wait for them in every port, just when idleness makes temptation most powerful. He acknowledged that he had not always been able to resist, that he had passed more than

one night on shore with companions as young and as
thoughtless as himself; that once—twice—Captain Moray
had advised him with a father's faithfulness and almost a
father's tenderness, sending for him to his cabin, that their
interview might be private. At length, emboldened, as
he blushingly confessed, by the very goodness which
should have made him more afraid of wrong, he was guilty
of such gross neglect of duty, that it demanded severer punishment. It was not withheld; he was reprimanded in
public. Exasperated, perhaps all the more because he was
obliged to acknowledge to himself that the reprimand was
well deserved, in a moment of passion he declared his determination to resign his warrant. The words once said, pride
did not permit him to retract. With an aching heart he
wrote the letter to the naval department containing his
resignation. Etiquette required that this should be trans-
mitted through his commander, who must, of course, be
acquainted with its contents. Here the tones and manner
of the young man grew so earnest, that Augusta drew
nearer, forgetting her fear of Mrs. Moray's raillery, in the
interest he inspired. He continued, "From the moment I
gave that letter, Mrs. Moray, my peace was gone. I had
taken a step which would shut me out from the career I
most ardently desired; but this I could have borne; it was
the thoughts of my mother's sorrow—I am a mother's boy
—her only boy, Miss Moray—this was what wrung my
heart, and but for my pride, would have made me entreat
Captain Moray to restore the letter to me before it could
have left the ship. A week passed, every day sinking me
deeper and deeper in depression and humiliation. I strove
hard to hinder it, but at length every defence gave way,
and I no longer made an effort to conceal that I was very
wretched. Just at this time Captain Moray sent for me to
his cabin. I supposed it was to tell me that my resignation

was accepted. I was so faint when I reached the cabin that I could scarcely stand. He saw it, and made me take a chair. Imagine my delight when, taking a letter from his desk, he said, 'Mr. Sutton, here is your resignation. I would not forward what seemed to me to be written in the heat of passion, till I had given you time to think on it. Now, if you please, you may withdraw it; if not, I will send it by this day's mail.' Oh! how happy I was, when I once more held that foolish letter in my hand, and how grateful I have ever since been to Captain Moray!"

"He is a very good-natured person," said Mrs. Moray, in a tone that grated as harshly on the nerves of Augusta as her "indeed" had done.

It did not seem to please Mr. Sutton any better. He answered quickly, "He is the best hearted man in the world; yet he is also one of the most decided and efficient officers in the service. His subordinates love, but they also fear him. For this reason it is that his ship is always well-disciplined. As to his men, they adore him; you can hardly meet an old tar anywhere who has not some story to tell of his daring or of his humanity."

"You are very kind, Mr. Sutton, to tell us all this," said Mrs. Moray, with a slight yawn, which might have escaped observation had she not raised her fan to hide it.

"I thank you a thousand times over, Mr. Sutton," said Augusta, warmly; "you must tell me some of those stories before we part. My uncle will be so glad to hear them."

"My dear Augusta! I am sorry to interrupt you, but really, you are treating Mr. Delamere quite rudely;" the observation was in a whisper, but scarcely Talma himself understood the art of so modulating the voice as to produce the desired effect, better than did Mrs. Charles Moray. In the present case it was intended that Mr. Sutton should bear, and he and Augusta both started and turned. Mr. Delamere, to whom Augusta was engaged for the quadrille that was forming, stood waiting to lead her to it. The interruption did not prevent her hearing from Mr. Sutton before they parted many of those anecdotes which in every military service become traditional of favorite officers. These were all of Captain Moray. They told of his daring spirit, evinced when almost a boy in the search for pirates in the Gulf; how he had bearded Lafitte, the terror of all tradors, in the fastnesses of his own island home; and inspired such respect for his heroism, that he had not only come off unharmed, but had won courteous treatment, and succeeded in the object he sought; how, when disease, from whose loathsome aspect all shrank appalled, made its appearance at an important naval depot, and all who could were finding excuses for getting away from it, he volunteered for the command, and though he was himself struck down and brought near to the grave, so long as he retained his senses, the comfort of the meanest sailor was his care, and his self-forgetful devotion to them, won a name which would fill a ship commanded by him with good seamen, sooner than all the press gangs in the world could do.

It has been said that every woman is born an *intrigante*; it is true, we believe, that few women are born without that nice sensitiveness from which proceeds the tact that wins its way to its object, through obstacles insurmountable to man's force. Without obtruding the subject upon Mr. Saville, Augusta managed that these anecdotes should reach his ear, and without taking the attitude of a petitioner herself, or suffering Captain Moray to appear at all, she had impressed him with the conviction that to advance the professional interests of Captain Moray was the surest way to win her favor. His own vanity deceived him into another deduction, to which her manner would have led no one else

—that with such a card in his hand, he need not despair of winning, not her favor only, but herself and the fortune of which report gave a somewhat exaggerated account.

"I will see about that," thought the shrewd Mr. Saville; "investments in Southern property are not always safe—there are apt to be as many debts as acres, or more."

Really good-natured, rather liking his uncle, and feeling more proud of him since listening to Mr. Sutton's stories than he had ever expected to be, Charlie readily lent himself to her plans, and at her instigation, solicited Mr. Saville to let them see him at Elizabethtown on his way to Washington. And so they parted.

It was October when Mr. Moray of St. Mary's arrived. He brought startling news with him. Measures of the utmost importance to the South, and to the party with which he had ever been associated in politics, were to be acted on during this session of Congress, and he had been prevailed on to accept a seat in the National Senate. He had refused to take any active steps for his own election, but he had remained at home, at the request of his friends, till the election of the State Legislature was passed, and the success of his own party in that, had made his appointment certain. He had already secured a furnished house in Washington, having made the journey to New York by land, and stopped a few days in the Capital for that purpose. It was here, as the acknowledged mistress of his house, that Augusta was to make her *début* in society.

"You will need some chaperone, of course," he said to her; "I will invite either Mrs. Charles Moray, or, if you would prefer it, Hugh's elder sister, who seems to me staid enough and mature enough for the purpose."

A few months before, and Augusta would have answered instantly, "Esther—pray ask Esther;" but now she hesitated, colored, met her uncle's eyes, fancied some peculiar meaning in them, and said, "Mrs. Charles Moray, if you please."

"And her son? of course we must invite him with her; if Miss Moray were with us, I should ask Hugh to come to us as soon as he arrived, and he may arrive any day, as he writes me that there is only one missing link in the chain of evidence he is searching for, and he will not delay a day after the attainment of that."

Mr. Moray paused, but Augusta seemed to consider the subject as settled.

"Then I shall ask Mrs. Moray and Charlie?" Mr. Moray said, in rather a questioning tone, fixing his eyes upon her, as he lingered by the table at which they had breakfasted together, and from which he had just risen.

"If you please, sir," answered Augusta.

Mr. Moray rested his searching eyes for a moment on her downcast, glowing face, then turned away with a smile that had in it more of bitterness than of mirth, repeating to himself,

"Varium et mutabile semper fœmina."

That day he went to Elizabethtown, and the invitation to Mrs. Moray was given and accepted. Charlie was not at home.

"Though I do not often venture to accept invitations for him—he is so seldom disengaged—this I can quite confidently answer, for I know he will be but too happy to come; and I have so wished that he should go to Washington and hear the debates in Congress. Charlie has excellent talents for elocution, and I think when he settles down, he will take to public life—so Washington will be a capital school for him."

Mr. Moray was decidedly verging on the school of

Democritus, for again a grim smile passed over his face. His words were few and simple.

"I shall expect you both, then, to be ready to leave New York by the last week in this month. In the meantime, I have a favor to ask of you."

"I am delighted to hear it; pray let me know what it is."

"To give Augusta the benefit of your taste in her preparations for her winter in Washington. She will have her own carriage, and be at the head of my establishment, and I wish her to enter into society with the distinction due to her name, and to her position as my acknowledged heiress."

He had risen, hat in hand, prepared to make his adieus, but was arrested by a gentle sigh and the words, "Ah! my poor Charlie!" from Mrs. Moray.

Neither sigh nor word rang true on Mr. Moray's ear, and there was a little impatience in the quick glance of inquiry which he threw at her.

"I was afraid you would be angry," she said, deprecatingly, "and I know Charlie would be desperately so, if he ever had reason to believe that I had betrayed his secret; but I really think it is hardly fair to let you invite him to your house, without telling you that he is coveting, and may steal its richest ornament."

"You mean he is in love with my niece,"—Mrs. Moray almost started to hear her euphuistic phrase translated into such plain, unmistakable language—"but I do not see," Mr. Moray continued, "why he is to be pitied for this."

"Not for this, certainly; but because the position in which you are about to place her, must surround her with admirers, many of whom may have greater advantages than he of position and fortune to commend them to your favor."

"I would rather marry her to one of my own name, than to the greatest fortune in Christendom."

Mr. Moray's answer had been quick and decided.

"You delight me—then you will give your consent."

"Let him win her's, and mine shall not be wanting. Good morning!"

"You have made me perfectly happy. Tell dear Augusta I will be with her early to-morrow. Good morning!"

"How easy it is to manage these men who think themselves invincible! My only trouble will be with Augusta. But somebody said once he could move the world if he only had a fulcrum for his lever; her pride is a good fulcrum, and I will soon find the lever."

Such were the lady's thoughts as she turned away from this interview. Let us listen to the gentleman's as he walked toward Captain James Moray's.

"Well! so after all it is Charlie—a fickle boy—instead of that noble fellow, Hugh, whom Mortimer as well as I thought she preferred. I wish it had been Hugh; but at least it will be a Moray, and I will do all I can to enable Hugh and his father to distinguish the name here, while I am building up for its representatives in the South, one of the largest landed estates in the country. It is little enough for a man's life-work—the thing by which he is to be remembered; but I have wasted so much time," with a heavy sigh, "this is all that is left to me."

It was the first time that Mr. Hugh Moray and Captain Moray had met. There was a simplicity and frankness about the brave old officer, which at once won Mr. Morny's esteem, and touched his kindlier feelings. Hugh furnished them with a subject of common interest. When all had been said and heard on this subject, they grew silent. Suddenly, with almost startling abruptness, Mr. Moray exclaimed, "You are now a post captain, I believe, Captain Moray?"

"Yes, poor ———'s death promoted me."

"What command have you had since your promotion?"

"None—there is little hope of a command for any one who has no interest in Washington."

"Are they not obliged to employ you in your turn, when there is no charge against you at the department?"

Captain Moray smiled, threw back his head proudly and said, "There are some whose turns come very often. It is true they dare not positively overslaugh me, and put a younger officer into the regular line of service over me; but the old favorites are sent again and again to commands, and the young favorites have special service created for them, while those who have grown gray in a life of hard service, who, for the sake of their wives and children, have clung like desperate men to the commissions which were their all, after hope and ambition had been both crushed out of them, doing the disagreeable duties from which the perfumed pets of the department shrink—these—" the veteran broke down, his voice was choked, and rising, he turned from Mr. Moray to the window, that he might hide the emotion of which he was ashamed. A moment after, returning to his seat, he said, "Excuse me; this is a subject on which I cannot speak."

Captain Moray had said that all ambition had been crushed out of him; but it was the ambition of a heart at once noble and tender, under whose pent up fires his heart was agitated by such uncontrollable emotion. He knew that those he loved would care little for the privation that poverty brought, could they only know that his name was honored as it deserved; but that to them, as to him, it gave a bitter pang to have the world receive the impression, which the slights of the Government could scarcely fail to give, that he was unworthy of any office of trust. Mr. Hugh Moray remained silent for several minutes after the Captain had reseated himself. To a stranger it might have seemed, from the outward quiet, that the agitation of the past moment had been forgotten, but to those who knew him well, that very quiet, in Captain Moray, was a proof that he was struggling against a strong tide of feeling; and to an accustomed ear, the quick tapping of Mr. Hugh Moray's fingers upon the arms of his chair, would have told that his mind was full of a thought which he found it difficult to express. Yet it was but a delicate scruple at assuming the position of superiority indicated in the power to help—he who had been all his life an idler, to offer help to one who had so faithfully performed its duties. Think of it as he would, however, there was but one way, and he spoke out.

"I am going to Washington as one of the Senators from Georgia. Tell me how I can serve you, and I will use all my influence in your behalf."

"Thank you! thank you, heartily, Mr. Moray! All I want is service, and the more work the service brings, the better."

"The Gulf, if I mistake not, will soon be our most important command," said Mr. Moray.

"If we have war with Mexico, as everything seems to threaten, it would be," replied the Captain.

"Suppose, in anticipation of it, you should apply for that command; you are entitled to a squadron now."

"I may apply, but I shall never obtain it."

"I think you will; try—make your application—I will soon be in Washington to back it. Perhaps it would be better if you made it in person."

"Excuse me for interrupting you—that would be impossible."

However, it proved not to be impossible, for the very next day Captain Moray called to say that he had decided to go himself to Washington. An invitation was immediately given him by Mr. Hugh Moray, to consider his house as his home while he should be in the Capital.

"Dear Captain Moray is coming to us in Washington, and I am so glad!" said Augusta to Mrs. Charles Moray, that day, in the presence of her uncle.

"I wish he were not so unstable," exclaimed her uncle, "with his Impossible one day, and his readiness to go the next."

The instability admitted of easy explanation, and Lily, proud always of Esther's good deeds, gave it to Augusta.

"Esther has been working all summer," she said, "working for money—writing little stories for a magazine, and copying for a lawyer—one of Hugh's friends—no one knew anything about it, except mamma, and she helped her to do it—and now they have given the money to papa."

"And does he know how it came? Have they told him about Esther's working?"

"Oh, no! We are afraid it would grieve papa to know that it was necessary—so please do not let Aunt Charles hear it, or Charlie either."

"And how does Captain Moray think the money came?"

"Oh! he thinks mamma saved it, you know," she continued, with a laugh; "papa knows nothing about money, and then he has such confidence in mamma's powers, that he would not be at all surprised to find her performing miracles."

"May I tell my uncle?"

"Yes, I should like him to know how clever and good Esther is."

CHAPTER V.

"There is what is called the highway to posts and honors, and there is a cross and by-way, which is much the shortest."—LA BRUYÈRE.

"PARIS is France," it has been said; but Washington is not America. Washington lacks the most important of our social elements. It has, it may be, our best, it has certainly a fair proportion of our worst, but it lacks that middle class which bears up the one and keeps the other in subjection—which fills the great space between the wise counsellor and devoted patriot, and the political adventurer and scheming speculator. It is in association with this class that the sentiment of expediency, which is disproportionately cultivated in political life, becomes subjected to the eternal and universal principles of right. Without it, it must be a strong man, indeed, who does not find himself in danger of rushing to the goal at which all are aiming by some short cut, when he believes that to preserve the straight path would be to see himself certainly distanced by more unscrupulous competitors. As the diver must occasionally rise to the surface and breathe the air, so must these sometimes leave the troubled waters of politics to breathe the purer air of our common life, and to receive the light of Heaven through a less refracting medium, if they would preserve their souls alive.

But not such was Washington in the eyes of our young heroine. Too proud not to be reserved and shy in the expression of feeling, there was in her nature a lofty enthusiasm suspected by few. To her, Washington was the seat of life whence the body politic drew its forces. The statesmen congregated there, were men who lived not for themselves, but for their country. It was still possible for her to preserve such an illusion. Men yet stood too near the grand old fathers of our country not to desire to *assume* some likeness to them, if they *had* it not. They wore robes of the same fashion, if they moved less freely in them. Our Senate had not yet become a debating club for the discussion of abstract questions, a discussion for the most part conducted with a puerility of thought, and a noisy declamation that would scarcely do honor to youths fresh from college, nor was our Representative chamber yet converted into an arena for pugilistic combats. Webster, Clay, Calhoun—the triumvirate to which, it is to be feared, we shall long have to look back as to our last, were still living; and as Augusta Moray gazed on the dark, melancholy eyes of the first, shadowed by that wonderful brow, or looked into the face of the second, where if prescient thought sometimes rose as a flitting cloud, it was chased away before the glow of the warm heart and the quick kindling fancy, or turned to the sharp angular lines and firmly compressed lips that marked the iron strength of the third, she felt that she stood in the midst of her dream's fulfilment. The session was one of peculiar interest. Great questions agitated the public mind, and were treated greatly. Two great parties, springing from the very foundations of our civil polity, strove for supremacy in our legislative halls. The one, looking into the depths of our colonial history, took its stand on the unquestionable truth that each State of the Union was sovereign over herself, from which was drawn the corollary that she was as free to leave as she had been to enter the Union. The other contended that the present Constitution of these UNITED STATES defined the boundary of the powers of each State as well as of the great whole into which they had been voluntarily fused; that to look behind that was such a resort to first principles or natural rights as is involved in revolution, and must be decided as revolution ever is, by the relative strength of the ruling and the revolting forces. Denying the premises, the first yet accepted the conclusion, reminding their antagonists that though there was no doubt of their numerical inferiority, it was not the first time in the world's history that a weaker party had stood opposed to a stronger, and supported by the determination to dare all, and, if necessary, to lose all, for a principle, had worn out the patience, even where they could not subdue the power of their antagonists, taking at last from their relaxing grasp what they might in vain have sought to wrest from their determined hold. On neither side was there any trickery, any bullying, any flimsy display of rhetorical power. All was grand as the subject for which they contended, solemn as the doom to which they seemed approaching. In the Chief Magistrate of that time all saw the unflinching executor of the nation's will—a man whose words were the sure prefigurements of his deeds. Their verdict must be carefully weighed, for it would be surely executed. In stern silence each sat to hear, to deliberate, to judge. The sharp logic and fiery vehemence of Hayne called up no angry flash, roused no personal vindictiveness; and the deep tones of Webster found as ready an entrance to Southern as to Northern hearts, while in those powerful words which seemed the fit weapons of a nation's champion, his mighty mind swept away all that opposed it save that principle which lay embedded in the very deepest stratum of the life of his opponents, and which could not be torn away from them till feeling and life were extinct.

It was in the capital and in the presence of these great men that Augusta best liked to find herself. We are afraid she did not always listen when men of more ordinary power occupied the floor—the gallery was an excellent dreaming place at such times.

But this was only one phase of her life at Washington. Under the chaperonage of Mrs. Charles Moray, and with the escort of Charlie and sometimes of her uncle, she went much into its gay society. Mr. Hugh Moray was fully aware of the power derived from social influence. It was with difficulty that his party had persuaded him to enter again into the cares of a public life; but now that he was in the arena, he *must* succeed—it was essential to his personal, and yet more to his family pride. It must not be through him that the name of Moray should be connected with failure—so every means of influence was studied and seized with avidity. Augusta acquired new importance in his eyes, when he saw "grave and reverend seigniors" pause in their conversation to gaze admiringly upon her beautiful face, or to follow with their eyes the proud grace of her retreating form.

"We are greatly indebted to you, Mr. Moray," said one of these, Mr. Mellen, of Virginia, on being presented to Augusta; "you have shown that there is something in which the South cannot be surpassed."

"Ah, Mr. Mellen!" exclaimed Mrs. Moray, who stood near, "we shall not permit you to claim Miss Moray as Southern property."

"I heard it surmised, madam, that one of your family held her in mortgage; but he cannot prevent us from claiming her as Southern. What say you, Miss Moray; do you not belong to us?"

"Certainly, sir; I have been six years at school at the North, but the South is my home."

Augusta spoke with a steady voice, though her face was dyed with a crimson, the source of which Mr. Mellen strangely misapprehended, as his rejoinder proved.

"Forgive me, my dear young lady, for calling up your blushes—I am sorry to see them, beautiful as they are, for I suppose they testify to the truth of Washington rumors, and so we cannot hope that the South will continue to be your home. I must not introduce my son to you, I see." This was said in a subdued tone to Augusta, then raising his voice he added, to Mrs. Moray, "At least, Mrs. Moray, we have furnished you with the material for the beautiful manufacture, and of genuine Sea Island, too."

There were some things in this conversation which grated harshly on the ears of Augusta Moray. She thought she must remonstrate with Mrs. Moray—surely she could not be aware herself of the impression her words must make on those who heard her. Could she really mean to insinuate that she was engaged to Charlie, or—or—to any one else? Oh, no! it was impossible. She would probably laugh at the idea if it were suggested. Such were Augusta's thoughts, and having come to such a conclusion, to speak of taking a bull by the horns, or of attacking a lion in his den, or any other of those actions which are the conversational standard of difficulty, would have given a faint idea of the effort necessary on her part to approach Mrs. Moray on this subject. It was simply impossible.

Captain Moray had been detained a few days after them. When he arrived, Mr. Hugh Moray announced his intention to give a dinner for the purpose of introducing him to the Secretary of the Navy, whom he had never seen out of his office, and to some influential Members of Congress. If Captain Moray could have remonstrated against this, he certainly would. The bold seaman, and hospitable and courteous entertainer on board his ship, was mastered on shore by a shy reserve, which forbade his finding much enjoyment in the society of strangers. His reluctance, however, would not have been noticed had it not been forced into observation by Mrs. Charles Moray.

"I hope you will not run away from Washington to-day as you did from Elizabethtown, to avoid Mr. Jackson's dinner," she said to him; and if her playful manner hid a deeper meaning, neither the simple-hearted old captain nor his frank host suspected it.

"Run away from a dinner! That casts at once an imputation upon your courage and your appetite, Captain," exclaimed Mr. Hugh Moray.

"I am obliged to plead guilty to it, sir; but I will try to redeem myself in your opinion, by my gallant assault on your good cheer to-day."

Too modest to explain that this reserve and avoidance of society on shore had originated in an indisposition to receive courtesies which his small pay did not permit him, without a disregard of prudence and even of justice, to return, the Captain left Mr. Hugh Moray, himself a lover of society, associating that taste with all that was manly, energetic and daring in character, with just such impressions as Mrs. Charles Moray had probably wished to produce.

To Augusta, presiding for the first time on such an occasion, over her uncle's table, the dinner would have been as formidable an affair as to Captain Moray, had she been at liberty to think of herself; but, in truth, that Captain Moray should make a favorable impression, was to her a subject of much more anxious desire than that she should. He was seated on her uncle's left hand, Mr. M———n, the Secretary, on his right, and before she left the table, she was gratified by seeing the open-hearted, kind old Secretary's handsome face expand with cordial smiles, as the conversation between them drew out traits of mingled shrewdness and simplicity from the gallant officer. The arrangement of guests at table had not quite satisfied Mrs. Charles Moray; indeed, she had ventured to suggest playfully, that her place was the one assigned to the Secretary, who ought to have the post of honor at Augusta's right hand; but the suggestion was overruled by Mr. Moray, who said that Augusta might need an occasional hint from Mrs. Moray, suppressing his most forcible reason for the present plan, which was that it brought the Captain and the Secretary together.

"You have done me a great favor, sir, in introducing me to Captain Moray," said the Secretary, in shaking hands with Mr. Hugh Moray. "I like him; I wish there were more such in the service."

"I am very glad to hear you say so, Mr. M———n; I have an application to make to you in his behalf, this week, and I was sure you would receive it more kindly if you had seen him," replied Mr. Hugh Moray, as he accompanied his guest to the door.

They were alone; for the Secretary was compelled to leave early for another engagement, while the remaining guests went from the dinner table to the drawing room, where they were met by others invited for the evening, ladies as well as gentlemen. Mr. Hugh Moray joined them with a somewhat cynical smile upon his lips, excited by the involuntary coldness which had shadowed the Secretary's open, cordial manner, at the mention of an application.

Among the guests of the evening was Mr. Saville, invited at the special request of Augusta, who introduced him to her uncle and to Captain Moray. Mindful of Mr. Sutton's instructions, she was nervously anxious that her gallant old friend should make a favorable impression upon this "chief of the chief," and a little vexed to find that Captain Morny, though sufficiently courteous, as he would have been with her introduction to a coal-heaver, showed no particular *empressement* in his reception of Mr. Saville. Following him to another part of the room, Augusta found an opportunity to say, "Mr. Saville, whom I just introduced to you, is the chief clerk in the Navy Department, sir."

"I know he is, my dear; I have heard of him before," was the quiet reply.

"Mr. Sutton told me he could do a great deal more for the officers than the Secretary himself; at least, he said the Secretary would not do anything without Mr. Saville's advice."

"And did he tell you that the officers paid their court to Mr. Saville?"

This was said with a laugh, which made Augusta believe that he saw through her manœuvring, and with a laugh and a heightened color, she said, "I see I must pay the court for you, sir."

Captain Morny turned his eyes in the direction of Mr. Saville, with an unusual intenseness of expression in them, then letting them fall on the glowing, sparkling face at his side, he said, taking her hand as he spoke, "Better not, my good child, better not; it might be dangerous; that is not a face to be trusted; he is a young man still, and might presume."

Augusta's only answer was a proud little motion of the head, which said, as plainly as possible, that such a degree of presumption could not be imagined.

Captain Morny smiled. "I see I may trust you, my dear, not to compromise your own dignity or mine."

"Indeed you may, sir; but I shall get you a squadron notwithstanding," she added, as she moved gracefully and smilingly away.

There was something peculiarly soft yet sparkling about

Augusta this evening. The ice seemed to have melted. She was always dignified, but to-night the dignity was without a touch of haughtiness. Mrs. Charles Moray was struck with the change now as she approached her, and said, "Augusta, you look as if you had found a treasure, and were willing to bestow a little of it on your neighbors. Pray do not forget me if it be so."

Again the glow and the sparkle were on her face as she said, "My treasure is incommunicable, Mrs. Moray, and indeed I feel much more like asking alms to-night, than bestowing them."

"You look like it," said Charlie, laughing; "'so pale, so sad, so woe-begone'—it moves my compassion; what can I do for you?"

"Give me a cup of coffee, if you please." It was handed her from a waiter just passing, and she added, with an effort to look grave, "If every one would be as compassionate, my wants would soon be supplied."

A glance to Mr. Saville, who stood near, had drawn him within their circle.

"Who would not be proud," he said, "of contributing to such an object! May I supply the cake to the coffee?"

"Is that all, Mr. Saville? I hoped you would offer me a fine frigate, if not a squadron."

"A squadron let it be; there is one trifling difficulty, however: you have no commission. How shall we get over that?"

"Oh! easily enough; I will get some one who has a commission to command it for me."

"Captain Moray, for instance."

"Exactly; how fortunate that he should happen to be here just at this time."

"Then, for form's sake, he will receive the squadron, and for form's sake, the Secretary will give it; but you and I will understand the matter, and you will know that the squadron is yours, and that I have given it."

"Of course, and I will be your debtor forever; how shall I begin to repay you? Shall I promise to dance one quadrille with you every evening this winter?"

"Unfortunately, I do not dance; but do not trouble yourself to devise means of payment. I like the thought of being your creditor."

"You are very kind, and I have no more wants."

"Where is your squadron to go?" asked the laughing Charlie, and at once destroyed, by his tone of badinage, the feeling of reality which mingled with this trifling on Augusta's part, at least. He was called away, and Mr. Saville, suddenly dropping his voice, and changing his tone to one of great earnestness, said, "Your friend, Captain Moray, may command my best services, Miss Moray."

"Thank you, Mr. Saville, thank you a thousand times; I shall indeed be your debtor, Mr. Saville." She spoke with a throbbing heart, and extended her hand, scarcely conscious of what she did.

The pressure it received recalled her to herself.

"Creditor—debtor—that bond may go farther yet," murmured Mr. Saville, as he pursued his way homeward that evening.

"How glad Hugh will be when he comes! and he is coming! I heard his father tell my uncle that he had arrived, and that he knew he would be impatient to accept his invitation;" so much in words, then in that deep under current of thought, which she refused to shape into words, yet which had throbbed in her heart, lent its fire to her eyes, and its soft grace to her movements through all that evening, came the conviction, "He looked at me—I am sure he looked at me as if I had something to do with Hugh's coming when he said it."

Such were Augusta Moray's last waking thoughts that evening.

Captain Moray's application for a squadron was made the next day. It was backed by influential friends, and the Secretary, having consulted with Mr. Saville, somewhat to Captain Moray's surprise, appointed him to the command of the squadron in the Gulf of Mexico. This was particularly grateful to Captain Moray and his friends, as there seemed little doubt that war between Mexico and the United States was not very distant—an event which would render the post one of peculiar difficulty, and therefore of peculiar honor. Mr. Hugh Moray expressed very warmly his sense of the Secretary's kindness in this appointment, and Augusta, perhaps with more reason, thanked Mr. Saville. Each accepted the thanks, without any attempt at disclaiming their agency in the favor bestowed. Captain Moray was no courtier, but he was a very exact disciplinarian. He could not condescend to fawn on Mr. Saville, but he was very respectful to his chief, the Secretary; and really liking him, there mingled with his respect a cordiality which overcame his usual reserve. The consequence was that at every visit to the department, he gained ground with the Secretary, and lost it with Mr. Saville, who would have been ready to revoke his decision in his favor, had that been possible, or had he not felt himself rewarded by the smiling reception he was always sure of obtaining from the beautiful Miss Moray, whose smiles were the more valued because they fell not on all. In the mean time, while Captain Moray was losing favor with this potential individual, Mrs. Charles Moray was gaining it. Soon after the appointment of Captain Moray to his squadron, she seemed to become suddenly aware of Mr. Saville's claims to consideration, and treated him with such distinguishing respect that they soon came to stand upon somewhat intimate terms.

"Really, Mr. Saville," she said on one occasion when they found themselves together at an evening entertainment, "we are all under great obligations to you, for your advocacy of my brother-in-law's claims."

"You owe me nothing, nothing at all, madam; it was all the Secretary—of course I have no power; all I could do, and more, if it had been possible, I would have been happy to do for your beautiful niece."

"Ah, Mr. Saville! Now you have touched my only cause of dissatisfaction with you."

Mrs. Moray kept her smiling eyes rivetted upon him. She was not surprised to see his eyes fall, and his face flush as he uttered the one word, "Madam!"

"Can you wonder at it, Mr. Saville? but I forget you do not know my reasons. See her," she continued, directing his attention to Augusta, who was just passing them, leaning on the arm of Captain Moray, who, much against his own inclinations, had been induced by her persuasions to accompany her to this *soirée*, dressed in the uniform of his rank, which he rarely wore except when acting officially; "now, Mr. Saville, can I help wishing to secure her for my daughter?"

"It is a very natural wish, madam; but pardon me if I say you cannot very much blame others if they wish to secure her—not—exactly—as a daughter," and Mr. Saville smiled his most insinuating smile.

"Not at all—not at all, Mr. Saville; but to give one competitor such advantages over all the rest as you have just given to Captain Moray's son, is a little annoying, to say the least—it almost throws the game into his hands, sir."

Mrs. Moray spoke in lowered tones, yet with such playful grace that her words might pass for jest or earnest, as her hearer pleased. Mr. Saville seemed quite disposed to take her in earnest.

"Captain Moray's son! I was not aware he had a son."

"Nevertheless, he has a son—a very decided son, Mr. Saville; a son whom it is impossible to ignore and mistake, as you will feel when you have seen him. The only element of success in this suit which he appeared to lack, was a position and prospects that would recommend him to Mr. Moray. These, I think, you have done much to furnish him with."

"By helping to give his father a squadron? you do not think he would marry upon a clerkship—that is all which his father can give him."

"His father can give him nothing which he would take —he is a lawyer with very fair prospects in truth—but we are proud, we Morays, Mr. Saville; and Hugh would not say to Mr. Moray, 'Give me your niece,' till success was in his possession, not in prospect only—I see—I see what you are going to say—but hear me out: it is true, as you have said, that Hugh is not personally advanced by your efforts; but if Captain Moray should prove a successful commander, and there is little doubt he will, for he is a man of excellent judgment and undoubted bravery, the prestige of his honors will extend to all his family—at least in Mr. Moray's consideration."

"But I think you are needlessly alarming yourself and me, madam, after all. The young man will hardly feel that he has a right to wear his father's laurels, whatever Mr. Moray may do; and if I understand aright, the difficulty is that he will not seek till he is more assured himself of his position."

"Yes; but, Mr. Saville, a humbler man might be encouraged into confidence, and Mr. Moray,"—she glanced around and dropped her voice yet lower, " with him, family name is the first consideration; he cares for nothing so much

as continuing the old name in connection with his splendid
estate, except the making that name famous; now, if Captain
Moray does the last, and he will if there should be a war
while he commands, Mr. Moray will desire Hugh above all
others for his heir, and he will find no difficulty in making
him understand that he does; and I shall lose my daughter
and you your—what shall I say?"

Again her voice was light and playful—she was conscious it had become gravely earnest.

"Will you not walk?" asked Augusta, pausing as she
passed again with Captain Moray; "Mr. Saville must be
very entertaining; I never knew you a fixture before."

"Poor Mr. Saville! he has been very good, and I have
been entertaining him with eulogies on my own family, beginning with our Commodore here. Oh, Mr. Saville! I
am really ashamed of myself, but the truth is, I am as very
a Moray as my friend the Senator himself."

"You could scarcely have chosen a subject which would
have interested me more, madam; will you walk now?" he
rose and offered his arm.

"No—I will reward you for your patience—Augusta,
my love, will you walk with Mr. Saville and let me have
my brother's arm?"

The Commodore was perhaps the least satisfied person
in this arrangement, but he was one of those who could
never demur at any proposal made by a woman, so he submitted to the exchange of companions with what grace he
could.

"Mrs. Moray has been introducing me to another member of your family, a son of Captain Moray, of whom she
speaks very highly."

He watched Augusta as he spoke, and saw the quick fall
of her eyes till their dark fringe seemed to sweep her flush-

ing cheek; but she said nothing, and he determined to try her still farther.

"You are acquainted with him, of course," he said; "is he really so noble as she represents?"

Augusta could not remain silent to so direct a question, but there was a tremor in her voice which showed the effort she was making as she answered, "I know not how Mrs. Moray represented him; but of his nobleness of nature she could not have said too much."

Mr. Saville almost fancied he felt the reflection from her burning cheek upon his own, as he bent toward her. He was satisfied.

"I will take care that our new commodore reaps little glory from his command; she loves that man, but she is as proud as Lucifer, notwithstanding all her softness. She will all the sooner be won by another if she fancy herself neglected by him, which she will be sure to do, if, as Mrs. Moray thinks, he can be kept from proposing to her by doubts of his position. Her daughter! She will never marry that brainless fellow—I am not afraid of him."

Such were Mr. Saville's evening meditations on this occasion. Augusta's were expressed in one intense heart-cry, "When *will* Hugh come?"

The two who rose earliest in Mr. Moray's house were Augusta and himself. Captain, or Commodore Moray, as according to usage in the American navy, he was called since he had obtained his squadron, had the self-indulgent habits in this respect common to most seamen when on shore, and Mrs. Moray and Charlie were self-indulgent everywhere and at all times. The morning after the *soirée* mentioned above, at seven o'clock, Augusta entered the little room where her uncle usually wrote and read, and where the morning papers were always left. Expecting to find Mr. Moray there, she came to ask if he would come into the breakfast room and take his coffee with her. It was a sunny room, and, what with the sun shining through the crimson curtains of its one window, and the glow of the coal fire casting its reflection on the bright steel bars of the grate, it seemed on this especial morning to be all alight. The door had been left ajar, and Augusta, treading with velvet slippers on the thick carpet, entered noiselessly. A gentleman was seated beside the table, writing. His face was turned away from her, yet by a sudden light that flashed to her eyes, and the crimson that rushed over cheek and brow, it was evident that Augusta was at no loss respecting his identity. No one who looked in her face could doubt that she was glad, very glad; yet there was a wavering in her movements, a sudden dropping of the clasped hands lifted in joyful surprise, a poise of the body, which seemed to speak rather of retreat than advance, when Hugh, though he could have heard no sound, seemed suddenly to become aware of her presence, and, starting from his chair, approached her with outstretched hands, and the one word, "Augusta!" uttered in a tone that said as plainly as any words could have done, "I love you dearly," and "I am rejoiced to meet you again."

One flashing glance from her eyes, a deepening flush, a half smile, were Augusta's only answer. Hugh lifted the still clasped hands which he had taken in his, to his lips. Just then her uncle's voice was heard at the door of the room giving an order to a servant, and, springing from the detaining hand, Augusta escaped from the room, passing Mr. Moray, who was entering, without a word.

"Where are you going, Augusta? Is breakfast ready?" he called, turning and following her across the next room.

"Yes, sir; will you come?" The answer was given without pausing or turning around.

"Very extraordinary," thought Mr. Hugh Moray, who

was somewhat punctilious on the subject of deference from the young to the old.

And while he turned back to invite Hugh to come and take his breakfast with him, Augusta went on to the breakfast room with face and heart all in a glow. Where was the coldness gone now? It had fled with the doubt and fear and mistrust for which, if she thought of them at all, she was ready to reproach herself at this moment so bitterly. "Doubt Hugh—good, true-hearted Hugh? How could she have done so? He was too brave and resolute as well as too true, to profess anything he did not feel—she should never forgive herself for having doubted him."

Such were the thoughts that floated through her mind, while, hardly knowing what she did, she managed, with the aid of the waiter, to pour out coffee for her uncle and Hugh, with only the mistake of putting into one cup all the sugar intended for both.

Mr. Moray was particular in the matter of coffee, and he called sharply to Gib to give him some coffee; what he had, he declared, was syrup. The color on Augusta's cheek deepened and, with a little touch of consciousness, she turned her eyes inquiringly to Hugh; but they fell in a moment before the smiling glance that met them.

"I am afraid that your coffee"—she began, stammeringly.

"My coffee is excellent," he hastened to say, " but I will take a little sugar," extending his cup and saucer to her, and continuing to hold it to the manifest disapproval of Gib, who had offered to take it. "I have not lost my boyish taste for sugar, you perceive;" he added, smilingly, as he withdrew it at length, becoming conscious that several lumps of sugar had been dropped into it while he was trying to gain a look from the eyes too steadily intent apparently upon the task of sugaring, to lift themselves from the cup.

"I must have had all yours as well as my own," said Mr. Moray, innocently, as he watched this operation.

"And so, Hugh, you have succeeded in the object of your journey?" began Mr. Moray when these important preliminaries had been settled.

"So entirely, sir, that I think our case will be won by a simple recapitulation of testimony."

"I heard you spoken of very handsomely the other day by a New York lawyer, whom I happened to meet at a dinner. He said that the resources you had shown in your search after testimony, and the acumen in testing it when obtained, had gained you a position in your profession which you must have been years in acquiring in the usual course of affairs at home; he talked of your having had several partnerships offered you—is that true?"

"It is. I have accepted an offer from Mr. Holton, to whose kind interest I was indebted for the appointment."

"You have done well, Hugh—I congratulate you. Mr. Holton is one of the first lawyers in the land. A partnership with him ensures your reputation and your success."

"He is most kind and generous," said Hugh, thoughtfully.

"How long can he spare you to us, Hugh?"

"I have not entered on the business of the office yet, Mr. Moray; and as the courts are not sitting at present, I have told Mr. Holton that I should be absent two weeks—perhaps three—if my father require me so long."

There was a smile in his eyes, as he pronounced the last words, which, as Augusta met it in one hasty glance, seemed to her to say that this was not the only contingency in which he might be induced to extend his visit to three weeks—at least so the sudden drooping of her eye and flushing of her cheeks would intimate.

"How do you like your father's appointment, Hugh?" asked Mr. Moray.

"Very much, sir; nothing could be better if the department only acts fairly by him and gives him, with the appointment, the means of holding it honorably."

"They cannot help it, Hugh—they cannot help it—the public would hold them responsible for failure; besides, the Secretary is very friendly to your father."

"Sincerely so, I doubt not, sir; but secretaries are not omniscient—they must trust much to their agents—their four years of power scarcely sufficing to give them any insight into the details of their office, and it would be extravagant to expect that their agents should be always high-toned men, incapable of being warped in their judgments by selfish influences."

"But, Hugh," said Augusta, quickly, yet with a little timidity of manner, very unusual but very becoming to her, "Mr. Saville has promised to do everything he can for your father."

"To whom did he make this promise?" inquired Hugh.

"To me," Augusta answered.

"To you!" exclaimed Hugh, surprised and not altogether pleased; then, trying to speak lightly, "It is dangerous for a lady to incur obligations—and if I have heard aright, Mr. Saville is not one to be satisfied without a *quid* for his *quo*."

"But indeed, Hugh, the officers all say that you can get nothing at the department unless Mr. Saville stands your friend, and they think that he did help your father very much."

"I have little doubt of it, if you condescended to ask his help," said Hugh, trying to smile, yet evidently unable to chase away the shadow from his brow. Just then Gib was called out, and returned to announce a gentleman who wished to see Mr. Moray.

"Sit still, Hugh," said Mr. Moray, as he rose to leave

the room, "I may return in a few minutes, and if I do not, your father will soon be here."

Hugh reseated himself silently. Augusta lifted her eyes to his face—the shadow was still there.

"Hugh," she said, with a little tremor in her voice, "you think I did wrong to speak to Mr. Saville?"

"Wrong! I think you did what was most kind, most generous; but, dear Augusta"—there was a touch of tenderness in his voice as he pronounced those simple words, which made her heart thrill, and bowed her head yet lower, "do you not know that it is just where their generous impulses come into play, that your sex are in most danger of committing themselves?"

There was a little flash from Augusta's eyes, quite different in character from the humid light that had lately filled them, as she said, "You need not fear for me; Mr. Saville will hardly presume upon anything I have said or done."

Hugh shook his head, yet he gave her a smiling and admiring glance, as he replied, "Ah! it is impossible for you to tell how presuming men are."

There was a pretty daring in her manner as she smiled back at him, and exclaimed, "I would take the risk again for the prize—to get the commodore another squadron when he wants one."

"Wait a while—see first that this does not prove one of the devil's gifts."

"One of the devil's gifts! I do not understand you," said Augusta, slowly.

"You are not read in necromancy, I am afraid. Have you never heard that when a poor man was at the lowest, the devil sometimes appeared to him and offered gold, which, if he accepted it, always brought to him more terrible evils than any he had yet known?"

"Oh, Hugh! How could you say that?—but it is impossible—he cannot harm him—I will not believe it;" yet her color faded perceptibly.

"Do not believe it," Hugh hastened to say, "indeed, the same old tales assure us that if the gift passed through a pure hand before it reached the poor man, it lost its evil properties; no—there is no danger for my father."

"A very comfortable conclusion, Master Hugh," exclaimed the old Commodore, who had entered just in time to hear the last words; "pray, have you brought a suit of armor from Europe proof against Mexican balls?"

Hugh had risen to meet his father, and while he gave and received a greeting so glad and affectionate, that in one less manly and self-possessed, it might have seemed boyish, he said, laughingly, "I shall leave you to face the Mexican balls as you may, sir; my armor is only proof against attacks at home."

"In general, by far the most dangerous. But I really believe, Hugh, they are going to do the right thing this time; they have given me the Congress for my flag-ship; she is a noble frigate—you must go on board to-day with me. We shall drop down to Norfolk in a few days to take in the remainder of our crew, and while they are being shipped, I shall spend a few last days at home."

While saying this, the old Commodore had bent over Augusta, and laying his hand on her dark, glossy hair, had touched her glowing cheek with the fatherly salutation she was accustomed each morning to receive from him. Scarcely had he seated himself at table, when Mrs. Moray entered, followed soon after by Charlie, and the conversation became more general, and, Augusta thought, less interesting; it was interrupted suddenly by Mrs. Charles Moray, who, pushing her chair back and rising quickly, exclaimed, "We ought to be ready, Augusta; you know Mr. Mellen and his daughter are to call for us this morning on their way to the Senate. Hugh, do you go with us? If you do, you must go trebly armed, or you will be compelled to surrender to the fair Virginian."

"Has Charlie found her so irresistible?" asked Hugh.

"Oh! Charlie is out of the question; he, long ago, was made captive by another," by *whom*, her glance sufficiently intimated.

"I am equally safe, and for the same reason," said Hugh, significantly.

Mrs. Moray looked surprised, and, for once in her life, the look was the true reflex of her feeling—she was surprised; not surprised at the attachment which Hugh's words intimated—that had long been no secret to her—but at the acknowledgment of it. A few skilful questions to the unsuspicious Commodore, had made her *au fait*, as she believed, of all that both he and Hugh felt on this subject. She glanced at him now, expecting to see surprise and disapprobation in his face; but no, he was smiling broadly in Hugh's face. What could it mean? She was resolved to discover, and she did.

"So Hugh has made up his mind to pocket all the honorable scruples of which you talked so eloquently, and win the heiress if he can?" she said to Commodore Moray when next she saw him alone.

"Oh, no! Hugh's pocket was not capacious enough for my scruples, though it might have disposed of his own—Mr. Moray himself demolished them."

"Demolished them! I am curious to know how; pray tell me—that is if there is no secret involved; you know I never pretend to keep a secret."

"And I never have a secret to keep—the whole thing was as simple and open as day. When Mr. Moray talked of inviting Hugh, I could not let him do it without telling him what Hugh felt, and what had passed between us on this subject; and so, as I told you, he demolished all my scruples, declaring that it was the very thing of all others he wished."

"And does the lady herself know all this?" asked Mrs. Moray, endeavoring, not very successfully, to assume an indifferent tone.

"Oh no! of course not; Hugh is very desirous that she should not even suspect it, so it must be a secret from her, at least."

"The timidity of love, I suppose," she suggested, with a sneer.

Timidity was a word the veteran particularly disliked, and he answered, "Well! I should not be disposed to think it was *timidity* of any kind with Hugh. I don't think he knows much of that feeling; but then, every man, in such affairs, likes to tell his own story in his own way, and at his own time."

"I should think he would be in some hurry to tell it, seeing how many rivals he is likely to have here, unless he is pretty sure of his ground."

"I don't think he has great reason to be in apprehension about it, do you?" The open, kindly smile with which this was asked, might have charmed away any demon less obstinate than envy.

Two weeks of Hugh's visit passed rapidly and happily away. Commodore Moray's ship lay off the Portsmouth Navy Yard. He himself had returned home for those last, few, precious days into which the sweetness of years seemed to be distilled. Precious in succeeding years, was the memory of these days to those who loved him. They were as a glowing twilight between a dull, lowering day, and the blackness of night.

Hugh lost these pleasant days. He still remained in Washington. He hoped, as he said, to be able to remain till his father should actually sail; and again Augusta's cheeks glowed, and her pulses beat more rapidly as she asked herself, "What keeps Hugh? Why did he not go home with his father?"

These were questions to which Hugh only waited an opportunity to furnish an answer. He had sought this opportunity daily during the last week of his stay, but had been always baffled by the superior tactics of Mrs. Moray. When Hugh first suspected her design, he smiled derisively and repeated to himself, "Where there's a will there's a way; I can bide my time;" but he found before the week was past, that his will was not all-powerful, nor his patience inexhaustible. Let us record the trials to which he was subjected in one day—the last day, as it proved, that he was at this time to pass in Washington.

"It is a very pleasant day, and there is nothing especially interesting in prospect at the Capitol this morning; may I hope that you will fulfil your promise of making me better acquainted with Washington and its environs?" Hugh asked Augusta, as he took his seat at the breakfast table on his return from an early walk. Mrs. Moray, who had become an early riser, was present.

"If my uncle can spare the carriage this morning," answered Augusta, glancing at her uncle, and speaking with a little more hesitation than so natural a proposition seemed to account for.

"Certainly," said Mr. Moray; "I will only drive to the Senate and send it back to you. I had a severe vertigo yesterday when walking, and my head is still a little confused, or I should prefer walking. I shall not want it more than fifteen minutes, however."

"Do not hurry yourself, uncle; I shall not be ready in less than half an hour," said Augusta.

"Might I ask you, my dear," said Mrs. Moray, as soon

as the door had closed behind Mr. Moray, "to go a very little out of your way, to put me down at the house of my poor invalid friend, Miss Drayton? as you will be engaged all the morning, it will be just the time for me to make her a long, quiet visit."

Of course there could be no dissent from such a proposal, and soon Mrs. Moray, Augusta, and Hugh, entered the pleasant, roomy, open carriage, and were borne by a pair of spirited horses, in a few minutes, to Miss Drayton's door. It was one of those balmy days in winter, when the stern old tyrant seems to have yielded to the blandishments of spring, who has twined her flowers around his crown and sceptre, and melted the icicles from his beard, and the snows from his garments by her odorous breath. At Miss Drayton's, Mrs. Moray descended from the carriage, but paused a moment on the step to say, "Will you wait one moment, that I may see whether she can receive me," then glided into the house. Five—ten minutes passed away, during which the coachman held in his impatient horses with difficulty, and Hugh, more impatient even than they, watched the door and the windows for some signal that should set them free. At length, the door opened, and he turned his eyes eagerly thither. Mrs. Moray appeared in the open doorway, but not unaccompanied. Beside her was a lady who appeared about thirty-five, perhaps forty years of age. Her face was destitute of every tinge of color—not only the cheeks over which her dark hair was plainly folded, but the very lips were pale. In spite of this, the face was beautiful, from its indescribable sweetness of expression.

"My dear Augusta," cried Mrs. Moray, "I have prevailed on Miss Drayton to take a drive with you this pleasant morning. I told her that I knew it would give you pleasure to take her."

"I could readily believe anything kind of Miss Morny, from the report given me of her by my niece, Annie Mellen," was said in a tone so gentle, that it would have breathed peace, as Augusta thought, into stormier hearts than any there that morning.

With a little glance at Hugh, perhaps with a little sigh of disappointment at losing the pleasure of that long *tête-à-tête* drive, with its longed for, yet dreaded disclosures; with an inconsistency which every woman will understand, Augusta turned to welcome Miss Drayton with her most cordial manner, a manner which was entirely free from the pride she sometimes exhibited. Hugh did not so quickly recover himself; he was courteous, but silent at first, and by no means sympathetic. It was impossible, however, long to retain his coldness to one so gentle and unobtrusive, yet so intelligent and well-informed as Miss Drayton. He was first won to listen; the hard lines of his face relaxed, he replied by a smile to Augusta's glance appealing for sympathy with her pleasure, and at last found that she had sunk into silence, while he and Miss Drayton were in the full flow of talk, narrating incidents of European travel, sketching points of scenery, or commenting on national characteristics; for Miss Drayton too had been abroad. It was a triumph indeed to have made one's self an agreeable companion under such circumstances, and we have no doubt Miss Drayton enjoyed it. Gifted with the most delicate tact, she had seen in a moment that Mrs. Morny's blandishments and irresistible persuasions had made her one of a party in which she was completely *de trop*. It was seen too late, however, to retreat with dignity. Under such circumstances, a selfish woman would have made the drive painful to herself and her companions, by a cold and supercilious tone; but it was a principle with Miss Drayton to add as much as possible to the sum of human happiness in little things as in great. There are some who reserve their powers for great occasions. Miss Drayton was eminently practical. She knew that she would rarely have opportunities of "binding up a broken heart," or, "ministering to a mind diseased;" but that every day, perhaps every hour, she might dissipate the threatening clouds of temper, and call back the light of cheerfulness to a face shadowed by care, by only cultivating the habit of studying rather to please others than to win pleasure for herself. In the present instance, trusting to the generous nature of youth, she began by letting her companions see in a simple, quiet way, how much enjoyment she was deriving from what had cost them some sacrifice of pleasure, and the result proved how true was her judgment. The drive which had begun so unpromisingly, ended with a cordial feeling of admiration and interest between Miss Drayton and her young friends, for friends they had become.

But Hugh's trials were not yet past. As the door was opened to admit Miss Drayton, a more youthful form and face issued from it. It was that of the young and animated daughter of Mr. Mellen. Annie Mellen was a warm-hearted child of nature. Just seventeen, and educated in her own paternal home in Virginia, she had seen even less of the world than Augusta Moray. In her whole style of character and manner, there was less depth, less power than in Augusta. She had not the slightest claim to be called beautiful, yet there was a charm in her bright fresh face, a charm in her simple, natural manner, and yet more in the glow of feeling which accompanied all she said and did. She had felt for Augusta from the first hour they met, one of those enthusiastic, devoted friendships, not unfrequently awakened in young girls toward those somewhat older, and somewhat more richly endowed than themselves; a friendship repaid by Augusta with more of interest and regard than any of the acquaintances she had made in Washington had attracted from her.

"Augusta," said Annie, passing her aunt and Hugh, and coming toward the carriage quickly, "Mrs. Moray invited me to lunch with you, and said you would take me home with you in the carriage, when you brought Aunt Lizzie back."

"Certainly, Annie," said Augusta, cheerfully, "come in."

But again Hugh's glance seemed to Miss Drayton not quite so cordial. She hesitated a moment whether she should recall Annie; but, besides that it would be a great disappointment to Annie, she could think of no good reason to give Augusta, so she contented herself with bending forward as Hugh was about to leave her, and saying in an undertone, "Persuade Miss Moray to make me a visit tomorrow morning, and come with her yourself, Mr. Moray; my quiet room is an admirable place for a *tête à tête*, and you will find me a most accommodating hostess."

Both laughed, but Hugh gave her another clasp of the hand, which told that her conjecture was right, and that he was grateful for her sympathy.

Annie Mellen remained not only to luncheon, but to dinner. The interval between these repasts was filled up with the reception of visitors. Hugh, while he remained in the house, devoted himself to Annie Mellen. Their gay chit-chat attracted Augusta's attention more than once from visitors who were less agreeable to her. She knew not that Annie's bright, cheery tones were conveying to Hugh's intently listening ear more of her Washington life than he could have obtained from herself in a much longer time; she only saw that he was unusually interested, and felt toward her who had excited that interest, a little touch of envy, not of jealousy; she knew Hugh too well to fear any rivalry from an acquaintance of a day. His, she knew, was not a heart to be won so easily.

After dinner, the ladies withdrew to prepare for a ball at the house of the Russian Minister. This was the ball of the season in Washington; nothing was wanting to make the scene attractive, which wealth, guided by taste, could furnish. All the greenhouses of the city or of its environs had been stripped to supply the orange and lemon trees that made the halls and staircases a bower of fragrance and beauty. Every doorway was wreathed with rare and costly flowers, every mantle shelf or *console* was a miniature garden, where, from beds of soft green moss, rose flowers, sometimes of purest white, without mixture of any color, sometimes of the most rich and brilliant and varied tints in nature; pansies of purple and gold, scarlet verbenas, many-colored orchids, camellias and azalias of every shade, from the most delicate pink to the deepest crimson. Through this scene of enchantment moved the young and beautiful hostess, fit dweller in such a temple. Beautiful as she was, with that *riant*, sparkling beauty whose charm is felt by the most insensible, she dazzled no less by the brilliancy of her dress, its exquisite arrangement of graceful drapery and harmonious coloring, and the diamonds which, like mimic suns, flashed their rays as she moved. Yet there was one moment that evening when all around her felt that there was a beauty which, without these adventitious aids, could throw hers into the shade. Mr. Moray would have desired always to see his niece magnificently attired. He had presented her with valuable jewels, among which were complete sets of pearls and of diamonds. But Augusta's better taste taught her that the fresh loveliness of youth needed not these ornaments, and she wore them only to gratify her uncle. This evening she had followed in her *toilette* the suggestions of her own taste, it may be, not without some conviction that it accorded with Hugh's, and as she stood for a few minutes beside her beautiful hostess, even Mr. Moray was satisfied with the result. Her dress, of spotless white, fell in soft folds, rich and glossy, *to the feet,* not below them—for according to the fashion of the day, although it swept the carpet behind her, it left visible in front the satin slippers, and even the arched instep. Lace of the most exquisite Point d'Angleterre dropped " like a powder of snow from the eaves," softening the full, yet delicate outline of the rounded bust and the perfect symmetry of the arms. A cluster of the delicately tinted flowers of the myrtle, a sprig of its glossy green leaves, with two or three flowers and a single leaf of scarlet geranium, formed her *bouquet de corsage.* The graceful line of the beautifully formed and well-set head was broken only by some of the same flowers tastefully disposed, from which there drooped, touching one white and rounded shoulder, a green vine hung with bright red winter berries.

" Now, that's what I call beauty, Mr. Moray," said Mr. Mellen, always a great admirer of Augusta, " that with two or three flowers and green leaves, and just a white frock without even a bit of ribbon, can out-do all the diamonds and feathers and gewgaws. She just looks like a fresh white flower herself."

" Doesn't she, papa?" cried Annie Mellen, warmly; "just like a white flower on a tall, graceful stalk?"

" Yes, Nannie, and the rest of you like things made of paint and patches."

" Oh, papa! that is too bad."

" Indeed, I think so, Miss Mellen," said Mr. Moray, good humoredly; " too bad, and very unjust."

And certainly nothing looked less like paint and patches than the animated young face, glowing with enjoyment, on which his smiling eyes were turned.

Later in the evening, Hugh was standing opposite a group of dancers looking with very evident admiration upon the graceful movements of Augusta and of Charlie, as they went slowly through the mazes of a quadrille, when he heard some gentleman near him say, in a tone which showed evident dissatisfaction: "She shall learn that I am not her glove to be put on and off at pleasure."

"Hush—sh—sh!" said another voice, on a lower key, "that is he."

The last words were so low that one not remarkable for acuteness of ear, could not have heard them; Hugh not only heard them, but recognized also the voice in which they were spoken, and was not therefore surprised when he turned, to find Mrs. Moray standing not far from him accompanied by a gentleman whom he had never seen, but whom by one of those intuitions which all have experienced and none can account for, he at once felt to be Mr. Saville. It may seem equally intuitive, it was not less certain, that he applied the pronouns "she" and "he" of this fragment of a dialogue to Augusta and himself. How she could ever have given Mr. Saville occasion to believe that he stood in any relation to her that might be symbolized by the close fitting of a glove was certainly somewhat of an enigma. Perhaps Hugh's professional habits of thought aided him in his conclusions. His experience as a lawyer had assuredly given him cause to know that a man readily believes what he wishes, and that the most innocent actions of a generous, unsuspicious woman, may be distorted by a designing man into the shape that suits his purposes. Whence he drew his convictions, he might perhaps have found it difficult himself to say, but they were not the less positive that Mrs. Moray and Mr. Saville had been speaking of Augusta, and that they feared to have him hear what they said of her.

"There is always danger in secrecy where a woman is

concerned," said Hugh to himself. He looked at Augusta as this thought passed through his mind. "How ingenuous, how superior to everything like intrigue she looks! How impossible that she should suspect it in another!" His heart swelled with new tenderness to her—a lonely orphan —no mother to counsel—no father to defend her—her only guardian so unsympathizing. It gave a fresh impulse to his desire to win her, that he might become to her father, mother, and more and dearer still. "I will speak this very night—I cannot bear this distance longer—we have lost the old brotherly and sisterly position—I doubt if she would come to me now with her perplexities as she would have done a year—no—it has been longer than that—two years ago. That can never come back—we must be more to each other—or less."

A pang of doubt shot through Hugh's heart. Augusta had certainly been more distant of late; was that the timidity of new-born passion, or was it the estrangement of growing indifference? Such thoughts had flashed on him before—perhaps they had aided Mrs. Moray in her desire to prevent the speaking those decisive words which might render all her plans abortive; but to-night they came with fiercer strength, rushing through the deep recesses of his soul, and threatening to overthrow its most cherished hopes.

Such is the rapidity of thought, that scarce a minute had passed since he had been gazing with free, bright spirit on the gay scene around him, from which he now turned away feeling that his mood was not in accordance with it. From the glare and heat of the ball room, he found his way to a library, cooler and less brilliantly lighted than the other rooms. No one was there. Lifting a heavy crimson curtain which fell again behind him, he entered the recess formed by a bow window, and looked out upon the tranquil night. He drank in its stilling influence, and soon his pulses throbbed less rapidly and his thoughts grew calmer. He was about to reënter the room when he heard steps approaching, and through an opening in the curtain saw Augusta come in, attended by the gentleman whom he believed to be Mr. Saville. With instinctive repugnance to meeting that man, he drew back into his retreat, supposing that they would pass on to the rooms lying beyond, but they paused, and Mr. Saville, drawing forward a chair, asked Augusta if she would be seated. She declined it with a slight bow, saying, in a cold and somewhat haughty tone, "Excuse me, sir; I understood that Mrs. Moray had sent you for me."

"And so she did, Miss Moray, that I might have an opportunity of asking to what I was indebted for the coldness of your reception this evening?" The tone in which this was said betrayed uncontrollable irritation. Hugh made a quick step forward, but again he checked himself, as throwing back her head with a movement of startled pride, Augusta spoke.

"May I ask you so far to explain yourself as to inform me what reception you expected from me, sir?"

"What you were ready enough to give me as long as you had anything to gain by it." The tone was as insolent as the words.

"I should forfeit my self-respect should I answer demands made in such a tone." Augusta spoke low but very distinctly, and then moved to the door.

"You don't get away so easily, my proud lady," cried Mr. Saville, intercepting her; "you shall hear first—"

What she was to hear was never known, for Hugh, unable to endure more, strode hastily forward, and Mr. Saville found himself suddenly dashed aside by a nervous arm. Not a word was spoken, not a glance bestowed on him. Silently Hugh drew Augusta's arm in his, and led her from the room; not so rapidly but that they heard the muttered curse and the "not loud but deep"—"I will make you rue this, if I die the next hour."

"Oh, Hugh! your father! I am so sorry—I ought to have been more patient—I believe what you said of him had made me a little afraid, and I did try to avoid him this evening. What shall I do? Had I better try—"

"Do nothing—try nothing—he is not worthy of a thought—and fear nothing for my father. I do not believe such a contemptible being as that can injure him."

Alas! Hugh forgot that the smallest insect may have the keenest sting. For his part, he dismissed Mr. Saville from his mind, and occupied himself wholly with Augusta, giving expression by look and manner to the admiration and tenderness of which his heart was full, while he longed for the moment when he might speak what he could say in no presence but hers.

The hour came at last, though Mrs. Moray delayed her departure to the latest possible moment. Hugh handed Augusta to the carriage in which Mrs. Moray was already seated. She watched him with impatience, she even called to them to hasten, but Hugh still lingered. He was saying, "I must see you alone, Augusta, though it be for a few moments only—I fear you have not always understood me. I would put it out of your power not to do so in future; could you not give me a few minutes in the library to-night, after Mrs. Moray has retired? I will not detain you long."

"It is so late—but—I will try," Augusta faltered, in a voice that trembled even as did the little hand that lay in Hugh's warm clasp.

There was no time for more. They were at the carriage—in a few minutes they were at home. It was Hugh who opened the carriage door for them. He had ridden with the coachman on the box, while Charlie preferred to walk. He gave his hand to Mrs. Moray, for Augusta had drawn herself away into the farthest corner.

"I think she is asleep," said Mrs. Moray; "I spoke to her twice, but she did not answer."

In truth, she had not heard anything but the throbbing of her own heart, and the echo of those words, "You have not always understood me—I would put it out of your power not to do so in future." She scarcely ventured to touch Hugh's hand in descending from the carriage; she hurried before him, before Mrs. Moray into the house; she would not for worlds have appeared to linger. Should she grant his request and see him in the library? She could not decide. "I will see how he looks, what he says," she thought, "perhaps he will have forgotten it." She glanced at his face as the lamp in the hall flashed on them; she met his eyes—no, he had not forgotten.

"Gib," she exclaimed, turning hastily away, "where is my uncle?"

"Gone to bed, Miss 'Gusty—he a'nt very well—he head is troublous, ma'am, and Mister Hugh, sir, here's a letter for you, an' Master said you must read it *mejantly*, sir—it comed by a gen'leman from New York. Master saw the gen'leman."

Before Gib had finished an explanation given with all his usual precision, Hugh had torn open the letter, and found it was from his partner and kind friend, Mr. Holton, written in great haste, and containing but these words:

DEAR MORAY:—My little daughter lies in a dangerous state; Mifflin's case comes on on the 20th—I fear I shall be wholly unfit to appear in it, or at least, to take the whole burden. You have studied it; besides, you can take my notes. Can you come to my aid? If you can, lose not a moment. You will have this, I hope, Thursday night. I think there is a 3. A. M. train. Take it if you can—I am almost distracted.

      Your friend, O. HOLTON.

"Half past two," exclaimed Hugh, looking at his watch, "stop that carriage, Gib—bring my carpet-bag—no—stop—I must do it myself."

Hugh rushed upstairs, and in a few minutes was down again, bringing his carpet bag and travelling cloak. Mrs. Moray and Augusta were in the reception room opening on the hall. The door was open. Hugh entered, and took a hurried leave of both.

"You will come back, Hugh?" Augusta said, in a voice which she strove in vain to render steady.

"The moment I am free," he said, turning back and clasping her hand once more for an instant.

Little did they surmise how they were next to meet.

CHAPTER VI.

"When to mischief mortals bend their will,
How soon they find fit instruments of ill."—POPE.

A LOUD knock on the door of her chamber, and her name called in a tone of alarm, startled Augusta from the late sleep of the following morning.

"What is it, Gib?" she cried, springing to the door.

"Miss 'Gusty! I believe Master is a dyin', ma'am."

There are some natures which such terrible shocks overpower at once—to others they give a strength never felt before, as the electric spark before which one falls senseless, only braces the nerves of another to tenser resistance. Augusta belonged to the last class. She had caught up her dressing gown as she hastened to the door, and before Gib had ceased speaking, she had opened her door and stood ready to follow him to her uncle's room. Long before she reached that room, she heard the stertorous breathing which had first alarmed Gib, and caused him to enter his master's room at an unusual hour. It was a sad thing to see the strong man lie there so helpless. His face was very pale. Masses of waving brown hair, mixed with gray, had fallen over his low, square forehead. Augusta pushed the hair aside and laid her hand on the forehead, but withdrew it quickly, startled by the coldness of that she touched. There was no movement in the stout form except as the heavy breathing stirred it.

"Oh that Hugh were with me!" was Augusta's first thought—but her first words, and they seemed to come without delay, were an order to call Mr. Charles Moray, and when Charlie came, it was only to receive her earnest adjuration that he would go himself for the physician whom Mr. Moray had occasionally consulted since he had been in Washington. Charlie had seen enough to urge him to activity, and he soon returned with Dr. Weston, though, soon as it was, the time seemed long to Augusta. Dr. Weston looked at the sick man, touched his wrist and turned at once to Augusta, saying, "This is no place for you, Miss Moray. You must leave your uncle to our care."

"Is he dying?" she asked, with husky voice, and tremulous white lips.

"No; but he is threatened severely with apoplexy."

And the threat was fulfilled, and when next Augusta was permitted to see her uncle, she saw that his tide of life had ebbed, and though none whispered such a fear, though even in thought she could not have borne to shape it into intelligible words, she felt that that tide would never flow again—nay, that it would recede—it might be slowly, it might be rapidly; but slowly or rapidly, it would recede till its last wave had swept beyond mortal vision. It gave to her feelings and to her manner an indescribable tenderness. His will was more powerful with her than it had ever been in its strongest and most despotic hour, yet with this submission there mingled strangely somewhat of the ineffable gentleness, the pitying tenderness of a mother to a sick child. His lightest wish outweighed with her not only her own inclinations, but those of every other person. She did not *say*, we can scarcely say she *thought*, but she *felt* it was to be for so short a time.

Mrs. Moray was very attentive to the invalid, but she lacked the inimitable tact possessed by many of her sex, less gifted in other respects than herself, by which the possessor seems to divine what will best please the sufferer before it has shaped itself into a wish. Mr. Moray had not lost his gentlemanly self-control, but Augusta, by virtue of her new power of sympathy with him, knew that Mrs. Moray by her cold, shallow nature, often irritated him when she meant most to charm. Surely there is no labor so utterly unrewarded as that to which hypocrisy condemns its unhappy followers; for, however closely they may study their part, however perfectly they may act it, there is some principle in the most guileless and unsuspecting, nay, in the most stupid of human souls, if it be also a true soul, which clearly recognizes that it is but acting. Especially is this the case when the deeper emotions of our nature have been stirred; a discord may pass unnoticed if it clash with a feeble tone, but if it break across some full deep organ tone, how our hearts quiver and shrink from its sharp clangor. Mr. Moray's nature had ever been far deeper and stronger than Mrs. Moray could understand, and it was increasing every hour in depth and strength, from the solemn shadows that were gathering around it.

Charlie, though not less light, was truer than his mother. His gay chit-chat sometimes amused the invalid, and Augusta never permitted him to evade his daily visit to the sick room. But there were thoughts and wants in that sick room in the heart both of the sick man and of his tender, pitying nurse, which they never breathed to mortal ear, which they would have felt it a sort of sacrilege to breathe to spirits light as these, and which made them both turn with longing to Hugh.

These feelings did not lessen in intensity even when, after a week, Mr. Moray resumed his accustomed habits, though his movements were slower than formerly, and had something of uncertainty about them, and on his face rested the shadow of a great fear. In one respect, he was greatly changed. He had always shown superabundant activity of nature, sleeping but little, and never in the day. Now, after the least exertion, even that of a short walk, he would fall asleep, and after dinner he invariably slept in his large chair by the study fire. It was a pretty picture, while he thus slept, to see the beautiful young face that watched beside him with a softness in the dark eyes which gave a new charm to them. As they sat thus, one afternoon, in stillness, the book which Augusta had been reading to her uncle lying half closed upon her knee, the study door opened with a click which startled Augusta, and aroused Mr. Moray. It was Mrs. Moray who entered.

"Did I wake you?" she exclaimed, forgetting or ignoring that few things annoyed Mr. Moray more than to be told that he had been asleep. "I am very sorry; but I wanted to know if you had any message for Hugh—I am writing to him. Shall I say anything for you?"

The question was addressed to Augusta, over whose face and neck rushed a quick crimson tide, as she answered, softly, "No, I thank you."

"Have you any message, Mr. Moray?"

"Yes; tell him I want to see him as quickly as possible. I was thinking of writing to him myself; tell him to come as soon as he can. Of course, I know he must stay while he is absolutely necessary to Mr. Holton."

The last words were said in a sort of *sotto voce*, as if they were addressed to himself rather than to her, and were intended to moderate his impatient longing. They were scarcely effectual for this last purpose, for after Mrs. Moray was gone he sat silent some minutes, and then said, with a strength of desire in his tone which made the tears spring from Augusta's eyes at the thought that she could not satisfy it, "I want Hugh very much. I hope he will come soon."

Let us follow Mrs. Moray to her own room and see how far her letter was expressive of this strength of desire. The apparent subject of her letter was the request that Hugh would attend to some business at home for her—then followed, "I suppose you have heard of Mr. Moray's strange attack. We were a little alarmed about him at first, but it has passed away, and so have our fears. I have been to ask if he or Augusta had any message for you. She had none, but he charged me to say that he should be very glad to see you here again whenever it suited you to come, though, he added, you must not think of doing so while your services were needed by Mr. Holton. I know somebody who I think would be glad to have you come, whoever might need you in New York. Had I asked Miss An—a Me—n—I use a few letters only of names which I am sure you are in no danger of mistaking, because I think we have no right to run the risk of compromising the delicacy of a young girl by the use of her name in relation to such a subject, especially when what we write is to pass through the Washington post office—but, I say, had I asked the young lady whom those initials indicate, the question to which Augusta answered with such an indifferent "No," I can imagine how the eloquent blood would have spoken in her cheeks, and enabled me to divine the message to which her modesty might have refused utterance. Ah, Hugh! You see, I have penetrated your secret. Not much of a secret either, for your unveiled devotion made itself manifest to all. This is my excuse for saying what it would otherwise be cruel treachery to a young, pure heart, to tell you. I know you are too much of a *preux chevalier* to value less the heart you have sought, because it has surrendered to you."

About this time it was that Commodore Moray sailed from Norfolk to his cruising ground. Two days before he sailed, he came to Washington to receive his latest verbal instructions from the Navy Department, and to grasp once more the hand of his kinsman, between whom and himself there had sprung up a cordial friendship based on esteem.

"I am wanting to see Hugh very much—when is he coming?" asked Mr. Hugh Moray.

"The moment he can get through with this case in which he is assisting Mr. Holton," said the commodore; "but, if you want him particularly—"

"No—oh, no!" exclaimed Mr. Moray, with that readiness to disclaim the possibility of any one being needed by him which is often seen in elderly gentlemen, and especially in invalids, proceeding probably from the fear that others may suspect that failure in their self-reliance of which they are beginning to be dimly conscious themselves.

During this visit of Commodore Moray, and for some days afterward, Mr. Moray seemed decidedly better. He resumed his habit of daily attendance at the Senate chamber, though he took no active part in what was done there, beyond giving his vote when called upon. This return to public life became the event of his day, the rest of which often hung heavily on his hands in spite of the unceasing tenderness which watched around him, and invented employment or amusement for his idle hours. In a society full of excitement like that at Washington, the man who runs not with others, is soon left behind and forgotten. But a short time had passed since Mr. Moray's house was a favorite resort of the powerful and the gay, and now, except kind old Mr. Mellen, who made a point of seeing him at his own house once in the twenty-four hours, though it might be only for a few minutes' call, in going to the capitol, or returning from it, few entered his doors. Augusta perhaps felt this seeming desertion more than he did. She could not bear that he should have cause to think himself already forgotten. So completely did she lose herself in him, that she was positively grateful to Mr. Saville, who called frequently, and sometimes passed an hour or two of the evening in playing backgammon with Mr. Moray. In his kindness to her uncle, she completely forgot his offence against herself, while Mr. Moray grew almost confidential with him, and one evening when Augusta had left them at their game, and gone to the tea table in the next room, he asked if Mr. Saville could recommend an honest lawyer to him, as he wanted to make his will, adding, that though he had quite recovered from his sudden attack, it had made him feel the necessity of adjusting his business.

"If we believe the general verdict, sir," said Mr. Saville, with a smile, "an *honest* lawyer will be somewhat difficult to find; but perhaps I can do what you wish myself. I have studied law and practised it for several years, though, disliking it exceedingly, I was not sorry to relinquish the practice for my present position."

"You are very kind," said Mr. Moray, with a little hesitation of manner, "but—"

"But you are afraid to trust me," interrupted Mr. Saville, laughing, "you are quite right, if the will is at all complicated—perhaps Mr. Hugh Moray will be back in time to meet your wishes."

"It would not help me if he were—I have particular reasons for not wishing him to do it." Mr. Moray spoke in a tone of annoyance.

"Is not Mr. Mellen a lawyer of some eminence?" asked Mr. Saville.

"He is—and he commenced the practice of law in my own State, Georgia, though he removed on his marriage to Virginia: yes, Mellen would suit me exactly—and I spoke to him about it, and he promised to do it as soon as he could; but he is so engrossed, and I—I am impatient, perhaps."

"Well, sir, suppose you give me the necessary items, and I draw up the instrument and bring it to you—then let Mr. Mullen examine it; that will not take much of his time. If it be correct, all is well; if not, and he will point out the errors, I can correct them."

"But I shall be taking so much of your time, Mr. Saville," suggested Mr. Moray, looking at the same time, however, much pleased.

"Oh! say nothing of that—it will only deprive me of one or two of my pleasant evenings with you here."

"Thank you! thank you! I shall always remember your kindness as that of a friend; but I cannot accept your time unless you permit me also to regard it in the light of a professional service."

"You shall do just as you please in that as in all the rest."

"Then will you close that door, and I will give you the memoranda at once—there is no time like the present, you know."

The door was closed, and the memoranda given. At ten o'clock, Mr. Saville entered the parlor where the ladies sat; Charlie had gone out.

"Miss Moray, I am afraid I have kept your uncle up too long—he looks wearied."

If Mr. Saville had intended to send Augusta away, he could not have chosen a more certain measure. With a hasty good evening, she went to the library, leaving him just in the act of taking leave of Mrs. Moray. From the library she went first to her uncle's room, to see that everything was arranged for his comfort, and then to her own. As she said "Good night" to Mr. Moray, his eyes rested on her with an expression of such affection as she had never seen in them before. Augusta's heart overflowed with a tenderness which she knew not how to express, and taking the hand Mr. Moray had held out to her, she raised it to her lips. Suddenly a great sob broke from Mr. Moray, and drawing Augusta closer to him, he kissed her on her cheek, and said, in an agitated voice, "When your old uncle goes, you will find he has taken care of you."

"And now you must take care of yourself, dear uncle, for which I care a great deal more than for anything else." She tried to speak in cheerful tones, and left the room immediately, fearful that he would continue to talk if she remained. She went to her own room, very weary, yet too much excited to sleep. It was so new, so strange, to have her uncle gentle and affectionate in manner. "It was pleasant, certainly, very pleasant," she repeated to herself, feeling all the time a painful sense of loss and want. This kind, caressing uncle might be pleasant, but he was not the strong, self-relying, despotic, yet just and honorable man of whom she had been proud all her life. Him she should no more see. It is wonderful how much more such a character is missed by those who have lived within its influence, than one more amiable even, if less powerful. But Augusta's thoughts at last rested on one who seemed to her to combine the strength and self-reliance, and even, on certain occasions, a little of the despotism of Mr. Moray, with all that was tender and good, and her soliloquy terminated, as most of her soliloquies had done of late, with, "Oh! when will Hugh come?"

These thoughts had held her long awake, and as she turned restlessly on her pillow, the clock in the hall below struck one. Soon after she heard the front door creak on its hinges, and she knew by that very creaking, that it was opened slowly and cautiously; for she had made quite a study during her uncle's illness, of opening all the doors about the house with the least possible noise, and she had found that this door, while it creaked under her slow, careful manipulation, was perfectly silent under Charlie's careless fling. The very conviction that this person did not mean to be heard made her nervous. Could it be Charlie returning home? No—she was sure it could not be, for she heard this person descending the steps. Her chamber was at the front of the house, and a full moon was shining on the opposite side, though her windows were in shadow. She started from her bed, and looking out, saw—could it be Saville?—crossing the street. She drew nearer the window; he was now in the middle of the street. Suddenly he paused, and turned toward the house, lifting his eyes toward her room. The moonlight streamed full upon his face, and she saw it as if she had stood beside him. There was a smile upon it, and yet she shrank back and drew her breath as if from actual pain as she encountered the glance which seemed to flash directly upon her. It was a glance she never forgot, and never recalled without a shuddering thrill—the exulting glance of a demon whose prey was delivered to him. It haunted her even in her sleep that night; the morning light could not drive it away, and though the pleasant, friendly look which Mr. Saville wore when they met, made her say to herself, "It was my fancy,"—when he was gone, and she recalled his face, it was as she had seen it in the moonlight.

Mr. Saville brought a rough copy of the will, and left it with Mr. Moray for Mr. Mellen's examination.

"Clever fellow, that Saville," said Mr. Mellen, after he had read it carefully over; "there is scarcely anything to correct; but we cannot be too cautious in such matters, especially as your niece will doubtless marry one day, and her husband may try to pick a flaw—so I will make one or two pencil marks here on the margin."

And with these pencil marks it was returned to Mr. Saville, with a request that he would bring it at four o'clock the next afternoon, if possible, as Mr. Mellen would be there at that time, and Mr. Moray would like to have him witness his signature, and take charge of the instrument for him.

"It is a sort of *memento mori* that a sick man does not greatly like to keep in his thoughts," he said with a smile, which he strove in vain to make cheerful; "when once it is sealed up and put in his hands, I shall dismiss it from my mind altogether."

Mr. Saville was detained "accidentally"—we use his own words—coming at eight, instead of four o'clock. Of course, Mr. Mellen was not there.

"I am very sorry," said Mr. Saville, "but I have brought the original copy with his pencil marks, and if you will look over that while I read the other, you will see that I have exactly conformed to his directions; then we can complete the signing and sealing, and it will be ready for your delivery to Mr. Mellen when he calls again, and you may dismiss it as completely from your mind as if it were already delivered."

Mr. Moray hesitated a moment, for he had wished Mr. Mellen's signature; but he was very anxious to complete the business—he was afraid of delay, and there was more earnest than jest in his desire to dismiss it from his mind; so he held out his hand at last for the rough draft, saying, "Very well, I will look on while you read the other, and then we will call in Mrs. Moray, and she and you can witness my signature."

Mr. Saville took from the table where he had laid it, a plain black morocco portfolio, and handed Mr. Moray the rough draft; then, holding the portfolio in his hand, read the will, very slowly and deliberately, glancing occasionally at Mr. Moray to see if all was right. All was right; not a word, not a letter out of place. Mr. Moray asked to look at it; it was handed to him, still in the portfolio. He read it carefully to himself, while Mr. Saville, with an unnatural pallor on his face, watched his every movement.

"And now the signatures," said Mr. Moray, looking up gravely; "ring the bell, if you please, and I will send for Mrs. Moray."

Mr. Saville rung, the message was sent, and Mrs. Moray entered. Mr. Moray sat at the table with the portfolio before him; a glance quick and furtive passed between Mrs. Moray and Mr. Saville; she was flushed and restless—he, ghastly white, with a still fixedness of manner.

"Mrs. Moray, I troubled you to come in that you might witness my signature to my will; pray, take a seat." He turned, as he spoke, to the inkstand on the table beside him. "Where is my pen?" he asked; "I am sure it was here a moment ago."

And so it had been, but Mr. Saville had dexterously removed it.

"Never mind, sir, take mine; you will find it writes very well."

He dipped it himself into the inkstand, but *not into the ink*, as he spoke, and handed it to Mr. Moray, who received it silently, and signed, in a bold, full, and somewhat heavy hand, Hugh Moray. The seal had been already affixed.

"Now, Mrs. Moray," said Mr. Saville, in a tone which seemed as rigid as his movements.

With another quick glance at him, Mrs. Moray drew near the table, took the pen, and signed, Ellen Moray, then handed it to Mr. Saville, who wrote underneath, Richard Saville.

"And now, Mr. Saville, will you please fold it the size of this envelope?" turning to the drawer beside him for an envelope as he spoke. While he was thus engaged, Mr. Saville had drawn a paper from within the one thus signed.

It presented a precisely similar appearance in every respect, seal and signatures occupying the same position in each. Rapidly, Mr. Saville folded it to the size of the envelope given him, and placed it within it. Then he lighted the little candle in the inkstand, and gave the envelope and a stick of sealing wax to Mr. Moray, who immediately sealed it, impressing on it his own private seal.

Each of the three gathered there, drew a long, full breath as this was done.

"I shall sleep the better for that to-night," said Mr. Moray, "and I think if you will excuse me, Mr. Saville, I will retire at once. Good night! Good night, Mrs. Moray!"

He passed out of the library. Those he left, spoke not, moved not, till they heard him speak to Augusta two rooms away, and then, attended by her, ascend the stairs, enter his chamber and close the door. Then Mr. Saville turned to his companion, slightly opened his portfolio, and gave her a glimpse of the paper just signed.

"These copying machines are invaluable," he said, in a low voice; "you see that sheet in the portfolio which looks somewhat like a black slate; there must be some pigment upon it—it does not come off except on considerable pressure; but when this pen, which I suppose contains some of the same pigment, is pressed on a sheet above, the sheet immediately in contact with that leaf receives exactly the same characters. Capital idea, isn't it?" And Mr. Saville closed this seeming portfolio, and buttoned it up carefully in the breast pocket of his coat, as if it had acquired new value in his eyes.

"Had you not better burn that copy at once?" asked Mrs. Moray, in a whisper, and glancing quickly around as she spoke.

"Burn it! Oh, no, thank you! I shall keep it."

Mrs. Moray made no remonstrance, but she felt that

her punishment had already begun. Verily our sins do find us out, and that without long search! This thoughtless, selfish, false woman of the world, had still been held to the days of her innocence by one memory—the memory of the evening prayer said first at her mother's knee, and continued ever since with something of the superstitious feeling with which an African recites the charm that is to secure him from witchcraft. To-night she dared not repeat that prayer.

The next day, Mr. Moray was in unusually good spirits, and talked, as he had not done since his illness, of his return home as soon as Congress should adjourn.

"I am glad I did not let you write Mr. Mortimer of my illness," he said to Augusta, "he would come to me immediately, I know; but such hurried journeys do not suit an old man like him, and I could not have delayed here even to give him rest; as soon as I am free, you and I and Hugh, if he will, must set out for St. Mary's. By the by, I have a promise to exact from you." Mr. Moray spoke almost gaily, regarding Augusta with a smile that had more of playfulness in it than she ever remembered to have seen upon his face in health. She had not time to question what the promise was, for just then Mrs. Moray entered with the papers and letters delivered by the postman at the door.

"There is one from Hugh, I think," she said, as she handed the package to Mr. Moray.

"Yes," he answered, and quickly breaking the seal, and glancing over it, he added, "It is to say that he hoped to be here a few hours after his letter. His cause is gained; Mr. Holton is able to resume business, and there is nothing further to detain him. You must give orders to have his room ready, Augusta; this letter must have arrived in the night, and I should not wonder to see him at any moment now."

Augusta rose immediately and left the room. Perhaps she was not sorry to escape with her burning cheeks and beating heart from the eyes, which, as a momentary glance had shown her, were fixed on her while her uncle spoke. If so, she did not attain her object, for she was instantly followed by Mrs. Moray, who arrested her just as she was crossing the hall to ascend the stairs.

"Come with me to my room, Augusta; I want to speak to you a moment," said Mrs. Moray. There was a tremor in her usually steady voice, which Augusta had never heard there before.

"What is the matter?" she exclaimed, with a startled manner. "Has anything happened to Hugh?"

"Nothing has happened to him; and yet what I have to say relates to him. But come with me; I cannot tell you here."

Mrs. Moray began to ascend the stairs, and Augusta followed, wondering and agitated, for there was something in Mrs. Moray's voice and manner that told, as plainly as words could have done, that she was to hear what was painful. This impression did not decrease when Mrs. Moray, having held the door of the room open till she entered, locked it after her, and going to her desk unlocked it with a little key fastened to her watch chain, and taking a letter from a private drawer, placed it in her hand, saying, "Read it."

"The letter is to you," said Augusta, drawn by curiosity, yet repelled by some feeling to which she could not give a name, from opening it.

"It is to me, from Hugh. I received it a week ago and ought to have shown it to you sooner, but I wanted courage; now, Hugh is coming, and if it be done at all, it must be done quickly. Read, then."

Augusta no longer hesitated. The paper trembled in

her hand, and her color came and went. She soon forgot Mrs. Moray, who sank upon a chair, as if unable to support herself, but who never for a moment removed her keen eyes from the face of her victim; she saw the very moment in which her arrow entered the heart at which it was aimed, and a quick drawn breath, a sudden collapsing of her whole frame, showed that she had not yet become wholly insensible to the pang she was inflicting. That it was a pang of no ordinary bitterness, the sudden, ghastly pallor that overspread Augusta's face—the one wild glance that shot from her eyes to Mrs. Moray as if she would question the reality of what she read, sufficiently proved. For a moment Mrs. Moray feared that she would faint; but that single glance, the consciousness awakened that she was keenly observed, roused into action what had, till of late, been the dominant passion of her being—pride. The current of life which had retreated to her heart rushed back in a swollen tide, dyeing face and neck and brow, and filling her pulses till the throbbing of her heart and temples became evident to the onlooker.

It has been said by one of the best physiologists of our time, that man contains within the circle of his being the sum of all vegetable and animal life, with that higher life superadded, which was breathed into him by the Creator at his birth, and in virtue of which he became a "living spirit." There certainly are moments when the human countenance seems to wear a wonderful likeness to the type of some particular animal. As Mrs. Moray cowered before the flashing eyes that Augusta turned upon her, the fox, cunning, yet fearful, looked strangely out from her handsome features. Augusta had drawn herself up to her utmost height as she held the letter out to her. Her lips moved, but no sounds issued from them at first. She was not to be conquered, however; one struggle more, and the words came in a voice soft and clear.

"I cannot understand by what right, madam, you have made me the subject of such a correspondence."

"Correspondence, my dear? indeed, I said nothing at all—a mere jest on a subject which I thought a perfectly understood affair; and I never should have showed you this, but I thought you ought to see it before Hugh came."

"It was perfectly unnecessary, madam; I was under no mistake such as you seem to have been; it would have been better to commit it to the flames, as you were requested to do."

A little deeper tone of voice, as if some effort was necessary to keep it steady, was the only mark of unusual emotion which attended these words. Mrs. Moray was bewildered, and began to think that she had intrigued very unnecessarily in this instance. However, she comforted herself in the belief that at least she had done no harm, and taking the letter, she said, with something like a sense of relief, "I will follow your advice and burn it, and we will never speak of it to any one. Especially, I must beg of you not to mention it to Hugh—he would be so angry with me for showing it to you. Will you promise me this?"

"You need have no fear that I shall ever recur to it again—even in thought," she added, after the slightest perceptible pause.

"But promise; will you promise?"

There was in Mrs. Moray, as she rose in uttering these words and placed herself between Augusta and the door to which she had turned, an eagerness of tone and manner, that sent a sudden dart of suspicion even into the agitated mind of the proud and passionate girl. She fixed her eyes on Mrs. Moray's face; it grew visibly paler under her gaze.

"Permit me, if you please, to see that letter again."

Mrs. Moray hesitated, but only for a moment. To refuse would be to strengthen the suspicion which she saw had already been excited. The letter was given. Augusta moved to the window, and by the full light there examined the address, the seal, the post mark; then she unfolded the letter, subjected the interior to the same close inspection, and then read again, "You must pardon me if I say that I have never given you or any one the slightest foundation for attributing to me any desire to establish other than friendly relations with Miss A—— M——. That you have been equally mistaken in the young lady's views I feel as certain. She has too much innate dignity of character to have given such feeling as you intimate to one who has certainly done nothing to deserve it from her. It is only my haste to free her from insinuations which I am sure she would resent, that gives me courage to use even her initials in such a connection. I entreat you to burn this letter immediately, as I have already done yours." This passage read, the letter was folded again and returned to Mrs. Moray.

"Will you promise now?" asked that lady as she received it; "will you promise that you will never let Hugh know I have shown it to you?"

"If you consider such a promise necessary, it is yours; I could have little pleasure in speaking of it—least of all to him."

There was a world of painfully suppressed passion in her tones.

"Then here ends the whole foolish affair." She lit a match and held it to the paper as she spoke. "I beg your pardon for the mistake I made in thinking that you needed this to guard you from a more fatal error. There—the last word has vanished in smoke, and you 'pass on in maiden meditation, fancy free.'"

She moved from the door as she spoke, and Augusta passed out with a somewhat more stately and deliberate step than usual. As the door closed after her, Mrs. Moray smiled and said to herself, "I was right; she almost deceived me at one time by her proud endurance; but I was right, and she has carried away with her the sharpest arrow that ever pierces a woman's heart." She moved twice across the room, and then the almost fierce gleaming of her eyes softened, and she added: "After all, it was really the kindest thing I could do for her; there will be nothing now to prevent her from marrying Charley—so no harm will come to *her* from Saville's plans; after all, they were more *his* plans than *mine*."

Augusta left Mrs. Moray's room, intending to proceed to her own; but before she had reached it, she was met by her uncle's attendant, Gib, who said: "Master wants to see you, Miss 'Gusty; I been a looking for you, ma'am."

"I will come directly, Gib," she replied, still moving on in the opposite direction; for there was a tempest in her heart which she felt must have way—she *must* be alone.

"Dere he is a calling now, ma'am; won't you please to come, Miss 'Gusty? Master has such *inviolate* ways, ma'am; I'm feared he'll hurt hisself."

Augusta had immediately turned at her uncle's voice, for it sounded sharp and imperative, so that Gib's concluding words were spoken as he followed her down stairs. They entered the library together. Mr. Moray looked quickly up.

"You may go, Gib; I want to speak to Miss Augusta; I am expecting Mr. Hugh; look out for him, and send him here as soon as he comes."

Gib went, leaving the door open behind him.

"Sit down, Augusta; what is the matter? you look pale." He paused, but she did not answer; indeed, it is probable that, though her eyes were fixed upon him, she did not know what he was saying. He resumed: "Poor child! you have had too much anxiety of late; but Hugh will take better care of you." A visible shiver passed over her frame, and Mr. Moray took her cold hand and placed her beside him, just in front of the fire.

"You are certainly not well. I have been selfish in letting you do so much for me; when have I not been selfish? I have never cared for you as I should, but you will find I have taken care of your interests, and you will be happy, you and Hugh; you will marry him by and by."

"Never! never!" she exclaimed, starting from her seat; the face just now so pale, flushed crimson, her pulses throbbing, her form, which had seemed ready to sink beneath its weight of trial, suddenly instinct with life and passion. Mr. Moray looked at her with something wilder than surprise gleaming from his eyes.

"What do you mean?" he asked, sharply; "you do not know what you are talking about. I said you would marry Hugh."

"And I say I will never marry him; I would sooner beg my bread from door to door; no, there is no imaginable degradation that would be equal to that."

She glanced upward, as if appealing to Heaven, and in the mirror that hung above the mantle shelf, she caught the reflection of a tall, manly form and of a white, stony face, from which dark, fiery eyes glared on her. She did not dream that Hugh's eyes could look thus. Perhaps he had not himself dreamed of the volcanic fire in his nature which that moment unveiled to both. Involuntarily she looked back; Mr. Moray glanced in the same direction, saw Hugh, and rose with an agitated smile to welcome him. He took one step forward, held out his hand and strove to speak, but instead of words there came a gurgling, gasping sound; he tottered, and ere Hugh, who sprang forward instantly, could reach his side, he fell heavily back into his chair with convulsed features and rigid limbs.

When Augusta had seen her uncle ill before, though agitated to the very depths of her soul, she had never lost her self-command; but now self-reproach gave new bitterness to her suffering, and pressed from her heart a despairing cry, and "I have killed him! I have killed him!" burst from her quivering lips.

Completely paralyzed by this horrible thought, all those tender cares which had given a safe outlet and noble expression to her burden of sorrow in Mr. Moray's former attack were surrendered to others. It was Hugh who summoned aid, despatched a messenger for the physician, and having aided to bear the unconscious sufferer to his room, stood beside him to offer the ministrations of pitying tenderness. While stooping over Mr. Moray in some of these ministrations, he heard a slight movement on the other side of the bed, and raising his head, saw Augusta there. The proud fire had gone from her eyes, the color from her face, while instead of the haughty carriage and the passionate life with which her whole frame had seemed to thrill but an hour before, her form was bent as if under the weight of years. Never had his heart yearned over her with such unspeakable tenderness as at that moment. He longed to fold her to his bosom, to soothe, to comfort her; but the memory of what he had seen and heard on his first arrival repelled him. Only their eyes met; how differently from that last glance of fire; her's were now beseeching and humble, his sad and tender. Words might have followed, and the barrier so artfully raised between them have been swept away in the flood-tide of feeling, had not the physician at that moment entered.

"He is better again, dear lady; he will recover from this," said good Dr. Frampton to Augusta, whom he found, an hour after, standing beside her uncle's door, looking more like an unquiet ghost than like a creature of flesh and blood.

"It was I, doctor. It was I who made him ill," came in husky tones from her quivering lips.

The doctor had been accustomed to minister to the wounded mind as well as to the body, and asking no questions, he took the ice-cold hands in his and said, "My poor child! that is not so; this attack has been threatening for days; I knew when I left your uncle this morning that it could not long be warded off. Only your devoted care has kept it off so long."

"Are you sure, doctor? are you quite sure?" she asked, as a slight tinge of color returned to her cheek and a little life to her eye.

"Quite sure; so sure that I do not feel satisfied for my patient till I see you at his side; your cousin is very kind and very considerate, but there is no nurse like a woman."

Augusta breathed freely again; the blood flowed again through the veins in which it had seemed to stagnate; she was like one awakening from a frightful nightmare. Every sorrow which brings with it no remorse is endurable, and this she felt as the doctor led her to her uncle's side, and she looked from his pallid face, now resting in a deathlike sleep, to the sterner and scarce less composed features of Hugh, whose eyes, after one rapid glance, no longer sought her face. Thus they sat through the darkening shadows of the evening, and the long, still hours of the night, together, yet apart. Their eyes never met; their hands occasionally touched each other while busied about the patient, but it was as stone touches stone. As the gray light of the early dawn made yet paler the pale light of the lamp, Hugh stole around the bed, and stood beside her.

"Will you not leave your uncle to me, and rest for a few hours?" he said, softly.

"I will rest here," she answered, leaning her head, as she spoke, against the side of the large cushioned chair in which she sat, and closing her eyes. He did not attempt to remonstrate, but went cautiously back to his former place. She did not sleep, and there was little rest in the thoughts which kept up a wild tumult in her soul while she reclined there with closed eyes, and all the appearance of perfect tranquillity. About an hour had thus passed when her excited ear became conscious of a slight movement. She opened her eyes upon her uncle. He lay as he had done for hours, breathing quietly; but Hugh had left his place, and was speaking to some one outside of the door. Again she lay still, till a stealthy tread beside her, and a whispered, "She are 'sleep, Mas' Hugh," made her look up to see Gib standing beside her with a tray, holding a cup of coffee.

"I am not asleep, Gib; but I do not wish anything."

"Set the tray down, Gib; Miss Moray will take the coffee presently."

Hugh spoke in a low tone, but with something of quiet decision more powerful by far than the most vehement urgency. It seemed to say, "No reasonable being can contest a point so trifling yet so clearly right," and Augusta, with a little irritation, both of feeling and manner, at being thus ruled, stopped Gib by a touch on his arm, took the cup from the tray, drained its contents, laid it back, and resting her head, closed her eyes again, without a word.

Mr. Moray awoke from this long sleep apparently well. By his physician's direction, all appearances indicative of the night's watch or of his previous illness had been removed, and it was soon evident that he was not only unconscious of his attack, but also of the circumstances that had immediately preceded it. Hugh's presence was a pleasant surprise to him. He had insisted upon being dressed as usual and going to his library, and though compelled to acknowledge himself somewhat feebler than he had been, he was greatly irritated by Gib's well meant but injudicious efforts to induce him to remain in his own room. He complained to his physician of it in a vehement tone, declaring that the associations of Washington and his long indulgence had made Gib quite forgetful of their relative positions. Dr. Frampton met these complaints with his usual tact, careful neither to deny their validity nor to treat them with indifference, yet mingling with his sympathy so many allusions to Gib's fidelity and traits of his conduct manifesting his devotion to his master, that he left Mr. Moray greatly mollified, and rather disposed to consider Gib's peremptoriness as a new proof of his attachment.

"Will you come and see my new horse, Miss Moray? I consider him the greatest beauty in Washington," said Dr. Frampton, as he prepared to leave the library.

Augusta rose and followed him to a window of the front parlor, which was separated by a long middle room from the library. As they entered this parlor, they found Hugh there, waiting to learn from the doctor what he thought of Mr. Moray's condition. Hugh rose to leave the room as he saw Augusta enter, but Dr. Frampton laid his hand on his arm as he was passing him, and said, "Stay, Mr. Moray, I wish to speak to you both about your uncle."

"Not *my* uncle, sir," said Hugh, quickly; "I am but a distant cousin to Mr. Moray."

"But a very devoted friend, as I can testify," observed the doctor.

"He has a claim on me stronger than kinship, sir," Hugh replied, meeting the doctor's kindly smile with much gravity of manner. "To his generous aid I am indebted for my profession."

"Then you desire to serve him," rejoined the doctor.

"I am here for no other purpose," said Hugh, with an emphasis that sent the crimson blood in a rushing tide to the very temples of Augusta for one fleeting moment, leaving her the next more pallid than before; "I am waiting," he added, "to know from you how I may do it most effectually."

"And it is to tell you this that I brought Miss Moray here, and that I have now requested you to stay; sit down, my dear young lady; you look pale and feeble this morning, and you will need all your strength."

Hugh glanced at Augusta's pallid face as she sank into the chair the doctor had placed for her, and for a moment his eyes softened into somewhat of their former tenderness; it was but a moment, and they gleamed again with a light as keen and cold as if it had been reflected from an iceberg.

"Dear lady, I am sorry to give you pain," Dr. Frampton continued, retaining the hand of Augusta, which he had taken to place her on the sofa; "very sorry; but it is my duty to tell you that I have no longer any hope of being able to do more than alleviate your uncle's sufferings." He paused a moment as he saw the spasm of pain which contracted the marble features he was watching; but it passed instantly, and as it came, without a sound, and he continued: "Mr. Moray's symptoms this morning mark more rapidly progressing disease of the brain than I had suffered myself to anticipate. You have too much good sense to be shocked at my asking you whether his business arrangements have been made in reference to the possibility of a sudden death."

"His will was made more than a week ago," she said, in a low, but steady voice.

"That is well! then I shall not need to speak to him on the subject, which in his present state I somewhat feared to do. It only remains for me to give you both the best directions I can for his treatment. Medicine can do little for him, but your cheerful society and tender care may lengthen out his life for weeks, perhaps for months, and make it peaceful and comfortable to the close. You must be cheerful, yet sympathising; above all, you must not permit the brain to be wearied by argument, or excited by opposition. However extravagant may be his propositions you must assent, if you can, and when assent is impossible, temporize; divert, if you can, but never contradict or oppose. On you, my dear Miss Moray, I rely principally in this, for I know how unfailing is womanly tact under such circumstances; here, every man must acknowledge the superiority of your sex; your cousin must, in all difficult cases, follow your lead."

"I do not know," Hugh began, paused, dropped his eyes for a moment, then lifting them to the doctor's face, continued in a more resolute tone: "I am not quite sure that it will be best for me to remain."

"Best! for yourself, do you mean, or for Mr. Moray?" asked Dr. Frampton, somewhat sharply.

"Best for Mr. Moray," said Hugh, adding, with slight hauteur, "the question of what is best for myself I should scarce submit to another."

"Then, sir, since you consent to let me judge of what is best for Mr. Moray, I must say that from what he said to me this morning of his delight at seeing you, and his expectations from you, your leaving him at present would be a great injury and a cruel disappointment."

The doctor spoke very decidedly—perhaps he was a little vexed by Hugh's manner. If so, he must have been mollified by the reply he received, given with an impulsive warmth all the more valuable because it was so rare in Hugh Moray. Stretching out his hand and grasping the doctor's, Hugh said, "Enough! enough, my dear sir! I am grateful for the privilege of ministering in any way to Mr. Moray's pleasure or advantage; I will bid you good morning and go to him at once, leaving Miss Moray at liberty to take the rest she so much needs."

Augusta did not take advantage of the liberty thus given. A quarter of an hour after Dr. Frampton left her, she entered the library with a very composed manner, and an almost smiling face.

"You look as if you had heard some pleasant news, *ma cousine*," said Charlie, who was making his usual morning visit to Mr. Moray when she entered.

Hugh turned to her and read that studied air of cheerfulness very differently. The manner was too still; it marked to him the heavy, crushing weight by which the usually impulsive nature was held down, and beneath the smile, he saw, or thought he saw, a sad, weary, hopeless look, that sent a pang to his generous heart, all the more bitter because he was no longer privileged to offer to her either sympathy or support.

Charlie, always impatient of quietude, soon withdrew, inviting Hugh to accompany him to the capitol. Hugh declined.

"It is kind of you, Hugh, to stay here with a complaining old man," said Mr. Moray, looking gratefully upon Hugh, as Charlie closed the door behind him. "Though," he added, as his smiling face was turned toward Augusta, "I do not take the compliment wholly to myself, I am none the less pleased with it."

Had his perception been as acute as formerly, he would have been startled by the impassive faces that met his kindly glances. Perhaps he was dimly conscious of missing something he had expected to meet, for after a moment's silence, pressing his hand to his forehead, he resumed, "There was something I wanted to say; oh, now I have it;

you are engaged?" and he looked again from one to the other.

There was no answer. Hugh knew not what to say, and Augusta's heart seemed for the moment to have stopped its beating. It was on her that Mr. Moray's glance rested last and longest. While thus resting, it suddenly changed its expression. Something of their former fire shot into his eyes, his head was flung back with the haughty gesture so familiar of old, as he said, "I hope, Miss Moray, you are not playing off the coquettish tricks of your sex upon my friend and relative here."

"Dear uncle, I have not the least intention to play the coquette, I assure you," said Augusta, trying to take his hand as she spoke.

"You are trying to evade giving me a positive answer, I see," he rejoined, flinging off her hand with increasing irritation as he spoke, "but you will find I am not so easily deceived as you think. What do you say to all this, Hugh?"

"That you must not let your kindness to me make you unkind to your niece, Mr. Moray; Augusta and I perfectly understand each other, I assure you; there is no danger of any further mistake or misconception between us."

The words were assuring to Mr. Moray, but in spite of all Hugh's efforts, he could not suppress a tinge of bitterness in the tone which made itself sufficiently apparent to one intently listening ear and throbbing heart.

"Ah!" said Mr. Moray, while the fire faded from his eyes, "you speak as a man should, openly and honestly; I wish Augusta could be as open, but it does not belong to her sex."

"Indeed, uncle, I am quite as open and honest in what I say as Hugh is!" it was a retort she could not suppress, and to which her burning cheeks and quickened breath gave double force.

"If that is true, let me see you give him your hand and promise that you will be his as soon as we are all at St. Mary's again."

"Better not exact any promises from me, uncle. Remember your own theory, that the more solemn a promise is, the more pleasure a woman has in breaking it." Her heart was trembling within her, yet it was scarcely possible to distinguish from the truth it aped, the mockery of mirth in her tone and eyes; she had recovered from her first terror, and was beginning to feel an excitement not altogether without a strange kind of pleasure in this conversation of double signification.

"You see, Hugh, she will not promise; I told you no woman was to be trusted."

"No woman that makes promises, uncle," said Augusta, in the same seemingly flippant tone.

Hugh looked at her with astonishment. Recollecting the warnings of Dr. Frampton, her terror of the past night, her sadness but a few minutes before, he could not understand the change, nor tell which was real, the sadness or the mirth, or whether both were alike untrue. He found nothing to help his conclusions in the eyes that met his with a touch of defiance in their clear, unfaltering glance. It aroused an answering spirit in him, and there was haughty carelessness in the smile with which he turned to Mr. Moray, saying: "Be at rest, sir; I already have Augusta's promise to share my home when it is prepared for her; she will, I doubt not, gratify you by giving me her hand in token that she will fulfil that pledge when—," he paused, seized the hand which had been scarcely lifted to meet the one extended by him, wrung it in a moment's passionate

grasp, whether of love or hatred, he could scarce himself
have told, and concluded, "when I shall claim it."

"Do you promise this, Augusta?" asked the persistent
Mr. Moray.

"Yes, sir, I think I may do so in a spirit as truthful and
earnest as Hugh's; but now I must run away from you for
a little while."

She rose quickly and moved to the door—not too
quickly; Hugh had already seen the sudden fading of the
flush from her face with something like remorse for the
selfish passion of that clasp and those sneering words.
Faint, dizzy, almost blind, she stumbled to the door, and
finding herself unable to proceed, rested for a moment
against it.

Mr. Moray did not see her, Hugh did.

"Permit me," said he, springing to her side, as if only
to open the door, but as he did so, receiving her sinking form
upon his arm, and bearing her to a sofa in the next room.
Her eyes were closed, her features still, her face ghastly
white.

"Augusta!" Hugh's voice trembled a little; there was
no answer; "Augusta!" he repeated more sharply, but
with as little effect. For an instant he was almost as pale as
herself; but before he could utter the wild cry which even
remembrance of Mr. Moray could scarce have given him
power another moment to repress, the cool air from the
window beside her recalled her to life. Her cheeks became
faintly tinged, her eyelids quivered. With life came the
consciousness of suffering, and too feeble to exercise any
self-control, and, it may be, not yet sufficiently aroused to
know that she was not alone, the varied agitation of the last
night and of this morning found for the first time expression
in tears, which trickled through her closed lids and fell in
heavy drops from her cheek upon the sofa pillow on which

her head was resting, while not a feature, not a muscle of her face, was moved. Such weeping comes only from hearts that have been utterly crushed. Hugh stood beside her, deeply moved, longing to soothe her as he had often done in lesser griefs, yet feeling that he had lost the power and the right, and fearing even to stir lest the discovery of his presence should inflict on her an added pang. A sigh, which he could not suppress, startled her; she opened her eyes, and instantly started to her feet and brushed away the tears that were yet hanging on her lids.

"You have been ill, Augusta; sit down, and I will ring for your maid," he said, gently.

"I will not give you that trouble," she answered, coldly, and took a step forward; but her trembling limbs refused to sustain her, and she sank back upon the sofa.

Having rung for her maid, he returned to her, and standing before her, said "Augusta, I have spoken and acted under the dictation of selfish passion this morning, and I am ashamed of it; can you forgive me?"

She did not speak; she could not, without an outburst of emotion which she would rather have died than yielded to. He resumed:

"You cannot; well, I deserve it, perhaps; but I must not lose these few seconds, my only opportunity, it may be, of saying that, though I overheard your scornful rejection of me in the character in which your uncle presented me to you yesterday evening, I will yet, if you permit it, prove myself your friend. Be still, as you have ever been, dear Augusta, my friend, my sister, and let me feel that you confide in me; let me only help you in your present great trials, and I will ask nothing more."

"God help me! I have no other hope—no trust in any human creature!" burst in a wailing tone from her overcharged heart.

At that moment steps were heard approaching, and he had only time to say, "Trust me or not, I will be your friend, and you shall one day acknowledge it," when her attendant entered.

CHAPTER VII.

> "When sorrows come, they come not single spies,
> But in battalions." SHAKSPEARE.
>
> "Pride requires very costly food—its keeper's happiness."—COLTON.

THE pledge with which the last chapter closed was well kept by Hugh Moray. During the month which followed, Mr. Moray grew feebler hourly both in mind and body. At first he was peevish and impatient, but this phase of his disease passed away, leaving him unusually passive and gentle. In both conditions one thought alone seemed to give him pleasure: the thought that Augusta was to marry Hugh, and that they would live together at St. Mary's.

"You will take better care of my poor people than I have done, though I have tried to be kind to them," he would often say; sometimes he added, "Let Mr. Mortimer do all he will for them; I wish I had not opposed him, but things seem so different to me now."

It was strange to see the apathy with which Augusta heard these observations. They brought no color to her cheek, her eyes remained calm and impassive, an unnatural stillness marked her whole aspect and manner, except when she was seeking to amuse her uncle, or ministering to his wants. Then her countenance lighted up; there were smiles on her lips even while they quivered with a grief she would not express, and her eyes shone through tears which never fell till she was secure within her own room. Never had she been so dear to Hugh as at such moments. The tender, protecting sentiment with which her almost unfriended childhood had inspired him, the more impassioned feeling awakened by her grace and beauty as the child grew into the woman, were now blended into one, while each had acquired new intensity. There were times when the touch of her dress, as she passed by him, thrilled him with emotions which all his manhood, aided by all his conviction of their hopelessness, could scarcely repress; there were times when, as he heard her utter words of cheerful hope, in tones which she strove in vain to render steady, as he saw her smiles trembling through tears, he was compelled to rush from the room, that he might combat in silence and solitude the strong impulse to fold her to his heart and entreat her to weep out all her sorrows there. Mr. Moray often fell asleep in the midst of conversation with them, and as he was always annoyed at finding either of them gone when he awoke, they were obliged to pass hours of the day completely tête-à-tête. Generally, these tête-à-têtes passed in perfect silence, while Hugh would read, or seem to read, and Augusta would take up some piece of embroidery or other feminine work. One day, however, Augusta started, as Hugh, whom she supposed to be on the other side of her uncle, spoke, and she found that he was standing beside her chair.

"Augusta," he said, in low tones, "I am not satisfied at suffering your uncle to continue under such misapprehensions in regard to our relations to each other."

The hot blood rushed to Augusta's temples; it was the first time she had felt its flow for many days. Before the quick, proud words could follow, Hugh spoke again.

"We cannot indulge a hope that he will ever be better,

and he sometimes uses words that make me fear his impressions regarding us may influence his disposal of his property."

"My uncle's misconception is as annoying to me as it can be to you," she answered, coldly and haughtily, "but after what Dr. Frampton said, I cannot undertake to undeceive him; I can only promise you that any arrangement of property which you desire, hereafter, shall meet with no opposition from me; if you still fear that your interests may be compromised—"

"I will not permit you to finish a sentence as unworthy of yourself as it is insulting to me," he exclaimed, looking with dignified composure on her flushed and agitated face; "it is enough that I have your unconditional promise to consent to any arrangement of property that I desire."

He was turning away, but she stopped him by a motion of her hand, and said, "My promise is not unconditional; I will consent to any arrangement that is not intended to subject me to obligations more humiliating than the most abject poverty."

It was Hugh's turn to redden, yet his words were calm and cold: "I understand you; Dr. Frampton must undertake the communication which I cannot in honor delay."

He took his hat from the table as he spoke, but before he could leave the room, Mr. Moray awoke and called him to his side. When he had an opportunity of speaking to Dr. Frampton, he found, if evil had been done, it was irretrievable, as the doctor declared no disposition of his property made by Mr. Moray now could be regarded as valid, and that it was therefore worse than useless to disturb his mind by a reference to the subject. "Besides," he added, "before this last attack, his reason was unimpaired, and any will he made then was probably free from the influence of any misconception whatever."

With this, Hugh was compelled to be satisfied.

During all this time Mrs. Moray had scarcely shown herself in Mr. Moray's presence; there was, indeed, such actual fear expressed in her countenance and manner when on a few rare occasions she had been forced to enter it, that even Augusta pitied and excused her. Charlie never failed to make his morning, noonday, and evening visit. His bright face and pleasant voice were always welcome to Mr. Moray, yet he never expressed any desire for his longer stay, or wished for him when absent. Evening after evening, mother and son continued to show themselves in the gay saloons of Washington, strange contrasts to the silent watchers in the dimly lighted room where a shadow deeper and more enduring than that thrown from the dusky wings of Night was hovering. Sometimes they met Mr. Saville; one evening he accosted Mrs. Moray, who had just entered, and was leaning still on her son's arm, with "I am glad to see you out of that dreary house; and how is my friend, Mr. Moray, getting on?"

"I do not believe there is much change; it is very sad; I am really obliged to come out of an evening, that I may keep up my spirits, for poor Augusta's sake."

"The truth is," said Charlie, who had no mock sentiment about him, "that neither my mother nor I are of the slightest use to poor Mr. Moray, while he can have Augusta and Hugh, and so we may as well enjoy ourselves while we can."

"True," replied Mr. Saville; "and so," he added, turning to Mrs. Moray again, "Mr. Hugh is very devoted in his attentions to poor Mr. Moray?"

"Very devoted, indeed," said Mrs. Moray.

The words were all very well, but Charlie thought the tone not sufficiently emphatic, and rejoined, "Entirely so; Mr. Moray can hardly breathe without Hugh. I do not know another young man who would confine himself so. I hope he will be rewarded for it as he deserves."

"I hope he will," said Mr. Saville, with a glance at Mrs. Moray, from which she turned somewhat hastily away. "By the by, Mr. Charles, will you ask your cousin what he hears from his father? the department hears nothing from him, and we begin to think he is a little slow in his movements."

There were several gentlemen near, over whose faces there passed a smile, not unobserved by Charlie. His blood fired, and resisting his mother's efforts to draw him on, he said, in a low but distinct tone, carefully modulated to reach the ears of those who had heard Mr. Saville, "If I had not a lady on my arm, sir, I would say that your words are a little insolent."

"Charles! my son!" exclaimed Mrs. Moray, "you are mad! Pray excuse him, Mr. Saville; he does not know—"

"His obligations to me," said Mr. Saville, bowing to Mrs. Moray with a smiling face, yet with a gleam in his eye which the lady little liked. "Do not be alarmed; I have no intention to quarrel with your son, and I am sure that he will not quarrel with me when he knows that I exerted all my influence with the Secretary to obtain the squadron for Commodore Moray, and that I must, therefore, feel especial interest in his proving himself fitted for a command which, now that we are at war with Mexico, is decidedly the most responsible in the gift of the department."

"Those who know Commodore Moray will never doubt his fitness, and if I was a little quick, Mr. Saville, put it down to his account, and don't call him slow again;" and with a good-natured laugh, Charlie held out his hand, which Mr. Saville took.

Later in the evening, Mrs. Moray found an opportunity of saying a few words to Mr. Saville apart.

"I hope," she said, "you will not heed Charlie's boyish folly; anything that touches his sense of family honor is so keenly felt by him."

"I assure you I am not at all sorry to find him so sensitive. It will be all the better for me by and by."

"Mr. Saville! What *do* you mean?"

Mrs. Moray's bitterest enemy might have pitied the agony in her pallid face and quivering lips as she asked that question. The dread future which crime ever brings, had started up before her, and she shrank cowering before it. "What *do* you mean?" she repeated, as Mr. Saville looked silently upon her with a gleam of malice in his cold, hard eye. He turned away and left her, without an answer.

"Why, Mrs. Moray! what is the matter? You are fainting; pray lean on me—this room is very close; we will get into the air," said a gentleman who, in passing, had been struck by her pallor.

"My nerves have been too much tried by Mr. Moray's illness," she answered, slowly and feebly. "I should not have made the effort to come out this evening. I will sit here," placing herself on a sofa, "till my son comes, if you will be so kind as to call him for me, and say that I am ill, and would like to return home."

Charlie was soon at her side, and was too much shocked by her look of suffering to express any reluctance to return, even if he felt it.

Mrs. Moray pleaded illness for her silence as they went, but she was in truth busied with the one thought, "How shall I free myself from Saville?" She almost persuaded herself that she could bear the contempt and reproaches of those whom she had most deeply injured, if by so doing she might escape the malice of Saville, and disappoint his hopes of gain. When she arrived at home, Charlie would have seen her to her room, but with an impatient gesture and tone, she bade him leave her, and as soon as he was out of sight, she went to the study where Mr. Moray, Augusta, and Hugh usually sat. All there was dark and still. It had been the scene of her crime, and from its corners, dimly lighted by the candle she carried, the malignant eyes of Saville seemed to gleam mockingly upon her. She turned away with superstitious fear, and hastened up the broad stairs, feeling that Nemesis was already treading fast upon her steps. Up the stairs, through the hall, fleeing, though no man pursued, she went straight to the door opening into Mr. Moray's room: it was slightly ajar, and she paused to breathe, and to listen if any one were moving there, before she should enter. There was no movement, but a low, soft voice, was reading in reverent tones, and these were the words that first fell on the listener's ear: "Make us ever mindful of the time when we shall lie down in the dust, and grant us grace always to live in such a state that we may never be afraid to die."

Mrs. Moray hurried away, feeling that a new and deadlier fear had entered her heart, from being brought into contact with the "powers of the world to come." She hastened to her own room, and set down her light there; but thoughts of terror pursued her; something seemed to whisper in her ear, "Make us mindful of the time when we shall lie down in the dust;" she crept back in the dark, to Mr. Moray's door. The reading was ended, and Mr. Moray began to speak.

"Hugh," he said, "I was always thought a brave man, but it is one thing to go forward in the strength of manhood to meet *possible* death, and quite another thing to lie here and wait for his certain coming."

"Certain! What makes you say that, dear uncle?" remonstrated Augusta.

"Because my mind is very clear to-night, Augusta,

clearer, I think, than it has long been, and I feel it is certain, and want to say something to you while I have the power. Tell Mr. Mortimer, when you see him, that I learned at last to love the prayers that I listened to, at first, only to please you, and prevent your asking me to see a clergyman; tell him I am able to forgive, as I hope to be forgiven—he will understand you; and that he must help you and Hugh to do all for my people, that I failed to do. And now, child, do *you* forgive *me!*"

"For what, dear uncle? Have you not been the kindest and most generous of friends to me?" said Augusta, kissing the hand which she had clasped in her own, and on which her tears were fast falling.

"Generous!" he repeated, "I never gave you what you most wanted, poor child! but you will not want it now. Hugh will give it to you in full measure," and turning to Hugh, with a wistful smile, he added, "You must love her for me as well as for yourself, Hugh; will you?"

Mr. Moray held out his hand to Hugh, who stood on the opposite side from Augusta, and placing his own in it, Hugh answered, clearly and firmly, "I will, Mr. Moray." Even there, within the shadow of that presence, before which pride ordinarily stands rebuked, Augusta lifted her head, and something of scorn flashed from her eyes, wet as they were with tears of tender sorrow, upon one whom she believed to be perjuring himself.

"And now, I have said all, I believe; good night. I shall sleep to-night, I think."

Mrs. Moray heard steps approaching the door, and again hurried to her room, saying to herself, "I will see what I can do to-morrow; to-night it is too late."

To-morrow proved to be too late, for before its sun arose, Mr. Moray was beyond the reach of all earthly feeling. There are few who do not think sometimes of the irrevocable character which their own death stamps upon their actions, but it is doubtful whether we as often remember that the death of another as surely precludes all change in the character of our acts and feelings toward him. Have we been unkind to a friend, ungrateful to a benefactor, unjust to our fellow man? We may live on, and our hearts be wrung with remorse long after they have passed beyond the reach of our atonement. Oh, the pangs of unavailing regret! Who that has felt them finds too strong the imagery of the worm that never dies, and the fire that is never quenched? "It is too late!" was the thought that impressed such haggard misery on Mrs. Moray's features for many days after Mr. Moray's death. And yet it was not too late to have done justice, by her confession, to those who had been wronged; but with Mr. Moray had died the only power that could shield her from the consequences of her crime, and these she was not sufficiently sincere in her penitence, to meet voluntarily. Mr. Moray, she had hoped, could, and, to protect his family name from dishonor, would destroy the will now in Mr. Mellen's hands, and make another without revealing the cause of his doing so to any one; now, her confession, to be available, must be known to many. How could she bear to see her own son turn from her with shame? How could she meet the world's scorn? No; it was too late; things must now take their course.

The funeral rites were over; the body deposited in a vault till it could be carried to the home which Mr. Moray had so loved, there to be laid beside kindred dust. Of all the long procession of Senators and Representatives, who, according to that reverent custom observed ever toward those whose death had left a vacant place in their country's councils, had followed the remains of Mr. Moray to their temporary place of rest, none but Mr. Mellen returned with the family to the house which had lately been his home.

Charles and Hugh Moray were both in the carriage with him, and neither of them was surprised to hear that he had in his possession the last will of Mr. Moray.

"I think it had better be read at once," said Mr. Mellen, "and for that purpose I put it in my pocket. I read and corrected the first draft, so that, though I did not write this, I am acquainted, as I believe, with its contents. Mr. Saville wrote it, and as he and your mother, Mr. Charles, were the only witnesses, it would be well for us to call for him and take him along with us."

"I fear it will be a very agitating ceremony to Miss Moray, and she is still suffering so much from the shock of her uncle's death, that if it could be delayed—"

Hugh paused, and Mr. Mellen replied, "My sister-in-law, Miss Drayton, is with her; I will get her to speak to Miss Moray, and be guided entirely by her wishes; in the meantime it will not be much out of our way to stop for Mr. Saville, and have him on hand. It is not necessary, but it is as well that he should acknowledge his signature."

Mr. Saville was at home, and consented to take the vacant place in the carriage. As he did so, he handed a letter to Hugh, saying, "This letter from Commodore Moray arrived under cover to me with a request that I would forward it immediately if you had returned to New York. I thought I should see you to-day, and so put it in my pocket."

Hugh thrust the letter into his pocket, feeling that the present hour was sacred to other interests. Augusta, overpowered by the shock of her uncle's death—sudden at last—and by previous days and nights of agitation and fatigue, had lain on her couch almost ever since his death, in the stillness of exhaustion. Miss Drayton was the only one whom she had willingly admitted, and she had sat beside her through much of this day, not conversing, for of this,

Augusta seemed incapable, but repeating, in a gentle voice, at intervals, some passages from the Bible, or some of those hymns in which the truth and tenderness of the Bible have been reproduced, and which touch the heart with such soothing gentleness in the hour of sorrow, even where that heart has not learned to love truth for the sake of its Glorious Giver. During all this time of sorrow, Augusta had declined seeing any one but Miss Drayton, and now, though she heard a knock at her door, she lay with her eyes closed as if asleep. Miss Drayton obeyed the summons, and found Judge Mellen standing there. His errand was told in a whisper. Miss Drayton looked back for a moment to the pale, still face upon the couch, and answered, "It is impossible; she could not bear it."

"What is impossible, Miss Drayton?" asked Augusta, without opening her eyes or making any movement except of the lips.

Miss Drayton drew near and explained it to her.

"Is it necessary? is it not very hurried?" she inquired.

"So it seemed to me," said Miss Drayton, "but my brother says that all who are interested are now present, that each of them has some reason for desiring to leave Washington immediately, and that it may be long before they can meet again."

"Very well; I will go."

"But have you strength for it, dear?"

"Oh, yes! I have strength for anything that will bring me sooner to St. Mary's. There I shall have rest." Augusta rose as she spoke, but she became conscious as she did so, of greater weakness than she had suspected. Miss Drayton saw that she trembled, and passed her arm around her tenderly.

"You love your home," she said, hoping to calm Augusta by drawing her thoughts away from the present.

"Oh, dearly! When I breathe its air again, I shall feel as if a mother's kisses were on my brow."

"And you will have a great work to do there; so many souls dependent on you!"

"Will you not come and see me there, and help good Mr. Mortimer to teach me how to do my work?"

They had reached the door of the parlor, and Miss Drayton could only reply by pressing the white hand which lay upon her arm. Augusta's pale cheeks became slightly tinged with color as the door opened, and they entered. Hugh started forward to meet her, but checked himself, as if at some sudden memory, and suffered Judge Mellen to support her to the chair which had been placed for her near Mrs. Charles Moray's. Had Augusta raised her eyes, she might have been surprised at the deadly pallor of that lady's face, and the languid faintness of her usually quick glancing eyes. Miss Drayton, who, not having seen her before during the day, shook hands with her, did wonder at the cold, clammy touch of her hand.

"Miss Moray," said Judge Mellen, as soon as they were all seated, "I was sorry to disturb you for what may seem to you a mere form, as our lamented friend made no secret of what had been his disposition of his property; but as my sister told me it was your wish to return home as soon as possible, and as all our friends, indeed, are anxious to leave Washington, I thought if you could make the exertion, it would be better."

Augusta answered only by a bow, and all having seated themselves, the Judge drew the will from his pocket, and proceeded, very deliberately, to break the seals of the envelope, and withdraw the paper from it. As he threw down the envelope, Mr. Saville raised it and examined the seal.

"Do you use this?" he said to Charlie, who, somewhat shocked at the levity in calling attention, at such a time, to anything extraneous, answered, shortly, "Mr. Moray did."

The seal had the thistle and the "Nemo me impune lacessit" of the royal arms of Scotland, to which the Morays claimed a right in virtue of certain ancient matrimonial alliances. Had any one been sufficiently at ease to make observations on others, he might have seen Mr. Saville carefully remove the seal and put it in the pocket of his waistcoat. While the carelessness or indifference of his manner was a little overacted, Mrs. Moray had lost all power over herself. We have spoken of her pallor and coldness; equally remarkable was the wild expression of the eyes fastened on Judge Mellen, as if from his lips she awaited the sentence of doom. All this was unnoticed by the Judge, who commenced reading in the somewhat measured tones usual to him, the sentences in which the testator expressed his wishes respecting his removal to St. Mary's, and burial there; then followed a few legacies—the place on which he lived, five hundred dollars per annum, and the use of his library, being left to Mr. Mortimer during his life, as a mark not only of the esteem and friendship of the testator, but of his gratitude for the services he had rendered to the people on his plantation, in which he hoped he would hereafter meet with no obstruction; to his friend and relative, Commodore Moray, was left five hundred dollars and a signet ring with the Moray crest, which had come from Scotland with the first emigrants of the name, and which, on Commodore Moray's death, was to descend to Hugh. All this was exactly as it had been in the will seen by Judge Mellen, and he read it without a change of tone. Then came the enumeration of certain shares in Bank stock, canals and railroads, as well as of some thousands of ready money in the hands of his factor, all which was hereby willed and bequeathed to—Judge Mellen made a pause—could it be possible?—to "Mrs. Charles Moray, of Elizabethtown, widow;" the last words were read rather in a questioning tone, as if the reader doubted the evidence of his senses, and the glance around the circle which followed, seemed to ask if he could be right. Receiving no answer, unless the surprise on all faces except Mr. Saville's, and a gasping sob from Mrs. Charles Moray might be considered an answer; he turned again to the instrument in his hand. Now followed the mention of St. Mary's; its acres of woodland and cleared fields, its houses, whether for dwelling or for plantation use, then the negroes, named by families and enumerated, then the horses, carriages, &c., nothing was omitted, and all was willed and bequeathed to Charles Moray, son of the before-mentioned Mrs. Charles Moray. Never did such simple words excite such varied sensations as were caused by these. As they were uttered, Augusta lifted her eyes and fixed them on Charles Moray's face, which burned beneath her gaze as if the brand of a shameful deed were blistering there. She never removed that gaze while Judge Mellen continued to read that the testator had made no especial provision for his dear niece, Augusta Morny, because she would find her home with these dear friends at St. Mary's, which, he hoped, would eventually become her own by her marriage with Charles Moray, which event would fulfil his most earnest wish.

Before Judge Mellen had finished reading, Hugh Morny, obeying an uncontrollable impulse, had risen from his distant seat, and placed himself beside Augusta. Judge Mellen was the first who spoke. Still holding the will in his hand, he said, with emphasis, "This is a most extraordinary document. Mr. Saville will, I am sure, bear witness, as well as I, that it is entirely unlike the will first dictated by Mr. Moray. That, if I am not greatly in error, placed Miss Moray and Mr. Hugh precisely in the positions occupied by Mrs. Moray and her son—am I right, sir?" turning suddenly to Mr. Saville.

"Yes; but I suppose a man may alter his will at any time during his life," said Mr. Saville, in a tone of studied carelessness.

"A man *may*, but *does* he without some good reason? I do not hesitate to say that, if this will be genuine—and after careful examination of the signatures, I see no reason to doubt that it is—it must have been dictated when my friend's mind was so much affected by disease as to destroy the validity of his acts. Indeed, he more than once, after his document was in my possession, alluded to Mr. Hugh Moray and his niece as his successors at St. Mary's. This testimony I am willing to give before a court of justice, and if you will take my advice, my dear," to Augusta, "you will contest the will."

Before Augusta could reply, Charles Moray exclaimed, "That you need not do, Augusta; for I am as well satisfied as Judge Mellen himself, that this will is no expression of your uncle's real wishes, and I here relinquish at once all claim that it gives me on his property."

"Thank you! thank you, Charlie! for giving me back my old confidence in you; as for anything more, I cannot receive from your bounty, what would have been welcome from my uncle's affection. If I have been wronged, I commit my cause to Him who is the orphan's friend. May He defend the right!"

Augusta had risen as she addressed Charlie, and her appeal to Heaven was made with an earnest look and an emphatic gesture, which made Mrs. Moray visibly shudder, and awakened a momentary terror even in the heart of Saville. She turned as if to leave the room, and Hugh offered his arm with a manner of such graceful deference as a princess might have claimed, and as he had never offered to Augusta Moray before. She accepted the support she greatly needed, but ere she had made a step forward, Mrs. Moray laid her hand upon her arm to detain her. Augusta shook it off as if it had been some unclean thing, and turned to her with flashing eyes and heightened color.

Mrs. Moray's contrition had not been sufficiently deep or sincere to make her humble. Its chief effect was to add intensity to her desire for Augusta's marriage with her son. For the injury to Hugh she had little compunction. "Hugh is doing so well he does not need it," she said to herself, "and he had no more natural right to it than Charlie." Were Augusta married to Charles, she believed that conscience would cease its perpetual sting, and moreover, that Saville's power to intimidate her would be lessened. All these considerations gave earnestness to her manner, as she said, "You will remember, Augusta, that St. Mary's is your home, and we shall be ready to set out whenever you wish."

"Excuse me, madam," replied Augusta, "Your home can never be mine, and I have no desire to influence your movements."

Again she would have passed on with a haughty bow, but Mrs. Moray, with increasing, almost with impertinent vehemence, exclaimed, "Do you intend to treat your uncle's last wishes with contempt? Remember! St. Mary's will be forever closed to you if you refuse our offer now."

"Mamma!" cried Charles Moray, "you must not say that. If St. Mary's is indeed to be mine, it will ever be Augusta's rightful home, where I shall esteem her more mistress than I am master, whenever she shall honor it with her presence."

Charlie's open, boyish face was flushed, half with shame, at what seemed to him his mother's strange rudeness, half with eagerness to mark his own different feeling. Augusta could not answer. Indignation and pride had lent her temporary strength, but it was fast failing. Hugh felt the trembling of the hand that rested on his arm, and putting back Mrs. Moray, who would still have urged her point, with a decided gesture, he led her from the room. Scarcely had the door closed behind them, when Augusta sank upon a chair in the hall, faint and gasping. Hugh felt that she must not be exposed to farther trial, and, disregarding her faint resistance, he lifted her in his arms and bore her up the stairs to a small room opening on her own apartment, where he laid her on a couch.

"Thank you!" whispered Augusta, feebly; "will you ask Miss Drayton to come to me?"

"In one moment, dear Augusta—never so dear as now—only let me say before I go that if not permitted to assert a nearer claim, I have at least a brother's right to cherish and to guard you."

He pressed his lips to the hand he held, then, alarmed by her increasing paleness, he hastened down stairs and sent Miss Drayton to her. That lady was the only one he found in the room he had just left. Judge Mellen and Mr. Saville had left the house, and Mrs. Moray had carried off Charlie to her own room, to consult him, as she said, on business, but, in truth, to try to reconcile him to the new dignities which, she could see, sat somewhat uneasily upon his indolent but kind nature.

When Miss Drayton had left him, Hugh continued long to pace, with slow, measured steps, through the deserted room which seemed to him, at that moment, to bear the aspect of death. Suggested by the contrast, there rose up the vision of that last gay, untroubled evening, when Augusta, radiant in beauty, with the flush of excitement on her cheek, and a softened light in her eyes, had stood just where he had seen her stand to-day in her plain, black dress, with colorless cheeks, and eyes flashing with proud disdain, or dim with clouds of sorrow, yet not less beautiful to him.

That evening there had been no scornful rejection in her eye or on her lip. If he could have but spoken then—and what had made the difference now? Was she indeed so fickle that a few weeks of absence had thus changed her?, that could not be. Had an enemy come between them? that might be—and his thoughts immediately reverted to Mrs. Charles Moray. "She never loved me," he said to himself, "and I think she has positively hated me, since she has regarded me as a possible rival to Charles." Still the utmost act of enmity he thought of ascribing to her was misrepresentation of some thoughtless word or action on his part. He had always thought her skilled in giving a gloss to language which the speaker little intended—skilled in interpreting all things so as to advance her own ends, but of conscious, wilful untruth, of absolute fraud, he did not suspect her. In regard to this will, he believed, with Judge Mellen, that there had been some unfair influence exerted over the failing mind of Mr. Moray; if there had been more, and the remembrance of the many conversations in which Mr. Moray seemed to consider him as his successor at St. Mary's, sometimes suggested the doubt, he believed that Saville was answerable for it. "That man hates both Augusta and me. I have read it in his eye, spite of all his cunning; he would do us an injury if he could. It has been no injury to me. I should be sorry enough to relinquish my career at the bar for the burdensome responsibilities of a Southern planter, and as for Augusta, we cannot offer her a splendid home; but my father—by the by—his letter," and throwing himself into a chair, Hugh drew from his pocket the letter handed to him by Mr. Saville, and was soon absorbed in its contents. They ran thus:

U. S. FRIGATE CONGRESS,
Gulf of Mexico, March 21, 18—.

I have been trying to write to your mother, Hugh, but find it impossible, and so I write to you that you may tell her what I have no heart to tell myself. My bitterest enemy could have chosen for me nothing more humiliating than my present position, a position accepted with the hope that I should be able at last to prove myself worthy of the confidence so long withheld from me. If the department should continue its present course toward me, I shall come home a dishonored man, while it may be that some perfumed pet of theirs will be sent out to supersede me as an incapable, and obtaining what I have in vain petitioned for, will cast a deeper shadow on my name by his success. Three or four vessels, of not over one or two hundred tons, would enable me to make our naval power as much dreaded as our army has become under the gallant Taylor; but here I am with ships of such heavy draught, that I cannot approach the coast near enough to throw a ball on shore; and yet all my remonstrances and appeals are met only by expressions of surprise that with such a gallant force at my command, I should have done so little. I am tempted to believe that my letters have not all reached the Secretary's eyes. From what I know of the ways of the department, I know it would not be at all impossible for this to be managed by a clerk who had a grudge against me, and, God—forgive me if I wrong him,—I have no trust in Saville. I believe he suffered me to obtain this squadron because he hoped by it to ingratiate himself with my rich relative, Mr. Moray, and now that he, poor fellow, is too ill for him to hope for much future service from him, I should not wonder if he were intriguing to give it to some other. As you wrote last from Washington, and seemed uncertain when you should leave it, I hope this letter may find you there. If it should do so, go at once to the navy department, see the Secretary himself, and tell him what I have here written you. Tell him I know the harbor of Vera Cruz thoroughly, and that with three or four vessels of light draught I will engage to land men enough to make themselves masters of the city, and of the whole country indeed; but without such vessels it is simply impossible—it would be throwing away the poor fellows' lives to send them in open boats, when I could not bring a cannon near enough to protect them. Make some inquiries where Commodore Puffer is; I have had a hint from an old friend in the service that he has been a good deal in Washington of late. He is the only man in the service, I think, who would supersede me without reluctance; not that I think him bad-hearted or dishonorable, but he has such an opinion of his own powers, that I honestly believe he considers it an act of injustice to the country that any important service should be committed to another. Exert yourself, my son, to save your father from this last and worst humiliation—the last, I say, for certain I am that I should never outlive it. Send this letter to your mother, and tell her that though I do not write to her by this opportunity, my best comfort is the memory of her love and her prayers. Love to your sisters. Your affectionate father,

JAMES MORAY.

Hugh looked at the date of the letter. "This ought to have been here a week ago," he said, "I have not an hour to lose; but first I must see Augusta."

He went quickly up the stairs and to the room, where he had left her. The door was closed, but his light tap brought Miss Drayton to it; she came into the hall to Hugh, closing the door after her. Without waiting to be questioned, she said: "She has been terribly agitated; it could scarcely be otherwise; but her greatest dread seems to be that any one should see her in that state. I have promised that no one but myself shall enter this room."

"I must not ask you to break your promise, and yet I know not how to leave the house without seeing her."

"Leave the house! You are not going away!" exclaimed Miss Drayton.

"No farther than to the navy department on important business for my father."

"Oh! you will return here, then? I feared you were talking of leaving Washington."

"I hope, when I do that, it will be to take Miss Moray with me to Elizabethtown, where my mother and sisters are—they love her dearly, and would be grieved, indeed, if she should choose any other home. Has she spoken at all to you about the future, Miss Drayton?"

"Not very coherently; one thought, only, seems in connection with it, that she must make herself independent by the exercise of her own powers. She has been much calmed by my promise to find work for her."

"Work! I must see her, Miss Drayton," and Hugh looked resolved.

"You will not, without her permission, Mr. Moray; to-day, especially," said Miss Drayton, remaining quite still, though Hugh had stepped toward the room, and even put his hand upon the latch.

Her confidence was not misplaced; Hugh withdrew his hand, and stepped back again.

"You are right, Miss Drayton," he said, "it must not be without her permission; and yet I must see her. Tell her, dear Miss Drayton, that I have an important commission from my father, which requires my immediate attention; but that I cannot and will not leave the house till I have seen her. Will you do this, dear Miss Drayton?"

Miss Drayton could not refuse, and soon re-opened the door to tell Hugh that he might enter.

The incidents of his life, the training even of his boyhood, had given Hugh Murray a power over himself, possessed by few men. Even now he was calm in appearance, self-possessed in manner, though his heart throbbed and his pulses beat as they had not done when he first rose to address a court, notwithstanding that was under circumstances which induced the belief that his success or failure in that first effort would influence his whole future career. He had now a cause to plead requiring more delicate tact than any he had yet approached, and the verdict he should obtain would affect the well-being of one dear to him as his own soul. The events of this day could not make Augusta more dear to him, but they had so touched the springs of his tenderest feeling, that he would have guarded her with his very life from the lightest touch of pain. This feeling grew acute almost to agony as he entered the room in which she was, and, taking in with a quick glance, its luxurious and tasteful arrangements, he contrasted them by a lightning flash of thought with the home likely to be that of a woman who should make herself independent by her own work. Yet Hugh was very calm—if any complaint could have been alleged against his manner, it was perhaps the complaint of an excess of quietude. Augusta sat on the couch where he had left her. A crimson spot on each cheek served only to make the surrounding whiteness more distinct, while her eyes glowed with excitement. Over her, too, the thought of the injustice done to Hugh, had exercised some softening influence. She would now have risen to meet him, but he stepped quickly toward her couch, and taking the hand she held out to him, gently reseated her, and placed himself in a chair at her side. Retaining her hand, he said, "I wanted to see you before I went out, that I might know when you would be ready to set out for Elizabethtown. Do you think you could go to-morrow?"

Hugh, it will be acknowledged, was adroit. The place was only touched in his question, and touched as an ascertained fact, the time was dwelt on as the great point at issue. In ordinary states of feeling such a *taking-for-granted* by one whose opinion she values, has a wonderful effect on a woman; but to-day Augusta Moray was in no ordinary state of feeling. All in which she had most trusted had deceived her. The very pillars of her life had been shaken, and she stood among the crumbling ruins of the past with proud self-assertion, saying to herself, " They shall not crush me. I will build to myself a new world, and though it have in it no beauty and no joy, it shall suffice." Ah! how different would it have been, could she have seen that it was the hand of love which held the bitter chalice to her lips,— that the selfishness of men was but working out the loving designs of Him who " chasteneth those whom He loves, even as a father chasteneth his children."

" You are very kind, Hugh; but I do not think I shall go to Elizabethtown," she replied to Hugh's question.

" We will talk of that at another time, when you are more composed; at present we will only settle the time of our journey; you must be impatient to get away from this house," Hugh began, with a smile; but his face grew grave before he concluded.

" I am more impatient to be understood by you, Hugh. You must not put me off as if I was a feeble child, incapable of deciding for myself. I have no guide left; I must mark out my own path."

" Dear Augusta! If Mr. Mortimer were here I think he would remind you of the Psalmist's petition, 'My Father, be Thou the guide of my youth;' and of his assurance, 'Commit thy way unto the Lord, and He will direct thy steps.'"

" He guides and directs us, not by sending an angel to

clear our way before us, but by giving us the power and the will to act for ourselves."

"Or by sending friends to act for us."

"He has left me none on whom I have a natural claim. I could not be happy in dependence on others. The best thing that those who wish me well can do for me, is to help me in finding something to do for myself."

Hugh thought of the loving, trustful child, who had said, "Hugh, I will live with you anywhere," looked up in the proud face beside him, and with a pang at his heart, which he could not wholly control, rose and walked to a window, that he might betray to no other eye what he suffered. When he returned and again seated himself at Augusta's side, his face had regained its composure. Yet there was a change in its expression—there was less tenderness there and more sternness.

"Perhaps you are right," he said, "at least, no one living has the right to constrain your freedom of action. I will only say that you may command my services in any way you please, and until you have found your work and are ready to begin it, you will not, I hope, refuse to make your home with my mother and sisters at Elizabethtown. You can have no cause of displeasure with them, Augusta," he added, as he saw her hesitate, "and no one whom you do not wish to see, will intrude on you there."

The color flushed to her face at his last words; but before she could reply, Hugh rose, and holding out his hand to her, said, "I must not weary you now. You may trust my advice—it is as disinterested as a brother's; at least, you may trust the affection of my mother and sisters. But I will say no more now, for you look weary; good afternoon."

One lingering pressure of her hand, one questioning look from the door, as if he hoped yet to read some softening in her glance, and Hugh was gone.

Months passed ere they met again.

When Miss Drayton returned to Augusta she found her weeping with an uncontrollable violence, which was the result of the almost superhuman restraint imposed on her by her proud determination to show that she needed not even sympathy from those around her. Reproach of Hugh was mingling with these tears, for, with the inconsistency of which most are guilty where the passions are excited, she accused him of coldness and hardness, because he had carefully guarded himself from the expression of any warmer sentiment than friendship, completely ignoring that she had more than once, of late, manifested her disdain of professions of deeper interest from him.

"He need not have been so careful to assure me of his disinterestedness—to make me feel that I could give nothing in return for all this ostentatious kindness."

Such were her thoughts. Yet when Miss Drayton, after letting her weep for some minutes in silence, drew her at last within the shelter of her arms, and with soft caresses said, "My poor child! has he wounded you too? I thought his truth, at least, might be trusted," she lifted her head proudly, and answered, "You know little of Hugh Moray if my tears can make you doubt him. Since I cannot relinquish my plans for my own support, he urges me to go to Elizabethtown and remain with his mother and sisters till I am ready to begin my work."

"And trusting him as you do, you will go, of course?" said Miss Drayton.

Augusta had unconsciously set a trap for herself. If she would have Miss Drayton trust Hugh, she must show that she herself trusted him, and she assented, though the assent was faint, and with the addition, "Unless you should hear of some place for me immediately."

"That is not very probable; there are places enough,

but few such places as I could conscientiously recommend you to. To know how to recognize the claims of a lady in the position of a governess, the employer must be a lady herself."

"And are there so few ladies?" asked Augusta, little disposed to submit to unnecessary delay.

"Very few, I fear, in my acceptation of the term; though there are a thousand counterfeits which, in the ordinary exchanges of society, will pass current without detection."

"I must not hope, then, for one of those few, but be satisfied if I find nothing worse than the common lot."

"Well, we shall see; in the meantime, I am truly glad that you have such a friend. Have you appointed any time for your journey?"

"No; if I must go, I suppose I ought to go at once. Hugh's business must require his presence in New York; he has been here more than a month; but if I could hear of something first—" She paused.

"I think you are quite right not to wait for it; Mr. Moray must, as you say, have already sacrificed much; and I shall be as busy for you after you have gone as if you were here."

Speech is a gift of Him whose every gift is good. Thought becomes clear, passion submissive to reason while we exercise it, provided passion have not so acquired the sway of our whole natures that speech has itself become its slave. These conversations, though not all that Hugh Moray or Miss Drayton could have wished, left Augusta more composed in mind than she had yet been. The future seemed less a tangled, pathless forest than it had been. Unconsciously, perhaps, she derived comfort from the thought that, for a time, at least, she would be within Hugh's home, the object of his friendly care. The next morning she woke after a night of deep and almost untroubled sleep. Her first thought was, of course, of her bereavement and of the altered circumstances of her life. It is that first waking thought which brings to our hearts the keenest pang of sorrow. That pang sent Augusta's thought not to a heavenly, but to an earthly comforter. Hugh would come this morning to know her decision. She must rise, for much was to be done to-day, if she were to be ready to set out with him to-morrow. Prompt as the thought came the action; she arose and breakfasted alone in the little music room that opened into her own apartment. Soon after her breakfast, as she was still there, giving some orders to her maid respecting the arrangements for her packing, a knock was heard at her chamber door.

"Say that I am here, Alice," she said to the Irish waiting maid, who turned to attend the summons.

"It's Gib, ma'am," said the girl, opening the door of the music room.

"Yes, Miss 'Gusty, it's me, ma'am; Master Charles sent me, ma'am, to see how you is, and to ax to speak to you."

"Master Charles?" Augusta repeated. "You are sure it was he who wanted to speak to me?"

"Oh yes, ma'am! Sure for true. It couldn't be nobody else, now poor Master Hugh's gone."

Gib spoke with emphasis. He had seen a little, and suspected more, of what had been passing in the house for the last four weeks, and it was his own private opinion that Master Hugh had been badly treated on all hands, and he strongly suspected that "Miss 'Gusty" had now put the finishing touch to the injustice he had suffered, by sending him away.

"Master Hugh gone!" repeated Augusta, with a half bewildered expression.

"Yes, ma'am, gone," repeated Gib, and this time with a little fierceness in his tone. He had expressed his pity for Master Hugh; the next thing was to show his readiness to do battle with all his enemies.

"When did he go, Gib?" Augusta's voice trembled slightly in spite of her efforts. Gib began to be appeased.

"Well, ma'am, I don't rightly know when he's left Washington; howsomedever, he isn't been home to my knowledge sence yesterday one o'clock; I know it was one, because I heard the big clock strike just as Master Hugh went out the door, and I was looking after him and saying to myself, Well! who'd ha' thought that Master Charlie would be our master, instead o' Master Hugh; that Master—"

"And has not Master Hugh been back since that time?" asked Augusta, interrupting the flow of Gib's eloquence.

"No, ma'am; leastways I ha'n't seen him; and he hasn't been in his room all night."

"And have you heard nothing of him, Gib?"

"I only hearn the man that came for his valise and cloak say he was a-going away with some gentlemen from the hotel."

Augusta sank back upon the couch by which she was standing. Now she felt how she had rested on that strong arm and faithful, courageous heart. Pride might still rule her words; it might press back the tears from her eyes, and close her lips against the moan that rose to them, but it could not scare away the agony from her wistful eyes, nor renerve her shaking frame. Gib's emotions changed their direction.

"I think it's very strange in Master Hugh to go off so; and may be he's a coming back."

"Yes, that was surely it; he was coming back," and a little color returned to Augusta's pale cheeks.

"And Master Charles. What must I tell him, Miss Augusta?"

"Say that I will see him here, Gib."

She spoke with alacrity, for she thought that Charles must have some communication from Hugh; it might be that he was coming to bring her some message from him.

"You will go on with the packing," she said to Alice; "I shall probably leave this place to-morrow."

The girl returned to the chamber, as Charles Moray entered at the door of the music room.

"You still look pale, Augusta," he said, after the usual salutations and inquiries had passed; "I must see a little more color in your cheeks before I can ask you to set out for St. Mary's."

What a pang that name on his lips cost Augusta he little knew! She could not speak for a moment, and Charlie continued: "When we do go, would you prefer to go by land, or water? If you are not strong enough for the land journey—"

"I am not strong enough for either, Charlie."

Augusta's tone was kind, even affectionate—far more so than it had been to Hugh.

"Not now, but you will be soon, and we will wait till you are."

"I shall never be strong enough to be at St. Mary's as a visitor."

"Not as a visitor; I would not have you feel as a visitor, let it be your home as it has always been."

"That cannot be, Charlie. If I was not my uncle's child, I was, at least, his nearest living relative, and was taught from my infancy to feel that I had the claims of a child in his house."

"And you would say that you are nothing to me; but,

Augusta, I have no sister, and I have always envied Hugh his sisters. Come with me and be my sister."

Augusta remembered Mrs. Moray, and the color flushed her face and the proud light came again to her eye, as she said, "Such ties are of Nature's making; I am not your sister, and cannot fancy myself so."

"Augusta," Charlie began, and paused, rose from his chair and looked out of a window, reseated himself, and again said, "Augusta, there is a tie we make for ourselves; will you be my wife? you know your uncle wished it."

"No, Charlie; I could not be your wife, even if my uncle had wished it."

"And do you doubt that he did, Augusta?" and Charlie's face grew hot.

"I do not doubt, for I feel quite sure that he never did."

"Why, then, should he have said it in his will?" Charlie spoke rapidly, as one who was becoming roused by the doubt insinuated.

"The *will* said it, certainly."

Augusta's emphasis was significant; there was a festering doubt in Charles Moray's own mind, and this emphasis was like a touch upon "*the raw*" to a mettled horse. He sprang from his chair.

"I think it would be more just, if you have any belief that the will is a forgery, to say so at once, and let the case be decided by law; do you suspect me of fraud?"

"I suspect *you* of nothing dishonorable; but sit down, Charlie, and let us talk of other things; I cannot afford to quarrel with the few friends I have left, and I should be sorry not to count you as one of them."

"I am glad you will permit me to be anything to you," said Charlie, reseating himself, though with a shade of irritation still, both in tone and manner.

"That I regard you as a friend, I am going to prove, by asking a favor of you," said Augusta, trying to smile.

Charlie was easily propitiated, and assured her that she could not gratify him more than to show him how he could be useful to her.

"It is only, Charlie, by fulfilling what I know to have been my uncle's desire about his people. To Hugh and me, who were with him constantly during those last few weeks, he expressed it very often, and I promised him to use all my influence to secure for them the kind treatment and care of their future master."

"You are not going to suspect me of cruelty, Augusta?" Charlie questioned, still a little angrily.

"I believe no man ever was more incapable of cruelty, Charlie; but my uncle was not cruel; he was considered, I believe, not only a humane, but a kind and generous master, and yet he was not satisfied with himself; indeed, he seemed often troubled by the feeling that he had not done all he should have done."

"That must have been nothing but a sick man's fancy, Augusta; for I am sure no set of laborers I have ever known were so happy as your uncle's negroes. They were comfortably lodged, well fed, not overworked, and free from all anxieties for the future. I am sure I have thought of them with envy sometimes, when I have incurred a heavy debt, without having a red cent to pay it with. Depend upon it, all that was a sick man's fancy."

"I don't know that that is at all against it, Charlie; I am afraid none of us think as we should do about these things till we are sick and feel ourselves drawing near to the eternal world; I seemed to be brought near to it myself when I talked with him toward the last, and I must relieve my conscience of my responsibility in the matter, by telling you that my uncle felt grieved at remembering that he had sometimes objected to some of good Mr. Mortimer's plans for the improvement of the people, and that he hoped that whoever was at St. Mary's after him would suffer Mr. Mortimer to carry them all out; and it was this I was going to ask of you as a favor to myself: it will make Mr. Mortimer so happy."

"I fear it will have a tendency to make the people very unhappy; but, of course, what you ask shall be done. And now, Augusta, let us come back to yourself. If you will not make your home with us, you must remember that your uncle intended that your home should be provided out of his property, so that, wherever it is, you must draw on me—"

"You must excuse me, Charlie, I cannot place myself under pecuniary obligation to any one."

"Pecuniary obligation it would not be—"

"I should feel it as such; and, once and for ever, let me say that if you would have me regard you as a friend, you will never make such a proposition to me again."

"And how are you going to live, Augusta? With all your finespun fancies, you are human, and must eat, drink, and be clothed."

Charles Moray spoke warmly.

"It is true I am human; but with human wants I have also human powers, and can work for what I need."

"Work! Are you going to put up a card, 'Washing, and going out to day's work, done here'?"

There was a sneer in the tone of the question.

"Not quite so bad as that," said Augusta, while her eyes flashed. "I am only going to seek, through Miss Drayton and my old teacher Madam B——, a place as a governess."

"A governess! I advise you to change your plan and take my proposal—it will be decidedly the easier life; but, in the mean time, till this delectable governess-ship is found, what are you going to do? Will you remain here?"

"Till to-morrow morning, with your permission," said Augusta, haughtily.

"And may I venture, without offence, to ask where you may be going then; as I understand, this 'place' is yet to seek."

"I might well refuse to answer such questions; but I have nothing to conceal. I shall return with Hugh to Elizabethtown, and remain with his mother till I find employment."

"With Hugh? Is not Hugh gone?" asked Charlie.

"What makes you suppose so?" Augusta's heart sank again with a sickening dread, and her cheeks grew pale.

"I did not *suppose* anything about it. Gib told me he was gone; but, of course, that is a mistake, if you were going with him. There is the door bell now; perhaps it is he;" and Charlie hurried from the room, glad, it must be owned, of an excuse for escaping from Augusta's presence, for Charles Morny was of too pleasure-loving a nature willingly to endure what gave force to a painful thought; and at the sight of Augusta, all his mother's glosses vanished, and he could only feel that she had been deeply injured, and that he, more than any other, had profited by the injury. This thought, which should have made him peculiarly gentle with her, did truly, from some of those strange vagaries to which this poor, frail nature of ours is subject, make him irritable and impatient. It was not Hugh who rang, but Charlie did not return to say so. A new idea had seized him. He would go and see Judge Mellen and Miss Drayton. Augusta seemed to regard them as friends; they might, perhaps, induce her to give up her unreasonable pride and accept a decent annuity from her uncle's large fortune. And so Charles Morny sauntered out, and, finding Miss

Drayton just preparing to visit Augusta, prevailed on her to stay and listen to him, and even to promise that she would advocate his cause with Augusta herself, though she acknowledged she had little hope of success. As to Judge Mellen, he declared it was the least Mr. Charles Moray could do, and it would be folly, it would be madness in Miss Moray to decline it.

While this was passing at Judge Mellen's, life was not standing still with Augusta. Charlie had left her but a few minutes when a card was brought to her from Mr. Seton, the midshipman whom she had first met at Saratoga, and who had continued his acquaintance by occasional calls in Washington. His present call seemed to Augusta somewhat intrusive, as he must have heard of her uncle's recent death.

"Say to Mr. Seton that Miss Moray is indisposed and receives no visitors," was her careless order to the servant who had brought the card.

"I did tell him the ladies were not at home to-day; but he is the most obstinatest young man, and didn't mind me at all," said the man in a grumbling tone, as he turned away.

Half an hour later there was a light step in the hall, followed by a knock at the door of the music room. Augusta opened the door herself, believing it to be Miss Drayton. It was Mrs. Charles Moray. What an intensity does crime give to the emotions of the most frivolous and shallow being! Here was a woman that had lived all her life with no higher motive than her pleasure, no deeper stirring of her heart than a child experiences to the giver of a toy; she had been led by a stronger spirit into crime, and the lowest abysses of her nature had been stirred, and fear and hate and cruelty had started forth: whatever she might be henceforth, she could not be frivolous. Something of this change was already marked in her face, as she stood there gazing for one moment silently upon Augusta. Augusta, too, was silent, and returned her gaze with a look of haughty questioning.

"I have not intruded on you for my own pleasure, I assure you," said Mrs. Moray, answering that look as if its sense had been put into spoken words. "Mr. Seton, whom you refused to see this morning, requested me to give you that, and to say that Hugh gave it to him for you, just as he was going off yesterday evening to join his father in the Gulf of Mexico. Mr. Seton wished me to say that he did not seal the envelope, because Hugh thought the receiving it so, would show you the hurry he was in, and you would understand then why he did not return to make any explanation to you."

Augusta had had time to recover herself sufficiently to ask with tolerable composure, "Is Commodore Moray ill?"

"No. I suspect, from what Mr. Seton says, that he has been showing his incapacity, as I always thought he would, and there is some danger of his being superseded. I suppose Hugh has gone to give him some help in commanding his squadron. I have no doubt he thinks himself quite equal to it."

The sneer drew no answer from Augusta, and she might have appeared quite calm, but for the slight trembling of the hand in which she held the unsealed missive from Hugh, and for a bright red spot that burned on each cheek.

"I will see Mr. Seton," she said, with sudden determination.

"You are rather late for that, I suspect. Mr. Seton sails himself for the Gulf at two o'clock to-day. He said he must be on board his ship immediately; his ship is the schooner 'Porpoise,' and if you have anything to send to Hugh, and will get it on board that vessel to him within the next two hours, he will take it with pleasure: he will probably see Hugh within a fortnight."

"I will read my note, if you will excuse me, madam, and send him my answer, if I find that it requires one."

"To which pleasant employment I will leave you. Good morning!"

To the last the sneer was in her tone; but Augusta thought little of it as she closed the door after her and sat down to learn what could have taken Hugh Moray from her side at such an hour, when he had just promised to guard and cherish her as a tender brother. She opened the envelope and drew forth its contents—a narrow slip of paper; it was printed. What could it mean? The burning flush rose to her temples as she read a check for one hundred dollars, drawn in her favor by Hugh Moray on the State Bank of New York. She looked again into the envelope, hoping there might be some word to explain this. No—not a word.

"He might have spared me this," said Augusta to herself. It was not her own humiliation that occasioned her keenest pang, even when she remembered that the open envelope had probably made those through whose hands it had passed as well aware as herself of its contents. It was the vanishing away of her ideal; it was the conviction that all noble delicacy, all true generosity must be absent from the mind of one capable of such an act. The Hugh Moray she had loved and trusted, was as much a creature of the imagination as was Hamlet or Othello. Here was the sharpest thrust, the cruel thrust which killed at once both hope and memory. But this was no time for thought; neither, as she said proudly to herself, was she a love-sick girl, to waste her life in vain regrets.

"Call Gib to me, Alice," she said, as she roused herself to action. While Alice was gone, she selected an envelope from her desk, enclosed the check, carefully sealed and addressed it. By the time she had done this, Gib was waiting.

"Gib, I want this note for Master Hugh taken to Mr. Seton, who is on board the schooner 'Porpoise,' lying at the Navy Yard. He is to sail in two hours, so you had better call a hack and drive to the Navy Yard, for it is very important you should be there in time; and, Gib, you must give the letter into Mr. Seton's hands yourself, and you had better tell him that it contains money, and that I will be obliged to him to hand it himself to Master Hugh."

She emptied her purse on the table, that Gib might take the money necessary for his drive; and then turned to packing her trunks with an assiduity which would speedily have accomplished the labor, had she not been interrupted by the entrance of Miss Drayton.

"Ah! you are busy packing, I see; what time do you intend to set out?"

"To-morrow morning," and Augusta busied herself with finding a comfortable seat for Miss Drayton, and assisting her to take off her shawl and bonnet.

"I am very glad you can go so soon," said Miss Drayton, as she kissed the flushed cheek bending down to untie her bonnet. "I was afraid, from what Mr. Charles said, that something had called his cousin off, and you might be detained."

"Hugh has been called away," said Augusta, in a low tone, turning, as she spoke, to lay aside Miss Drayton's wrappings.

"Where?" inquired Miss Drayton.

"To his father, in the Gulf of Mexico. He went out to him in a ship which sailed last evening."

"You saw him before he went?"

"No; but he sent Mr. Seton to let me know all about it."

"And to make arrangements for your going, I suppose.

How grieved he must have been to leave you so! Is Mr. Seton to go with you to-morrow?"

"No; he is ordered away, and sails this afternoon."

"How unfortunate! And who goes with you, then?"

"Nobody. Governesses, you know," with a faint smile, "may travel without protection."

"But pretty young girls may not. Mr. Charles will go with you, I do not doubt, when he hears that Mr. Hugh cannot; if he did not go, I am sure my brother would not suffer you to go alone; one of them will see you safe to Elizabethtown. I could not answer it to my own conscience, to say nothing of Mr. Hugh, if I should part from you without knowing that you would have proper escort to his mother's care."

Miss Drayton was surprised at the still, determined face that met her, as she looked up, at the end of this little speech.

"Miss Drayton," said Augusta, "you have been so kind, so good—I shall be sorry to seem ungrateful; but I must have my own way in this—I must go alone; it is a proper beginning to my independent life. I do not ask this as a favor, I insist on it as a right," she continued, as she saw Miss Drayton prepare to remonstrate.

"Of course, no one can dispute your right to direct your own actions, my dear," Miss Drayton replied, in a manner which, though still kind, was marked by more than her usual gravity.

Augusta turned away with more sullenness in her manner than any one had ever seen there before; for, though quick in temper, she had never been sullen.

"It is but the loss of one friend the more," she said to herself; "well—let them go."

But she was less stoical than she fancied herself. As she raised her eyes after a while to Miss Drayton's face, the gravity there seemed to her more like sorrow than anger. She could not bear it; and drawing near, she said: "Dear, good Miss Drayton! my last friend! forgive me for those unkind words! I am sorry to do anything you disapprove, and I feel all your generous kindness in my very heart of hearts."

"My dear! do not talk of my kindness; I would gladly do something for you, if I could, for I love you tenderly, Augusta, and so does my poor Annie too, whom I left weeping at home, because I would not let her come to you to-day;" and Miss Drayton, with an affectionate caress, drew Augusta down beside her on the sofa, adding, "I have better matters to talk of than my kindness: I have a proposal to make to you, that may alter all your plans."

Then and there, Miss Drayton fulfilled her promise to Charles Moray, enforcing, with all her feminine ingenuity and all the energy of her affection, his proposition respecting the annuity; but ingenious reasons and affectionate entreaties were all in vain. Augusta was firm, though the fire in her heart did not again show itself in any ungentle word or action. She entreated Miss Drayton to be her friend, and to believe that she knew what was best for her own happiness in choosing as she did.

"I have heard Mr. Mortimer say that work was the best cure for unhappiness—let me try it."

"But, my dear, you may not obtain the work, and what will you do then? Would you rather be dependent on Mrs. Commodore Moray, who, from what I know of our naval officers' families, is not likely to be very rich, than take that which is equitably, if not legally your own."

"I shall not be dependent on Mrs. Moray," said Augusta, with lowered voice, while her eyes fell.

"Ah! I see. Her son will take you off her hands," and

Miss Drayton looked at the down-cast face with a benevolent smile.

The smile died away before the flashing glance that replied to it, as Augusta said, "I shall not even go to Mrs. Moray's or to Elizabethtown at all. I shall go to Mrs. Brenton, in New York. I have no doubt she will consider my services in her school to be a sufficient compensation for my board, till I can get some better place."

"Well, my dear, you may be right—I would not discourage you for the world; but you know we ought always to be prepared for possible failure in our plans; it is possible, you know, that Mrs. Brenton may have no place for you. Now will you let me be your Aunt Nancy, and do for you just what I would for my name-child Annie," and Miss Drayton drew out the purse which she had filled this morning for just such a possible occasion.

"Oh, dear Miss Drayton! indeed—indeed—" Augusta began vehemently, laying her hand, as she spoke, upon that in which the purse was held.

"My dear, listen to me; the obligation would be mine —it would relieve me from so much painful apprehension—"

"But, indeed, there is no cause for apprehension; besides I am not quite penniless, and if I could only part with some jewelry, which is entirely useless to me with my present prospects, I should be rich."

"Let me see the jewelry."

Augusta unlocked her jewel casket with a little key, suspended to her watch chain, and showed two morocco cases. Touching the spring of each in turn, the lids flew back, and displayed in the one a necklace, earrings, and pin, of very large and beautiful pearls—in the other, earrings, pin, and ring, of diamonds of unusual size and purity.

Miss Drayton raised the case containing the pearls, and

said, "I should like to take these for Annie, if they are not beyond my purse. Do you happen to know what they cost, my dear?"

"I do; for my uncle took me with him to make the selection in New York—they were three hundred dollars; but they have been worn two or three times—"

"Which only adds to their value; if you really wish to part with them, I will gladly become their purchaser at that price."

And so Miss Drayton was comforted by knowing that Augusta would not be without the means of supporting herself for a few weeks at least, should Mrs. Drenton be unable to receive her. A small sum was also brought to her by Charles, as remaining in the Washington Bank, in which Mr. Moray had deposited his money, after all claims against him had been satisfied. As this had not been named in the will, it of course belonged to her as nearest of kin. This paid the milliner and dressmaker for the simple mourning, which Miss Drayton had procured for her, and furnished her with travelling expenses, leaving her three hundred dollars untouched for future contingencies.

With all the alleviation thus given to their anxiety, her friends, Judge Mellen and his daughter, and Miss Drayton, who drove to the depot to say farewell to her, felt their hearts sink with a weight of pity as they saw her stand in the yet gray light of the early morning, with her black drapery falling gloomily around her, while the faithful Gib was attending to the safety of her baggage. They could not forget how lately crowds had been officious to proffer their services to her who was abandoned thus to the care of a menial. These externals, which so deepened the sadness of the picture to them, were, however, scarcely felt by her. Deeper sorrows had made her insensible to them. They found in her none of that girlish shrinking from her lonely travel for which they were prepared. Indeed, when Judge Mellen would have introduced her to a lady and gentleman, who were going in the cars, and with whom he was slightly acquainted, she declined the introduction with a decision that did not permit him to press it.

"Where is Mr. Charles Moray?" asked Judge Mellen.

"In his bed, asleep, I suspect," answered Augusta, smiling.

"He ought to be ashamed of himself," and the florid face of the kind-hearted judge flushed a deeper red.

"Pray, do not blame poor Charlie! He meant to come with me, but he did not wake in time."

Her friends Annie and Miss Drayton wept, and even Judge Mellen's eyes were not free from the mist of sorrow, as the cars moved off, and the crape veil was thrown back for a moment from Augusta's pale, mournful face, that she might look her last upon them; but her eyes were tearless. Be thankful, ye who weep, that severer grief has not frozen the fountain of your tears.

We will not detain the reader by details of a journey without adventure. Mrs. Brenton received her former pupil with kindness, and sooner than her friends could have hoped, procured her a situation as governess in the family of Mr. Price, a very wealthy banker, whose house on the Fifth Avenue, was one of the show-houses of New York, while Mrs. Price was acknowledged by all to have the handsomest carriage, the most beautiful horses, and the richest livery ever seen in Broadway. Mrs. Price had been herself a pupil of Mrs. Brenton's, but had left her school some years before Augusta's appearance there. Her old respect for her teacher exercised still a restraining power on the lady of fashion, and she did not bloom out in her presence into that overpowering ostentation, which she displayed elsewhere.

"You will not forget that Miss Moray is a lady," said Mrs. Brenton.

"Oh! certainly not. It is really very important to get one who will not teach the children vulgarities—why, do you know, my dear Mrs. Brenton, that I positively saw my last governess turn out her egg into a glass; I really saw her do it with my own eyes. Now, really, you know, all the Latin and mathematics in the world would never repay one for having children taught such absolute neglect of the rules of polite society."

"Well, my dear," said Mrs. Brenton, with a good-natured laugh, "since you are no longer my pupil, I do not mind confessing to you that I rather enjoy taking my own egg from a glass—but do not be alarmed; Miss Moray is, I am sure, quite free from such solecisms."

And Mrs. Price soon made it known to all her acquaintances that she had been so fortunate as to secure for her governess Miss Moray, who had been the belle of Washington all last winter. "Not that I think her so very beautiful—at least that style of beauty is not my favorite style," the lady added; at which one could scarcely be surprised, as Augusta was tall, with dark hair, and eyes whose brown seemed to deepen into black when shadowed by excited feeling, while Mrs. Price was a pure *blonde*, "fat, fair, and forty." Sometimes the friends of Mrs. Price felt some curiosity to see the "belle of Washington," and a message was sent by the accommodating hostess requesting Miss Moray to come down and play a little for the young people to dance. Doubtless among the guests on these occasions there were some who pitied the young and beautiful stranger, at whom the impertinent levelled their glasses, and the cold and selfish carelessly glanced; but to pity and to impertinence alike, Augusta Moray opposed the shield of a manner as cold and as impassive as if she had been indeed the marble statue she resembled in the delicate chiselling of her features and the colorless purity of her complexion.

On the whole, there was no want of material comfort in Augusta's position. Mrs. Price was not a cruel or unkind woman. Vanity and selfishness were the deepest shadows in her not very marked character. Augusta's room was in the fourth story; but it was large and airy, lighted by gas, and its cold tempered in winter by the warm air from the furnace which, do what they would, could not be kept from ascending beyond the rooms occupied by the family, while her table, at which her pupils,—two young girls, the one ten, the other twelve years old,—ate, was supplied with good, healthy food, if not with luxuries. One complaint often made by persons in her position, could not be made by Augusta. Those who served her were never negligent or insolent. With an intuition, which we often see in a greater degree in that class than in any other, they recognized her as a "*real lady*," a term which means a great deal with them, and they did willing service to one who, even in her poverty, had not lost the open hand or liberal heart, and who, however haughty to her equals, or to those who considered themselves her superiors, was always gentle to her inferiors.

While thus fortunate in externals, Augusta's heart and mind lived only in the past. She performed her duty faithfully to the children entrusted to her, but with no affectionate interest in them. Their improvement was of less moment to her than was the proud consciousness that she had paid for all she received. Could she have forgotten herself, could she have loved her work and those for whom it was done, how different would have been her life! Love is the spirit of Heaven; pride, of Hell. She lived only in the past, we have said, but even from that, pride drew not nutriment, but poison. Her former life seemed completely dissevered from her present. She heard nothing from St. Mary's, nothing from Hugh. Miss Drayton was the only one of those she had formerly known, from whom she occasionally received a letter. It was at this period of her life that the autobiography, with which we commenced our little history, was begun, and the picture to which it alludes, was painted. The other picture, of St. Mary's under a stormy sky, was also painted then. And here we leave her, while we follow the steps of one, in whom we hope our readers feel some little interest.

CHAPTER VIII.

"Mine honor is my life: both grow in one,
Take honor from me, and my life is done."—SHAKSPEARE.

WHEN Hugh Moray parted from Augusta, he supposed it to be only for an hour or two. He was going to the navy department, to see the Secretary himself. In his honor he perfectly confided. He would show him his father's letter; if there had been any treachery practised, this would unmask it; the Secretary would see the reasonableness of his father's request, and the wisdom of his plans, and so all would be arranged. "L'homme propose, et Dieu dispose." The Secretary's office was closed at the navy department. He was at a cabinet meeting. Some naval officers were waiting to see him—some with anxious faces, which strove in vain to look careless, others with faces stamped by the recklessness of dissipation, who strove in vain to look thoughtful. Among the younger men was Mr. Seton, to whom Hugh bowed, having occasionally met him at Mr. Moray's.

"Can I see the Secretary?" asked Hugh of an official, presenting his card, and adding, "I am the son of Commodore Moray."

"The Secretary is not here, sir; but Mr. Saville is."

"When will the Secretary be here?'

"I really do not know, sir; he is at a cabinet meeting."

Hugh turned away, and was leaving the department, when he was joined by Mr. Seton, who said, "I am very glad to see you, Mr. Moray; I could not venture to call so soon after Mr. Moray's death, and yet, as I sail for the Gulf to-morrow, I wanted to say that I would be glad to take anything you might have to send to the Commodore."

"Thank you, Mr. Seton."

The gentlemen walked silently on for a few minutes, and then Hugh said, "May I ask in what ship you are going?"

"In the 'Porpoise,' a little schooner of about two hundred tons—just the thing for the Gulf service."

"I am glad they are waking up to that fact at the department; my father says he cannot do anything without some vessels of light draught."

Mr. Seton made no comment.

"I believe you have served with my father, Mr. Seton," said Hugh.

"I have, Mr. Moray; and every man who has done so, I believe, loves him—certainly, every careless youngster, over whom he has exercised the influence he did on me, must do so. You must lay it to that love, if I ask what may seem to you an impertinent question: Do you know— do you think the Commodore knows that Commodore Puffer is to be sent out to the Gulf? It is not positively said that Commodore Moray is to be recalled, but that is the conclusion; as every one who knows Commodore Puffer knows he would not accept the position of second in command, and he is the junior of Commodore Moray."

"Are you sure of this, Mr. Seton?"

"*I know* that Commodore Puffer lies in Hampton Roads waiting for his orders, which will be carried to him by the Porpoise to-morrow; *I know* that the Porpoise is to go out in company with the Flint, which carries the Commodore himself; *I know* that both these vessels are to carry out soldiers; and, without looking into the Commodore's sealed orders, *I know* we are going to the Gulf of Mexico; *I know*, too, that the schooner Dolphin, the fastest sailer in the navy, leaves the navy yard within an hour, and carries despatches to Commodore Moray. What these despatches contain, I do not know, of course; but the belief is that they will offer to Commodore Moray the option of asking for a recall or of being superseded by his junior. You have heard, of course, that the troops have not yet been landed, and that the General is becoming impatient."

"I know that it has been impossible to land them for the want of armed vessels of sufficiently light draught,—just such vessels as you tell me Commodore Puffer takes with him, and my father has in vain applied for. Do you call this justice, sir?"

"No, sir," said Mr. Seton, with emphasis, and with excitement equal to Hugh's. "I was sure there was a cloven foot in the business somewhere, and now I see it was Saville's. I would give my next year's pay, badly as I want it, if Commodore Moray would hold on in spite of them till he had accomplished the business, and then, when there was nothing more to be done, request to be recalled."

"Could he do so? would it not be regarded as disobedience of orders?"

"I do not see how it could be, if the despatches that precede Commodore Puffer are only to give him the permission to resign; he certainly may refuse that, without any disobedience; and for the rest, if he had everything prepared, he might go into action as soon as the vessels he wanted arrived, and read Puffer's despatches afterward, when he had leisure."

"Do you think I shall have time to write by the Dolphin?"

"Not much," and Seton shook his head; "if you could go now—"

"Go I could, if I felt sure that—that—" Hugh hesitated; he feared to offend one who certainly wished to serve his father.

"Sure that my advice was good; I am but a middy; yet I think all who love your father would give the same advice. Come with me to the yard and consult Captain Rapall. He is one of your father's warmest friends, and a man of excellent judgment."

"I will; but should he advise my going, shall I have time to go back for my trunk before I must be on board?"

"No; there will not be ten minutes to spare now when we get to the yard; but stop, here's a darkey who'll drive there, get them, and have them at the yard as quickly as you can be there yourself. If you don't go, you know, it is only to take them back. Holloa, Hannibal!"

Hannibal, who was a hackney coachman, received his order, drove to Mr. Moray's, and executed it, as we have seen.

The young men walked rapidly on. Hugh was thinking too busily to speak. He was weighing the necessity there was of his presence *here* for Augusta and *there* for his father; he was trying to subdue the almost intolerable pain which the thought of her imagining that he could leave her at such a time for anything but an absolute necessity, caused him.

"If I should go, Mr. Seton," he said, suddenly, "will you do me a great favor?"

"Your father's son may command me to the extent of my power." Mr. Seton spoke earnestly, for Hugh's tone was very earnest.

"After all," said Hugh, smiling, "it is not quite a Herculean task I am going to demand of you. The greatness of the favor lies in its importance to myself. If I go, I must send a few lines to Miss Moray, explaining my not being able to attend her to my mother's. Will you see that she gets it? I would not like to trust it to an ordinary messenger."

"I will deliver it myself before I sail to-morrow," Mr. Seton replied.

"Into her hand?" urged Hugh.

"Into her own hand, if she will permit me."

They were at the navy yard. Captain Rapall was in his office. Hugh was introduced by Mr. Seton, and detailed the information he had received, and the suggestion that had been made by the young midshipman. Captain Rapall read Captain Moray's letter through with a grim smile, then laying it down, he spoke: "That is just your father, sir; honorable, unsuspecting, too keenly sensitive for this common, work-a-day world. Such a notion as Seton's of being too busy to read despatches till the action was over would never suggest itself to his guileless soul. He ought to have lived in Arcadia. But if you can go and induce him to do that very thing, you will save both his life and his honor. No fear of his being tried for disobedience of orders. They know here that a courtmartial would bring out their own crooked dealings; besides, if he be successful, which he is sure to be, he could afford to be tried; they would not dare to touch him."

"Then I will go," exclaimed Hugh.

"You must be quick; the sailing signal is flying," said the Captain, pointing, as he spoke, to the trim schooner that lay a few yards from shore in the Potomac.

"I must write a letter first," exclaimed Hugh; "it is impossible for me to go without."

"Be quick, then; Seton, run down to the wharf; the Dolphin's boat is just pushing off; call them back—tell them to hold on for ten minutes."

"Shall I order Mr. Moray's trunk on board, sir?" asked Seton.

"Certainly, if it be here; but we can't wait."

"Here it is, sir," and Seton hurried off with willing obedience.

Captain Rapall seated himself to write a few lines of introduction for Hugh to the commander of the Dolphin, while Hugh himself filled up the check that Augusta had received, and wrote the following note:

DEAR AUGUSTA:

Though I know I am doing what you would not forgive me for leaving undone, it is with infinite pain that I leave you at such a moment. Nothing less than my father's honor, in which I believe his life also bound up, would I put in competition with your need of a friend, who is vowed to do you service as a brother, whether you will honor him by admitting his claim to a brother's place or not. I have no time for explanations; I must trust them to Mr. Seton, who has promised to put this in your own hands. Let me only entreat you, by the memory of your childhood, trust me as your brother, and as a proof that you do so, use the enclosed, and draw on me for whatever you need afterward. It is the only way in which you can show me that I have not offended you in what I am now doing. Charles will go with you to my mother's, where it will be my delight to find you on my return. They will not allow me another moment. H. MORAY.

"Fold it quick, Moray; here is an envelope," cried young Seton.

"Mr. Moray, the boat will leave you," cried Captain Rapall; "your ten minutes are gone."

"Give it to me, you may trust me; I will seal it, or,

better deliver it as it is; it will show her what haste you were in, and that will plead your excuse for all omissions. Good-by; I hope you will persuade the Commodore."

"Good-by; give that to Miss Murny herself; I can trust you more fully than I can some others in the world," said Hugh, as he sprang into the boat, which had been held within a short distance of the wharf by a signal from Captain Rapall.

The Dolphin was a fast sailer, and little more than three weeks of northerly winds brought them off Vera Cruz. There lay the Congress, her sails reefed, her anchors down, everything about her trim and clean, and her beautifully proportioned hull and tapering spars reflected in the still, blue water,

> "Just like a painted ship,
> Upon a painted ocean."

A peaceful picture it was indeed without, but within the idle soldiers scoffed, enraging the brave tars who loved their kind commander, by wondering if he had come there to show his ship to the castle; if he was afraid that he should get his pretty toy-boats knocked to pieces, or more red paint on them than pleased his fancy, that he kept them there broiling in the sun, while there stood the Mexicans waiting for them. "Ah! if the old General could only get ashore, one sight of his noble face, rising a head and shoulders above any other man's, would send the rascals off in double quick time, before we had time to fire a shot. Just look at him up there now; wouldn't he like to be at that castle! I'm afraid he wouldn't be careful enough of your boats to please your nice Commodore."

Such taunts, daily and hourly repeated, and growing more bitter as time wore on, but for the vigilant eye and strong hand of discipline, might have caused some danger of outbreak between the saucy, idle soldiery and the brave tars, each holding their own especial commander free from blame in this enforced delay, for which, in truth, both were responsible. If the commander-in-chief of the land forces chafed at this idle time—he who had already won his crown of laurels in combat against a nobler foe, on the field of Chippewa—how must it have galled the sensitive nature of Commodore Moray, now for the first time entrusted with a large, independent command, and supposed by his countrymen at home to be in a position in which he might show what were his true qualities as a leader. Never was sight more welcome to him than the Dolphin, as, with white wings expanded, she came sailing up that noble harbor, and as she passed the Congress to anchor in her stern, fired her salute of twenty-one guns to the Commodore's flag. The schooner had scarcely anchored when, in obedience to the Commodore's signal, the gig was lowered and her commander, accompanied by Hugh, took his way to the frigate.

"Hugh! my son! what brought you here?" cried Commodore Moray, pressing his son's outstretched hand as he stepped upon the deck, and hardly refraining from a tenderer greeting than he thought becoming before so many witnesses—while his troubled eye showed that he felt sure only some sorrow experienced or apprehended could have sent Hugh to his side.

"All well at home, sir," said Hugh, briefly, and the Commodore's eye brightened as, with an unspoken thanksgiving, he turned to give a courteous welcome to the gray-haired, weather-beaten commander of the Dolphin. They descended together to the Commodore's cabin, the General accompanying them. A quarter of an hour passed, and the General and the commander of the Dolphin again appeared, and with a courteous salute, the first returned to his walk upon the quarter deck, and the other, after a few hurried words with the officers standing around, went over the ship's side into his boat, and was pulled back to the Dolphin.

"Confound his unsociality; I'd have given him a glass of my best sherry to know that they were going to send us one or two more boats like the Dolphin," cried one of the younger lieutenants, older men only looking their disappointment.

Hugh had been introduced by his father to the ship's captain, and stood in conversation with him for a few minutes; but as soon as he saw that Commodore Moray was alone he became abstracted, and kept both eye and ear intent upon the door of the cabin, beside which the sentinel paced to and fro. It was not long before he was summoned. The door closed on him, and Commodore Moray held out his hand again, saying, in a voice he strove in vain to make firm, "So you have come to show your father you, at least, are not ashamed of him, Hugh."

"I should hardly have taken a voyage for such an unnecessary object. I had other designs, I assure you, in coming."

"You do not know, then, that the despatches brought by the Dolphin permit me to resign my command and return in her to the United States, as another will be sent out immediately to take my place."

"Yes, sir, I know that, and yet more; I can tell you who your successor will be."

"Puffer, of course?—I see I am right. Well, I must bear it; but a Mexican ball would have been a less cruel death."

"Father!" exclaimed Hugh, as Commodore Moray turned away to hide the heaving chest and moist eyes, of which he need not have been ashamed, "Father! listen to me, and all this may be redeemed. I come by the advice of your best friends in the navy, to entreat you not to accept this treacherous permission—not to resign."

"I have no such intention, Hugh; I shall never turn my back on yonder shore till I have seen the stars and stripes floating there. I shall leave the Congress and go on board the Dolphin; I will not interfere with Puffer's command; I will hoist no broad pennant; but, since the department has graciously given me command of the Dolphin, I will take her as near to that shore as I can without putting her on it, and every shot she fires shall tell the world I am no craven."

The brave old man's eyes flashed, and the veins on his temples stood out like cords.

How Hugh longed for his mother at that moment, for he felt that only a woman's gentle caressing touch could soothe that agony. He had no words of comfort for it; he could only say, "This was not what I hoped you would do, father; it was not what your friends, especially Captain Rapall, through whose advice I came, advised."

"What then?"—the tone of the question was abrupt.

"They thought you should retain your command, make all your arrangements for landing the troops—"

"They were made long ago; I have had nothing to do but study the coast and make plans."

"Then, they said, order the schooners up as soon as they were near enough to make out your signal, put the troops on board, and commence the attack at once; they were sure General S—— would coöperate with you."

"And where would Puffer be all this time?"

"Perhaps in his own ship, perhaps in yours, but he is your junior, and the despatches superseding you, you would be too busy to read till the action was over." Hugh ended with a smile, for he had talked himself, if not his father, into very cheerful anticipations.

"A very pretty plot, Hugh, a very pretty plot; but your father was not made for a plotter."

"But, dear father, there are those at the department who are at war with you, and stratagems are permitted in war."

"Still, an honorable man would never practise them in a private quarrel."

"But, father, indeed I can see nothing wrong here. You are the commander of the squadron till displaced by the positive command of the department, which cannot take effect till you receive their despatch."

"And I, knowing that Commodore Puffer has that despatch in his pocket, refuse to see him, or refuse to receive it till I have executed my own will! No, Hugh. While I hold my commission I am bound to obey the orders of my government, issued through its legitimate channels; I do not deny that there are occasions—rare occasions—when an officer may run the risk of disobedience, but it must not be for his private advantage."

"Captain Rupall assured me they would not dare to try you, for fear of exposing their own game; moreover, he said, the country would sustain you if you were successful, and of your success he did not doubt."

"Nor do I; it is certain, if we can get within cannon shot of the shore, though it will not be as bloodless as people at home believe; but is an honorable man obedient only because he fears punishment? or shall we do evil that good may come? Wilful disobedience it would be, and I should deserve to be cashiered; I dread my own verdict quite as much as I do that of a court; the world may condemn me, but, thank God! my own conscience will acquit me."

"Father, will you speak to General S—— of this before you decide? he is a brave and honorable man, and if he—"

"No, Hugh; I will take counsel of none but my own conscience; I will strive to do right, let what will come of it, and when Puffer's pennant is in sight, I will haul down mine, though I would rather cut off my right hand than give it such work to do; and I will go on board the Dolphin, simple Captain Moray."

And from this determination, though sleepless nights and days of painful thoughts left their impress on his pale, stern face, Captain Moray never swerved. When, two days after Hugh's arrival, Commodore Puffer's flag appeared on board the Flint which entered the harbor, followed at no great distance by two other sloops of war, Commodore Moray himself drew down his pennon, and with his son and secretary descended to his gig and was rowed to the Dolphin. It was a touching scene, and perhaps, could Commodore Moray have known the feelings of admiring deference with which all, from the gallant General to the humblest tar, regarded him at that moment, he would have felt himself repaid for his outward humiliation. Something of it he did know, for, as soon as it was rumored that he was to transfer his flag to the Dolphin, and suspected that it was his intention to bring her into action, more officers and sailors volunteered to accompany him than the little craft could have accommodated. Hugh knew by the glistening eyes and heaving bosom of his father how these demonstrations touched his heart. It was then first that it became known to all on board that Commodore Moray was to be superseded by Commodore Puffer in the command of the squadron, and that he would return home in the Dolphin.

It was a lovely day when Commodore Puffer at length arrived. The clear, blue summer sky was reflected unbroken in the almost waveless sea, as Commodore Moray descended for the last time the frigate's side. Every man was at his post, and as, after shaking hands with the officers, the Commodore looked around him with a mute gesture of farewell, one loud spontaneous cheer burst from the men.

That heart-stirring sound had scarcely died away when it was echoed back from the Dolphin, as Commodore Moray stepped upon her deck, and again the men on board the frigate caught the dying sounds and sent them back across the wave, and as the Commodore's flag streamed out from the little vessel, it was saluted by the cannon of both ships.

"I am afraid that will not please Puffer," said Commodore Moray, as he saw the first flash from the frigate, " and, indeed, Mr. Pitman," turning to the lieutenant commanding the Dolphin, "I did not intend to hoist my flag on board. I have no command now. I am but your passenger; though, with your permission, I shall detain the Dolphin till after the attack is made, and assume command of her for that one day."

"We shall all be proud to be so commanded, sir; and we hope you will let us bear your pennant. Commodore Puffer will not break his heart, we may hope, at carrying a blue flag instead of a red for a few days."

"We will not try his magnanimity so far," said Commodore Moray, with a melancholy smile, "he is Commodore of the squadron, not I; that pennant must be lowered, Mr. Pitman."

The last words were in a tone that admitted of no remonstrance, and the order was obeyed promptly, though with reluctance.

Commodore Puffer's flag was soon after saluted. A really active and meritorious officer, notwithstanding the vanity which made him sometimes forgetful of the claims of brother officers as deserving as himself, but less self-conscious, he lost no time in entering on his new duties. The salute had scarcely ceased when he presented himself on board the frigate to confer with the commander-in-chief. He had expected to meet Commodore Moray also on board, but finding that he had already withdrawn to the Dolphin, he sent his secretary to that vessel with a note, requesting the Commodore to join their conference. Commodore Moray declined to do this, but sent back the plan which he had himself drawn up for the landing of the troops and the assault to be made by the ships upon the castle and town, for the purpose of covering their landing. In this plan there was one point marked, "Important, but, I fear, not to be attained. It may be held with comparative safety, if it can be reached." In his note the Commodore wrote, "It is my intention not to leave the harbor till after the attack, for personal reasons, as well as because I believe the Dolphin may do good service on that day. You will find on the plan sent a point marked 'Important, but, I fear, not to be attained, &c;' if you will leave that to the Dolphin, her commander will try to give you a good account of it; I ask this as a favor to myself."

The favor was, of course, granted, in a note in which Commodore Puffer acknowledged the value of the plan submitted to him, and said that, as the commander-in-chief entirely approved of it, and as it was of the first importance to act immediately, he should not delay for any further examination, but would commence the action the next day at 8 A. M. This was followed by information respecting signals, and the note concluded thus: "If more men are wanted on board the Dolphin, they may be detached from the frigate." Commodore Moray sent a note that evening to Capt. Keeler of the frigate, requesting him to send him twenty men, adding that, as it was a sort of "forlorn hope" that he was about to lead, he should like to have volunteers for it. Accordingly Capt. Keeler, after assembling the men on deck, and making a little speech, in which he said that their gallant old Commodore wanted twenty men for the Dolphin, which he should himself command during the fight the next day, and which he meant to station where she would get the most balls of any ship in action, asked, "Who will be one of the twenty?"

"I—I—I—" rang over the ship, in such a shout that it was difficult to know, not who had spoken, but who had been silent; and after he had selected the twenty whom he supposed most serviceable from those who offered, ten others urged their claim so earnestly, that they were permitted to present themselves to Commodore Moray, who would not reject the brave fellows.

The morning sun rose calm and clear; the healthful breeze stirred the blue waves into quicker life, and filled the white canvas as the ships, no longer held by their anchors, were turned with their prows toward the shore. Those ships looked little like bearers of wounds and death; as their gay flags streamed out upon the air, their bands played their inspiriting marches, and officers and men, dressed as for a gala day, and wearing the cheerful faces that would befit a gala day, took each his post. It has always seemed to us that in naval warfare a courage of nobler character was required than in contests on the land. In the last, the blood is stirred by the rush to meet the enemy, by the actual fight, often hand to hand with a visible foe, so that something of personal feeling almost necessarily mingles in the encounter. But he who stands to serve the cannon, to pilot the ship, or to direct the manœuvres in a naval engagement, must do all with the cool, collected courage of one who stands there to do his duty even unto death, yet with nothing to give a quicker flow to the blood, or to awaken the feelings that are stirred in the most peaceable by a personal assault.

The narration of this morning's events belongs to history. Our business is with the little schooner, which carries those in whose fortunes we have an especial interest.

Commodore Moray would have had Hugh go back to the Congress, telling him that it was not his duty to remain, and even that his presence would interfere with his own calmness in action; but Hugh suggested that it would discourage his men, if they saw him sending his own son out of the battle into which he was leading them.

"But remember your mother and sisters, Hugh, how much they will need you if anything happen to me."

"I will not forget them, father, I will not expose myself unnecessarily; but I may be of use to you—I shall at least know all that happens to you."

Commodore Moray yielded. He had taken the command of the Dolphin, and now stood upon her deck dressed in the full uniform of his rank, with a face that was pale with concentrated feeling, but with a more cheerful countenance than he had shown for many weeks. There was a smile in his eyes, if not upon his lips, and the men on board, taking their tone from what they supposed to be his, laughed lightly as the formidable artillery of the Castle opened its fire on the approaching ships, while they were yet too distant to be touched by it. The sound of that laugh aroused a new train of thought with Captain Moray. He measured their distance from the Castle with his eye, glanced at the course he had himself marked for the ship, and ordered Lieutenant Pitman to direct the men to come aft, while he said a few words to the chaplain of the ship.

"My men," he said, when all except the helmsman stood there before him, "we are going into no child's play,—we are not afraid of death when we meet it in our country's service; but we shall not meet it with less courage for knowing that it will give us entrance into heaven. A short prayer from the chaplain, and then every man to his post."

Every head was uncovered, and bowed with at least the aspect of solemn reverence as the chaplain asked the mercy of Heaven on the bodies and souls not only of those present, but of all who were that day to meet in combat, whether friend or foe.

We know there are those to whom such prayer, under such circumstances, would seem an impious mockery; but not so do we regard it—not so are we taught by Him to whom all human wisdom is but folly. It was when the hands of Moses were lifted to Heaven that Israel prevailed. Little do those know of magnanimity who cannot conceive of a man praying for the enemy and doing good to him as he has opportunity, against whom he will yet fight so long as he stands in opposition to his country, or to the cause which he has pledged himself to support.

"Every man to his post; and remember, live or die, our country will know how we have done our duty this day."

The order was obeyed with alacrity; and if after this the tone of the men was less gay, it was not less manly. The merriment of the scoffing infidel, in the presence of death, is a poor bravado, meant to hide from others the heart which he feels to be trembling within him. It is the Christian alone who can be at once wise and brave.

Still, for some minutes after this, the Dolphin pursued a course outside the line within which fell the shot from the castle; but when she had arrived opposite the point marked out for her station during the landing of the troops, the prow was suddenly turned shoreward. The men had been ordered to shelter themselves, as far as it was possible to do so, till the station at which they aimed was reached. The guns of the little schooner could do little against the castle, but she could do good service, first by drawing its fire upon herself, while the boats from the other vessels were landing the soldiers, and after she had reached her proposed station, by preventing sallies from the castle, as her shot would completely rake the plain between the castle and the spot selected for the landing of the American forces. Within a few minutes after the Dolphin's course was changed, the shot from the enemy began to fall thick and fast around her. The men were sheltered, as we have said—the helmsman alone excepted. Some attempt had been made, by order of Commodore Moray, to strengthen the shelter provided for him, but it seemed only to offer a mark for attack, and was soon knocked to pieces, and the man himself so wounded, that he fell helpless on the deck. Another started forward to take his place.

"Back! back, sir!" shouted Commodore Moray, as he stepped at once to the spot, beside which he had stood to deliver his orders more rapidly, and seized the wheel himself.

"Pardon me, sir," said Mr. Pitman, springing to his side, "but that is my place rather than yours."

"Your place is the one I assigned to you, sir! back to it, this instant!" again shouted the Commodore, too imperatively to be disobeyed.

Fast and furious fell that iron hail; and still, though some of her spars were carried away and her sails torn, the gallant craft held on her way with one form only rising above her bulwarks—the form of Commodore Morny. Every eye on the deck was turned to him, and none saw an instant's change in that smiling eye and calm face. Hugh saw him not, for his father had taken care to give him employment with the surgeon below. Long it seemed as if he bore a charmed life, but at length a sudden spasm contracted his brow, and his right arm fell helpless to his side. Scarcely paler than before, scarcely less cheerful was his face, as he laid his left hand on the wheel, and moved so as to use it with effect; the blood soaked his sleeve, and ran in a little stream where he stood, but the strong spirit did not falter. Another ball shattered his thigh; he bent to his knee, yet still his hand grasped the wheel, and even as he sank into unconsciousness, his fainting voice uttered, "Not yet! back for one moment!" to those who approached to bear him below. But there was little further need for such an order. They had got beyond the line which it had seemed madness to enter. Her hull leaking badly, her sails hanging, one mast shot away, and lying a helpless ruin on deck, the Dolphin slowly, with the help of a single sail, reached her station and began the work assigned her. It was brave work, and those who saw it felt that no ship had done more for the cause than had the Dolphin, as her fire, steadily and skilfully delivered, again and again drove back the advancing foe.

Two days after the landing of the forces, the Congress was sent home with those who had been seriously wounded. Commodore Moray occupied his former cabin, in which a hammock had been slung for Hugh. His leg and part of his thigh had been amputated; but the surgeon still hoped that his arm might be saved. He was too weak to do anything but look his wishes, and to Hugh's anxious inquiries the surgeon could only answer with hopes. Before they arrived in New York, to which port the ship had been ordered by Commodore Puffer, principally on Commodore Moray's account, fever had set in, which lent him temporary strength, even while diminishing the chance of his ultimate recovery. The surgeon, though desiring to keep him silent, could not prevent his speaking to Hugh at this time. "Hugh, there is one thing I must say to you," he began, as soon as he had strength for speech.

"We shall have time enough for it by and by, father, better not exhaust yourself now."

"We know not what time we shall have, and I must say it. They told you, I heard them, that I had exposed myself madly—thrown away my life. That would have been unchristian. They did not know, Hugh, that there was some personal feeling mingling with the motives that made me volunteer for that service—I am afraid the personal feeling was the strongest," and a groan, which his physical suffering had never wrung from him, quivered from his pale lips: "God forgive me! I felt when that poor helmsman fell at my feet—he is better now, Hugh?"

"Yes, father."

"I felt then as if he had fallen, not in the service of his country, but in my personal quarrel; it was a terrible pang, and I determined none but I should take that exposed place while God gave me life and strength to hold it. Tell your mother how it was, Hugh, and do not let her think I threw away the life she valued, and which was God's, not mine."

"You will tell her yourself, dear father," said Hugh; "to-morrow evening we shall be in New York."

Before the Congress had reached New York, the news of the landing of the forces by the fleet under the command of Commodore Puffer, had been carried there by the telegraph from New Orleans. For some days the daily papers, throughout the country, were as eulogistic of that officer as if he had himself written the articles treating of the event. How bitterly fell these articles, full of ungenerous comments on the incapacity of him whom Commodore Puffer had superseded, upon the hearts of the little household at Elizabethtown. They could have borne any wound better than one that reached them through his sensitive heart. Mrs. Moray never lost her faith in him for an instant.

"Oh! mamma, if he had only landed them!" cried the weeping, excited Lily.

"Wait, Lily, you will find he has done all that was his duty."

A few days before the arrival of the Congress, a new

light began to dawn upon the public. A letter from the commander-in-chief had given honor where honor was due, without breathing the spirit of a champion against wrong. By a simple detail of facts, it was seen that no means of covering the landing of troops had been given to Commodore Moray; that Commodore Puffer had been able to act so promptly only because he found everything prepared for him; that the plan of operations, which had been so much lauded, had been given by Commodore Moray to his successor, and that the most difficult and dangerous part of that plan had been undertaken and executed by himself.

The papers, with more or less grace, unsaid their says, so far as they reflected on him who was now acknowledged to be the true hero of the day. Transparencies of Commodore Puffer's full-length likeness figured, it is true, at all the illuminations, and over the doors of the Whig headquarters in every town—Commodore Puffer was a whig—but every one knew that the transparencies, having been painted, must be used, and the democratic party soon had Commodore Moray suspended over their headquarters. It is true, the likeness was not very good, as Commodore Moray had never been thought a man of sufficient importance to be asked to sit for his picture; but the transparency was, we must acknowledge, much handsomer than the Commodore himself, so he surely had no reason to complain; and besides that, the artist had guarded against mistakes by labelling his picture, Commodore James Moray. It could scarcely have been mistaken by any who had read the letter sent by Mr. Seton, though without his name, to the New York Herald, giving a detailed account of the action, since the moment chosen for representation was that in which the Commodore was sinking to the deck under his second wound, while his left hand still grasped the wheel, and his right hung useless at his side. The city of New York had promised itself the enjoyment of a grand demonstration in a public reception of the Commodore, in expectation of which one alderman had bought up large quantities of powder, and another had speculated in fireworks, both intending to sell out to the city, of course, doubling their money. Both these gentlemen felt themselves aggrieved when they understood that Commodore Moray's condition was such as to render rejoicings at his reception somewhat ill-timed. Had not an astute associate suggested that public rejoicings at the success to which he had so largely contributed would be admissible, even if the Commodore should prove to be mortally wounded, they would have changed sides and backed Commodore Puffer as the hero of the day. The same gentleman added that, should the Commodore die on his way home, the city would doubtless pay well for funeral honors, out of which a pretty thing might be made with good management. So the two city fathers took the Commodore's reputation again under their guardianship, hastening their preparations for the rejoicings, lest the funeral at which the fireworks and much of the powder would be unnecessary, might interfere with them. It was in consequence of this haste that the Congress anchored amidst a blaze of light thrown across the bay from the illuminated city, and that the wounded men, many of them delirious with fever, were disturbed by the booming of cannon long after the surgeons had hoped to see them lulled to repose by the cessation of motion in the ship. Early the next morning, when the sun was scarcely an hour high, a boat approached the Congress from the navy yard. In her stern sat the Commodore of the yard, and beside him a lady, who was so closely veiled and shawled that it was not easy to distinguish either face or figure; yet, as she was handed with respectful attention to the deck, Hugh Moray recognized his mother in the movements so full of gentle dignity, and hastened to her side. She raised her veil, and all read in the pale, but beautiful face, the sorrow which has no words. To the mute questioning of her melancholy eyes, Hugh answered, "Alive, dear mother, and I hope he will know you, and be better for the knowledge," yet there was something in his voice which forbade her to hope.

"You may trust my mother's self-command," said Hugh, turning to the surgeon.

"I hope so," was the reply, in a tone which showed how needful it was considered, and the surgeon preceded them into the Commodore's cabin, intimating by a gesture that they should wait a moment at the door.

It was but a moment, and he passed out, bidding them enter. Commodore Moray looked up with an agitated smile, "My wife!"

A silent, quivering kiss upon his trembling lips, a soft, caressing hand upon his gray locks, was her greeting. She could not speak, lest sobs should come with her words—she turned aside her face that the big, silent tears should not drop upon his. He closed his eyes for a moment, and brushing away her tears, she pressed her lips to his broad forehead. He looked up with a faint smile, and whispered, "Did you know I had left part of myself behind me?"

"I know you have brought me all I value in your own great heart, my hero!"

He smiled; such praise was sweet to his childlike, loving heart.

"How did you hear?" he asked a moment afterward.

"Through the papers; letters were sent by the way of New Orleans—all the world knows now what I knew always—" Her voice was choked—it was not the present sorrow that overcame her, for that she had nerved herself. It was the memory of those long years of injustice under which his life had faded away in silent sorrow, and to vindicate himself from which he had faced such deadly peril.

Dr. Maxwell, the surgeon, soon became convinced that Commodore Moray could have no nurse like his wife; and as it was impossible that he should remain on board the Congress, which Commodore Puffer had requested should be ordered back to the Gulf, it was determined to attempt to convey him to his home at Elizabethtown. This was rendered comparatively easy by the ready civilities of railroad corporations and steamboat directors, all pleased to bring their names before the public in connection with one whom all now delighted to honor. A steamboat came alongside of the Congress, and received the Commodore, who was lifted on board in his couch, and accompanied by his surgeon and son, and by eight or ten stout sailors who were to bear him from the steamboat at Jersey City to the special car, which had been offered by the railroad company for his use, and from which several seats had been removed to make room for his couch. The same men attended him in the car, and bore him with careful tread to his own home, asking as their reward to be allowed before they went, to press their old commander's hand, in token of their love and reverence, and positively refusing the money that Hugh would have pressed on their acceptance. And at every place at which they stopped on the route, crowds paused to gaze with eager eyes upon the carriage, or the curtained couch, that contained one who but a little while ago had walked among them with "none to do him reverence."

Let us close this sad and "o'er true tale." The summer passed away with varying hopes and fears to those with every cord of whose loving hearts, the brave old veteran's life seemed bound. Autumn came, and clinging to the hope which grew fainter day by day, they said, "The bracing air will revive him;" but he shrank from it. What braced them, chilled his exhausted frame. He had been able, after his leg had healed, to sit in a large chair for several hours each day, and even occasionally to take a turn or two across the room with Hugh's assistance and the use of a cane; but day by day, as the winter came on, his strength decreased, he sat up less, and at length there came a day when he begged to have a couch placed beside his bed, and only to be helped from the one to the other. These changes formed sad epochs to the loving heart which had shared his griefs and watched beside his bed of suffering without one selfish thought. When the couch was brought, her gentle hand smoothed its pillows, and as he laid his head upon them, he looked up with his old, sweet smile, and said, "How sweet it is to have you to nurse me, darling."

She could bear no more. Falling on her knees beside him, the long repressed agony burst forth. Her tears and kisses, mingled, fell upon his hands, his cheeks, his lips, and when he passed his arm around her neck and drew her head to his bosom, she lay there and sobbed as a weary child sobs on its mother's breast. Not a word was spoken till her sobs had ceased, though her tears still dropped and her kisses were pressed upon the hand that embraced her; then he said, "I am glad, darling, since we were to part, that it was so—they cannot refuse you the pension now."

"Hush! hush! it would be to me the price of your blood," she answered, in a hoarse whisper, and with a shudder.

"You must not feel so, love. You know if they had left me undisturbed, we must have had the fight just the same."

"No! oh no! not the same. You would not have been *there!*"

"Some one must have been—and this was God's ordering."

Yes—there was the one stilling thought. It was God's ordering; and more and more, as the gloom settled down upon them, they anchored themselves upon it. Some earthly consolations they still had. Commodore Moray's native State, New Jersey, voted him, by its Legislature, the gift of a handsome sword. As he could not go to the capital to receive it, it was sent to him. His name and Vera Cruz were engraved on the golden handle.

"You will keep it for your children, Hugh," said the veteran, as, after examining it, he placed it in his son's hand.

Congress met, and in the speeches of senators and representatives, allusion was made to the gallantry of Commodore Moray; and the navy department was questioned why one who had proved himself fitted for any command should have been displaced, and a life so valuable to the country, imperilled by the position which it was rumored he had been compelled to assume in vindication of his own honor; to which questions the department replied somewhat oracularly, yet in terms of high compliment to the wounded Commodore. Last of all there came a letter from the Secretary himself, written with his own hand, and marked *private*, in which, without alluding to the past, he complimented Commodore Moray's gallantry, regretted his wound, and assured him the government as well as the people of the country were ready to do everything that could manifest their regard for him.

"Then they will not refuse a pension to my family," was the Commodore's thought as he read these words.

We have narrated these testimonials, because, trifling as they may seem, they were very dear to the dying officer. Little do those who, to serve some party end, cast a slur upon our gallant navy, representing the vices or indolence of a few as characteristic of the whole, know how coldly and heavily fall their words upon the men who have looked to their country's approbation as the great reward for all their years of self-denial and of hardship.

But, pleasant as they might be, there came an hour when these things sounded like the far-off murmurs of a dream, when the loving hearts around that couch would have given all the fame, all the hope of fortune, for one word more from the still lips, one glance from the closed eyes, when the last tender whispers were dearer than would have been the loud huzzas of millions. But all was over, and to him who lay there so still and cold, human love and human glory were alike nothing.

CHAPTER IX.

> "Not so sick, my lord,
> As she is troubled with thick coming fancies,
> That keep her from her rest."—SHAKSPEARE.

AND during all these months had Hugh been quite forgetful of Augusta? That was impossible. The love, which has its birth in the untouched heart of a boy, which has grown with his growth, and strengthened with his strength, which has given life to his hopes and vigor to his action, being the very mould in which his life has shaped itself—such a love is not forgotten easily even in one of ordinary firmness of character and tenacity of affection; and the firmness of Hugh's character, the tenacity of his affections, was not ordinary.

Mr. Seton had been faithful to his trust; he delivered, what he supposed a note from Augusta, safely. Hugh waited till he was alone to open it, and found his check returned, without a word. His first feeling was of indignation. "Proud, foolish girl!" he exclaimed, as he tore the paper into bits and scattered it to the winds; "you may live to feel the want of the friend you have rejected."

For a few days this conviction brought with it a certain sense of satisfaction, but softer feelings were soon awakened.

"Poor child! What does she know of the life that is

opening before her. She must be saved from it, if possible," and Hugh wrote to Mr. Mortimer, asking his aid in accomplishing this object.

"I owed her uncle for money expended on my collegiate and professional education. I always intended to pay it as soon as I could. I can now, and as he is not living to receive it, it is justly hers—not only justly, but legally. Impress this upon her, I entreat you, since she refuses to hear me."

To this letter Mr. Mortimer replied that he did not even know where Augusta was, his correspondence with her being carried on through Miss Drayton, whose address in Virginia he enclosed to Hugh.

"I cannot be your medium of communication with Augusta," he added, "for she has declared that any mention of any one, with whom she was associated in the past, except Charity, her old nurse, will at once put an end to our correspondence. Poor child! Her trial has been great, and with no true faith in the divine, how can she be otherwise than distrustful of the human! She says, if she is ever to recover strength, it must be through forgetfulness; her own words are, 'my past is indeed dead—let it be buried out of my sight.'"

Miss Drayton, to whom Hugh next applied, had also promised not to mention anything connected with Augusta's past life in her correspondence, but her womanly ingenuity found a way to reconcile her promise with her wishes. Painful and inconvenient as travelling was in her imperfect health, she went to New York and found her way to Mrs. Price's door. It was between eleven and twelve in the day when she rang at the door. Visitors were not usually admitted at that hour, and the man who opened the door hesitated for a moment; but Miss Drayton was wrapped in an India shawl, and Mrs. Price's servants had been taught to pay respect to India shawls, so Miss Drayton was admitted into the reception room—as a small, tastefully furnished parlor was called—and her card was carried to Augusta, who was engaged with her pupils. The next moment Mrs. Price, who was languidly descending the stairs to her carriage, was astonished beyond the power of expression at being, as she afterward expressed it, "literally swept out of the way" by her governess, who, haughty to all others, had ever been proudly deferential—proudly humble, we might have said, for there is no contradiction in the words—in her manner to her employer. She was scarcely less surprised, when she looked up to question the meaning of this, to see that there was color on the marble cheeks, and the play of feeling on the chiselled features, which, till then, seemed to her so sternly still.

"Why, Miss Moray!" she cried, but cried in vain; Augusta did not hear her. "After all, she is beautiful," she said to herself, "but she must have a lesson."

Perhaps the lesson was none the less sharp for the perception of the beauty. She had seen a card in Augusta's hand, and watched her till she entered the reception room.

"Edouard!" she cried, as she reached the door of the reception room, raising rather than lowering the tone of her voice as she spoke, "Comment a-t-il arrivé que vous avez admis un visiteur á Mademoiselle Moray á cette heure; ne savez vous pas qu'elle est engagée, de rigueur, jusquo deux heures?"

All Mrs. Price's servants were French, and it would have shocked her to give an order in the English language.

"Mais, Madame—" began Edouard.

"Il n'y a pas de raison pour une telle chose. Ne le faites jamais encore—c'est tout."

Augusta was in Miss Drayton's arms, feeling her heart beat with a sensation unknown to her for months, pressing her tremulous lips again and again to the hand that rested on her shoulder, when these words reached her ear. Disengaging herself from Miss Drayton's arms, she stood haughtily erect till the "c'est tout," told her that all was said; then she stepped toward the door; but Miss Drayton arrested her, and passing before her, presented herself to Mrs. Price just as that lady's velvet mantilla was disappearing through the inner door of the vestibule, while Edouard stood prepared to throw open the outer one at her approach.

"Permit me, madam, to speak to you for one moment, if you please," said Miss Drayton.

There was something in the very tone which announced a woman of gentle breeding, and when Mrs. Price had turned and seen Miss Drayton, there was a quiet dignity about her, aided a little, perhaps, by "that love of a cashmere," which enforced courtesy.

"You will pardon my having called at such an unseasonably early hour; I was impatient to see my young friend. Indeed, the desire to see her, after so many months of absence, was the only incentive to a winter journey from Virginia to New York—a formidable thing to an invalid; but I will not now trespass on your courtesy and Miss Morny's time longer than to ask if she will be at liberty to come to me this afternoon, after two o'clock, at my friend, Mrs. Gerald Rashleigh's?"

Now it so happened that Mrs. Gerald Rashleigh was to Mrs. Price what Mordecai had been to Haman. Mrs. Rashleigh's was the only desirable circle in New York into which she had vainly sought to obtain her *entrée*.

"And she has such delightful foreign society, you know. Why, do you know, she came to church one Sunday last winter with an English lord and a French count in her carriage at the same time, and one of them, the Englishman, I believe, stayed with her for several days; I should really like to know her, for the sake of my daughters." A degree of forethought for her daughters, this, which was truly honorable to her maternal love, considering the very tender age of those daughters. This little digression will explain to the reader the cause of that almost obsequious deference with which Mrs. Price was according her permission to this arrangement, when Augusta stepped forward, saying, "I shall be quite at liberty at—" she glanced at her watch, "say a quarter past two. I have some minutes to make up, you know."

"Then Mrs. Rashleigh begged me to say that she would be here in her carriage at, shall I say a quarter to three? can you be ready in half an hour?"

"Oh yes! but Mrs. Rashleigh's coming is quite unnecessary."

"She insists on it, and she says you must take it as a call, which would have been paid long ago, if she had known where to find you."

"She is very kind, but I neither receive visits nor pay them, except to you; and now I must leave you. Goodby."

Augusta bent to receive her friend's kiss.

"Pray do not go, Miss Moray," began Mrs. Price, who had stood in the vestibule during this colloquy.

"Excuse me, madam; I am engaged, *de rigueur*, until two o'clock," and with her usual bow of proud deference, she ascended the stairs, leaving Miss Drayton still below.

"Our young friend is *un peu trop fière*," said Mrs. Price, with a smiling glance at the ascending form.

"She cannot readily adjust herself, perhaps, to her new circumstances?" said Miss Drayton, kindly.

"Oh! I cannot say that; she makes a capital governess, and never obtrudes herself, which saves a great deal of awkwardness—I mean to herself," said Mrs. Price, hastily, suspecting by a slight tinge on Miss Drayton's check that she was not commending herself to the friend of Mrs. Gerald Rashleigh; "we should be glad to see more of her."

Miss Drayton only answered by a bow, and moved toward the door, beside which Edouard still stood. He opened it, and both the ladies passed out. Mrs. Rashleigh's carriage was in waiting for Miss Drayton.

"Pray come whenever it suits you to see your friend," said Mrs. Price, as she turned to hers, which was also there. "It was on her account that I gave the order you may have overheard to Edouard; she dislikes very much to receive visits."

Miss Drayton bowed coldly and went on her way, quite as well au fait of the lady's meaning as was Augusta herself, and feeling that her house, with all its grandeur, was not the place in which she would have chosen that her young friend should commence her new career.

Mrs. Rashleigh was punctual to the appointed hour. Augusta was punctual, too, and presented herself as soon as she heard the footman inquire for her, not permitting Mrs. Rashleigh to descend from her carriage, as she was preparing to do.

A single glance at Mrs. Rashleigh, as she held out her hand to assist her, and seated her beside her in the carriage, was enough to disarm Augusta of half that reserve from which, as from a shield of glittering ice, the obtrusive sympathy of the little minded, or the insolent assumption of the vulgar crowd fell harmless. So far did this lady win her confidence before they parted on this day, that Augusta promised sometimes to visit her.

"Will you let me call for you sometimes on Sunday? or are you, like your friend Miss Drayton, too much of a churchwoman to go with me—we are Presbyterians—at least the church we attend is Presbyterian; where do you go?"

"Nowhere, in New York; I have no pew, you know," she added to Miss Drayton, who had exclaimed at this.

"You must not say that again, Miss Morny," said Mrs. Rashleigh, taking her hand kindly in hers. "I shall call for you on Sunday next, and you will remember, after that, you have always a seat with us; it will be vacant if you stay away," she added, with a smile.

"You are very kind, madam," and a faint smile from Augusta's face reflected that on Mrs. Rashleigh's; "but—"

"But you cannot go the Presbyterianism. It is not very deep dyed. Come and try us."

"I have no objection to that. I was accustomed from childhood to its simple forms, and love them for the sake of the lips from which I heard them, though I feel the beauty of the English service. I will go with you, Mrs. Rashleigh; I only hesitated for fear there were others of your family whom my coming might annoy."

"Do not fear; my family is—"

"A unit," said Miss Drayton, smiling.

"At most a duet," replied Mrs. Rashleigh, returning the smile; "Mr. Rashleigh and myself."

Almost as soon as she was left alone with Augusta, Miss Drayton began upon the subject which had brought her to New York. Augusta had been expressing her warmest gratitude to her for the interest which had induced her to travel so far only to see her, and Miss Drayton replied, "There is no one in the world, except my own Annie, whom I would go farther to see; and yet, I scarcely deserve all the gratitude you are giving me, for I should have waited till the winter was over for my visit to you, had I not hoped to do you an important service by coming."

"You have done me an important service; I had begun

to doubt whether there was such a thing as pleasure in the world, and to-day I have felt it."

"My poor child!" and Miss Drayton lifted her eyes, full of a tender pity that made them beautiful, to the face that was bending over her as she lay upon her couch; "have you seen no pleasure around you in your new home?"

"Much of what they call pleasure, for I often am obliged to join their evening parties, to minister to their enjoyment; but my eyes have been touched with the magic ointment; I see now how little truth there is in all that charmed me so much but a year ago."

"Perhaps, my dear, there was more truth than you are now disposed to think; the position you looked from then, and that at which you stand now, are extremes both; neither, probably, would give you a view that was quite true."

"You may be right," said Augusta, listlessly.

"I have something to say to you which I hope may introduce you to a better point of view than either; it will, at any rate, prove to you that the world is not destitute of truth and honesty. I would have written to you about it, but it concerns one of those of whom you had forbidden me—"

"To write or to speak equally; you must excuse me, Miss Drayton, if I say it is cruel thus to disturb my hardly-won equanimity," and Augusta rose, trembling with agitation, and turned as if to leave her friend.

Miss Drayton also rose.

"Augusta," she said, and her hands were outstretched and her eyes humid with tenderness, "you will not leave me—leave me in anger, when I have come so far, through such difficulties, to visit you?"

Augusta stood still, but did not return to her seat.

"Come back, dear Augusta; sit down, and hear me."

Miss Drayton sank back, with an exhausted look, on her

couch, and pointed to the chair at her side, from which Augusta had risen; but she paid no heed to the gesture, and placed herself in one at a greater distance.

"Then I must come to you," and Miss Drayton was rising; but Augusta took the seat she had indicated, saying, coldly, "I will not put you to that trouble."

"Thank you, my dear," said Miss Drayton, gently; "and now, if you will read that letter, you will see that I could not fail to communicate its contents to you."

Augusta took the letter and glanced at the address. It was in the well-known handwriting of Hugh. She laid it down.

"I will not read it," she said, passionately; "it is cruel, I say again, to persecute me thus; they are happy; let me, at least, enjoy such peace as they have left me."

"Augusta," said Miss Drayton, "this letter is written by one who, as far as I know, has committed no offence against you; and if you knew where it was written, you would not call him happy."

Augusta glanced at Miss Drayton and then at the letter.

"Where was it written?" she asked, slowly, as if the words dropped from her without any effort of her will.

"Beside his father's dying bed."

"His father's dying bed?" in the same way, as if but half conscious that she spoke; then, with sudden force, "Commodore Moray's dying bed?"

"Even so; did you not know he had been dangerously wounded in that battle at Vera Cruz?"

"I saw the pictures, and I heard people say he had come home wounded; but—dangerously—dying—" Augusta's voice altered.

"It is a very sad affair altogether; people blame the Government very much. They superseded him just on the eve of the battle, when he had made all the preparations for it. I have heard that some of his friends urged him to retain the command till after the battle, which, as the oldest Commodore on the station, he was entitled to do; but he is very punctilious, and would not palter with what he thought his duty; so he resigned the command of the fleet, but took the little schooner that had been offered him for his return home, into the very thickest of the fight. She was not built for a war vessel, they say, so the helmsman was not sufficiently protected, and he took the helm himself. Every one admired his gallantry, though some think he was wrong to expose himself so madly; the wonder is, he was not killed immediately. He was wounded in the thigh and in the arm very badly."

Miss Drayton paused, for Augusta had grown very pale; but she faltered out, "Tell me all; was Hugh there?"

"He was, for he had resisted all his father's persuasions to leave him, and a young relation of mine who was on board, and from whom I had some particulars not mentioned in the papers, says he seemed entirely to forget himself after his father was wounded, and exposed himself almost as madly as the Commodore had done, but the worst of the danger was over then."

"And Commodore Moray?"

"Had his leg amputated and returned home to die among those——but, my child, you are fainting!"

Augusta's pale lips moved to say no, but the room was reeling, the air was darkened, her eyes closed, and with a faint sob, she sank back upon the cushions of the large chair in which she sat. Miss Drayton threw some water into her face from a goblet that stood beside her, and with a convulsive gasp, life came back—life and consciousness—and dropping her face into her hands, she wept with passionate emotion.

What strange revelations of our own nature do we find in those moments when its depths are stirred. With what rapidity does the past rush upon us. It can scarcely be said that we recall it. It lives, and we live in it, though for years we may have thought it dead and buried. We live in it, not as we once did, minute by minute, hour by hour, but all its hours seem concentrated into one flash of full, perfect life—a life which is an agony, whether of joy or sorrow. Is it thus that in the future state of being, the life of earth is to flash on our consciousness, kindling in the hearts of the redeemed a more intense fervor of grateful love, and adding keener tortures to the imperishable regrets of those who rejected the only refuge for sinful man?

To Augusta, at that moment, little things—at least they seemed little when they were passing—words, looks, full of the tender, gentle, chivalrous, yet childlike character of her old friend, were distinctly present;—his joy at the opportunity given by the command of the squadron to show what was in him—not for his own vain glory, but for the justification of those who loved and confided in him. And this squadron she had taken some pride in believing had been her gift, a fatal gift. And he would die without her seeing him; he had loved her, she knew. She had thought little of it through all those weeks and months when she had shut herself up in proud isolation, saying, "They do not care for me, neither will I care for them."

Now she knew that he had cared very tenderly for her; she had had it in her power to add a pleasure or a pain to the life which was so rapidly passing away, and she had chosen to add the pain. And this she had done to one who had been so unoffending! Suppose Hugh had been cruel—had sported with her love, and trampled on her pride—was this gentle and noble heart to be slighted for Hugh's fault? And now, when she saw this plainly, when for one look of tender forgiveness—one gentle "My child," one word of guidance from those wise and loving lips, she would have given the best year of her future life, she heard the fatal words, "He is dying," and that wail "It is too late!"—earth's bitterest cry—went up from her full heart.

"But is it too late?" she said, with gasping breath, uncovering her pale face, and turning her tear-swollen eyes on Miss Drayton. "Is it not possible for me to see him yet?" Then, as pride, too strong to be wholly subdued, even by that agony, awoke, she added, "If I was sure he would see me; but, perhaps, he has forgotten me; he would hardly think of any at such a time, but those most tenderly beloved."

"Read your letter, my dear, and you will see," said Miss Drayton.

The letter, Hugh's letter, was in her hand; the color flushed to her pale cheek as she opened it—not "the blush to wooers dear,"—but the angry flush of pride, which expected again to be stung by the indelicate offer of money as of alms to a beggar. She read:

ELIZABETHTOWN, Nov. 23d, 18—.

DEAR MISS DRAYTON:

When you know that I write beside what I fear to be my father's dying bed, you will readily believe that no common interest could claim a thought, or win me for one moment from the duties that have become our dearest solace. That you will sympathize with us in our dread of a sorrow whose bitterness can be in some degree appreciated by all who had any knowledge of *him*, I am quite sure, from my past experience of your kindness; but not even to claim this sympathy, dear as it would be to me, could I have written at this time. You will see, then, the force of the feeling which prompts this appeal to you, and you will not refuse to help me if you can. Mr. Mortimer, from whom I have just heard, tells me that you only know where Miss Muray is. That you do know is an unspeakable comfort to us all—to none more than to my father. He loves her very tenderly, and has never ceased to mourn the strange circumstances that have acted so fatally upon her finely-strung nature, making her forgetful of the suffering she is inflicting upon all who love her. Knowing her as you do—knowing how, amid all the faults of ungoverned impulse, and an almost insane pride—her innate nobleness manifests itself in every movement of her life, making us almost forgetful in the deeper feeling it excites, of her unrivalled personal beauty, and of the witchery of her manner, you will not wonder that we, to whom she has been as a daughter or sister from her childhood, cherish the tenderest regard for her, and cannot rest until we know something of her present condition. I have sad reason to know that I have in some way excited her displeasure; but I feel sure that if she knew my father's desire to see her, she could not in his present state refuse to gratify him; he says this is his only unsatisfied wish."

"I must go," cried Augusta, looking wildly around her, when she had read thus far; "I must go to him."

"Not to-night, my dear, not to-night," said Miss Drayton, coming to her as she began to cloak herself for her intended journey; "see, it is already growing dusky."

"Do not stop me, I have not a minute to spare; see,"—pointing to the clock on the mantlepiece,—"it is half past four; the last train leaves at five."

"But listen, my dear child, you will be too late; you cannot go alone at this hour; besides, you have no money with you," said Miss Drayton, glad of any excuse that might stop her.

"That is true," exclaimed Augusta, as she put her hand in her pocket; "you must lend me some."

"I do not think I can; to-morrow I will go with you."

"No—no; if you cannot lend me, I must beg my way; to-morrow will be too late; he wants to see me! Oh, Miss Drayton, why did you not come sooner? Why not send the letter?"

"I came as quickly as I could, darling; and I feared to send it, lest you should send it back and withdraw yourself from me too."

Augusta groaned; it was all her own fault. How poor and mean seemed now that isolation which pride had counselled! She had thought only of herself. *She* might suffer, she had said, but she would prove that she could live without *them*. It had never occurred to her till now that *they* might need her ministrations—that she was resigning the blessed privilege of soothing as well as of being soothed, of serving as well as of being served. She had steadily continued to prepare herself for going out in spite of Miss Drayton's remonstrances, and was now half way down stairs, followed by Miss Drayton.

"Where are you going, Miss Moray? Surely you will not leave us before dinner; we dine at five," cried Mrs. Rashleigh, who was coming up in her bonnet and shawl.

Augusta turned her pale face toward her, and tried to speak; but the voice would not come.

"What is the matter?" cried Mrs. Rashleigh, turning to Miss Drayton.

"She insists on going to Elizabethtown to-night, to see Commodore Moray; she had not heard of his illness before."

"But, my dear Miss Moray, you cannot go to-night; there is a snow storm coming on—see—" pointing to the window—" to-morrow—"

"It will be too late; I must go."

"Then John shall drive you to the boat. Run, Florine,

tell John to bring the carriage to the door again and drive Miss Moray to the steamboat for Jersey City; she will hardly have time for the train now."

The carriage, in which Mrs. Rashleigh had just returned from a visit of charity, was driven to the door, and Augusta ascended it, without a word of thanks for the kindness thus extended to her. Poor child! her heart was full of one thought: Would she be in time? Miss Drayton thrust her purse into the hand that continued to grasp the letter with an almost convulsive tenacity.

"I wish I could have gone with her; but I was afraid I should only add to their troubles," said Miss Drayton, as she shivered at the chill air of the damp November evening, and drew her shawl more closely around her.

It was dreary, indeed; a red glow in the west was all that relieved the dull, leaden line of the sky. Through the thick air a few snowflakes flew, presaging the night, and the wind already swept in gusts through the streets of the city, and lashed the darkened waters of the bay into angry waves. Augusta saw nothing of all this, and if she heard the wind, it was but to wish that it would sweep her onward on its wings more rapidly than boat or car could bear her. It was not only that her affections had been touched at the thought of her friend, her "father," as she had sometimes called him in the intimacy of their intercourse, bearing her on his heart, suffering for her, in the midst of his own great agony; it was not only that bitterest of all thoughts, that he should die with an unsatisfied desire to which she could have given its fulfilment—her trouble lay deeper than this. The depths of conscience had been stirred, and its waves were overflowing her soul. There was a voice within her, saying, "You have chosen your way, and you must walk in it; you separated yourself from them, and God will separate them from you. He will die without your seeing him, and they will remember you only as the troubler of his peace—the cruel one who added another pang to those under which he was already sinking."

"How exaggerated!" does the reader exclaim. True, for passion is ever an exaggerator, and Augusta Moray was still the slave of passion; nothing was changed but the direction in which it propelled.

She reached the boat in season, and in less than two hours from the time she had left Mrs. Rashleigh's door, she was set down in Elizabethtown.

"Did you see that tall woman in black that got out just now?" asked the conductor, of a gentleman in the car.

"No; why do you ask?"

"Why, she seemed sort o' queer to me, and I thought maybe you noticed her, as she sot just before you, and I was going to ask if you thought she was crazy."

"I was reading my paper, and did not see her; but what was there queer about her?"

"Why, she never seemed to hear me when I asked for her ticket; I had to take it out of her hand, and I don't think she knew it then; and just now the horses in a carriage were jumping about so the driver could hardly hold them in, and she walked right straight under their heads; and though the driver hallooed at her and cursed her, and the people ran to her to pull her away, she didn't walk a bit the faster; the fact is, I don't think she heard the hubbub."

"And did she get safely by?"

"Yes; but if she wasn't such a young lady, and a pretty nice looking one, too, I'd think she was drunk, or crazy."

"Pretty people do get drunk or go crazy sometimes, and young ones too," said the gentleman, carelessly, as he returned to his paper.

In the meantime Augusta, absorbed as she had been represented by the conductor, was pursuing her way toward the well-known house where the happiest hours of her life had been spent. Her heart seemed to stand still for a moment, and then to hurry on with quicker beats, as through the thickening dusk and the falling snowflakes she caught the first view of its dimly-defined outline.

"If he still lives, I shall feel that I am forgiven, and may yet hope," was the thought that flashed upon her at that moment.

She drew near. There was no bright light streaming out upon the stormy night. She entered the porch. No cheerful voices, as of old, were heard within. With a trembling hand she touched the bell, but it gave no sound. Again she tried, throwing into the effort more power than was needed. The sharp, clear ring startled her, and made her hold her breath in alarm. No one came; yet she waited long before she dared ring again. When she did, it was with a lighter touch, yet it was more effectual. A dim light was seen through the glasses at the side, the key turned in the lock, the door opened, and Augusta, trembling with cold and fear, looked once more upon the familiar objects in the hall. She turned to the face of the servant who had opened the door; it was the face of a stranger; she tried to utter the question she had come so far to ask, but her trembling lips refused to shape the words; she raised her heavy crape veil, and the servant afterward said, "She was jist that skeered, she was ready to let the lamp fall, when she seed sich a white face, with the two eyes a starin' so."

"Please, ma'am, would you tell me what you want, for we haven't got no time to spare, seein' the poor Commodore's jist after dying."

"Dying—then he is not dead!" and Augusta stepped forward.

"And sure, ma'am, he is dead enough, though it hasn't

been for long, an' I'd ask you in, ma'am, but the missus an' Mister Hugh an' all, is more dead than alive, an' couldn't see no strangers."

Augusta turned silently away. It was true, she was a stranger—made so by her own act. What place had she within their home at such a time? Through the increasing storm and the now almost rayless night she made her way with some difficulty back to the railroad station. She could have wished the difficulties greater; the struggle with them seemed to dull somewhat the sharp pain in her head, and to interrupt that never ceasing wail, "Too late; too late!"

Arrived at the depot, Augusta found a seat in its darkest corner, where she might await the coming in of the return train. This seat was behind the stove, whose red hot surface sent out the smell of burning iron through the room, and scorched, with almost intolerable heat, the face of Augusta, and that part of her person which was presented to it, while on the back of her neck and shoulders there poured a stream of cold, damp air from the window behind her, in which there was a broken pane of glass. Unconscious of these physical ills, or if she was conscious of them, too much absorbed in more intolerable pain to think of relieving herself from them, Augusta sat, while hour after hour of that inclement night passed heavily away. The cars were due at a quarter before nine, but nine, ten, struck, and still they came not. At length the shrill whistle was heard, and a red, fiery light shot past the windows of the depot. People rose and hurried out, and Augusta rose too and followed them with a sort of automaton movement; they entered a car, and so did she; again the steam whistle shrieked, and they were in motion. A few minutes after, the conductor passed around. It was the same who had gone up on the last train, as far as New Brunswick, and was now returning to Jersey City, where he resided. He came to Augusta, and immediately recognized her as the woman who had acted "sort o' queer" on his up trip.

"Ticket, ma'am," he said, touching her on the arm, for she did not notice him, and he supposed her to be asleep.

There was no answer to his appeal, no apparent consciousness of it, except that she moved slightly, as if to escape his touch. He raised his lantern and cast its light directly upon the face of ghastly white, which had so alarmed the servant at Mrs. Moray's. Augusta's eyes closed to shut out the light, which it gave her intolerable pain to look at, and she murmured "Too late! too late!"

"Well, we was late!—there was a smash up this morning just above Trenton, and the cars was a long time getting by. Ticket, ma'am, or,"—meeting the bewildered expression of her eyes, which were at last turned upon him—"if you haven't a ticket, I'll take the money."

The last word seemed to carry some meaning to her mind, for she handed him her purse; but when, setting down his light, he had taken from it the amount of her passage, and would have returned it, he found some difficulty in making her take it.

Those who have travelled in the United States cannot have failed to perceive the kindness with which the conductors of public carriages watch over the comfort of ladies who, travelling without a gentleman, seem peculiarly dependent on their care; especially is this the case when age or illness increases this dependence. The conductor of the car in which Augusta Moray was returning to New York was no exception to this honorable class, and when they reached Jersey City, he came to see whether his interesting passenger needed his aid. He found that she had not risen from her seat, though the car was already nearly empty.

"We're to Jersey City now, ma'am, and if you want to

cross, you'd better be quick, for it's so late the boat won't wait long, I'm thinking."

He received no distinct answer, but hearing a muttering sound, he bent down his head and heard: "Too late! too late!"

"No, ma'am, I don't think it's too late if you'll go at once, and I'll help you."

He tried to take her hand to draw it through his arm, but she drew it quickly away with a little cry, saying, "You shall not force me away till I have seen him. I do not believe he is dead; she says so because she is afraid I shall see Hugh."

Again he flashed the light of his lantern on her face. It was no longer pale. Fever burned on her cheeks and sparkled in her eyes.

"Now, my goodness! what am I to do, I wonder? I can't leave the poor thing here, that's certain; if I could get her to the boat, it wouldn't be no better. Suppose I was to take her to the hotel. She'd be a deal more comfortable in that nice, quiet room that Jean's just got ready for her sister, and I know Jean would tell me I ought to carry her there. It will only be for one night, for I dare say to-morrow, when the fever's off, she'll tell us where she lives, and I'll send her home, or Jean will go with her herself; and her clothes are handsome, and she's got a watch; I shouldn't wonder if her friends are rich; it may be a good piece of work for me, after all."

The first part of this soliloquy was spoken—the next was thought only; and so, with these mingled motives of generous kindness and self-interest, he assumed the care of Augusta, or, should we not rather say, accepted it from the Providence which had seemed so evidently to lay it upon him?

Hiram Brown, the name of the conductor, did not want

for ready wit, and after listening for a moment to Augusta's ravings, he said, in a kind, friendly tone, "Come with me, and you shall see him. Poor thing!" he added, as her large, melancholy eyes were lifted to his face, "I am sorry for you."

If she did not understand the words, she did the tone and the look, for they were of that universal language of humanity which is the first and the last to be comprehended by us; and when again he said, "Come with me, and you shall see him," she arose, took his offered arm, and accompanied him without a word. They had but a few steps to go, and he thought it best not to call a carriage, as she might be unwilling to enter it; so he led her at once to the little white cottage, containing only two rooms below and two above, in the clean, bright kitchen of which sat his Jean, impatiently expecting him. The delay in the arrival of the train had caused cruel suffering to her faithful heart; but she had heard the whistle which announced its coming, had piled more wood upon the warm, clean cooking stove, had placed upon it again the tin coffee pot, the beefsteak, and the covered dish of milk toast, which had been drawn away some time before, in despair of his return. These things done, she had only to listen for the well-known step. It came at length, but not till she had begun to fear again, and then it was slower than its wont. "Could he have been hurt?"

The door was opened before he reached it, and Jean peered forth into the darkness. She could just see approaching forms; one was his, certainly; she knew the movement; who was the other?

"Hiram, who've you got there?" called Jean.

Hiram did not answer immediately, and as they came nearer, Jean perceived, not altogether with satisfaction, that it was a woman who leaned upon his arm; but before the dissatisfaction could shape itself into word or action, Hiram entered, and indicating by a gesture that she must not speak, led the lady through the dark front room, and placed her in Jean's own rocking chair by the fire. This done, he turned to Jean, and before he had said a word, the little cloud had left her brow, chased away by his close embrace and his warm kiss, and when he said, "The poor lady is very ill, I'm afraid, Jean; the fever's got in her head, and she couldn't tell rightly where she was to go nor nothing; I know'd you'd say I ought to bring her here, and so I did."

Ah Jean! Well may your brown cheek glow so brightly. Let others talk of woman's rights as they will, you know that you are enjoying woman's highest privilege, and exercising her noblest duty, while you are thus keeping a human soul true to the best instincts which God has implanted within it.

"She thinks she's going to see somebody; 'twas the only way I could get her along," said Hiram, in further explanation; "I don't know how you'll get her to bed now."

Augusta's mutterings had ceased while in the open air, which had probably rendered her circulation less rapid. She still continued quiet, though her eyes were kindling, and her cheeks flushing again with fever.

"Will you come up stairs to bed, ma'am?" asked Jean, with a voice and look as soft as pity could make them.

"Can I not see him? Is it too late?" asked Augusta.

"Too late to-night, ma'am," said Jean, with a woman's ready tact. "He'll be asleep now, and you wouldn't want to wake him; but to-morrow morning, right early, you'll see him."

"Then he isn't dead. I knew it could not be; he would not die, you know, till he had seen me; it was his only ungratified wish."

"Then come, ma'am; I'll show you to your room; and

to-morrow morning, when he's awake, you'll see him."
Jean took the burning hand of her guest as she spoke, and
Augusta followed her without any apparent reluctance to
the tidy little room prepared for the young sister, who was
coming from her distant Western home to spend the Christmas and New Year with Jean. All was ready for her, even
to the little grate filled with coal, and the box of light kindling wood beside it. We are not sure that there was not a
little regret in Jean's heart as she touched the kindling below the coal with the flame of the lamp she had brought up,
and saw the ruddy flame spring up, thinking that the bright
polish would be burned off the grate before Carrie saw it.
It was a sacrifice, but the sacrifice was made. There was a
little rocking chair in this room too, and Augusta was seated
in it, while Jean untied her bonnet and cloak, and laid them
aside.

"How beautiful she is!" thought Jean, as she saw her
thus unveiled. Augusta's comb had been drawn out in taking off her bonnet, and her dark hair fell in thick waving
tresses over her face and shoulders. This seemed to rouse
her for a moment. She gathered the hair up as she was
accustomed to do, and asked for her comb. The familiar
action seemed in some degree to restore her to consciousness. She looked around her with surprise, regarded Jean
for a moment earnestly, and then said, with a little trepida-
tion, "Who are you? and where am I?"

"You didn't seem well in the cars, and my Hiram—he's
the conductor—brought you home with him," Jean answered, with a quiet simplicity that was reassuring.

"The cars!" exclaimed Augusta, in a startled accent;
then, after a moment's pause, "Oh yes! I remember; I
was too late! too late!" and again the wild look came to
her eye.

"Too late for to-night," said Jean, "but if you will go

to bed and sleep good, you will see him when you wake in the morning."

Again the promise had the effect of quieting the disturbed mind, and Jean was able to undress her, to put on her one of her own tidy little wrappers, which, if not fine, was as neat and clean, she herself said, "as any lady in the land could wear," and to lay her in a bed as clean as the wrapper, and very comfortable, though it was made of straw.

Ah Jean! I wonder if you thought that night of the good Samaritan, as you gave up that dearest pleasure of the twenty-four hours, getting Hiram's supper ready, and sitting to see him enjoy it, to pour out his steaming coffee, and to hear him say again and again what a dear little wife he had, what a comfortable home she made for him, and how much better a man could be when he was so taken care of, and when, instead of this, you knelt beside the bed to chafe the cold feet of the stranger with your warm hands, and sat all night beside her, listening to her strange, wild talk of persons of whom you had never heard, and when, hardest of all, at the earliest dawn of light, you woke Hiram, abridging by a quarter of an hour his little time for sleep, that he might be able to go for the doctor before he was obliged to be at the depot. Perhaps Hiram might have grumbled a little at this, as people are apt to grumble when first awoke, had he not seen that though his Jean had evidently not even lain down through the night, she had prepared his clean linen and warm socks, and hot coffee, and notwithstanding a little paleness, looked as cheerful and bright as if she had never known care or watching. Jean may not have thought of the good Samaritan, but I am sure she had something of the spirit of Him who has given us that beautiful example.

The doctor did not have a cheerful Jean to wake him, and he, like Hiram Brown, had been up late the night before; so he grumbled and growled terribly when he was called, declaring that "he would not go at such an unreasonable hour; that he would not be such a pack horse for the community." Hiram saw that he was sufficiently awake to understand him, and hurried off to his cars, quite sure that, in spite of all these cross speeches, the doctor would go; and so he did, and quickly, too, though he grumbled all the time he was dressing himself, only changing his decision not *to be* for an assertion that he *was* "a perfect pack horse for the community."

The doctor's cheerfulness had not been perfectly restored even when he reached Jean's pretty cottage, and he listened to her details of the lady's case with a clouded brow, "poh-pohed" all idea of anything serious, saying, "And so Hiram's going to take charge of all distressed ladies that travel in his cars? A perfect knight-errant! I hope he has something more than his thousand dollars salary to do it upon; that's all."

"But, doctor, who was to take care of the poor lady? Somebody must, you know, for she was all crazy like, and couldn't take care of herself."

"Let the public take care of her, then."

"But the public wasn't there, you know, doctor, and Hiram was," said the simple Jean, not at all satisfied to have Hiram blamed.

"Well, let me see her," cried the doctor, feeling somewhat puzzled to answer this, yet unwilling to acknowledge himself vanquished; "I've no time to talk here—without my breakfast, too, and very probably for nothing at all. I dare say this woman is one of those foolish people that have a fever whenever they are excited, and get delirious whenever they have a fever, and if you had only waited an hour, all this fuss—"

The doctor stopped suddenly; they were in the sick room, and as Augusta, roused from unquiet sleep by their entrance, raised herself in bed and turned her startled face toward them, there was something in her looks that filled his heart with pity, and something which told to his practised eyes that the case was more serious than he had professed to believe it. He drew near the bed, the little peevish expression all gone from his face, leaving nothing there but the large-hearted philanthropy and the acute sense for which he was noted.

Augusta drew away as he approached.

"It is the doctor, come to see you, to make you well," said Jean, on the other side of the bed, taking her hand kindly.

"The doctor! oh, sir, is he better? can I see him?"

"Him!" said the doctor to himself; "I knew it; a man's always in the case if a woman goes out of her head, and a woman, if a man does."

"Can I see him?" repeated Augusta.

"Certainly, as soon as you are well enough," the doctor answered.

"I am well enough now; let me go!" she said, vehemently, to Jean, who held down the covering she would have thrown aside, and prevented her rising. "Let me go, or he will die without seeing me!"

"You cannot see him yet; it would agitate him too much, and perhaps prevent his recovery; you must wait till he is better—then you shall see him."

"Are you sure? Will Hugh let me come?"

"Hugh? I cannot tell you unless you tell me his whole name. Hugh what?"

"Hugh Moray," she breathed, softly, almost in a whisper, looking around her with a stealthy glance, as if afraid some one was present whom she would not have to hear her. Jean withdrew quickly out of sight, but not quickly enough to prevent Augusta's seeing her dress just as it disappeared.

"There!" she said, turning to the doctor, "I knew she was listening; she will tell him—I know she will."

"She has gone now, and if you will only tell me where he lives, I will bring him here. Tell me, where does he live—this Hugh Moray?"

The partial gleam of sense was gone, and she repeated, "Hugh Moray, of St. Mary's; Hugh Moray, of St. Mary's," as a child sometimes repeats a name in sport, scarcely conscious of what he is doing, while her eyes closed wearily. The doctor touched her pulse; it bounded beneath his finger like a frightened steed. The conviction of her illness only made him more anxious to discover her friends and home. Her muttered tones sank into silence; he thought she slept. Joan went down to see if Hiram had left any coffee, that she might get a cup for the doctor. Suddenly Augusta's eyes opened.

"Good-by," said the doctor, as she turned them on him; "I am going to bring Hugh Moray from St. Mary's."

"But he is not there; don't you know he died in Washington? and we all died then; I died in New York; and then I came to—to—Elizabeth—Elizabeth—well, I don't know; I can't remember," passing her hand over her eyes, and speaking like one in a dream.

Generally, Doctor Foster would have said to a patient, under such circumstances, "Never mind—don't try;" but instead of this, he said now, "You came to Elizabethtown to see him—and he would not see you?"

"Yes, he would; he loved me—*she* couldn't help that—and he called me 'dear child,' and—and—oh! I must go; it will be too late," and she raised herself in bed; but the doctor's strong arm held her back.

"You must be quiet now," he said, "and do just as you are told, or I cannot promise that you shall see him."

Doctor Foster had gained, as it seemed to him, all that

he was likely to gain from this delirious ramble; the next thing was to do what he could for his patient's recovery; afterward he would see about informing her friends where she was to be found. Unfortunately for himself, and yet more unfortunately for those who came under his treatment, the doctor had not accepted fully the new medical light that had dawned upon the world. Yet, had he not been entirely without profit from it. Even on those who flee from its ray, there falls a twilight reflection from it which makes it no longer midnight with them. Doctor Foster called homœopathy a humbug; but it was the boast of his friends that he gave very little medicine,—scarcely any,—relying very much on the *vis medicatrix* of nature. "Only," said the doctor, "nature is sometimes unable to act from the state of the system, and we must remove what clogs her beneficent energies."

Well, we are not writing a medical treatise, for which we would be duly thankful, and so we need only, as veracious historians, record that in the present case the blood, according to Dr. Foster, clogged the beneficent energies of nature, and the lancet was employed with unsparing hand. The result was to render the patient, at least for a time, less troublesome. The ravings of delirium were exchanged for the stupor of exhaustion. During this temporary lull, Dr. Foster sent his own housekeeper to watch her, and administer the cooling draughts, which were all the medicine he deemed necessary, while Jean obtained some rest.

The next visit of the doctor was made at an hour when he knew that Hiram Brown would probably be at home. He knew that Hiram's three years as a conductor had given him an almost universal acquaintance with persons living on his section of the railway.

"Do you happen to know anybody of the name of Moray, living at Elizabethtown?" he asked.

"To be sure, I do; everybody about here knew the poor old Commodore that I see by the newspaper to-day is just dead."

"Dead! Was his name Hugh?"

"No; they call him James in the paper; but his son's name is Hugh; I've often heard that young cousin of his'n that's gone away, and had a great fortune left him, call him so."

"Well, I must write a note to this Mr. Hugh Moray, and you must get it to him this evening. The lady up stairs is some relation or friend of his."

"You don't tell me so! well, I'm right glad I brought her home to Jean, if 'twas only for the good old Commodore's sake; but, doctor, how will it do to trouble them just now; the Commodore only died yesterday—they must be in great trouble."

"But if this poor girl should have wandered away from their house in this delirious state, it would be a great relief to them to know where she is."

"That's true," said Hiram, reluctantly convinced, for he was too genuinely kind not to have that delicacy which shrinks from any intrusion on sorrow.

The doctor wrote his note, and Hiram took charge of it. Of course he could not himself stop at Elizabethtown long enough to deliver the note—he was almost glad he could not; but he committed it to an acquaintance whom he saw at the railroad station, with many charges that he should tell Mr. Hugh that the lady was comfortable, and had a good doctor and nurse, and "he need not be a bit troubled about her—indeed, that the doctor only wrote to keep him from being troubled."

It is not certain that Hugh Morny understood all these well intended assurances. The doctor's note gave such a description of the lady that there was no doubt in his mind who it was; he also learned from it that she had come to Elizabethtown in the afternoon train and returned at night. Could she have been at the house? The servant who attended the door was questioned, and her tale was heard. Hugh never hesitated for a moment on his own course. His father lay dead—he could no longer serve him. His mother and sisters were safe in the shelter of their home—a home not less sweet or less holy because of the consecrating presence of their dead; and this young girl, whose vision ever rose up before him as the embodiment of a free, bright childhood, or of youth crowned with all the best gifts of God, whom for long years he had treasured in his heart of hearts—not as a saint, to be worshipped, but as a woman, to be loved—not the less dear to his manly nature because, among qualities noble and beautiful, she had faults to be forgiven and weaknesses from which to be protected; she, whom he would have shielded with his life from the lightest touch of harm, who, but a few months ago, had never stepped beyond her threshold without a guardian, now presented to him a melancholy picture of unfriended womanhood, wandering alone through storm and night, and when mind and body had both failed beneath her trials, indebted to the compassion of a stranger for shelter and care. To read the note he had received to his mother, to tell her he should be at home again in the morning, and to take his place in the next train returning to Jersey City, were things of course with him. It was after nine o'clock when he was led by Hiram Brown to his home. Jean was in the sick room, but hastened down when she heard her husband's step.

"This is Mr. Morsy, Jean," said Hiram, "the lady's cousin," for so Hugh had announced himself.

"Oh, sir! I am so glad to see you. It seemed so sad,

like, that she should be ill and maybe die here, without so much as a soul that knew her name even."

Hugh thought he had nerved himself for all, but that word *die* had overpowered him. He turned away for a moment from the observation of Jean's tender eyes, and though he immediately mastered himself so far as to ask the question, "How is she?" his voice sounded husky and indistinct.

"Well, sir, I hardly know what to say to that; she was quiet all day, slept all the time, and didn't seem to have much fever; but now her face is all red and hot again, and she's begun to talk just the same. But won't you come up and see her yourself, sir?"

Come up and see her? Hugh's heart bounded at the thought. He had so longed to look upon her—so feared he never should see her more—and now, but a few steps separated him from her, what was to prevent his passing them? what was to prevent his watching beside her, unconscious as she was, through this night, ministering to her wants, and, it might be, listening to her voice? What was to prevent it? That which was stronger than bolts and bars: the delicacy of a noble soul, which would not debase itself by taking what another was powerless to withhold— nay, what would have no value unless freely yielded, was his second thought, as, with an unconsciously haughty gesture, he declined Jean's invitation.

Dr. Foster had purposely delayed his evening visit till a late hour, that he might see Hiram, and learn the result of his note. When he came, he found that the first effect of the bleeding had passed, and the fever had returned with increased violence. Later in the night the delirium became more violent than ever. She was less easily influenced than on the preceding evening, and, as Jean prevented her rising, cries of distress and terror thrilled through the house, and made Hugh start from his seat, and ascend the stairs toward her room. Did some influence, imperceptible to others, acting on her excited nerves and brain, tell her that he was near? We know not. Many such mysteries there are to tax the acuteness, perhaps to disappoint the hopes of the physiologist.

"He is there," she whispered softly, as if to herself, glancing at the same time at the door, behind which Hugh had stationed himself. She tried again to rise, but Jean gently laid her arm on her, saying, "Lie still, dear lady!"

"Hugh! Hugh!" cried Augusta, wildly, "Will you let them kill me?"

Then, as Hugh involuntarily sprang into the room, she held out her hands to him, exclaiming, "Oh, Hugh! why didn't you come sooner? She would not let me go to you, and now it is too late."

"No, dear Augusta! It is not too late; I am here now, and no one shall trouble you."

He took her hands as he spoke, and seated himself in the chair Jean placed for him beside the bed.

Her eyes softened, her crimson lips parted with a smile, and she said softly, "They won't trouble me while you are here. But what made you stay so long? Mr. Mortimer was waiting for me—no—not Mr. Mortimer—who was it wanted me, Hugh?"

"I wanted you, dear one," said Hugh, with a full heart in his voice, as he bent down and gently kissed the hand he held.

"Oh no!" she said, speaking again with a little wildness, "No, she said you didn't want me. Oh! let me go to my uncle—he will die before I get there."

"He does not want you now; you must rest and I will take care of him."

"And you will let me come when he wants me?"

"Yes, if you will sleep now."

"But if you go, Hugh, she will come back, and then she will never let me see you again," and Augusta held tightly the hand in which hers was lying.

"No, she shall not come; I will leave a kind friend with you, who will not let her come."

He beckoned to Jean, who had with instinctive delicacy withdrawn to the farther end of the room, and she came near.

Augusta clasped Hugh's hand tightly again and came near to him, whispering with a frightened look, "Hugh! she is coming!"

"No, dear one; that is a friend who has promised to watch by you till I come back. Look at her, see! she is not like her."

Augusta looked earnestly at Jean, who smiled kindly on her. The smile was returned after a little while; the hand relaxed its clasp, and with a gentle, submissive tone, Augusta asked, "Will you stay with me till Hugh comes back?"

Jean gave a cordial assent, and took the seat which Hugh gave her. How hard it was for him to leave her, no words can tell. How tenderly his eyes met the glance she turned upon him as he rose! How his very inmost heart seemed to leap forth in the kiss he again pressed upon her hand! It was his farewell, for the night had passed and it was within a few minutes of the time for the early train, by which he must return home. That day he must be at his mother's side.

"Hugh! you will come back?" said she, as he turned again to look at her from the door.

"As surely as I live!" was the emphatic reply; yet, even as he spoke, his heart was sinking within him with the fear that he might come back to find her no longer there. He had written a note to Miss Drayton, telling her of Augusta's illness, and giving her address, requesting that she would send the best nurse she could obtain, to relieve Jean, until his mother and sisters were able to come to her assistance, and he had forced into Hiram's hands a purse, which would procure whatever might be needed for her comfort.

Hugh's note was sent to Miss Drayton by the morning boat, and he had the satisfaction, a little after noon, to receive a few lines from her, written by Augusta's bedside, assuring him that she was sleeping quietly, that Jean reported her to have been more composed from the time he had seen her, and that the doctor considered her symptoms more favorable.

Much did he need the comfort and the strength thus given him. The father, of whom he had been so proud, whom he had loved all the more because the world had been unjust to him, was this day to be borne to his grave. In that procession walked many who had never looked upon his living face. All sought to render honor to the worth, known too late. His brother officers, from the Brooklyn navy yard, civilians of the highest dignity, all whose presence could give distinction sought a place there. Distinction they may have given, a short-lived distinction, but scarcely pleasure to the hearts of those whom his death had left desolate, for in them sounded ever the sad words that Augusta had so often uttered, "Too late! too late!"

But we will not dwell upon a scene which no pen can adequately describe. They bore him forth with reverent hands, they laid him tenderly to rest in his last bed, and gently covered his resting place with the green turf. There, watched by love, undisturbed will be his repose till He in whom he trusted shall appear. We may not linger there. From him, who has entered the haven, we turn to those who are yet tossed on the troubled waves.

CHAPTER X.

> "Oh! how this spring of love resembleth
> The uncertain glory of an April day;
> Which now shows all the beauty of the sun,
> And by and by a cloud takes all away."—SHAKSPEARE.

DECEMBER's dark, stormy days have come. Winter's snows have covered the fields around Hiram Brown's cottage. The winds whistle bleak and cold around it, but within there is brightness and warmth for the stranger who, after weeks of illness, is just able to rise and sit for a few hours each day, beside the fire in the little grate which had first been lighted to welcome her, and for the friends who have tended her with loving hearts and hands.

When Augusta awoke to perfect consciousness, feeble as a child, and with the child-like tenderness, the child-like longing for love, all reawakened in her heart, the first object on which her eyes rested was the face of Mrs. Commodore Moray, bending over her with anxious tenderness. For a moment she thought herself dreaming, and after one earnest gaze, closed her eyes, then opened them again to see if the vision had faded away. No! there it stood beside the bed, the hair a little grayer, the face a little sadder and paler than of old, but not otherwise changed, except by the deep mourning dress.

"Do you not know me, love?" asked Mrs. Moray, thinking there was recognition in the glance turned to her.

"Dear Mrs. Moray!" was breathed in a low, feeble voice.

"Say dear mother, as you used to do when you were a little child," said Mrs. Moray, pressing her lips tenderly to her forehead.

"Dear mother!" and Augusta smiled, as none had seen her do for many a month; then, with a little sigh of weariness, she added, softly, "But where am I, and what are you doing here?"

"Hush! you must not ask any questions till you are a great deal stronger."

"You will not leave me?"

"No, dear child!"

Augusta laid her wan, white hand on Mrs. Moray's; her eyelids fell wearily, and she slept again. From this hour her recovery, though slow, was steady. Who has not observed how dependent are the soul's manifestations upon the physical condition? Augusta Moray, with health which had never known disturbance, was, as we have seen, proud and self-reliant; Augusta Moray, enfeebled by illness, was touchingly submissive. Day by day, as her own dim memories prompted her inquiries, the past was unfolded to her. The months in which, repelling the kindness that would have soothed and cherished her, withdrawing herself from all that could have made life attractive, she had sat in chill loneliness—months, in which her life could have been symbolized only by a frozen sea, in the midst of whose desert vastness rose an icy statue of herself at once deity and sacrifice—such are the marvels wrought by pride—the blow which struck that statue from its pedestal, and revealed all that its glittering surface had hidden from her view—all, all came back to her. It was as if she had been under some strange glamour, such as we are told could make the meanest hovel seem a splendid castle, could transform a beautiful young prince into a hideous beast, or restore him to his proper shape. How magnanimous had seemed her conduct in withdrawing from all on whom she could be supposed to have any claim, in resting only on her own resources, relieving them of all draft on their sympathies or their aid. Now, this magnanimity was dwarfed into the littleness of selfish passion. Instead of relieving them, unless she could believe them all false and hollow, she saw that she had inflicted on them the deepest pain, and in the end far greater trouble and expense than she would have done by accepting their proffered care at first. And why had she rejected that care? Had it been indeed to spare them? The conscious blushes that dyed her cheeks said a thousand times—No! It had been the feeble revenge of a slighted woman. She had been willing all should suffer, if only she could reach the cold, stern heart that had—not wronged, not rejected,— that had offered her a brother's protecting and honoring affection. With the usual tendency to swing from one extreme to another, she saw these things, not as mistakes that might be rectified, not even as sins that might be pardoned, but as a total shipwreck of her life. Others had not been deceived, she argued; what was so clear to her now, must always have been manifest to them; and how they must have pitied her throughout! Yes, they pitied her— they were so noble that they had not cast her off, though she had so tried them; but veil it as they would, must not contempt mingle with their pity? And with this sentiment she must learn to be content—she, who had flung scornfully away all that was not the passionate devotion of a lover, must receive with gratitude *this*. And the one who was most tender, to whom it was so much a part of his nature not only to love, but to throw a sanctifying halo around that he loved, which permitted him also to honor it, he, on whose tender heart she had probably inflicted the keenest pang, had passed beyond the reach of her confession or atonement.

Such depressing thoughts weighed heavily upon her, making her recovery very slow, as we have said. She seemed to herself to have lost all self-control. In the shadowy twilight, and often in the day, when hidden behind the white curtains of her bed, tears stole from her closed eyes, quiet tears—no sobs, no distortion of her features marking passionate emotion.

"Will you see Hugh, dear?" Mrs. Morny had asked, the second morning that Augusta was able to rise from her bed and sit up, with a wrapper of crimson cashmere thrown over her white gown.

Scarcely less deep was the crimson that flushed to her pale cheeks as she asked, "Is he here?"

"Yes, he has never failed to call as he went down to his business or came back again, since he knew you were here."

"He is very good; I will see him if he wishes it."

"You must not agitate her, Hugh! she is very weak."

"I will be careful; I would not have asked to see her yet, but I think she will be better when she has seen us all, and has no more agitations of that kind to look forward to."

Hugh intended to speak cheerfully, as he entered—Augusta meant to meet him with a smile; but the first look at her hollow cheeks, tinged though they were with a faint flush, and at the pale thin hand extended to him, silenced the words on Hugh's lips, and the first glance into Hugh's eyes brought tears instead of smiles to Augusta's face.

"You will soon be well enough to come home with us, I hope," said Hugh, after some observations on her improvement, on the weather, on Jean's and Hiram's kindness, things that, lying within the range of their life, yet did not press too nearly on their hearts.

"I am well enough, I believe," with a little emphasis on "well."

"Not quite yet; but you will come when you are, will you not?"

The tears which had been just dried, came faster; the lips quivered, there was a little sob. Hugh was frightened.

"I did not mean to agitate you," he said; "forget it till you are stronger, and then, if my wish gives you pain, let it pass—forget it still."

"No, no, pardon me this weakness—I cannot help it. I am so weak; but I shall feel better when I have said just this: I will do whatever will be least troublesome to—to you all; I have tried my own way, and—and—"

"Dear Augusta!" and Hugh took again the hand he had suffered to fall from his, after one silent pressure; "do not use such a word as *troublesome;* let it be the way that will make you most happy, and that shall be our way as well as yours; but we will say no more now. Here comes my mother to turn me out. Do you expect Miss Drayton to-day, or shall I let her know how you are?"

"If you could send her a message, I should be very thankful—she looks so delicate, and is so little accustomed to exposure, that her visits, in such weather, lie heavily on my conscience."

"Your conscience is too tender, my dear cousin. You should think at present only of what will make you well. Good-by; I shall see you to-morrow."

"Hugh was mistaken; she is not more cheerful for having seen him," was Mrs. Moray's unspoken comment on Augusta's state after this visit.

"How foolish I am! Am I never to be taught that kindness is all I can expect from him? Shall I never be able to imitate his indifference, his composure?" was Augusta's.

"I am afraid I betrayed a little too much of my agitation at first; but she will learn in time that she has nothing to fear from me, and then she will trust in me again. Poor child! when in her delirium she had forgotten my foolish hopes, how she returned to the tone of her childhood! If I dared, I should like to ask her about some things she said then; but it would not do. I dare say, after all, it was only a vague feeling that my good aunt had done her some injury, applied in her delirium to what occupied her thoughts just then; yet it may not have been. I wish I knew all—nonsense! I dare say there is nothing to know,— as if there must necessarily be some special cause for her not giving me—I will not think of it again—" and Hugh, whose musings we have thus jotted down, took out his notes on a case he was to argue that very day; and Augusta, could she have seen the attention he gave to them, and the steady hand with which he made further comments on the margin of his paper, would probably have felt her envy of his calmness increase. And yet, Hugh Morsy felt even when thus engaged that a change had passed over him, that had left him not only a graver, but a harder man; that he had less trust in others, less sympathy for them, than he had once. Many, who would have pitied the unfriended boy, probably envied the fortunate barrister, who was fast winning both fame and fortune; but Hugh would gladly have exchanged his near prospects of both, for the confiding tenderness which had made the boy's heart soft and glad.

In a week from this time, Augusta found herself again at Elizabethtown. It was a removal she would fain have resisted. Far rather would she have buried herself in the little cottage with Jean and Hiram. There were moments when she felt that she would rather bury herself beneath the white heaps of snow, or the ice of the sullen, gloomy river; for suffering, mental or physical, had not changed this proud and passionate nature; it had only made her less confident in her own decisions, and burned into her heart the conviction, scarce welcome at this period of her life, that she could not immolate herself without bringing suffering to others. There is a mood of mind in which even this may be braved; but such was not Augusta's at present. She could not so soon forget him who had passed away, with " but one ungratified wish." To Mrs. Moray's question whether she felt strong enough to go, she answered, "Quite strong enough; but—" and here she paused.

"But what, my dear child? Speak freely to me, Augusta; you shall do nothing you do not wish."

"I have no wishes," she said, a little petulantly; then, as she met the sad eyes that looked pityingly into hers, her heart smote her, and with a sudden gush of tears, she added, "Do with me, dear Mrs. Moray, what you please. I have no wish but to give as little trouble as I can to you, who have been so kind to me. Do not think me ungrateful for all your goodness! Who but you would have come to me at such a time?"

Augusta raised the hand which Mrs. Moray had laid caressingly on hers to her lips.

"Any one, dear Augusta, who had loved you as we do. You once confided in my love, my child, and spoke out your heart to me; and why not now?"

A slight color rose to Augusta's pale cheeks as she said, "I have nothing to speak; I only thought it might be better for me to go back to Mrs. Price, and finish my engagement, now that I am better."

"That would be, indeed, to trouble us. Indeed, I believe," Mrs. Moray added, smiling, "that Hugh has put that out of your power. You must excuse him; you know that Hugh does not often lose his self-control, but I do not think he was quite master of himself when he did it; Miss

Drayton's account of what passed on her visit to you had made him so angry, that he wrote a note to Mrs. Price, informing her of your illness, asking that whatever you had left at her house might be sent to his office, and requesting her to release you from an engagement which you were unable to fulfil. Are you angry with him, my dear?"

Augusta's cheeks had flushed to a deeper crimson; but it was not with anger.

"I cannot be angry with what was so kindly intended," she said, softly.

"You are right, my dear, it was kindly intended—it was just as Hugh would have felt and acted for his sisters," rejoined Mrs. Moray.

The glow faded from Augusta's face.

"Still," she said, "Mrs. Price's was not a bad place— her impertinence never did more than excite my contempt."

"Well, a place is not a very good one which gives us frequent occasion for the exercise of such an unchristian emotion as contempt. Good or bad, however, you are not fit for any place now—you still have fever every evening."

"I think I must often have had fever before my illness. I had violent headache often all night; sometimes, indeed, when I was playing for them to dance, I was almost wild with it."

"That proves what Dr. Foster thought. He said this illness could not have come on so suddenly as we supposed; he thought the exposure and the great shock you had received," and Mrs. Moray drew Augusta's head toward her till it rested on her bosom and pressed her trembling lips to her forehead, as she remembered what that shock was— "he thought that these," she resumed, after a moment's pause, "had only brought on more rapidly and aggravated, perhaps, an already existing disease."

18*

They were silent a little while; then Augusta returned to the subject.

"I have no doubt Dr. Foster is right," she said, "yet even in that condition I was able to teach with satisfaction to my employer; ought I not, then, to do it again?"

"It was not with satisfaction to yourself, Augusta; it would now be with exquisite pain to your friends. Will you give us this pain, child?"

"Oh, no! dear Mrs. Moray—never! never again!"

"Then you must come to us, at least for the present. We will talk of the future when you are quite well. Come and be my daughter and Hugh's sister,—will you?" and she bent over and kissed her.

"I will be anything you wish," said Augusta, but so listlessly, that Mrs. Moray turned away with a sigh at her powerlessness to give pleasure or inspire confidence.

Often, very often, did Hugh, during the succeeding month, have to sigh for the same cause. How could it be otherwise, while with success unattainable to one less practised in self-mastery, he was striving to prove to her that she might rest in his affection as in that of a brother; an affection too unimpassioned, too free from selfish desires, to require that she should repress it by reserve, or fear to encourage it by yielding to its guidance; while she was seeking in all their intercourse for some proof that the past had not been all a dream; or, at least, that the dream had had some better foundation than a mere girlish vanity, the very suspicion of which, humiliated her beyond endurance.

"Was not that," she asked herself, "the very window at which I sat when he said those words which confirmed, more than confirmed, all I had dared to believe? did not his father think as I did? And yet, had we not both mistaken him? Did not what followed show that we had?

But then, that parting scene! there he sat now on that very spot, reading a letter, and what meant the long neglect of his absence; on the other hand, what meant that meeting at Washington, those happy days that followed? ah! but that letter!—his own hand and seal; there was no mistaking that. Fool! fool that I am!" and with an impatient movement she threw her head back, as if to cast off the thoughts that at once irritated and mortified her. In doing so, she met Hugh's eyes fastened upon her with something like a smile in them, and as bright a flush rose to her cheeks, as if he thought he could have read what had been passing through her mind.

"What subject occupies you so deeply, my cousin? my mother spoke to you twice without your perceiving it."

"Don't look so shocked, my dear," said Mrs. Moray. "It was only to call your attention to this beautiful sunset."

"I beg your pardon; I was thinking—" then, as her conscience reproved her for the untruth, she changed her phraseology; "I am thinking that I am really quite well enough now to be doing something, and that I ought not to be idle any longer."

"Do you call your present life idle, my dear?" asked Mrs. Moray, with a pained expression of countenance; "a very busy idleness, as I could prove by the exhibition of various articles of your neat handiwork."

"Are you weary of us, Augusta?" asked Hugh, drawing near, and leaning against the casement of that very window outside of which he had stood that summer afternoon.

Augusta made a little impatient movement with her hand, which was peculiar to her, and which Hugh well understood.

"Those who have few friends do not readily grow weary of them," she said, as he continued to look at her smilingly, yet as if he would have an answer.

"That is not your case, Augusta, and I can prove it to you. Do you see these three letters? I have received them all to-day, and they are all full of you. First Miss Drayton writes that she and Miss Mellen are very anxious about you, that she does not like your own account of your present condition, and she wishes me to ascertain from your physician, whether he thinks a change of climate would be of service to you; if he does, and you will consent to come to her, Judge Mellen will himself come on to escort you. Then Charlie and Mrs. Moray—"

"Mrs. Moray!" with an expression of contempt, "pray let her pass!"

"I am content; but we cannot let Charlie pass."

"It would be as well while he is with his mother. He is but her echo, understanding, too, as little as does the echo, the sound it repeats."

"Well! the sound he repeats at present is a very kind, pleasant sound; they are anxious to know how you are, and Charlie would himself come for you, if you would go out and spend the rest of the winter with them. His mother has been very ill—he hopes she will be able to travel next summer, when you can return with them, if you wish."

"That proposition has been answered already. I cannot be a guest in my early home, with Mrs. Moray for my hostess. Is that all?"

"No; I have a third letter. It is from Mr. Mortimer. He is very anxious about you; but read for yourself," and opening the letter, Hugh handed it to Augusta, pointing to the following passage as that which he wished her to read.

"I believe a return to her native climate and to a life as

free as that of an intelligent being can ever be from responsibilities, will be her best cure; but this is not my only or my strongest reason for begging that she would come. I want her for my own sake. I am old—I cannot come to her, and I long to see the child who is the only living thing that I can flatter myself will miss me a little when I die. Tell her that hour cannot be very far away for one as old as I—it may be very near; ask her if she will let me die with this my strongest, almost my only earthly wish ungratified."

"I will go," said Augusta; returning the letter without raising her eyes. There followed a moment of struggle on her part, and of embarrassed silence on Hugh's; then her head sank, her face was covered with her hands, and she burst into a perfect passion of tears. It was long since she had wept thus, and now it would have been hard for her to tell the cause of her tears. In truth, they were from very mingled feelings; tenderness to Mr. Mortimer, agitation at the thought of seeing the old home, regret at leaving the friends with whom she now was; and last, and strongest of all, perhaps, grief and humiliation at the thought that Hugh wished her to go, or he would not have shown her such a letter—all these emotions contributed to her tears.

Mrs. Moray had been called out of the room, while Augusta was reading the letter, so that she and Hugh were alone. To a nature like Hugh Moray's, the pain of estrangement from those beloved, is never so keenly felt as when they are in sorrow. Involuntarily Hugh approached Augusta at the first sound of her weeping. His arm was outstretched as if to draw her to him that he might soothe her as he had often done before; but with sudden recollection, he drew back and walked once or twice across the room, before he could master himself sufficiently to speak without betraying more emotion than was consistent with the calmness of a disinterested friendship. When he spoke, though his manner was composed and undemonstrative, his voice had still unusual softness in its tone.

"Dear Augusta! I would not have shown you this letter," he said, "fearing that it might agitate you too much, had not Dr. Foster, whom I went to see this morning, not feeling quite satisfied with your progress toward health, told me that he believed nothing but entire change of climate would restore you completely. It will grieve us all to part with you even for a few months. I shall write Mr. Mortimer that we spare you only on condition that you are to come back to us in May; Charlie will be glad to find so good an excuse for coming as your need of an escort, unless, indeed, I should be able to leave my business for two or three weeks, and you will let Esther and me come for you."

"Thank you!" said Augusta, recovering her voice during this speech, which had probably been prolonged for this very purpose; "you are very kind; but it will hardly be necessary to trouble you and Esther; travelling is very safe in our country."

"But travelling alone is not very agreeable."

"When must I go?" asked Augusta, waiving the last proposition entirely.

"The doctor said as early as possible; and as I found Mr. Mortimer's letter at my office, and thought it probable you would not refuse his entreaty, I have been making inquiries about packets and passengers. I find a vessel will sail a week from to-day, in which a clergyman, with whom Mr. Holton is acquainted, has taken passage for himself and his daughter. I have secured for you the refusal of a state-room till to-morrow—" Hugh paused a moment; Augusta's face was still downcast and somewhat averted from him; he could not read its expression; but there was no mistaking the dejection indicated by the attitude. Taking the hand that rested on her lap, he added, "You know not how painful it is to let you go without some of us accompanying you; but the doctor thinks it so necessary—and—and—" he paused again—he could not bear to refer to money, to acknowledge that he could not afford to meet the cost of more than one traveller at present, even if he were able to leave his business.

"And it would be the cost of three," he said to himself, "for she would not be comfortable with me, without Esther."

Suddenly Augusta looked up—she had been trying to gather composure for the very subject which Hugh was endeavoring to avoid.

"Before I decide, I must know what the expense will be," she said, somewhat brusquely, as people are apt to say things about which they are very decided themselves, yet anticipate a contest with another.

"Oh! very little—not worth speaking of. I will arrange that before you go, so that it will give you no trouble."

"I cannot decide till I know exactly what it will be," she repeated, very firmly.

Hugh saw the question must be met and answered. "The passage is twenty-five dollars, and surely such a sum—"

"Can be easily met by me," Augusta interrupted; "I have about one hundred and fifty dollars—part of it from my six months' salary at Mrs. Price's, and part of it from—" she hesitated a moment, not willing to speak of the sale of her jewelry, then resumed, "part of it remaining from the sum I brought with me; you would oblige me very much if you would get Dr. Foster's bill for me in the morning; till I have seen that—"

"That is paid already," said Hugh, somewhat coldly.

"And the amount?"

"Need not trouble you, Augusta; it is paid, I said."

"So I understood you; that changes my creditor; to whomsoever it is due, I must know the amount."

"Still so proud, Augusta?" he questioned, sadly.

"It is not pride, it is simple justice—for all your kindness and that of your mother and sisters, for your generous care of me in illness, your generous hospitality—"

"We give hospitality to strangers," Hugh interrupted; but she went on as if she had not heard him.

"For *all*, I thank you; but my heart would break under pecuniary obligation. I pray you do not force me to lie under its crushing weight."

"You are under no pecuniary obligation to me. I owed your uncle more than twenty times the fifty dollars paid to Dr. Foster. What I owed to him is now yours, since you are his heir-at-law, and this sum was not disposed of by will."

"It was not disposed of, because it was intended that it should remain with you. I have no more claim on it than I have on anything else that is yours."

"And must we be altogether as strangers, then, Augusta?" Hugh asked, in an accent in which, in spite of all his efforts, there was some bitterness.

"Should I have submitted to a stranger's guidance, and dwelt so long in quiet, in a stranger's home?" she asked, quickly. "Your kindness, in any other form, I repeat, I will accept—money, never; I have been humbled enough on this subject, let me hope that you will never name it to me again."

In saying this, Augusta looked, for the first time, steadily into Hugh's face. Her own was flushed with passion, and her lip was curved with an expression which he could scarcely interpret by anything except disdain. As she concluded, she rose from her seat; and though he began to expostulate on the injustice of her words as applied to himself, she seemed not even to hear him—she certainly did not heed him, not deigning even a glance as she withdrew to her own room, leaving him bewildered, yet indignant.

Her proud displeasure evaporated in another fit of weeping when she found herself alone, and when, at Esther's call, she descended to the parlor to tea, her face had lost its flush, and her manner its unusual excitement. But the sterner nature she had roused had not been able so quickly to regain its equilibrium. When she ventured to look at Hugh she saw that he was very grave; and though the courtesies of the table were offered with punctilious attention to her as well as to his mother and sisters, his countenance never lost its expression of grave reserve. After tea, Lily asked if he would not finish a poem which he had begun to read for them the last evening; but he answered that he should be engaged in his study, and they must read it themselves. As he said this, he withdrew into the said study and remained there all the evening, though Mrs. Morny expressed the fear that he must be very cold there, as the room was not easily warmed, and the fire had only been ordered by Hugh while they were at tea—and Augusta said to herself, "It is I who have made him angry and driven him from his family."

Before returning to their rooms, each of the family in turn, first Mrs. Morny, then Esther, then Lily, stopped at the study to say good night to Hugh.

Augusta and Lily had left the parlor together, lighted by one candle, which Augusta carried, for Esther and Lily occupied the same apartment, and Esther had already carried their light up stairs.

"You will come in and say good night to Hugh," said Lily, pausing, as they reached the study door.

"No; but I will wait for you." Then, in reply to Lily's

questioning eyes, she added, "Hugh is busy; he will not care to see me this evening."

"I will ask him," said Lily, tripping in with a smile on her face.

Hugh was sitting with his back to the door, which careless Lily left so far open that Augusta could both see and hear what passed within.

"Hugh, you are very unsocial, this evening," said Lily.

Hugh did not turn, nor did his pen cease its movement across the paper, as he said, in a dry tone, "I am very busy, Lily."

"Well, good night;" she bent down and gave him her sisterly kiss, exclaiming, as she rose, "I believe Augusta was right, after all, when she said you were so busy that you would not care to see her."

"She was mistaken," still in the same dry, curt tone; "tell her, if you please, that I shall be glad to see her here for a moment, if it will not give her too much trouble to come to me."

"Oh, no! she is just outside of the door. Augusta! Hugh wants to see you," said Lily, as she went out.

Augusta entered. The haughty air she had worn, when she left Hugh in the afternoon, was gone. Her eyes were heavy, her face pale, her movements languid.

Hugh rose, placed a chair for her, and closed the study-door. Augusta felt very weak, yet she did not seat herself, as his action had seemed to invite her to do; she only rested her hand upon the back of the chair. Hugh had gone to his desk, and now approached her with a paper in his hand.

"Augusta," he said, "here is Doctor Foster's bill. You will perceive by the little note appended to it, that he believed me to be your accredited agent; you will excuse, I hope, the liberty I took in permitting him to entertain that idea."

His voice had no softness in it; In his manner, though perfectly courteous, Augusta missed that peculiar deference which she had been accustomed to find there.

"Hugh!" she said, falteringly, "you are angry with me."

"Not *angry*—at least not *now*," he said, in the same restrained manner, "but I cannot deny that I was deeply wounded by your remarks this evening. It is too agitating a subject for you at present, however," his tone softening a little, "but some day I shall ask my cousin to be so kind as to tell me in which of my efforts to serve her I have been so unfortunate as to inflict on her a humiliation."

"It is better that I should tell you now, Hugh," said Augusta, in a voice that was almost a whisper.

"As you please," was the somewhat *nonchalant* reply.

It was very difficult for Augusta to speak on such a subject with so little encouragement; but she was determined to make the effort. Hugh might have some apology, something to say that would make that one ungenerous, ignoble action seem more in harmony with the rest. It could not be excused—it might be palliated. Yes! she would speak.

It was not very certain that she could, for twice her lips opened and no sound came. Hugh waited. Suddenly a flush came to her face and she spoke. Indignation had awakened again, and she was strong.

"When we give alms to a beggar, Hugh, we are taught to do it without ostentation; surely a delicate reserve is at least equally desirable when we would force our favors upon those who have not solicited them."

"Your proposition is incontrovertible; but excuse me if I say I cannot see how I have sinned against it." The manner and tone were alike haughtily repellant.

"By sending me money, or its equivalent, a draft, in an open envelope without a word of explanation or apology; I would rather have wanted bread," she went on warmly, "than to have been compelled to convict you of an act untrue alike to the principles of a Christian and the instincts of a gentleman."

"Somewhat hard words these, I should say, to one who, hurried away by the intelligence that peril to what was dearer than life, overhung his father—" Hugh's voice softened at that word, but soon grew hard again; "peril which might be averted by his presence, begged for ten minutes delay, and spent every moment of them in writing such a note as he believed would convince you that, in what he enclosed, you were only receiving a part of what was your own, and—"

"You wrote me a note, Hugh? You wrote me a note with that draft which you sent by Mr. Seton?"

"Exactly so; by Mr. Seton, whom you had introduced to me as a gentleman, and your friend, I think; and as I had used up my last minute in this poor note, which seems to have escaped your eye or your memory, Mr. Seton promised that he would seal it and deliver it himself."

"He did come to the house to deliver it; but, not knowing his object, I declined to see him, and he sent me by Mrs. Charles Morny, an open envelope, with the message that this would show me the hurry you were in; and, Hugh, I solemnly declare that the envelope contained nothing but the draft which I sent back to you."

Augusta thought this must free her from all blame in Hugh's mind; but she was mistaken. Instead of the return to his usual gentleness, which she had expected, his words were more indignant, his attitude more haughty than ever.

"And you could believe this of me?" he exclaimed, "*you*—there was not in your heart one memory of the past, to plead for me—nothing that would say 'he is incapable of such an act?' I do not wonder that you refuse so haughtily to accept a service from me. I do not wonder that you desired to withdraw from all association with one capable of such—I have no name base enough for it!" he cried, suddenly turning away, and striding across the room. As he turned at the farther end of it, he saw her standing where he had left her, with her eyes fixed upon him, and her clasped hands resting on the back of the chair he had set for her. He could not see that the eyes were full of tears and the hands trembling; yet something in the attitude touched him, and he came back to say, more gently, "It is enough, Augusta; I cannot deny that you are fully excused."

"Excused! but not forgiven, Hugh," she said, softly.

He was silent.

"What could I believe, Hugh?"

"Believe!" he cried again, with a force that made her start, "believe that Mr. Seton or Mrs. Moray had abstracted it, as one of them most certainly did; believe the paper had been blown away, had melted into thin air; believe any impossible marvel rather than this."

"I should have done so, Hugh; but—"

She hesitated for a moment, and he exclaimed, "You would have done so, *but* that you had already learned to distrust me—*but* that you had already ceased to esteem me worthy of your friendship."

This was not the truth; but it was something so like the truth, that Augusta knew not what to answer. She could not speak of the letter which had put an impassable gulph between them. Even had she made no promise to Mrs. Moray, how was it possible to name it without betraying the nature of the hopes it had crushed—of the affection it had outraged. Might there have been treachery here too? She grew bewildered, oppressed. Hugh was startled as he saw her press her hand to her forehead, and gasp as if her breath came with difficulty. He remembered her late illness for the first time during this conversation, and he came to her side with more quietness of movement and said, "I fear I have agitated you; do not let us speak of this any longer."

"And will you not forgive me, Hugh?" she said; "I do not know quite how it was—I was so sad and confused; I am confused now, I believe; but I wish you could say 'I forgive you;' can't you, Hugh?"

Hugh was subdued. There was no anger, but only sadness in his tone, as he replied, "I do forgive you, Augusta; will you forgive me, my poor child, for forgetting for a little while all you have been suffering lately? Good night, you must forget all this and sleep; Lily has gone, I suppose, but I will get a light for you."

He lit one of the candles that stood in bright silver candlesticks on the mantlepiece, and handed it to her. She went to the door, then turning round, looked at him with sad, weary eyes, and said, "You do forgive me, Hugh?"

Hugh had no words for such an appeal. "Forgive and forget!" that was just what he did. For a moment he went back to the old days when she was the little child she looked just then, and his heart was as free from any debasing passion and as full of tenderness as heart could be, as he folded her in his arms, and gave, in one soft pressure of his lips upon her cheek, the only answer of which he was at that moment capable. Only a few hours before, such a familiarity from Hugh would have been resented as an offence, and not the less deeply resented if supposed to indicate the freedom of a *brother;* but having discovered that she had so greatly wronged him in her thoughts, Augusta, with her *womanly* generosity, repaid the wrong by giving back to him all her childlike confidence. Even that letter was scarcely remembered for that night; and when it did force itself upon her thoughts, there came with it a conviction that could she only speak of it, which was, of course, impossible, it could be so explained that she would see there was no want of consistency in Hugh. He had not sought her—that was a point the letter clearly settled; well, let that dream pass—he was still her friend, and what was better, he was noble, and she might still esteem and trust him as of old. And so gentle and so trustful had these thoughts made Augusta, that Hugh found it harder than ever to keep within the limits of that calm friendliness of manner he had prescribed for himself, during the few days that intervened between this interview and her sailing.

"Hugh! will you take this?" Augusta said, the next day, offering him the fifty dollars he had paid to Dr. Foster. "I think I have enough without it," she added, with a deprecating timidity of tone and manner.

"You will not have too much *with* it," said Hugh, clasping the hand she held to him, for a moment, but leaving the money in it.

Augusta did not press it on him. She would show him how she trusted him, and Hugh understood and thanked her in his heart.

"Will you let me go to Jersey City with you?" she asked, after this point had been settled; "I want to see my good, kind Jean before I go; I will come back at twelve o'clock, under Mr. Brown's own care."

"I am afraid it will be too cold for you."

"I will wrap very warmly."

Augusta went. She found Jean neat and smiling as ever, sitting on one side of the bright, warm kitchen grate, while sister Carrie, a younger Jean, sat at the other—her visit had been delayed, but not prevented by hospitality to the stranger.

"Oh, Miss! I am so glad to see you, and looking so well, too," cried Jean, "with such a color in your cheeks."

It was pretty, that color, though only the frosty air had brought it there, and it faded even while Jean was speaking.

"I am much better, thank you, Jean; and so this is Carrie. I was sorry to disappoint you of your Christmas visit, Carrie."

"Oh, ma'am, please don't mention it. I must have gone home by this if I had come at Christmas, so you see it was all for the best, ma'am, every way."

"You are very good to say so. Here, Jean, I have brought you a few little things that I thought you might value because I made them."

Augusta unrolled a package as she spoke, and showed various knitted articles, over which Jean and Carrie went into raptures.

"They are for the little stranger, Jean; I brought them now, because I cannot be here to welcome it when it comes."

"Dear ma'am! you are so good."

"The goodness, dear Jean, was on your side and Mr. Brown's; what would have become of me but for you?"

"Well, I am sure, ma'am, we did no more than was our duty, and we've been paid for it over and over again; besides the pleasure of serving you, there's that beautiful picture you sent us Christmas day."

"It was a trifle, Jean, but I thought you would like it because I painted it myself, and I tried to make it like what you had told me of your home in the West."

"It is, ma'am, 'tis wonderful like. Hiram knew the big oak with one branch broke off, right away, though it stands t'other side the house; but then I always put it right in my mind, you see—and you painted that yourself for me! and there's the big rocking chair and the sofa in the parlor!"

"But I did not send you the rocking chair and sofa, Jean."

"You did not send them yourself, ma'am; but when we went to thank the gentleman—Mr. Moray, I mean, ma'am, because the men that brought it said he had sent them—he says, 'You mustn't thank me,' says he, 'it's all for the lady—though she'd rather you would not speak to her of it;' but, ma'am, indeed, I couldn't help speaking, and so I told Hiram."

"But, indeed, my good Jean, I had nothing to do with it—it was all Mr. Moray's own friendship for you; I never even saw them."

"Is it possible, ma'am? then you must come and see them, for they are *rale* handsome and no mistake."

Jean led the way into the little parlor and exhibited, with a glow of pride and pleasure, the really pretty sofa and chair, not being satisfied till Augusta had taken her seat in the last, and so verified her assurance that it was "the easiest thing ever was." Jean colored a little as she added, "Ah, ma'am! I didn't need them to tell me that the gentleman loved the very dust you walked upon, and couldn't do enough for anybody that was good to you. I seen that, the very first night he come here, when his own father was a layin' dead."

"Was he here before the funeral?" asked Augusta, half ashamed of questioning Jean, yet longing to hear all she could tell.

"Indeed he was, ma'am; he came soon as the train could bring him after he got the doctor's note, and he sat up all that night by the kitchen fire. When he first comed, he looked quite quiet like, though he was so sad; but when I was a telling him about you, he just broke down like and turned away, as if he couldn't bear to hear it; then I asked him to go up and see you."

"Go up and see me!" cried Augusta, with a quick flush.

"Yes, ma'am, I asked him; but he said no, and so I left

14

him and went to take care of you, and you was asleep. The doctor gave you something to put you to sleep, you see, and after a long time you woke up; and soon as you woke you tried to get up and you kept saying, 'I will go to him,' and when I held you back, you screamed 'Hugh! Hugh! come to me!' just as if you knew he was there; I declare I was that weak you might have knocked me down with your little finger, I was so scared; and I dare say you'd have gone from me, but the gentleman, he heard you scream, and come flying up stairs, and the minute you seen him and he spoke to you, you was just as quiet as a lamb. He went home the next morning, for you see his father was to be buried, and the lady from New York came; but when night came, there he was, sure enough, and all the sleep he got was on a bench in the kitchen, wrapped up in his cloak, and that he did for many a night after. I only wish the sofa had been here then!"

Augusta heard without a word. As Jean spoke, from the darkness of that delirium, looks and tones flashed forth like the shadows of a half forgotten dream. That dream hovered about her all the day, mocking her attempts to grasp its vanishing views. No wonder her head ached at night with the vain effort.

A fortnight later, Augusta was once more at St. Mary's. We will precede her, and see what changes she will find there.

CHAPTER XI.

"He who would fight the devil at his own weapon must not wonder if he finds him an overmatch."—South.

The reader may remember that Mrs. Charles Moray and her son had announced their determination of returning immediately to St. Mary's, before Augusta had parted from them in Washington. To tell the truth, Mrs. Moray did not expect much pleasure from that visit; ghosts, she knew, would meet her there, which it would be hard to lay; but ghosts would now meet her everywhere, and Charlie must go, must take possession of his property—the ghosts must be met. But she would not meet them in the loneliness which she had formerly known there. What good Mr. Mortimer enjoyed as the serene stillness of nature, would have been to her a frightful desert, peopled by demons impatient for their prey.

"And so you are really going to live on a Southern plantation, my dear Mrs. Moray!" exclaimed Mrs. Cullen, one of the gayest of the gay world of Washington, at that time. She was a widow, who had brought her only daughter there to introduce her into society. "Where could such society be found as in Washington?" she asked, and justly, too, "and how could mothers expect their daughters to marry well, if they did not give them an opportunity of seeing the world?"

Mrs. Cullen had conscientiously done her duty, in this respect. Her daughter had seen the world at one, two, sometimes at three balls, every evening, except Sundays, during the winter months; yet the great desideratum of being well married had not yet been attained. Not that Miss Cullen was without admirers. She was, in truth, very much admired. The term is cold; men called her beautiful, at least those men on whom she exercised the bewildering charm of her coquetry. Her mother's reputed wealth would have ensured her attentions, had she been less pretty than she really was. We know not how it was, and fortunately are not compelled to account for it. Some said her sharp tongue had spoiled the fortune of her pretty face; some that she was too great a flirt to be trusted by a wise man; however, this was certain, Miss Cullen had seen the world and been seen by it, and still remained unappropriated. Mrs. Cullen and Mrs. Moray had met often in their round of gaieties, had indeed been quite intimate, and Mrs. Cullen had been one of the first after Mr. Hugh Moray's funeral to call on the mother of "that fortunate young Mr. Moray," prepared to offer condolence or congratulation as the case should seem to demand. She found it well that she had thus provided herself, for both were called for. First, the condolence, for "dear Mr. Moray had been always so much beloved; he had won her heart the first hour she saw him by his partiality to Charles—strange as it might seem, considering how *talented* Mr. Hugh Moray, Jr., was, and having his own name, too, Mr. Moray had always preferred Charlie."

Then, as to the congratulation, "It was quite natural that she should be glad that Charles had come into possession of such a noble property—one of the finest in the Southern States, and she was glad, she could not be hypocrite enough to deny it."

"And they say you have something very handsome yourself?" suggested Mrs. Cullen.

"Well, nothing very great—fifteen or twenty thousand dollars—enough, with what I had before, for me to live on without troubling Charlie, when he gets another mistress to his house."

"That will be very soon, I suppose, as we understand that his marriage with his beautiful cousin is *une affaire arrangée.*"

"You do not believe all Washington reports, do you, Mrs. Cullen?"

"*Ma foi!* If I could do that, I might hope to move mountains."

"Then you would do well to put that among the things you do not believe. Mr. Moray wished it, but there are some things one cannot do to please even the best of friends. We offered Miss Moray a home, and would have provided handsomely for her; but—well—you must excuse me—Charlie would not like that I should talk of such things even to you, dear Mrs. Cullen; but you know there are some people who must have all, or they will have nothing."

"Ah! I understand; and when is she going?"

"Gone, my dear! actually gone! flounced out of the house in a passion at her disappointment, without even saying good-by to me, who have been a mother to her, as every one knows, and gone to Mrs. Commodore Moray, at Elizabethtown. She is the mother of young Mr. Hugh Moray. He is rapidly rising in his profession, you know, so he would be no bad *parti* for her. I sincerely hope he will marry her; I should be sorry, if only for her uncle's sake, that she should come to harm."

"And so you are going to one of those *triste* Southern plantations without even a companion?" cried Mrs. Cullen, compassionately.

"Indeed, I have no such idea; it would kill me; and though I would sacrifice my life for my son's interest, I would not choose to die of the blue devils. I don't intend that St. Mary's shall be *triste*. I shall remain in Savannah till Charlie has got through with the first sad scenes. It will do no good, you know, for me to go through them again."

"Of course not; and it is your duty to keep yourself cheerful for your son's sake; the Quakers say cleanliness, but I say cheerfulness, is next to godliness."

"I agree with you; so after that is over, I shall take with me upholsterers and all sorts of workpeople, to make the old house completely new, and refurnish it in every respect. The place has really great capabilities, but it has been horribly neglected. In a couple of months I shall make quite a different thing of it. All this will amuse me, you know, and as soon as it is in perfect order, we shall come away for the summer. Mr. Moray stayed there all the year, but I could not think of such a thing. We will go to Saratoga, or Newport, or somewhere where we can get a little life; and in October or November we shall go back with as many agreeable people as we can persuade to go with us. I hope you and Miss Cullen will be among them."

"You are very kind, but I am afraid my Elise,"—the name had been Eliza, but was Frenchified to please Miss Cullen's taste—"my Elise would never stand such a quiet life."

"A quiet life is not what I design, I assure you. Charlie has the promise of several young gentlemen to come and spend a month at a time with him to hunt—St. Mary's is full of deer. I shall try to have half a dozen pleasant young ladies always on hand. Of one thing you may be sure; the gentlemen shall be good *partis*—always; I have told Charlie if he wanted me to invite young ladies there, he must always make sure of that; for, you know, when young people are brought so near together for a whole month, something must grow out of it."

"Can you tell me some of the young gentlemen's names?"

Two or three names were given by Mrs. Moray.

"Very good—very good; I don't quite like Reardon; they say he plays; but the rest are capital."

"Reardon plays, my dear Mrs. Cullen, but they say he is always fortunate; I had a little hesitation about him on Charlie's account; but Charlie insisted on it. He says he is the most entertaining fellow in the world, and that as to any danger to himself, he has not the least fancy for play."

"Ah! but the fancy may come and the luck may change. Well, I must be going; I'll tell Elise what you say. You'll have a piano, of course?"

"A grand piano; one of Chickering's best."

"The young people can dance, I suppose, by that, sometimes?"

"Certainly; besides, every plantation has more than one fiddler on it; you know they call a violin a fiddle."

"Well, I think you may depend on us; but I will hear what Elise says."

Mrs. Cullen took an early opportunity of consulting her daughter on a subject which seemed to her by no means unimportant.

"They do say that this Mr. Moray was immensely rich," she said, "and the young man is good-looking and agreeable enough; what do you say to going?"

"I'll try it, if you wish; we shall spend nothing there, and I suppose, with riding, and driving, boating, and pic-nicing, and dancing, and flirting, if there are pleasant men there—"

"You will let the flirting alone, if you please, we have had enough of that this winter; if you go, I expect you to behave yourself discreetly ; do you understand, Elise ?"

"I am not quite destitute of understanding; I take your meaning to be that I am to do all in my power to become Mrs. Moray. I hope, before the bargain is consummated, you will make sure of the fortune. Remember, if that should be light, there are no brains to turn the scale."

"If you don't take care, your tongue will ruin all your bargains, and what good will your brains do you then ?"

"Teach me not to regret the loss of fools."

"The loss of their fortunes would be a more serious evil."

"I might gain the fool and Mr. Reardon the fortune. How then ?"

"It will be your own fault if it should be so ; I think it would be common charity to that poor young man and his mother to exert yourself to keep him out of the hands of a gamester."

Whatever might be the variance between this worldly mother and her daughter, they were agreed in accepting an invitation which promised them some gayety for the ensuing winter without expense, Mrs. Cullen declaring that she had spent the income of two years upon her winter in Washington.

"I shall give no more invitations till I go to Saratoga," said Mrs. Moray, on receiving this promise; "I want our little coterie to be altogether of the *élite.*"

In thus playing the part of "lady of the manor," Mrs. Moray had almost forgotten the poison drop in her cup of pleasures, when it was recalled to her one morning by a ring which she had learned to know, and a voice that made her heart leap with a strange sensation of terror. She was at the head of the stairs, going to her room, and turned hastily to bid the servant remember she was "not at home." It was too late, the gentleman was already in the hall. She heard him say, "Oh! Mrs. Moray will see me; just tell her I am in the study; say I am sorry to hurry her, but I cannot wait."

He had not seen her; she walked quickly to her room—she would delay going down—it might be that he would be obliged to go without seeing her. The messenger soon knocked at her door.

"Mr. Saville, ma'am, in the study; sorry to hurry you, but he can't wait."

Her door was partially opened, and she spoke from behind it.

"Tell Mr. Saville I am extremely sorry; but I am just dressing to go out."

A minute—it seemed to her a second only—and the man was heard reascending the stairs; there was another tap at her door, and when she opened it, a slip of paper was handed in.

"Mr. Saville send that, ma'am; he's a waiting."

The paper contained but a single line: "I must see you; it is of the utmost importance."

"Can anything have been discovered?" she asked herself, growing visibly paler at the thought; and without a word to the man who stood waiting her commands, forgetting that to give effect to her pretence of dressing for going out, she had loosed the cord that confined her morning dress at the waist, she went hurriedly down the stairs, crumpling the slip of paper nervously in her hand.

Mr. Saville, enjoying the thought of his triumph over a lady whom the world perhaps regarded as his superior, had followed the waiter to the hall, and stood looking up the stairs, and listening for the tones that might come from thence.

"Take care, madam! you will fall," he cried, springing forward with outstretched arm to catch Mrs. Moray, around whose feet the tasselled cord had become entangled.

She shrank back from his touch, saying, coldly, "There is no danger," as she drew the cord around her and knotted it carelessly. There was a smile upon his face which she would once have resented as impertinent, as he turned toward the study, and her cheek burned with an indignation she dared not express in words as she followed him. As she entered, he closed the door, and throwing himself into a chair, looked up at her and laughed. At that moment she would have been glad to see him fall dead at her feet; and yet Mrs. Moray was not generally esteemed an ill-tempered woman. Perhaps there was something in her eye which told him he was going too far; he may have remembered that a woman excited by passion will do mad things. His laughter suddenly ceased, and he exclaimed, "Excuse me, but, indeed, I could not help laughing at the thought of what a fright you must have been in to come down with your gown loose; what did you think had happened?"

"Something very serious, I supposed, since it had induced Mr. Saville so far to forget what belonged to a lady as to insist upon seeing me, although I sent him word that I was preparing to drive out."

A slight smile again curled his lip, as he said, "In the intimacy between us, such ceremonious observances may surely be dispensed with. I must confess I was hurt at your excuse; to put me off with a sham, as I knew it must be at this hour! Let me tell you, madam, it was scarcely grateful to one who has served you and yours as I have."

"I am here now, Mr. Saville, to hear your business; as to gratitude and service and all that, it is as well to be silent."

"Perhaps you are right; the service speaks for itself,

and the gratitude may show itself more worthily in deeds than words. To cut the matter short, and speak plainly, as I think we ought to do to each other, you and your son are enjoying fortune through my means; I want to know how I am to be benefited by it?"

"How you are to be benefited! I do not understand you, sir."

"Oh! you thought, doubtless, that I acted in this business from pure disinterested friendship? that is the style, is it not?"

There was deadly fear at Mrs. Moray's heart, but nothing in her words betrayed it, though they came from pale, trembling lips. She rose from her seat, saying, "I will not stay to listen to such language."

"You are mad, to brave a quarrel with me in this way," said Saville, placing himself between her and the door; "do you know that I have here," touching the breast pocket of his coat, "what, if made public, would cast you down in a moment to poverty and contempt?"

"Since you cannot gratify your malice without endangering yourself, I have little fear."

"Endangering myself!" with an accent of contempt; "you do little credit to my ingenuity or your own wit, if you suppose I have left myself so helpless. Are you aware that your son, not wishing to be detained in Washington, as *he* says, or hating all business, as *others* say, has given me a power of attorney to act for him here?"

"What of that? the power of attorney does not extend to the drawing up a new will for a man already dead, does it?"

"Not exactly; what I have done in that way has been under commission from you; but it places all Mr. Moray's papers in my hands to examine at my leisure, and I may find among them another will of later date by one week than the one entrusted to Judge Mellen."

"And both wills written and witnessed by you! How will you account for not having given notice of this later will?"

"I drew up and witnessed two wills; how should I know which was preserved; why was I to disturb people's minds, and do mischief, perhaps, by talking of another will when this had never been withdrawn from Judge Mellon, and the other had probably been dictated by a passing caprice, and destroyed as soon as made; of course, it becomes a very different matter when I find it carefully placed in an envelope, the envelope sealed with Mr. Moray's seal, and indorsed in his hand, 'My last will and testament, to supersede all others.'"

As Mr. Saville referred to the seal and indorsement, he exhibited each in turn on the packet which he drew from his pocket. They seemed incontestibly genuine to Mrs. Moray. Even the villain before her felt some touch of pity as she sank pallid and gasping into a chair, and threw her clasped hands up, as if in a sudden agony.

"I have no desire to quarrel with you," he resumed in a more peaceful tone, as he saw that she had recovered sufficiently to listen; "indeed, I have meant by all this to prove to you that we cannot afford to quarrel; all I want is that you should be my friend as I have shown myself yours."

"What do you wish me to do, Mr. Saville?" asked Mrs. Moray, in a faint, agitated tone.

Mr. Saville saw that the lesson had been taught—that he could now afford to be civil, and he said, "Nothing that will put you to any inconvenience, I hope; I shall always be glad to arrange our little affairs in the manner most agreeable to yourself. All I desire now is that you should give me your note for five hundred dollars, payable in sixty, or even ninety days, if you prefer it; you see how easy I make things for you; I have even drawn the note," placing the paper before her as he spoke, "so that all you have to do is to sign your name here."

The name was signed with a trembling hand.

"There, that is all," said Mr. Saville, carefully depositing the note in his pocketbook. "It was scarcely worth agitating yourself about that. As to the rest—for I think it would be as well we should understand each other fully, that we may have no more such unpleasant scenes as that of to-day—you have in Georgia Bank stock and Central Railroad bonds—stop, I have made a little note of it here, thirty-one thousand, four hundred dollars. Now you can empower me to sell out fifteen thousand, or less than half of this; if any questions are asked, you can say that I have promised to invest it profitably at the North. Mind, I don't say invest *for you*, but only invest profitably, for I never tell a story if I can help it. You will not object to this, of course?"

"If I did, it would matter nothing; I am the slave of your will," in a dreary, hopeless manner.

"Slave! oh no! no! my friend; if you were my slave, I should take the whole, and yourself too, perhaps, ha! ha!"

"If you are a man, spare me unnecessary insult. I am ready to do all you demand; only show me how."

"Oh! I will make it quite easy to you. You can rest a while on this; when I come next I will bring the form you are to sign, empowering me to sell. If it should require me to come out to Savannah, in order to accomplish it, I suppose you will give me a Christmas dinner at St. Mary's; I think I can get a fortnight about that time,—to visit my poor old mother, you know, ha! ha! ha!"

"Do the fiends mock us thus while they torture?" questioned Mrs. Moray with herself—but she said nothing.

"Well, good-by; we part friends, don't we?" he attempted to take her hand; but she snatched it from him. "Depend upon it, you are wrong; we must be friends; now be good and give me your hand—put it right into mine yourself, like a willing—*slave*, did you say?—no, *friend*, and I will tell you how you may draw my teeth, make me powerless, get this," tapping his pocket, "into your own hands, and burn it or do what you like with it. Will you hear?" and he held out his hand.

Slowly, with the reluctant movement with which one might put out the hand to touch a noxious reptile, she put her hand in his. He clasped it tightly, wrung it with a violence that made her writhe with pain; then, as he threw it from him, while his face flushed, and his eye sparkled with passion, he said, "Contrive to get that girl into my power, and you shall make your own terms." In another moment he was gone.

Mrs. Moray went hurriedly into her room, with a heart bursting with passion, to lock her door and give vent to tears—of penitence? no! to tears of rage and mortification. Repentance, atonement, were not in all her thoughts; not her crime, but its consequences she mourned; not how to make restitution, but how to escape this horrible thraldom, was the question that long engrossed her, and to which she found no sufficient answer, as was proved by the alternations of forced gayety and horrible depression in which her life passed for weeks, or until she had buried, under a crowd of self-created engagements, this terrible scene. It is thus we are prone to talk of the "dead past," and say we will bury it. Fools! it is not dead—it will never die; we think, perchance, we have buried it, but its Gorgon head rises when we least expect it from that grave, freezing us with a dread, more fearful because of our fancied escape.

Two weeks after, or about the middle of April, Charles Moray stood, the acknowledged master, in the house which had first received him a gay, careless boy. He could not be gay in that first hour at home, for there had been another arrival there.

Hugh Moray lay once more within the walls of his early home, on the soil he had so loved, and for the continued connection of which, with his own family, he had schemed. But the busy brain schemed no more; the feet, which had planted themselves so firmly there, were still; the hands were folded in a quietness never to be broken till time should end. The stranger might lord it in his halls, the niece, who was nearest to him of any living thing, might be compelled to give place to the woman he had regarded with contemptuous indifference; what mattered it to him? He had done with the relations of earth and time—there is no work nor device in the grave whither he had gone.

There was no grandeur, no pomp, in these second funeral rites; but there were more true mourners there. At night, and by torchlight, he was borne by his own people to his narrow bed beside kindred dust. Mr. Mortimer and the inheritor of his fortune followed next; and then a long procession of those whom he had ruled, and whose simple, affectionate natures, retained no memory but of kindness from him. As they wound their way along the narrow path, untrodden for almost twenty years, the torches threw a weird light upon the old oaks, under whose shadow he and his fathers had played, and whose long gray moss swept his coffin, as it passed along on the shoulders of its bearers. The sighing wind, which swayed gently those giant branches, seemed to Charles Moray a fitting requiem; he was startled when, about midway their sad march, there rose on the air of night, a wild mournful strain, sung by the blacks. Those who have ever heard this people sing, will not easily forget the wild melody of their music, or the readiness with which they improvise words to suit at once the music and the occasion. The music of this melancholy march required a stanza of eight lines, four of which were improvised by a leader, while the last four, in which all joined, was a chorus evidently familiar on such occasions. One stanza of it ran thus:

Leader alone.—We carry we massa to 'e long, long sleep,
  Tru de trees, wid de torch a shinin' bright,
  An' we lef' him dare in de grabe so deep
  All alone by hisself in de dark, dark night.

Chorus.—Jesus hab open de door in de heaben
  Higher dan eben de eagle fly,
  And to white wing angel de order giben
  To carry 'e soul clean up to de sky.

It was an impressive scene, and one not easily forgotten; and when, over the grave, Mr. Mortimer breathed the words of solemn prayer, uttered with the broken voice of one who mourned his lost friend, especially when he asked that "He, in whose hands are the hearts of all the children of men, would enable him who was to take the place thus left vacant, so to lay to heart this scene that he should remember his own latter end, and live so that he might meet it with a consciousness of having performed his duty to those whom God had committed to his care," Charles Moray thought the influence of that hour would remain with him while he lived. He thought of the time when these men around him, or their descendants, might bear him to the same place, and for the first time, they presented themselves to him in another aspect than as the representatives of so much gold. He resolved to keep his promise to Augusta, and rejoiced the heart of good Mr. Mortimer as they walked back by the light of a single torch—the rest had been extinguished at the grave—by expressing his wish to do everything that he should advise for the advantage of the people, whom he was now to consider as his.

Alas for human resolutions!

The next week brought Mrs. Moray; and in a vessel from Savannah came, nearly at the same time, the boxes of furniture, paper, &c., &c., with an upholsterer and a head carpenter, to direct the workmen on the plantation in the improvements to be made. All was bustle and life at St. Mary's, where stillness had reigned so long. Charles Moray found a friend or two from the mainland always willing to come down and hunt or fish with him. Mrs. Moray was busy every moment planning for the workmen, and sometimes aiding, with her own hands, the execution of her designs. Even Mr. Mortimer took some pleasure in arranging with the aid of this excellent carpenter, to spend some part of his legacy in the improvement of the little church, and more, in fitting up a room in his own house very neatly for the occupancy of Augusta Moray, whenever he could persuade her to come to it. The negroes, generally, were well pleased, proud of their new master and his works; but Charity looked on with a dissatisfied air, and often turned away with streaming eyes and clasped hands to ask, "Lord! what has dey done wid my chile?"

These exhibitions, on her part, became at length so disagreeable to Mrs. Moray, that she insisted on her being sent out of the house where, through all changes, she had continued to occupy the room which had been Augusta's from her babyhood.

"Send away Charity!" cried Charles Moray, with surprise; "why, where could I send her to?"

"Send her where you please," was the answer; "I should think in the field, to work, would be a very good place—it would teach her to be less impertinent."

"That is out of the question—I am sure you do not mean it; Charity seems to me to have a right here almost as good as my own; I could not think of sending her away."

"Then you may order the boat for me to-morrow morning; I will not stay in the same house with her."

"My dear mother!" and Charlie tried to take her hand, but it was passionately snatched away.

"Don't call me your dear mother, when you would rather keep an old negro in your house than me."

Charlie would have continued to remonstrate, but, with these words, Mrs. Moray rushed out of the room; and putting on his hat, he walked out and took the direction to Mr. Mortimer's.

How much he told that gentleman of what, in his own mind, he called his mother's unreasonableness, we know not; but that evening Mr. Mortimer sent for Charity and asked if she would come and live with him. At first she shook her head, saying, "I wouldn't hab no rejection, sir,—for de ole place don't seem like heself no more; but you see, sir, ef I come away, who's a going to take care o' my Miss 'Gusty's room?"

"Why, Charity, it is for that very thing I want you here," said Mr. Mortimer, as he opened the door of the room he had just arranged, and showed her into it; "this is Miss Augusta's room, and when I am gone, this will be her house. She will never live up at the big house again; and, you know, she would like to find you here."

"In course, sir, I know she would; and I'll come, if you'll let me bring all de tings she been laft behind when she was gwine."

Of course, a ready consent was given to this; and the next day Charity transferred thither not only herself and her own bedding and clothes, but the crib in which her nursling had once slept, the little dark mahogany bureau, in which were still kept all of her childish articles of dress, which had not been taken with her; the shells she had gathered for her play, the defaced set of cups and saucers, tho broken doll and picture books—all, all were brought with her and arranged, as nearly as possible, as they had been in the old home. Amidst these mementos of the past, Charity took her place, adding greatly to Mr. Mortimer's comfort by her oversight of his little household, and especially of his wardrobe, and looking confidently forward to the moment when Miss Augusta should come to take possession of *her* property, as Charity now considered Mr. Mortimer's house and all that it contained, to be. She even persuaded the good man, who loved to act upon her strong faith, though he might vindicate his understanding to others, by smiling at it a little, to make a flower garden before his door, because " Miss 'Gusty always loved flowers."

And so, while Augusta was pining drearily in the midst of the isolation she had herself created, fond hearts were building a bower of rest for her under the soft skies she loved so fondly! Of what happiness does self-assertion defraud us even on this side the grave!

Late in June, the " big house," so changed and so decorated that, as Charity said, " It didn't know its own self," was again closed, while Charles Moray and his mother sought health and pleasure in the waters of Saratoga and the breezes of Newport. They returned early in November, accompanied by Mrs. and Miss Cullen, and followed in a few days by the Harry Reardon of whom we have already heard, and by two of those brainless inheritors of wealth who seem born to disperse again, for the benefit of the many, the fortune which has been accumulated by some more gifted progenitor. In the present case, however, the ends of their being appeared likely to be disappointed. Instead of their fortune being dispersed, there was some apparent probability of their becoming united in the hands of Mr. Reardon. This gentleman was one of those who present a constant puzzle to that class of people who interest themselves in their neighbor's modes and means of living. He had no ostensible fortune, and nothing to do; yet he eat and drank of the best, was clothed with the finest, and, always gay and entertaining, found hosts of friends wherever he went. To men living in his own circle it was no secret how Mr. Reardon lived. When Charles Moray invited this very agreeable gentleman to come and kill some of his game at St. Mary's, he hardly understood, though others, it might be, did, the laughing answer, "I'm afraid I sha'n't find any of my game there, Mr. Moray."

"We have all sorts of game there," said Charlie.

"Have you a billiard table?" asked Mr. Reardon.

"I will have—I like billiards myself."

"Who will you have that I can play with?"

"There's Briggs and Douce coming in November, and several others have promised before the winter is over; besides, I will play with you myself, sometimes."

"Excuse me, Mr. Moray, but I never play with my host; it isn't safe." Then, in an aside to one of his intimates, —"I might kill the goose that lays the golden eggs."

"Isn't safe? Why, you don't think I'd quarrel with you for beating me?" said Charlie, laughing.

"Perhaps not, but it's a principle of mine. Every man has his principles, you know."

"Oh, well, you sha'n't sacrifice your principles for me. We shall both have people enough to play with; I'll take care of that."

"You may count on me for one, though I don't know that I shall add much to your game; I am not much of a shot."

"Then I will promise you some capital *misses*," and Charlie's laugh showed that he had perpetrated a pun, which might otherwise have escaped detection.

"I understand Miss Cullen is to be one of them," said Mr. Reardon.

"Yes, so my mother says; do you admire her?"

"I should, if I could afford it; she is the most piquant woman I know."

In such a society we need hardly describe the mode of life. All were bent on killing that time which it is the part of the wise to redeem. Around them lay the noblest work ever allotted to man, waiting to be done; the great Taskmaster who had made the work for them and them for the work, waited, gave them time, hour by hour, day by day,—waited, and they rattled dice, knocked about smooth, shining balls over a green cloth, handled painted cards, danced, rode, and yawned wearily, wondering what they should do next to get rid of the time so mercifully given.

Christmas came. Its approach gave promise of jollity to all but Mrs. Moray. She was very evidently depressed —she could not hide it; indeed, she did not seek to hide it; she edified all her acquaintances by declaring that she was very sad thinking of "dear Mr. Moray," whom this season brought strongly to her mind. Why this should be so might seem mysterious to her guests, *did* seem mysterious to Mr. Mortimer, who knew that she had never spent a Christmas at St. Mary's with Mr. Moray; but will be understood by the reader, who remembers that Mr. Saville had *threatened* to eat his Christmas dinner with her. As she believed him to be approaching, the Gorgon's head, which looked dimly forth from the gayest scenes into which she entered, grew more distinct and terrible. The day before Christmas brought her a letter, "From our kind friend Saville, Charlie—he cannot come now; indeed, he says it may be February before he can be spared."

"I am sorry; capital fellow, Saville—so kind; though he has so much to do already, is willing to undertake all sorts of unpleasant business for a friend."

Harry Reardon smiled—Charlie wondered what the

smile meant, but only for a moment. Reardon caught his look of inquiry, and soon diverted his thoughts to other subjects.

The Gorgon head retreated, and Mrs. Moray was gay once more.

"I don't understand her," said Mrs. Cullen to her daughter; "it seemed strange that she should be so gloomy about this Mr. Moray, who was a very distant relation, if he was any at all; especially as she thought it foolish in her son to stop our dancing for one week, at the time his own uncle died."

"But, my dear mamma! How could you be surprised at that? why, Commodore Moray didn't have a doit to leave to any one—how could he expect people to be sorry? Now, when one is paid generously for mourning—"

"Hush, Elise! you get such a sharp way of talking, you will make everybody afraid of you."

"Not everybody; it would take something more than a sharp tongue to make that rogue, Harry Reardon, afraid. I don't believe he fears anything alive, or dead either, indeed."

Mrs. Cullen did not like a certain little glow and sparkle about her daughter, as this was said.

"I hope you are not getting up any intimacy with Harry Reardon. His gambling is really becoming quite disreputable; I have no doubt, from the melancholy look of that poor Douce, that he went away from here quite cleaned out."

"Well, if people will fancy they can play when they can't, what is Mr. Reardon to do? I think he is very honorable, for my part, in refusing to play with Charlie Moray. This estate, and those 'loves of negroes,' as that simpering Miss Mills calls them, would soon be his, if he did."

"Simpering or not, Miss Mills understands her interests better than you seem to do yours; and I should not wonder if she was soon in a position to offer you an invitation to spend the next winter here with her."

"Poh! don't you believe it; Charlie Moray's not so spooney as all that. He does know a thing or two; I am a great deal more afraid of that cousin of his, who was thought such a beauty in Washington."

"Why! they don't even know where she is," cried Mrs. Cullen.

"They *didn't* know. It seems her madness—Harry Reardon says we are all mad about something—her madness is of the romantic style; she wouldn't be dependent on her friends, forsooth! as if there was anything else for a *lady* to do, when she has no fortune—so she went off to be a governess. Of course, she soon got sick of that; Charlie Moray has just heard that she is with some cousin or aunt of his, and has written to ask her here; though, he says, he is half afraid to tell his mother about it, for they are not very good friends, it seems."

"I think that shows Charles Moray to be very amiable," said Mrs. Cullen, who lost no opportunity of praising the possessor of such a fortune.

"He *is* soft-hearted, I think; but nobody gets much good from it; he's never of the same mind two minutes together. Why, before we came here, he had promised that old Mr. Mortimer to have plantation schools and all that sort of thing; and now his mother and Harry Reardon have laughed him out of the notion. It was a silly notion, to be sure, and, as Harry Reardon says, would only have made the negroes discontented with their situation, whereas now they are the happiest laboring people on the face of the earth; but I like to see a man carry out his own notions, if they are silly. I like to see people consistent."

"My dear! I heard some very great man, I don't remember his name, but he was one of those men that are so wise nobody understands them, say that 'consistency was the mark of a little, narrow mind.' I remember it because your poor, dear father had often accused me of being inconsistent, and it was such a good answer."

"That you used it, I dare say."

"Certainly I did, and your father said, I remember, then I had a very large mind."

"So must Charlie Moray have. Poor fellow! he has sometimes as much difficulty as Æsop's old man had with his ass. I was sorry for him, this morning, when Mr. Mortimer found him giving out the rum to the negroes instead of the molasses and coffee and sugar, and I don't know what else, that he had promised him to give in its place."

"Well! I think it was very unkind in Mr. Mortimer to wish them not to have it. It's hard to grudge them this one jollification in the year."

"They'll have a double allowance of rum this year; Harry Reardon made Charlie Moray give it."

And so had Charlie Moray kept his resolutions and his promises!

This conversation will give the reader a sufficiently correct idea of life in the "big house." To amuse one's self in the present—so to take care of one's interest as to secure the means of amusing one's self in the future—these are the two great commandments of this class of people. Unfortunately they can never perfectly attain their end; for even with them, there lingers some feeble spark of those aspirings after the Infinite, which the whole earth would fail to satisfy.

CHAPTER XII.

> "And as a bird each fond endearment tries
> To tempt her new-fledged offspring to the skies,
> He tried each art, reproved each dull delay,
> Allured to brighter worlds, and led the way."—GOLDSMITH.

"THE whole earth would fail to satisfy," we wrote, and yet ever we turn from one object to another, believing that we have at last found the panacea. Once the cry of Augusta Moray's heart had been "Home! Home!" the green shades, the blue sky of St. Mary's! In these she could die content. *Die* content, perchance; but not live so.

Little content was in her heart when she bade Esther and Hugh adieu, on the deck of the packet to which they had accompanied her; and her sad, almost pleading eyes, as he turned on the wharf to wave his hand once more to her, were present to Hugh that day in scenes that were strangely out of harmony with such memories, and caused him once even to lose a point in the argument of the opposing counsel.

Love presents itself under many aspects; and in saying this, we mean a genuine love, not its counterfeits, which are innumerable. There is a love born of what is bright and beautiful in its object, which lives and grows only in that brightness and beauty; there is a love, which takes root only in strong and noble souls, which is mellowed into deeper tenderness and nourished into more vigorous life, by the sorrows and necessities of its object. Such was the love of Hugh Moray. Augusta, proud, gay, admired, might be relinquished, not without a pang—perhaps a life-long pang—but Augusta in sorrow, Augusta forsaken by the flatterers of her summer days, had a hold on his generous heart strong as his own life. She walked mute and sad by his side; her face threw its shadow on his page and, as he thought of her return to St. Mary's, under such altered circumstances, of the coldness, perhaps the malignity, she might meet there, he could scarcely resist the desire to follow her, and, if he might not win her within the safe shelter of his love, at least to show her enemies that they could not strike at her with impunity.

The packet, in which Augusta sailed, arrived in Savannah in the night. The moon was still shining brightly on the sandy bluff, and the long, low stores under it, when she dressed herself, and wrapping a shawl around her, went on deck, to breathe once more the soft air of those southern skies, beneath which her life began. That air does not invigorate, but it heals—it does not give strength to resist, but it induces a languor which, like an opiate, seems to lull the senses to forgetfulness, and so to steal from sorrow half its bitterness. At least so felt Augusta on this night. Earth seemed very sad and lonely to her. Its glory had departed, but its storms also had past; she said to herself, "I have nothing more to lose," and with a languid despondency, which she called resignation, she believed herself reconciled to walk henceforth in the shadow.

Poor child!—for a child, notwithstanding her twenty years of life, she yet was—how little allied was this sensation, born of these soft airs acting on a mind wearied by its own frantic efforts to rise above a humiliating sorrow and on a body debilitated by illness—how little allied was this to the resignation which finds some sweetness in the bitterest cup that Divine Love has mixed, and when earth is all gloom, rejoices the more in the brightness of heaven. As yet, the eyes of Augusta were determinately fixed on the earth,—to the heavenly glory which yet shone around her, she was blind.

The day had scarcely dawned, when Mr. Mortimer, having been told by one of the waiters at the hotel, whom he had bribed to bring him the earliest news of the Isabel's arrival, that she lay at the wharf, rose and hastened thither in a carriage. Augusta had not expected him, yet the first glance at the white locks and the venerable face, unseen for nine years, was enough; and the languid step, with which she was still pacing the deck, quickened, as she stepped forward to meet him. There was no recognition in his eye, as it rested upon her.

"Dear Mr. Mortimer!" she exclaimed, drawing near him with an outstretched hand, "do you not remember me?"

"My child! my dear child!" he cried, as he folded her in his arms, and pressed a fatherly kiss upon her cheek; then, holding her off for a moment, as if to examine her more fully, he drew her silently to him and kissed her cheek again. They could not speak again for some minutes. Thoughts of the past were swelling the hearts of each almost to suffocation. Mr. Mortimer first recovered his voice, and said, with a little huskiness in his tone, and with a smile that gleamed through tears, "You were a good child to come—Charity and I will grow young again in the delight of seeing you."

Augusta looked up to smile; but the dear, kind face, the familiar voice, the old, unchanged love expressed in both, were too much for her; and dropping her face into her clasped hands, and yielding to the fatherly caress, which drew her to his side, she rested her head upon his shoulder and wept there silently and long, soothed by an occasional word of tenderness.

Charles Moray had always intended to meet Augusta in Savannah till the time of her arrival drew near, when he was easily persuaded that it would be better to send Mr. Mortimer for her, and to stay at home himself and assist his mother in the entertainment of the guests, with which she had, somewhat inopportunely, filled the house just at this time.

"You can go up in the boat for her, you know—that is, if you really think it necessary to meet her at all," said Mrs. Moray to him.

"Necessary to meet her! Certainly, I think it necessary,"—Charlie was always very decided in words—"I wish Augusta to feel that she is coming home, and we must both do everything we can to inspire her with such a feeling."

"Then I had better hold myself in readiness to depart; you know she has declared she will not make her home where I am."

"Words spoken in a moment of passion, and forgotten, I dare say, as soon as said."

"I do not believe it."

"At any rate, you will forget them, for my sake;" Charlie bent down and kissed his mother's cheek, as he added, "we can afford to be generous."

"Like a foolish mother, I will do just what you say; but I wish I could make you see this affair just as I do; depend upon it, it will be better for all parties that Augusta Moray should stay at Mr. Mortimer's—he wants her."

"And so do I want my cousin," said Charlie, with a flushed face.

"You must like tragedy better than I, if you do," said Mrs. Moray, with an emphatic shrug of the shoulders. "No,

Charlie! I do not want her; I do not want to have our pleasant coterie here broken up by her foolish conceits and mad suspicions, and I cannot pretend to want it—I am no hypocrite."

"But, pardon me, if I say you are acting upon what are only conceits and suspicions yourself."

"You are mistaken; I am speaking of what I know; and I tell you, when she comes into this house, all pleasure is at an end; her black robes and sombre face, if they do not frighten your friends away, will at least make them feel all gayety to be out of place in her presence."

This was not an alluring prospect to one of Charlie's temperament; and remembering Augusta's last days at Washington, he could not deny that his mother had some reason for her apprehensions; yet he still insisted that the invitation should be given. He wished very much that it should be given by his mother, as well as by himself—he made quite a point of this—'if she would write a note to Augusta, so would he; and he would send them both by the boatmen; for, after all, it was not necessary that he should go in the boat, as Mr. Mortimer would be with Augusta.' Mrs. Moray did not let him see her smile, though smile she did, at this abatement in his view of Augusta's claims. She saw that she had touched the right chord, that Charlie was beginning to fear lest Augusta should stand in his sunlight.

The two notes were written; and really, that of Mrs. Moray seemed the more cordial of the two. They ran thus:

"DEAR AUGUSTA:

"I am sorry not to be able to go for you myself; but it was impossible for me to get away. I know Mr. Mortimer will do everything for your comfort. Remember, however, that your home is with us, not with him. I received his letter announcing your arrival in Savannah, this morning, and I send the boat immediately, with orders to the men to await your coming and be subject to your commands.

"Believe me, ever,
"Your affectionate cousin,
"C. MORAY.

"St. Mary's, Feb."

"And so, my poor Augusta, you are once more in your native State and on your way to the home of your childhood. You will find things greatly changed—I hope you will find all the changes, improvements. We left your own particular room long untouched, dear, hoping that you would come to order your own alterations; but you gave us no hope, and at last we refitted and refurnished it, much to your old nurse's annoyance. It is very pretty. At present it is occupied by Mrs. and Miss Cullen. I wish they had gone away in time for us to prepare it for you; but, the truth is, our visitors all find St. Mary's so pleasant, that I believe nothing but the heat of summer, or the dread of fever, will drive them away. I shall be truly glad to see you, dear, and to have a little rational conversation once more. From the oldest to the youngest here, all seem equally mad in their pursuit of pleasure. I am quite weary of the click of the billiard balls all day, and the sound of music and dancing all night. They have driven good Mr. Mortimer away from us altogether. Tell him that I know he will come to see you, and so I shall be doubly a gainer by your residence with us. Only think of his expending so much money on his house with the hope of making it a pleasant home to you. I was quite touched when I heard it. But I cannot spare you to him; so come quickly, dear Augusta, to the home and the heart of

"Yours affectionately,
"A. MORAY.

"St. Mary's Isle, February 5th, 18—."

If Mrs. Moray really desired to secure Augusta to herself, she had certainly been peculiarly infelicitous in her mode of presenting the attractions of her house.

"She knew that, if I had entertained any design of going to her house, such a letter would have prevented it," said Augusta, as, with something of the hot spirit of her childhood burning on her cheeks and flashing from her eyes, she handed the note to Mr. Mortimer.

"I am glad of the result, my child; but you must not be too hard on this silly woman. This is her way of being happy; and you know she could not be expected to feel to your dear uncle as we did."

"My uncle! ah, true! Some respect was certainly due to his memory in the house which they owe to his bounty; but it was not of him I thought. Oh, sir! if you had known Commodore Moray, you would wonder with me how one so gentle, so noble, could be so soon forgotten. In his home—"

Augusta had spoken with effort from the time she named her dear old friend, and here her voice failed entirely, and she burst into tears.

Mr. Mortimer let her weep in silence for a moment; then, intent on his charitable design of peace making, he said, "We are all frail, human creatures, and must make allowance for each other's errors, my dear. It may be that your friends err by nourishing a gloom which is incompatible with the cheerful resignation that our Heavenly Father has a right to expect from us."

"Gloom! oh no, sir! Indeed, you are mistaken. Nothing can be farther from the truth than that word. They are peaceful, even cheerful—thankful for his noble life. But they cannot, they do not desire to forget, and in the presence of that memory, how can they be gay? Mrs. Commodore Moray herself said to a friend, who urged them to visit, 'We have been brought too near heaven to find much enjoyment yet in earthly pleasures.' Surely this is not gloom."

"No, my child, you are right—this is peace; but I am afraid it passeth the understanding of this poor lady, so we must not blame her that she does not entertain it."

A glowing sunset was turning the still waters of the sound to molten gold as Augusta neared the home she had so dearly loved. A breeze as soft and warm as that of a summer evening rustled the leaves of the old oak at the landing place, which threw its lengthening shadow far out upon the water, as if to meet and welcome her, and, as she stepped on the green shore, a mocking bird trilled out its glorious song above her head. The scene, the sounds, the very touch and odor of the soft air, woke a thousand memories, sweet and sad. Words are powerless, even if words were possible at such a time. Augusta did not attempt them, though deep down in her heart, "My *home!* my home!" went sounding on through every variety of tone and tune, gladsome or sad. Yes, it was her home by a tie which no human power could dissolve—hers as it could never be another's—a part of her life.

Accustomed as he was to the exuberant emotional nature of the African race and their uncontrolled expression of feeling, Mr. Mortimer was touched almost to tears by Charity's reception of her former nurseling, as, kneeling before her, she covered her hands with kisses, and even, before Augusta could prevent it, bent down and pressed her lips to her feet, exclaiming, "My own chile! my own Miss 'Gusty! Please Farra, I is ready for go, now I see your face once more."

She seemed never weary of gazing at her, noting with an outspoken admiration, which often gave a richer glow to the complexion she so much admired, the regal beauty into which her childish promise had developed.

"Just see how 'e step!" she would exclaim to some companion, as they stood together, watching her receding form, as she walked under the old oaks to some of her childish haunts, where she thought herself in little danger of meeting any of Mrs. Moray's gay visitors. "It seem like her foot neber tetch de ground. Dat Miss Moray to de building would gib all 'e money to be han'some as my Miss 'Gusty."

"I bin tought she an' me young maussa bin gwine to married."

"You young maussa!" said Charity, with an expression of the most withering contempt in voice and look; "you young maussa! when my Miss 'Gusty married, 'e'll married somebody what can hab 'tority. You young maussa!" and Charity turned away indignantly.

And Charity's criticism would have been accepted by Charles Moray's best friends and greatest admirers. He was certainly not one who exercised authority over other minds. On the contrary, he was bent and swayed by every passing influence.

When his boatmen returned, bringing him a pencilled note from Augusta, asking that he would come and see her at Mr. Mortimer's, whose quiet home suited her better in her present state of health, he was just leading Mrs. Cullen to the six o'clock dinner, which Mrs. Moray had introduced, to the great annoyance of cooks and waiters, accustomed to the unfashionably early hour of three.

"Augusta has come," he said to his mother, who passed him at the moment.

"Indeed!" said the lady, while a cloud gathered on her brow; "she will hardly care to join us to-day; I will—"

"Oh, she is at Mr. Mortimer's. I shall go to see her after dinner. Suppose you leave Mrs. Cullen to do the honors of the tea table, and go with me?"

"Excuse me; I do not choose to expose myself unnecessarily to rudeness. I did my duty in inviting her here; as she has not accepted or replied to the invitation—"

"She has replied to mine."

"That only makes the rudeness to me more marked."

"You ladies are such sticklers for etiquette," said Charles to Mrs. Cullen, as he seated her on his right hand at the round table, which was another of Mrs. Moray's innovations.

"You must pardon me if I say that this seems to me more than a point of etiquette, Mr. Moray; I have heard that Miss Moray was a little eccentric; I think this looks like it; to treat the mother with such disrespect, and yet expect to maintain friendly relations with the son."

"Of whom are you speaking, Mrs. Cullen; of Miss Moray, who was the belle of Washington a winter or two ago? By George! what an air she had! the handsomest woman I ever saw—and the haughtiest," he added, in a low tone, to Miss Cullen, "so the poison carried its antidote."

The depreciating words were met by a smile; but none the less did Miss Cullen remember the superlative of the commendation and resolve to exert all her fascinations that this haughty beauty should not win one adorer from her circle. Gifted herself with an energetic spirit, she had felt something very like contempt for the easy good nature of Charles Moray, and spite of her mother's exhortations, had refused to make any effort to win the heart which she believed at any time within her power. Now, that it might be in danger, she was roused to exertion, and from the moment he left the table, when she entreated him just to stop for five minutes and let her hear the end of that story he was telling her mamma at table, of which she had just caught enough to interest her, and which nobody could tell so well as himself, to that in which, starting from the piano as with silvery tones the mantle clock rung forth eleven tiny strokes, she exclaimed, "Oh, Mr. Moray, eleven o'clock! and I have kept you singing all this time! Well, indeed, you must lay the blame on your own delightful voice," she devoted herself to him unceasingly.

Had her mode of attack been the display of her own attractions, Charles Moray might have broken from her snares; but many a man of stronger spirit than his, has submitted unresistingly to the more delicate and more potent flattery of one who draws out his powers to charm rather than exhibits her own. Certain it is, though Harry Reardon cast many a smiling glance at the pair as they talked, waltzed, or sung together, Charles Moray's perceptions were only of a very pleasant evening which had slipped away so unaccountably fast that he had not been able to visit Augusta, as he had fully intended to do.

"Perhaps it is as well; my mother would have looked like a thunder cloud all the evening, and spoiled everybody's sport here, if she had seen me go; now, I can breakfast with Mr. Mortimer and Augusta in the morning, before a soul here is up." It was a well-arranged plan, but as Charles was not himself an early riser, he slept the next morning till the breakfast bell informed him that he would find the whole party collected below stairs, while he was two hours too late for Mr. Mortimer's early breakfast. After breakfast, Miss Cullen urged the accomplishment of a promise carelessly made many weeks before, that she should see a deer hunt, to which Mrs. Cullen would consent only on the condition that he would promise to give his undivided care to her daughter. So much was said of Charles's perfect command of his spirited horse, and of his wonderful accuracy in shooting, that the sport assumed new attractions for him, and again Augusta's claims were postponed. Indeed, he can scarcely be blamed if she was forgotten altogether, as he swept over the green savannas to the inspiriting music of the hounds as they pursued with fleet steps and unerring scent the monarch of the sylvan scene, who bounded away far in the distance, through low brushwood, or grass, above which, at every bound, rose his branching antlers, while beside him, as eager in the chase as he, rode a young and handsome woman, her eye kindling, her cheek glowing with excitement.

The hunt was ended; the deer lay bleeding before them; and now they turned, at a more moderate pace, homeward. The path they pursued led them near Mr. Mortimer's.

"Have you seen Miss Moray yet?" asked Miss Cullen, as she glanced at the simple yet pretty parsonage, embowered in oak.

"No; I have not been at leisure one moment since I heard of her arrival," said Charlie, reddening with a slight consciousness that the excuse was scarcely valid.

"That is my fault," said the lady, while the smile that played around her mouth showed that she did not consider the fault unpardonable; "I will not be answerable any longer for such neglect; you must call immediately."

"And leave you to make your way home alone? Augusta would be the last one to pardon me for such a departure from *les bienséances.*"

"There need be no departure at all; I shall go with you; of course, I intend to call on your cousin."

She wheeled her horse into the little cross road which they were just passing, as she spoke, and Charles followed, with the doubt whether it was quite the thing to bring a stranger to call in such an informal manner upon Augusta, contending in his heart with the relief from the dread of this first interview, which the presence of another would afford him.

Augusta was standing in the piazza, trying, with Mr. Mortimer's aid, to train the wild jessamine and rosa multiflora, now both in bud, to wind around the rude columns, formed of pine trees denuded of branches and bark, and to meet in an arch above the entrance. The glow of healthful exercise mantled in her cheek, and as she stood on the light steps used by Mr. Mortimer in mounting to the upper shelves of his study, and looked smilingly down upon him and Charity, who were busy disentangling the hitherto untrained branches and handing them to her, or winding them around the columns at her suggestion, Charles thought he had never seen her look more beautiful, in spite of the gloomy black which enveloped her from the tapering neck to the slender, arched foot. The riders came up rapidly, and the sound of the horses' feet on the firm earth was heard while yet they were at a distance.

Charity was the first to see them, as, turning, she shaded her eyes with her hand, and peered out into the half sun-lit and half shadowed road.

"Hi! Miss 'Gusty, here's Mas' Charles and dat Miss Cully to the buildin'; you better come down."

Mr. Mortimer and Augusta both turned in the direction of the sound for a moment, then Augusta reached out her hand for the branch he held.

"Had you not better come down to receive them?" asked Mr. Mortimer.

"There is quite time enough for that," she answered, quietly, receiving the branch, conveying it to its destined place, and securing it there. They had reached the steps to the piazza before she began to leave her eminence, and Charles, springing forward, cried, "Stay, Augusta, let me help you," but in vain. She moved gently, quietly, almost languidly; yet there she was on the piazza before he could reach her.

"Independent as ever!" he exclaimed, mercilessly shaking the hand Augusta placed in his, in his desire to appear cordial and unembarrassed.

"Pray assist Miss Cullen," was her rejoinder, as that young lady was ascending the steps, with her habit skirt, which had in some way slipped from her arm, falling around her feet. If the slip had been a ruse, intended to prevent Charlie's desertion, it had been ineffectual, and the flush that rose to Miss Cullen's brow, and the slight brusqueness in the movement with which she waved off the gentleman's assistance and recovered the trailing skirt, may have marked her disappointment. If so, it was not the only disappointment she experienced this morning. She had intended to meet Augusta with a condescending courtesy which should at once charm Charles Morsy and give "the governess," as she had lately been accustomed to style Augusta when naming her to her mother, her proper place; but she found herself powerless before an impassive calmness and indifference, which seemed impervious to attack as a steel coat of mail, while the most punctillous courtesy left her no legitimate subject of complaint.

"What a good memory you must have for faces. You called me by my name at once, and I should never have remembered you, though I dare say we met in Washington," was one of Miss Cullen's observations.

It was met with, "I may have seen you there, but I cannot remember it. My old nurse here mentioned your name as you were approaching."

"Do you correspond with Mrs. Price? I used to know her at Saratoga. I should like to hear something about her."

"I am sorry I cannot gratify you; but I know nothing of Mrs. Price; I was only the governess of her children," was the calmly courteous reply.

"Dear me! how you must have disliked it."

"Not at all; it was a very profitable engagement."

Miss Cullen gave up in despair; she might as well shoot her arrows against a granite wall. Besides, a glance at Charles Moray's face showed her that she was annoying him by her sharpshooting. This was far removed from her present intention, and fearing that she could not resist her warlike propensities, she gave the signal for their departure.

"You will come to see us," said Charles, retaining the hand which Augusta had given him at parting; "I want you to see the old house in its new dress."

It cost Augusta some effort not to say that she would rather have seen it in its old one; she only answered, "I will come as soon as I am strong enough to walk so far; you know I have not been very well of late."

"You must not walk; you must have your riding horse."

"My poor little pony? They tell me he is dead. If he were living, he would hardly be able to carry me now."

"Of course not—you must have another; I will see to that."

"Thank you for your kind intentions, but Mr. Mortimer keeps no stables."

"Oh, the carpenters can soon knock up a stable; I will see to it."

Charles Moray hurried away as he spoke, to join Miss Cullen, who was already standing beside her horse and looking impatiently back, as if to chide his delay.

"I hope he will do no such thing," said Augusta, in somewhat annoyed accents, to Mr. Mortimer; "I should dislike it very much."

"Do not be disturbed, my dear; I think he will forget it."

And Mr. Mortimer was right. Charles Moray found himself just at this time crowded with engagements; the late breakfast—unfailing result of the night's festivities—was succeeded by hunting, fishing, boat racing, picnicing on a neighboring island—engagements into which he seemed thrust without will of his own, and which were succeeded by the late dinner—and that by music, dancing, card or billiard playing, till the early hours of another morning sent him to his bed, to recruit his exhausted energies for another day of forced gaieties and wearied satiety. Charles Moray, light as was his nature, never asked himself if this were happiness —he knew it was not;—but he did sometimes ask, Why am I not happy? Here were all the elements he had ever asked for to constitute his Elysium,—fortune, friends, and nothing to do but to amuse himself. Ah! there was the rub: he had yet to learn that man withers without work as surely as a plant without water; that though labor—the labor which makes the brow to sweat and the back to bend, which dwarfs the soul and holds it down to the earth, may be a curse—work, the work which gives exercise to all man's faculties, and thus stimulates the growth of his whole nature, is an immeasurable blessing. His soul was even now withering within him for the want of it, and yet all around him lay, not work in the abstract, but his own work —work the highest and noblest that can be allotted to man, and for which his position of master gave him peculiar advantages. Indeed, it was not only work that could not be done so well, but work that could not be done at all by another, while he held that position.

Charles Moray was not the only one on St. Mary's Isle who was reaping the bitter fruit of neglect of this great principle of our nature. With a richer and deeper nature than his, Augusta Moray had been unable even to *fancy* that she could find her life in the sports that charm none but the lightest spirits for more than an hour. Her Paradise had been of another kind—more refined, ministering to higher enjoyment, yet bounded to herself and those whom love had made as parts of her own being. Could she have realized it, it would have been but to write on it as others had done before, "Vanity of vanities—all is vanity and vexation of spirit." It had been denied to her, and she felt that nothing was left worth a struggle, except to keep her pride intact from the soil of dependence, and thus to eat and drink and die. None, save one who has felt it, can conceive the bitterness of this aimless existence to a spirit conscious of power. It is a daily, hourly death. None need feel it—the world's great Creator intended it for none. He has given a place and a work to every creature to whom he has given life. He who leaves the place unfilled, the work undone, does so at his peril; on his head will assuredly fall the penalty sooner or later. Happy for him if it fall ere the curtain of death divide him from all the interests of his present existence, and the neglect and its consequences be therefore irretrievable.

Mr. Mortimer was grieved to see that though Augusta would enter with at least the appearance of pleasure into any scheme devised by him, or even by Charity, for her enjoyment; that though she would say, "Oh yes! that would be delightful!" as she took her book, or work, or drawing materials to the rustic seat under the great oak which he had arranged for her, or would declare that nothing could be more charming than a ramble with Charity to the old haunts she had loved as a child, the book, or work, or drawing often proved but an excuse for musings that left her sadder than before, and she returned from the rambles with an expression of weariness in countenance and movement, for which she could not plead delicacy of health, all symptoms of illness having rapidly disappeared under the soft ministerings of her native air.

Though grieved, as we have said, Mr. Mortimer was

long silent. One Sabbath evening they sat together in the shaded piazza, which the warmth of the advancing season—it was now the last of March—made the pleasantest part of the house, Augusta reading to her old friend, who had suffered much lately from increasing dimness of sight. The book chosen by him was "Taylor's Holy Living and Dying."

"Do you agree with that?" said Mr. Mortimer, as she finished one of those long rhythmical sentences in which we know not whether to admire most the clearness and force of the reasoning, the poetic beauty of the language, or the devotional feeling.

"Do you agree with that?" he asked again, as she hesitated.

To many, to most, perhaps, it would have been easy to answer "yes" or "no," or "I do not know;" but Augusta never equivocated in her life, scarcely ever evaded meeting a question fairly and fully; so now, after a minute's vain attempt to recall what she had been reading, finding that Mr. Mortimer still awaited her answer, she said, with a flushing cheek, "I am not quite sure that I understood it."

"And yet it was not difficult to understand. Are you quite sure you know what you were reading?"

"Oh yes, sir; it is 'Taylor's Holy Living and Dying,'" she said, but her eyes sank before the mild, steady gaze of his, that seemed to her, tenderly reproachful.

"My child, where is your heart?" asked Mr. Mortimer, gently; "I have seen from the first it was not with us," he added, mournfully. Augusta was touched. Tears sprang to her eyes. Again she seemed a little child, and he, her kind teacher, as she said, softly, "Forgive me, dear sir; I will be more attentive," and raising the book from her lap, she would have read again.

Mr. Mortimer laid his hand upon the book.

"No, my dear, I will not ask you to read any more this evening."

"Are you offended with me, dear Mr. Mortimer?" asked Augusta, with a little tremulousness in her voice.

"No, my child, not offended; I have no right to be that, nor have you given me any cause; but I am disappointed. Ah, my dear! you do not know what disappointment is to the old, who have but little left here to love or hope for, and who know that from even that little, death must divorce them soon."

"Oh, dear sir, say not such cruel words!" exclaimed Augusta, with streaming tears.

"Hush, hush! my child; I did not mean to wound you."

"Only tell me what you wish—what I can do; I came at your wish, hoping to give you pleasure."

"It was very kind in you, my good child, as kind as has been your compliance with all my wishes since you were here; but your heart has not been in these kind acts, your heart is not here; where is it, Augusta?"

The flush rose from Augusta's cheek to her brow, a thrill shot through her whole frame; she would have escaped from the piazza, but had no power to stir. To any other but Mr. Mortimer she would have answered such a question proudly, defiantly, perhaps; but for this gentle, good old man, this kind, constant friend, she had no pride.

"My dear," said Mr. Mortimer, again, as he read that flushing and downcast face, "do not think that I meant to ask an impertinent question, to pry into the secrets of a young and delicate nature; I want to know only so much of your life as will enable me to help you to the paths of peace; you seem to me now like a little child which has wandered away from its home into the solitude of a vast wood, where it stands affrighted at its loneliness."

"You are right—loneliness; yes, that is it."

"And yet, it may be, the home is just at hand, if some friendly guide would only point to the path."

Augusta did not speak, and her downcast eyes forbade his reading there her unuttered thoughts.

"Shall I try to be your guide, my child?"

The voice was so tender and gentle, and when Augusta lifted her eyes to the face, the flowing gray locks, the kind smile, laid such a bond upon her, that even the strength of her pride could not break it, yet she shrunk from the probe that might be applied, and could only answer with a faltering voice, "It is hard to guide one, sir, whose wanderings are aimless, who has no home and no hope."

"No home! no hope! God forbid that this should be your case! There is but one place in God's dominions over whose door is written 'No hope.'"

"I was speaking but of this life," said Augusta, sadly.

"Our life is one; the mistake—the fatal mistake—is to think of the portion spent on earth as the whole. Do not think that age has made me cold—that I have forgotten the force of human love and human hopes; memories, Augusta, grow very tender in the light that falls on them from the world to which I am so near."

He sat a little while in quiet thought, whose outward expression was not sadness, but peace; then resumed.

"What I would say is that these hopes and loves must bring us more disquiet than happiness, so long as they centre on ourselves, or on those whom love has made as parts of ourselves; it is only when their action is as wide as the world—as high as the heavens—that they bring happiness. It is not through self-seeking, but through self-renunciation, that we attain to a true peace."

"Self-renunciation? I do not quite understand," said Augusta, interested by the apparent paradox.

"Yes; it is he who is willing to lose his life for a good cause, who finds a higher, nobler, and even happier life even in that act."

"I understand *that*—the martyrs who lay down their earthly lives for their faith, win a richer, heavenly life."

"Your explanation is good; but you must bear in mind that martyrdom is but the highest expression of that principle which must govern the whole Christian life; it is only thus that we can reconcile the 'peace' and the 'tribulation' which were alike our Saviour's promise to his people."

It seemed to Augusta that Mr. Mortimer had forgotten her individual case in the enunciation of a general principle, and pleased at the change, she turned readily to what she considered a new subject.

"I fear," she said, "that a religious persecution would find few martyrs among us of the present day."

"I do not know," was the thoughtful answer; "there were many more than Elijah suspected who had not bowed the knee unto Baal; there are many, I hope, even in this self-seeking age, who live in this spirit; many who do not pause in their course of beneficent action for any pressure of personal sorrow, or absorption in personal joy—who seek not their own, but the things of others."

"It seems to me, my dear sir, that you are inculcating a stoical disregard to our own pain or pleasure, which may be very beautiful in theory, but which is quite unattainable, or attainable only by those whom nature has not endowed with very keen susceptibilities."

"Pardon me, my dear; the highest expression of my ideal was in one who was gifted with the tenderest of human hearts, and exposed to the extremity of human woes, yet who spent his life not in vain repining, but in going about doing good; who, even when dying a death of agony, prayed not for himself, but for his murderers—from whom no pang extorted a cry till he felt that desertion which,—blessings on His Holy Name!—no mortal need feel,—which none can feel or understand, perhaps, save those who have been banished from the presence of God into what the Scripture calls 'outer darkness.' Was this stoicism, or want of keen susceptibilities?"

Augusta sat awed and still. It appeared to her almost irreverent to make that Divine life, yet more that sacrificial death, the subject of conversation. Nor did Mr. Mortimer pursue the theme farther; he had cast the seed, he could now only pray that God would give the increase.

Another week had passed away, and again the aged teacher and the young girl, whom he had loved and prayed for, sat in the same piazza. The rustling of the leaves, stirred by a gentle breeze, and the singing of the birds, which had built their nests in the great oaks, were the only sounds that broke the stillness of the evening.

"Great peace have they whose hearts are stayed on Thee," softly repeated Mr. Mortimer. The words had furnished the subject of his sermon on the morning of that day,—a sermon in which, with a simplicity that placed what he said within the comprehension of the humblest intellect, and a directness that suffered no earnest heart to evade its grasp, he had elaborated and enforced the truth presented to Augusta in conversation.

"Do you not desire this great peace, my dear?" he asked, turning suddenly, but not ungently, to Augusta.

"I fear it would be a vain desire," she said, timidly.

"Try, my dear, try."

"How, my dear sir, how shall I try?"

"Get away from yourself—let your sympathies and work be no longer for yourself, or for those few beloved friends who are parts of yourself, but for the needy and sorrowing wherever you find them; and let your trust, your reliance be not on yourself, not on any human arm, but on God."

"This is very general, dear friend; I want to know what I shall do *now*—for whom can I work? with whom can I sympathize?"

"I think, just at present, the most unhappy person within your reach, the one who has the greatest claim on your sympathy and charity, is Mrs. Charles Moray."

The quick crimson flushed Augusta's brow; she raised her head proudly, and said, "I can do nothing for her."

"Bless your enemies—do good to them that despitefully use you and persecute you," said Mr. Mortimer, in the tone of one rather reciting to himself than addressing another.

"What good could I do to Mrs. Moray?" asked Augusta, hotly.

"I do not know; I only know that she needs all sorts of good, and I do not think you should so determinately withdraw from her as to make it, as far as your act can make it, impossible to act beneficially upon her."

"I have already declined Mrs. Moray's invitations, and I cannot now solicit them or approach her unsought."

"You cannot lay that much prized jewel of your pride on the altar of Him who is your peace? Well, in this case, it is not demanded; she told me this morning that since you would not come to see her, she was coming to-morrow to see you."

"Since she has delayed it so long, I wish she had omitted it altogether," said Augusta, haughtily.

"Hush, my dear! Remember, daily dying is the Christian's life and peace."

"Did she tell you at what hour she would be here?"

"No; only in the morning."

"You will not leave me alone?"

"Are you afraid of her?"

"Not of her, but of myself."

"You know where to turn from that fear—but I will be present and assist at the sacrifice," he added, with a smile, which Augusta had scarcely the power to return.

What had changed Mrs. Moray's tactics, so far as to induce her to seek one whom she hated with a bitterness, which only a consciousness of having done a great injury, for which we have no desire to atone, can infuse into the heart, we may perhaps learn by a more minute survey than we have yet made of her life at home.

CHAPTER XIII.

"Upon my head they placed a fruitless crown,
And put a barren sceptre in my gripe,
Thence to be wrenched with an unlineal hand."—*Macbeth.*

"Frailty, thy name is woman!"—*Hamlet.*

WE said, some pages back, that Mr. Mortimer was right in the opinion that Charles Moray would probably forget his promises to Augusta. He did forget them, in the ordinary sense of the expression—that is, he forgot to execute them; yet they did not altogether vanish from his sphere of thought. They returned to his memory at inopportune times, when it seemed impossible to take any step toward their fulfilment, rousing him for a moment from the dull despondency of *ennui*, to a keener pang of shame. Weary of others,—dissatisfied with himself,—this is precisely the condition in which a man, especially a self-indulgent man, is most in danger. It would be an interesting study to the psychologist to follow our present subject through daily and hourly alternations of feverish unrest and despondent inaction, to mark the sullen expression and jaded movements of the morning—to hear him again and again meet the first proposition of the day's amusements by the declaration that he must leave his guests to themselves, as business, too long postponed, demanded his attention, or as a message from the plantation required his presence; or, with an expression of unconquerable determination in the glance directed to his mother, as he had an engagement with his cousin, which he could no longer postpone. Then, to mark the gradual relaxation of his purpose, under the influence of the temptations presented, in which presentation his mother never appeared, though an acute observer would easily have surmised that she sat behind the curtain and moved the wires. Let us give but one example.

The scene is the old dining room, in which Mr. Hugh Moray had entertained the stranger, who had exercised so large an influence over the destination of his property; but it would scarce be recognized by one who remembered it only in its former state. The large windows opening to the floor were now richly draped; the floor was carpeted; the oak furniture is of the modern antique style, the breakfast table glitters with its display of silver. Charles Moray, Harry Reardon, and two young gentlemen, sons of planters on the main-land, are seated at the table with Miss Cullen, Mrs. Marvel, a gay young widow, and her younger sister, Miss Tanner, both Saratoga acquaintances of Mrs. Moray, who had only lately arrived to pass the weeks of spring, so dolorous in a northern clime, so *riant* and sparkling in a southern one, with "dear, darling Mrs. Moray and her charming son."

"What are you going to do this delightful spring day?"

"Suppose we take to the boats and show Mrs. Marvel and Miss Tanner one of the pretty islands in your neighborhood," said Mr. Reardon.

"I vote for a brisk canter to the other end of this island and a picnic under the oaks," exclaimed Miss Cullen, who, conscious that she looked well on horseback, always preferred riding to boating. "How do you vote, Mrs. Marvel?"

"Is there a carriage road to the other end of the island?" asked Mrs. Marvel, whose *rôle* was excessive timidity. "I am afraid Mr. Moray's horses are too gay for me, and as to the sea, it almost killed me when I came here —those great waves!" and the widow shuddered slightly.

"A beautiful carriage road, level and smooth as a bowling green—so you will be on my side; now, Miss Tanner, your vote."

"One moment's delay, Miss Tanner; let me assure you the sea to-day is as smooth as Miss Cullen's carriage road, an unbroken mirror for the bluest of blue skies, and that the island is a perfect Isola Bella."

"Oh! I dote on the sea, and the blue sky, and the islands and all that," cried Miss Tanner, enthusiastically.

"Thank you, Miss Tanner!" exclaimed Mr. Reardon; "now we have a tie, but I hope—"

"No, no! Mr. Moray, your vote; you will not deny me your vote," cried Miss Cullen.

"You must excuse me to-day; I shall have to leave you to your own devices; I must see my cousin, Miss Moray, to-day; but I am sure either Mr. Maxwell or Mr. Howell," glancing at the two young gentlemen visitors, "will ride with you with pleasure."

Both the gentlemen named, offered their services eagerly, though timidly, to the handsome, dashing Miss Cullen, whom they greatly admired.

"Thank you," she said, with a very slight bow and an expression of pique, "I shall stay at home; I believe I have letters to write."

"I protest against that," said Mrs. Moray; "the weather will soon be too warm for any active exercise, you must not waste this beautiful day in the house; Charles will not let you, I am sure, if it depends on him."

Harry Reardon bent his face over his plate with a smile, which called up a quick, bright flush, half of shame, half of vexation on Miss Cullen's cheeks. That smile did not speak the feeling she had hoped to excite. Charles Moray saw the flush, which he attributed to a more flattering cause, and addressing her alone, he said, "I wish I could go; I will try to join you at the picnic; but, indeed, I must see my cousin first."

"Let us all go there and carry her off with us. Mrs. Marvel will have a seat to spare in the coupé. I want you to sing that beautiful song, 'Woodman, spare that tree!' for us; I shall put my guitar in the carriage."

"But, indeed,—" Charles began, but after another glance changed what he was about to say into "Well! if we are going to the Northend, we must make our preparations quickly; we shall find it warm at midday, and it is a seven miles' ride."

"Shall we call for your cousin?" asked Miss Cullen, scarcely able to repress a little exultation in her tone.

"Oh no! it would take us quite out of our way. I must put off my visit till this evening."

"Miss Tanner, shall we go to Isola Bella?" asked Mr. Reardon, with mock earnestness.

"I am afraid it won't do," said Miss Tanner gravely, mistaking the tone.

Miss Cullen's eyes turned with mischief in their glance to Mr. Reardon, and with a readiness which showed that he had not outlived his gentlemanly instincts, he said to Miss Tanner, "Since we must submit to the majority and go to the Northend, permit me to have the pleasure of driving you in Moray's brougham. Mrs. Moray will, I dare say, accompany your sister."

The proposal was accepted, and in this order they went, not altogether to the satisfaction of Miss Cullen, as Mrs. Cullen and her maid, too, divined, from her captiousness and impatience while arranging her dress for the drive. Charles Moray lost half his value in Miss Cullen's eyes, when Harry Reardon was not by to bear witness to her power. Of course, Charles Moray returned too late and too much fatigued to walk over to Mr. Mortimer's that evening.

Notwithstanding the manœuvring of his mother and the easy pliability of Charles Moray, it was obviously impossible that two persons living within a mile of each other, and neither of them in strict confinement, should not sometimes meet, especially when Augusta's restored strength rendered her capable of the long, quiet rambles she loved. One day she was walking leisurely over the narrow, shaded path, strown with the sere leaves of the last autumn and winter, which led by the burial ground to the plantation, when the sound of approaching voices and steps made her draw closer the light mantilla she had thrown from her shoulders and exchange her languid, pensive movement for a quicker step. Move as quickly as she would, she was soon seen, and almost as soon overtaken by Charles Moray and Mr. Reardon.

"Augusta!" exclaimed Charles Moray, "how very glad I am to meet you! I was going to see you this morning—was I not, Harry? My friend, Mr. Reardon—my cousin Miss Moray."

Augusta bowed to Mr. Reardon in acknowledgment of the introduction, as she said, with a smile, which seemed to him to speak more of carelessness than of pleasure, "Your assurance needs no corroboration from another. It is well your intention was not put into action as you would have found neither Mr. Mortimer nor me at home."

"Where are you going? let me carry your basket—plants? What are you going to do with plants out here?"

Augusta glanced at Mr. Reardon; but he had stepped on ahead, and seemed out of earshot; so, lowering her voice a little, she said, "I hope you will pardon my coaxing the gardener to give me some cuttings from my uncle's favorite rose tree; I am going to plant them at his grave."

Charles Moray reddened with shame, and said, ingenuously, "It is a disgrace to me that this should have been left to you. I have been intending to call and consult Mr. Mortimer about an epitaph for a monument that I am going to write to Hugh to send me from New York. Dear old Hugh! how I wish he were here! Do you think he would come if I should write for him?"

The blood that flushed Augusta's cheek, was called there more by indignation at this expression of a weak selfish and increasingly indolent nature,—this *intending, was going,* and *wishing,*—than by the name of Hugh or the thought of his coming. To Charlie's question she answered somewhat coldly, if not curtly, "The best way to ascertain that, will be to write."

"Augusta," said Charles Moray, struck by her manner, "you must not think me the heartless fellow I seem. If you could only be one day in our house, you would see how impossible it is for a fellow to do as he wishes."

"Unless he will exercise a little decision to secure his independence," Augusta responded.

"A man may be decided with men; but what is he to do with the women, Augusta?" asked Charles Moray, with such an expression of helpless perplexity that, had Augusta been one whit less provoked by his weakness, she could not but have laughed. As it was she shrugged her shoulders and was silent.

Suddenly Mr. Reardon stopped, and as they came near, bowing to Augusta, said, "I am sorry, Moray, to disturb so pleasant an interview; but I find it is past ten, and I must remind you that the ladies will expect us."

"Will you go to them, Reardon, and say I am necessarily detained, but will join them as soon as I can—"

"Not detained by me—" said Augusta, hurriedly.

"Not *by* you, only *with* you—she is doing, Reardon,

what I ought to have done long ago; I cannot leave her to do it alone."

"It is a work which certainly does not need two to perform it; so, if you are really anxious to do it yourself, I will give you the slips and return home," and Augusta held the basket toward him.

For one who boasted of his *savoir faire*, Charles Moray both felt and looked awkwardly enough. He was provoked with Augusta for her cool rejection of his attendance, and scarcely less provoked with Mr. Reardon for being a witness to it.

"I have no desire to drive you home," he said, a little sulkily to the first.

"Then I would advise you to hasten on with Mr. Reardon, and not keep the ladies waiting."

As she said this, glancing toward Mr. Reardon, she saw a smile curl his lip; old kindliness to Charlie awoke in her heart; she would not expose him to that bold man's mockery, so holding out her hand with a friendliness, which at once restored his self-possession, she added, "You know, Charlie, I will not help you to break a promise; come to me when you have no other engagement, and I will take this walk with you with pleasure. Good morning."

Both gentlemen felt themselves dismissed, and moved on rapidly, and for some time, silently.

"What a complexion!" cried Mr. Reardon, suddenly, "what hair! what eyes! all glow and sparkle in her looks, and cool as an icicle in manner. Moray, you must pardon me, but I cannot help laughing," and he suited the action to the word, "I cannot help laughing, when I think how you looked—I never saw a man so coolly *planté* in my life; yet with that last word and look and movement, she made me envious of you. What a witch she is! That is the sort of woman who could move the world, if she chose."

"She is too proud to choose to exert her influence on any but her friends—I am used to being the butt of her caprices. With all her glow and sparkle, I prefer one who will not plunge me in a second from the genial glow of a summer's day into an ice bath, even though she should at last restore me to the sunshine."

The gentlemen had moved rapidly on; yet, when they reached the house of the manager or overseer on the plantation, they found the ladies collected in the piazza to await their coming, astonishing the staid wife and wild, sunburned children of Mr. Carter, the manager, by their gay dress and lively talk.

"I told you so, Mr. Reardon; I knew we should be here before you," cried Miss Cullen and Mrs. Marvel at once.

"How long is it since you arrived?" asked Mr. Reardon.

"Fully fifteen minutes," was the answer, as each lady examined the tiny watch hanging at her girdle.

"We should have been here long before that, had we not met the Queen of Fairyland in our walk, who turned poor Moray here into a tree, planted him, ladies; I could not leave him, of course, so there we should even now have been, had she not taken pity on us and 'with her rod reversed and backward mutters of dissevering power,' set him free again."

"What do you mean, Mr. Reardon?" cried the bewildered Miss Tanner, whose wits were somewhat slow at guessing riddles.

"What nonsense you talk!" exclaimed Miss Cullen, who had reasons of her own for disliking the account.

"That is the way truth is always discredited. Well, all I say is, try your power on him, ladies, and see if you are not attacking a charmed man."

Mrs. Marvel and Miss Tanner laughed; Miss Cullen

flushed, and her eyes flashed, and her lips settled themselves into a line of unwonted firmness. To her sensitive ear there was a challenge in Mr. Reardon's words, which the glance she caught, seemed to direct especially to herself. It was as if he had told her, "You have tried to play him off against me, you will henceforth find him as little impressible as you have found me."

"I will try, at least," was her inward response. Was it this decision which prompted the manner half advancing, half receding; the eyes lifted to his, then sinking before them; the burning flush, with which she met Charles Moray as he returned from a colloquy with Mr. Carter, in which he had been engaged during this by-play? Perhaps the gentle flattery of such a reception was more felt by Charles Moray from its contrast to the cool reception Augusta had given him; it may have been this, or it may have been the new character imparted to her face by the counterfeit emotion, which made him think her at that moment more charming than he had ever seen her. It was to her and not to Mrs. Marvel, as he had intended, that he offered his arm to lead the way to the sugar works, the ladies being desirous to taste the warm, luscious sirup, as it comes from its first boiling. It was a strange scene to them, and would have been stranger still, if they had waited till night and seen it lit by the red flames. Brawny men, with bared arms, flourishing dippers with long handles, were moving about among the boilers, where simmered the thin, clear juice of the cane, or where boiled with a bubbling sound, the dark, thick sirup. No one who had heard their laugh, blithe as a child's, or listened to the jests, with which they responded to the merry salutations of their visitors, could have deemed them oppressed or melancholy men.

While the visitors were in the sugar-house, Mr. Carter, by Charles Moray's order, had sent over for his horse and

Mr. Reardon's, and the whole party returned together by the carriage road.

"I say, Moray, were you afraid of meeting the Queen again, if you walked?" cried Mr. Reardon, gayly, but a little maliciously, as he mounted.

Charles Moray busied himself about the arrangement of Miss Cullen's drapery, not appearing to hear the question. The lady received his attentions with the same air of newly-awakened sensitiveness, which had already proved effective in drawing him to her side. This was revealed rather in looks and manner than in words; indeed, the near neighborhood of the coupé and the frequent interruptions from Mr. Reardon, rendered anything like confidential conversation difficult. Yet there was an undertone of feeling accompanying even the most commonplace observation, which, where the feeling is genuine, is a source of the most exquisite pleasure.

"How warm the sun is to-day, and yet it is only the last week in March," observed young Moray.

"The last week in March! May will soon be here!" cried Miss Cullen, in a voice which could not be interpreted as an expression of gladness.

"You will not leave us so soon."

"Mamma says we must."

"But what do *you* say?" in a low and very earnest tone.

The answer was a sudden lifting of the eyes to his, and as sudden a drooping of their lids, which quivered as with suppressed emotion.

Had they been alone, Charles Moray would at that moment have spoken the irrevocable words which would have placed St. Mary's and its master at the feet of Miss Cullen. Not that he was what might be called *in love*, but in pure idleness, and for the want of something to excite him, he had played around the flame till his wings were scorched, and

though half suspecting a snare, he was ready to drop into
it. Do not say, reader, such weakness is impossible. To
the young man who is a mere idler or pleasure seeker—in a
world where every reflective, earnest soul finds work that
tasks his utmost power, no weakness is impossible; he drifts
at the will of circumstance hither and thither, till he becomes unable to resist the current, even though he knows
that it is floating him to ruin. Charles Moray was not
wholly ignorant of the tactics of flirtation, as practised by
the frivolous of either sex; but he was not quite au fait of
that deeper coquetry of which practice had made Miss Cullen mistress, which could simulate successfully not merely
the sensitiveness of an awakened heart, but the modest reserve necessary to render that sensitiveness alluring. The
sensation it awakened in him was welcome; he fostered it,
he dwelt on all that was calculated to increase it, till he half
persuaded himself that the sparkle of fancy was indeed the
glow of passion. Then why should he pause or hesitate?—
he was his own master. He determined to speak at once.
But this was not so easy as it seemed. The lady liked to
display her power. Especially did she take pleasure in this,
in the presence of Harry Reardon; yet she shrank with a
reluctance which perhaps she did not herself fully understand from saying the words that would commit her irrevocably. Thus affairs rested for some days, affecting the
various lookers on with emotions differing, according to the
stand-point of each. To Harry Reardon it afforded at first
quiet fun, changing to a less complacent feeling as the flirtation became more serious; to Mrs. Marvel it was provoking to see the only marrying man in the company so engrossed; to Mrs. Cullen it was a source of exultation, the
expression of which, in manner, at least, it was difficult to
restrain; while to Mrs. Moray it brought vexation scarcely
disguised. Bitterly did she regret that she had not made

more honest and strenuous efforts to draw Augusta Moray into her circle. "Charlie certainly liked her once," she said to herself, "and she is so much handsomer than that girl— he could never have been made such a fool of, if he had had Augusta near him to compare her with; she would not have married him—of that I am sure; but so much the better, if she had only kept him from desiring to marry another."

And on that hint she spoke first to Mr. Mortimer, as we have seen, proposing to call on Augusta the next day, saying that she had waited with the hope that Augusta would come to her, but she had been disappointed, and she could no longer submit to this estrangement from one in whom she felt so deep and tender an interest.

The visit was made. Mr. Mortimer complied with Augusta's request that he would not leave her, the more readily, because he thought his presence might bring the interview to a more peaceful conclusion. Mrs. Moray never had studied more to ingratiate herself than on this morning. She acknowledged with a singular degree of frankness that she had not done her duty by Augusta, whom, considering her as a sacred trust from Mr. Moray, she ought to have made more strenuous efforts to win. "But you know, Augusta," she said, "you harbored most unjust suspicions of me when we parted, which showed themselves in your manner, if not in your words. You will not wonder that they made me indignant; I was very angry with you, my dear, and it has taken me all this time to get over it; but now I would gladly prove to you, if you will let me, that I love you too well to have injured you intentionally."

A courteous, general acknowledgment of her kind intentions was all that the exquisite tact of this address won for Mrs. Moray.

To her invitations the answers given were not more satisfactory.

"Come with me to-day," said Mrs. Moray.

Augusta regretted that it would be impossible.

"Mr. Mortimer, cannot you persuade her? She wants a little gayety to make her forget the past."

Mr. Mortimer looked at Augusta without speaking; their eyes met, and it was to him that she addressed her answer, in which she seemed to lose all consciousness of another presence.

"Neither my dress nor my feelings are suited to gayety," she said, as she glanced at her black dress, "and you would not desire me to forget the past; you know it is all I have."

There was a moment's embarrassed silence, and then Mr. Mortimer said, "I am afraid you must excuse her from the galeties, Mrs. Moray; she is hardly strong enough for them; but we will keep a little cheerfulness for you if you will come and see us often."

And unable to obtain any greater concession, Mrs. Moray went away, promising to come very often.

How strange are the revelations we sometimes obtain of the oneness—if we may so express it—between man's lower nature and the material world by which he is surrounded. We mark a mode of action in this material world and announce it as a *physical* law; but lo! when we turn our observation on the world within us, while its movements are unrestrained by those higher powers which connect us with the Infinite, we find the same law ruling there. Reaction is always proportionate to action, says the student of nature's laws; resistance but increases the force of that which it is not sufficiently powerful to overcome.

Harry Reardon had thought Elise Cullen, as he said to Charles Moray, the most *piquant* woman he had ever seen. Her beauty charmed, her wit entertained, her coquetry excited him. A languid wish had more than once been awakened in him that he could secure her for himself, yet the wish had been followed by a laugh at his own folly, for how could he, with his expensive habits, afford to marry without fortune?—and he had ascertained that Elise was wholly dependent on her mother, who was not likely to give, with her own good will, either daughter or fortune to him.

Such had been his cool reasoning while he believed this pretty sparkler had given to him all the heart with which nature had gifted her; but within a few days this had seemed not quite certain. It grew daily, hourly, less so, and as it did, the languid wish grew into a strong desire, a passionate determination. Under the frank, gay exterior of this man was concealed, almost from himself, a nature, slow to rouse, but, once roused, unsurpassed in the force of passion and the persistency of will. The experiences of his life had taught him not to subdue himself, but to bear down opposing circumstances. Left an unconnected orphan while yet but a boy, he found that his father had dissipated his fortune in the pursuit of pleasure, and there was nothing which he could justly call his own. In his father's life of pleasure he had shared, and the education his powers had thus received, and the direction given to his character, had neither fitted him for any employment by which fortune could be gained, nor given the habits of hardihood and self-denial which might have enabled him to do without fortune. Like the steward in the Bible, "he could not dig, and to beg he was ashamed," and like him, he found a resource in the habitations of his friends. These friends, the former companions of his father, invited him at first from pity, but he exercised his agreeable qualities with such success that the pity soon became liking. These associations gave him currency in what is called good society. How he maintained himself there, how he managed to be the best-dressed man of their acquaintance, and to ride the finest horse, they never asked. "Clever fellow that; see how he gets along—he never wants anything," they exclaimed; perhaps, had he *wanted* anything, these friends might have proved less constant. It was at this period of his life that Harry Reardon formed the wise determination never to play at games of chance with those who were his hosts, or who had been so and might be so again.

Such was the man who now found himself in circumstances in which a departure from the one self-restraining principle of his life opened to him the prospect of fortune; and with fortune, would not the faithless Elise be his too? The circumstances of his life had not been favorable to the cultivation of delicacy of feeling, or purity of taste. There was nothing repellent to him in the thought that before he could win her, she must prove that the graceful flatteries she was now lavishing on another, were only the tribute of a venal soul to fortune. Rather was it a pleasant thought to him that in her heart—if heart she had—she preferred him; and when prudence and inclination coincided, a new and warmer light would gleam from her eyes, and shed its red glow upon her lips.

Perhaps it will be thought that the new sentiment excited in Charles Moray would render the designs of Mr. Reardon innocuous, by steeling him against the attractions of dice, cards, or billiard balls. This would be a mistake. An engrossing passion might, indeed, have produced such an effect, but the pleasant excitement of his vanity, which he now mistook for love, rendered him only the more eager to seize, in the absence of his charmer, on all that might preserve the agreeable elation of his spirits.

And so it grew into a habit that, at night, when the ladies had retired, and the young men were left alone, instead of smoking their cigars together in the library, and then separating for their respective rooms, as had been their earlier custom, they repaired to the billiard room—one of the late additions to the house—and spent some time in "knocking about the balls," as Reardon expressed it—a process which somewhat depleted Charles Moray's purse, for Reardon very frankly acknowledged that play was no play to him without betting. The bets grew larger after some time; then Reardon grew delicate—"Moray must excuse him; the luck was so constantly in his favor, he could not consent to be winning his money in this way, yet to play without betting—he would as soon pitch quoits, play marbles, or any other boyish game."

Of course, Charles Moray, the new possessor of fortune, made light of his losses, and would not be so niggardly as to grudge a few hundreds a night for his own amusement and his friend's. Then the luck changed somewhat. Charles Moray won about one game in five—sometimes about one in three; he grew exultant, acknowledged he had begun to weary of being beaten all the time, but now that they played on *equal* terms, it was another affair. It was, indeed, another affair; the bets were doubled, quadrupled, in amount—the hundreds became thousands—but "what of that?" Charles Moray said to himself; "he would soon win them back."

But, somehow, in spite of all his success, he found, at the end of the week, that the account stood largely—more largely than he liked to think—against him. Then the wine and even stronger drinks began to show themselves at the board, and Charles Moray, when he grew heated with them, would play wildly and grow quarrelsome, if Reardon attempted in any way to restrain him. He lost his gay, *debonnaire* manner, grew moody with all but Miss Cullen, to whom he became more impassioned and less gracefully sentimental. She regarded these changes but as proofs of her power, and played off upon him the full battery of her coquettish airs. Mrs. Moray was provoked with her son's infatuation—of his play she knew nothing. She remonstrated with him, and the result was a coolness, which put the last seal on her unhappiness, for amidst all the worldliness and selfishness and cold inhumanity of this woman, she had still one green oasis in the barren desert of her heart—she loved her son. And at every new disappointment, every new pang, there was a voice within her which told her that the pain was punishment; and the present sorrow oppressed her not so much by its own weight as because it cast on her the cold, formless shadow of a deeper woe.

In the mean time, a change of a very different character was passing over the life of Augusta Moray. Very gently and patiently did Mr. Mortimer lead her half-reluctant steps toward the fountain of living waters at which her thirsting heart might drink and thirst no more forever. She had had sufficient religious instruction, but little religious influence in her life. This the Christian pastor, waiting with a serene spirit his dismissal from the ministries of earth to the enjoyments of heaven, was admirably fitted to supply. In the light of his life, so full of tender care and active labor for others, Augusta grew dissatisfied with her own. It was the dawning of a new life—the true life—within her. Feeble might be the germ, yet it lived, and would live, and attract all the powers of her nature into its own perfect development. Henceforth her voluntary life would be not for herself, but for Him who had redeemed her by that which was not only more precious than silver or gold, but more precious than all she had valued or coveted in the past. Already was there a stirring of this new life within her on that peaceful Sabbath evening, when she had asked of Mr. Mortimer, "What shall I do now, dear sir?—with whom shall I sympathize now?" The whole strength of her old nature had risen up against his answer that Mrs. Charles Moray seemed just then the person who of all within her reach most needed sympathy and help. In the spirit of the great captain of old, who had been prepared to do some great thing at the prophet's command, but whose pride revolted from the simple act of bathing in the Jordan, she thought that she would readily have made herself a servant of servants, devoting herself to the ignorant and sometimes disgustingly filthy negroes around her, who, she had heard Mr. Mortimer lament, sometimes needed more kindly and intelligent care than they found in illness. There would have been something of heroism in such ministrations to her peculiar delicacy of constitution—it would have been a sacrifice worthy of the altar on which it was to be laid. Oh! how little do we know ourselves! Here was the old pride showing itself under the very mask of humility, and many weeks was it before she detected the counterfeit, and accepting Mr. Mortimer's test, came to him with an ingenuous blush, and asked if he would go with her to see Mrs. Moray. They went, but the time had passed when Mrs. Moray believed that Augusta could do her service—the infatuation of Charles was beyond her help—and she received her coldly.

It was now the last of May. All the visitors except Harry Reardon and Mrs. and Miss Cullen were gone, driven north by the hot breath of the coming summer. On Charles Moray the coil of that which men call fate, but which superior intelligences see to be the serpent we have nourished in our own bosoms, was fastening with a deadly grasp. Pleasure had been the object of his pursuit; never had he resisted its siren voice, and now it was luring him rapidly down to ruin, and he knew it, yet could not resist its fatal attractions. There were times when something almost like fear crept along his veins, as he looked at Harry Reardon sending the ball with cool precision to its destined spot—times when the coquettish glance of Miss Cullen changed suddenly to one of mocking malice from which he shrank; but he quelled the creeping fear and silenced the misgiving with courage won from the wine cup.

Why linger on the tale—the end must come. Charles Morny reeled to his bed one night with confused noises ringing in his ears, which even in their confusion shaped themselves to the terrible words, "I am a ruined man."

Throwing himself on his bed dressed as he was, he slept heavily and awoke late. No noises now, but a silence which seemed like the silence of death. Was it not death, seeing there was nothing more for him to hope, or fear, or do? Suddenly he remembered Miss Cullen. There was something then for him to do. She must know that he was now a poor man; if she still loved him—why did his heart sink lower rather than bound at the thought? Why? Because the shock of a great misfortune shivers every false sentiment and silences passion, while it only brings out in added strength the true and simple affections of our nature.

Still, pleasant or unpleasant, he must see Miss Cullen; he had gone too far to leave her without explanation—he must give her the choice to accept or reject him; though, should she do the first, Heaven only know what he should do with such a wife.

As these thoughts passed through his mind, he made his toilet rapidly, and refreshed by his morning bath and by the very act of dressing, he sallied from his room, with less of despair at his heart or in his face. He was going to the breakfast table, but as he approached the room, he heard his mother's voice, and with a pang like the swift stroke of an arrow through his heart, he turned aside to the library, determining, under the plea of letters to write, to order his coffee to be brought to him there. He was still in slippers, which fell noiselessly on the carpeted floor; the door of the library was closed, but not latched—he threw it open, and stood for a moment bewildered by the sight before him. There stood Harry Reardon, his face glowing as he bent it above another face, all flushed and quivering—the face of

Elise Cullen—yet looking as Charles Moray had never seen it look—all coquetry and selfish scheming displaced for once by a genuine, though it might be, a light and shortlived emotion.

"How could I know you cared for me?" in the tremulous tone through which we seem to hear the heart's throbs; and "You never would have known it, if I had remained the poor devil I was some weeks ago," in the man's steadier voice, was all that Charles Moray heard. Without even waiting to close the door he had opened, he turned, and went, as noiselessly as he had come, back to his room.

Once there, he threw himself into a chair amidst a whirl of thought over which he had no mastery. His first word, spoken after many minutes' silence, was the exclamation, "Fool! fool! the sport of an artful woman. Well, at least I am quit of that perplexity."

He started from his seat as if there was relief in the thought. Then, as the scene he had glanced at flashed vividly up before him, his color rose, his brows knit, and "Rascal!" escaped through his shut teeth. "And yet I do believe she loves him—poor thing!"

The pitying epithet proved that, however his self-esteem had been wounded, his heart had not been touched; we forgive not so readily the wounds struck there. Thought had no softening influence on his feelings to Harry Reardon. Rather did it bring out darker shades in his conduct, and he began to suspect more than he saw. And St. Mary's, the treasured inheritance of Mr. Moray, for whose transmission to one of his own name he had so schemed,—the inheritance which Augusta had once believed her own, was to be this man's—and through him. The thought was maddening. And it was a *debt of honor*—not to be examined into—not to be postponed—and his mother! He started with a new pang at thought of the disclosure to be made to her. There was a knock at his door. It was from a bright-faced young negro lad, whom he had promoted to the post of his personal attendant. He came to ask if his master would have his breakfast brought to him.

"Where are the ladies?" asked Charles Moray.

"The young un is a ridin', sir, wid Mister Reardon—I year de ole ladies a talkin' purty loud in de library."

"Purty loud," with a certain wink of Sambo's eyes, meant quarrelling.

"Can my mother suspect anything?" thought Charles Moray, as the blood flushed to his brow. He felt it was impossible in his present condition to bear her reproaches, and before he had swallowed the coffee brought him by Sambo, he had made his determination—he would leave his home—his no longer—that very day—that very hour—he would write to his mother what he dared not say, and it would depend on how she bore the intelligence whether he ever saw her face again. The resolution was no sooner formed than he prepared for its execution.

"Sambo, tell Carolina and Will and July and Scipio, that I want them to get the boat ready as quickly as possible: I shall be at the boat house in twenty minutes; and, sirrah, if you tell any one I am going, I'll cut your ears off; do you hear?"

"Yes, massa, I year," and with a grin, which seemed to say that he had little faith in the execution of the threat, Sambo darted away.

To throw into a carpet bag and portmanteau as much of the contents of his bureau as they would hold, was Charles Moray's first work when he was left alone. The next was to write to his mother. Had he had time to think about this, it would have seemed impossible; but ten minutes of the twenty were already gone, there was no time for artful glosses, and he wrote:

DEAR MOTHER:

I am going away, because I cannot bear to see you after telling you that St. Mary's is no longer mine—it belongs now to Mr. Reardon, who will, I dare say, purchase whatever belongs to you in the house, and accommodate you in any other way he can—I am sure I have little reason to regret its loss; it was helping me to the devil as fast as I could go. I would give my right hand that it had been left to Hugh or Augusta. I am going to Hugh now for advice. Direct to his care, if you write; but if you cannot write without reproaches, better not write at all—it would not take much now to make me send a bullet through my brain.

Your worthless son,
CHARLES MORAY.

This was not all—another note was yet to be written; it was to this effect:

To MR. REARDON.

SIR: I am compelled to leave St. Mary's in haste, and consequently without seeing you. You shall hear from me in New York, and will find me ready to take the steps necessary to give you legal control of the property of which you may consider yourself now in actual possession.

Your obedient servant,
C. MORAY.

More than his twenty minutes were already gone. His room was in a wing of the house and on the ground floor. Beckoning to Sambo, whom he saw just returning from the errand on which he had sent him, he handed out the portmanteau and bag, saying, "To the boat; and half a dollar if nobody sees you."

A grin and a nod were the only answer as Sambo caught them and set off on his secret expedition, evidently considering the reward as already his. Charles Moray lingered a moment to look around him; then, putting the notes in his pocket, passed from the room and the house which he was never more to enter as his. Hurrying to the boat, he found Sambo awaiting him there, expectant of his reward. He was made perfectly happy for the rest of the day by the reception of a bright, silver half dollar, with a charge that he should go to the plantation and so be out of the way of any questions respecting his master till the boat should return in the evening.

The lingering summer's sun was nearing the horizon, when Mr. Reardon, who could not but feel some anxiety respecting Charles Moray's unexplained absence, found himself at the landing place watching the slow approach of the boat propelled against the wind by the wearied rowers.

"He is not there!" he exclaimed to Miss Cullen, who stood beside him; then, with a light laugh, "Surely, he can't mean to repudiate."

"Never," cried Miss Cullen, with emphasis; "he has no brain, poor fellow; but he would not do anything so dishonorable."

Mr. Reardon shrugged his shoulders—he had not much faith in honor when opposed by interest.

The boat touched the wharf.

"Where did you leave your master?" he asked, stepping toward the men, who touched their hats to him, as he approached.

They named the little town on the mainland, at which persons, going from St. Mary's to Savannah, were accustomed to land, and where they could procure conveyances.

"Has he gone to Savannah?" asked Mr. Reardon, with a darkening brow.

"I b'lieve so, sir; I seed the carriage a drivin' that road; but may be, sir, he's telled you," and the speaker, Carolina, a more than ordinarily intelligent negro, handed Mr. Reardon the two notes with which Charles Moray had intrusted him. Mr. Reardon opened his own, glanced over it, and turned, with a quick step and a smiling face, to Miss Cullen.

"Read that," he said, as he drew near, holding the note out to her. "Your mother must be satisfied with that, I think."

"Perfectly," was the reply, as the note was returned. "With that in your hand, you may make your own terms with her."

"And with *you?*"

"You did not need it with me," was the murmured reply, as the brilliant, yet somewhat hard face, softened as it did to no one else.

"Then you will be mine at once—this very evening; why not?" he asked, as she exclaimed quickly, "No, no!"

"To-morrow, then—stay, listen, before you decide;— here, in this lovely spot, we may remain in peace for a few weeks—'the world forgetting, by the world forgot'—but only for a few weeks; then I must plunge into business; I must obtain legal possession from Charles Moray, preparatory to selling the property—"

"Selling!" cried the lady, faintly; she did not like that —the *éclat* of a great landed property pleased her.

"Yes, you did not think of my keeping it and living here out of the world, did you? It will be, in some of its aspects, an unpleasant business. I shall certainly have to fight my way figuratively, and it may be really, to the end. You see I am perfectly candid with you; candid, because you are mine—are you not? Stop, not a step further till you answer;" he glanced around—they were alone, far from the sight or hearing of others. "Now lift your eyes to mine;" he had faced round upon her, holding both her hands; the eyes, on which his were fastened, were slowly lifted as by magnetic force; he gazed, for a moment, into them with a bold, smiling face; then, shaking his head, said, "No, it is no use for you to promise; I should never trust those wicked eyes—I must seize my prize here, before there is a chance of its being borne away by others."

"Impossible," said Miss Cullen, rousing herself to resist what she felt was an unreasonable demand, "even if I could consent, my mother—"

"Will readily forgive you when the act is done; though she may not be willing beforehand to sin against her silly conventionalisms; but listen to me, Elise, if we are not married before we leave this island, we never shall be; even should you remain true to me, your mother will not risk unpopularity—such as I shall probably encounter before this business is concluded; besides, she will fear for the end— she does not know that I never withdrew a step in my life and never will;" his face grew like iron in its hardness; "she will force you away; I am not one to be played with thus— so be mine now, if it may not be to-morrow—within this week, or we both move from this spot free as we were yester eve—speak, Elise; but remember, your words can never be recalled—I am not Charles Moray."

The name of his victim was spoken with infinite contempt; and, strange to tell, this girl, whom a gentler, a tenderer, and a more delicate love would have failed to win, was subdued by his audacity. He had dropped her hand at the last words, and drawn a little apart from her. She approached and said, softly, "I will do as you wish."

"That is right," he said, with a smile; "I will trust your lips," pressing his own to them, as he spoke, "though not your eyes. Now listen! With this note in my hand I will seek your mother and ask her consent to our engagement; that won, I may sound her on the question of immediate marriage; if she disapprove, I shall express a desire

17

to be absent when Mrs. Moray becomes aware that St. Mary's is no longer her son's, and propose that you shall accompany me on a boating excursion. I know where I can find both license and clergyman; and once off from mamma, I promise you, she shall not see you again till you are more mine than hers. What do you say? Is it well planned?"

She looked up with an embarrassed smile, for she could not but be conscious that there was little respect for her dignity or delicacy either in the plan, or the bold manner of its announcement. It was not thus that she had dreamed of being loved; yet here were the very qualities which had excited her preference for Mr. Reardon. He was only proving that she was right when she said months ago that he was afraid of nothing.

"You do not answer," he said, as she turned away again without speaking.

"Did you not have a note for Mrs. Moray? May not that tell her all?"

"You are right—it may," he answered, taking the note from his pocket, and examining the hastily written address, as if he had expected to find the contents there. "She shall not have it till we are gone to-morrow morning," he added, decidedly; "she will sleep the better to-night, and I shall avoid a scene, which, of all things, I hate."

Mrs. Moray was not very much surprised, though greatly mortified and vexed, when told by Mr. Reardon that he had a note from her son, who had been unexpectedly called to Savannah. The "unexpected call" did not disturb her; it was the thought "A stranger knows more of his movements than I do." Never had she been less in a condition to bear any sudden shock. Her correspondence with Mr. Saville had, of late, inspired her with such dread of his encroachments, that she had almost decided to pass the summer at St. Mary's, solitary as it would be, after the departure of her guests, rather than go North, where she could scarcely hope to avoid meeting him. To this source of nervous anxiety had been added of late the pain of estrangement from her son, and the irritation against Mrs. Cullen and Elise, excited by the belief that the latter was making a decided and successful attack upon the heart of her son. She would have been little pleased to yield her power as mistress of the mansion to any one; but Elise Cullen's sharp tongue had made her and, for her sake, her mother, peculiarly disagreeable to her. One of the terrible penalties of crime is, that it shuts up the soul of its victim in a kind of solitary imprisonment, forbidding it to seek the sympathy of others, secluding it from communion with all who have not drunk of the same unblessed cup. From the hour when Adam hid himself among the trees of the garden, the guilty soul seeks concealment, and the annoyances, which would shrink into scarce visible motes, if brought out to the light of day and sunned in the smiles of a friend, grow to portentous size in the twilight chambers of a heart which is thus shut and barred. Mrs. Moray had lost much of the graceful gayety which made her formerly a general favorite. A forced levity alternated with sullen reserve in her countenance and manner. For a few days past her depression had been increased by languor, which she attributed to the unusual heat, and which, when she forced herself to exertion, was succeeded by feverish irritation. She looked ill this evening, and no one felt surprised when, with a slight apology to the ladies, she withdrew to her own apartment. After her departure, Mr. Reardon became evidently *distrait*, and after answering several times at random, and with what seemed strange maladroitness, Mrs. Cullen's attempts at conversation, he roused himself, crossed the room, and seated himself on the sofa beside her, as Elise, at a glance from him, rose and left the room.

"Really, this place is getting to be very tiresome," said Mrs. Cullen, with scarcely concealed ill humor, as her quick eye detected the glance, "I shall certainly leave it the next week."

"I hope not; I hope to persuade you to remain till the middle or last of June—"

"Impossible!" interrupted Mrs. Cullen, with warmth.

"Do not say so till you hear my reasons; but, first, will you oblige me by reading this note?"

He placed the open note of Charles Moray before her. Mrs. Cullen glanced hastily over it, then read it with more deliberation. Harry Reardon, in the mean time, read her face as clearly, and a sarcastic smile curled his lip as he marked its gradual softening and the glow with which she turned toward him.

"Why, Mr. Reardon! you are indeed a fortunate man—the possessor of St. Mary's—why, it is the finest plantation in Georgia, I hear, and three hundred negroes—are there not? I congratulate you on being able to make such a purchase."

Mr. Reardon smiled. He believed that Mrs. Cullen knew as well as he did, that the acquisition had not been a purchase; but of this it was not his place to speak.

"Thank you!" he said. "You can put the crown upon my fortune, Mrs. Cullen. Give me Elise—she has promised, with your sanction, to be mine—to become the mistress of St. Mary's."

"Dear child! Ah, Mr. Reardon! I always knew she preferred you to any other, though I did all I could to discourage it—because I thought you, with all your charming qualities, a wicked creature,—not in the least a marrying man."

"Now, then, that you see how mistaken you were, you will give us your consent."

"Certainly; nothing could please me better—here is my hand upon it."

He received her hand in his, and pressed his lips to it; then, still retaining it, he said, "Grant me one more favor, and I am your debtor for life; let us be married immediately—we are neither of us so young as to make it necessary for us to wait to grow older."

"But, *immediately !* what would people say ? it would seem so strange."

"Not at all; we have been here, in the same house, the whole winter; the worst that will be said, will probably be, that we were engaged all winter and kept it secret till we were ready to marry."

He paused a moment; but she did not answer. She was considering whether there could be any mistake in that note, whether it was genuine; if she dared, she would have asked to examine it again.

"A moment's thought will show you that my plan is best for all. I suppose you would not think it proper for Elise to remain after Mrs. Moray leaves us, except as—"

There was a sudden change in the face into which Mr. Reardon was looking, and in a less deliberate, less hesitating manner, Mrs. Cullen exclaimed, "That is true; Mrs. Moray must go, I suppose. Does she know it ?"

"I think not—I have a letter for her from her son, which, I presume, will tell her of it. I kept it till the morning, lest it should spoil her rest."

"I should like to see her when she receives it; it will cost her something to lay aside the dignities she has worn so haughtily."

The lady little thought how much of the dignity of womanhood she was laying aside in this betrayal of the petty malice that can rejoice over the mortification of a rival. Even Mr. Reardon felt it, and shrugged his shoulders slightly, as he said, "*Chacun à son gout.* I should not like it; so I will leave you the note, and you shall have the enjoyment of the scene all to yourself, if you will only promise that when I come back with a license to-morrow evening, I shall find everything prepared to make me 'Benedict, the married man.' Come, you had better consent; it is the only way in which you can enjoy the pleasure of playing Lady of the Manor to Mrs. Moray."

"Well, I must see Elise first; I do not know what she will say."

"Send for her; I am sure she will say just what I do—stay, there is your maid in the piazza, I will give her the message."

"No, no; I will go to her," said Mrs. Cullen, doubting whether Elise would approve being thus brought down; but Mr. Reardon did not seem to hear her; and before she had ceased speaking, he was in the piazza, on the steps of which Mrs. Moray's maid and Mrs. Cullen's were seated together enjoying the evening breeze.

"Go to Miss Cullen's room," he said to the latter, "give Mr. Reardon's compliments to her, and say he asks her to step to the library—her mother wishes to speak with her."

The woman looked surprised, but did not hesitate to obey the order. She found Elise sitting in a window, through which the moon shed a flood of golden light. She had removed the combs from her hair, and it fell like a rich veil around her, sweeping the floor as she sat.

"I cannot go," she said, laying her hand on the shining tresses, as she heard the message, which was delivered word for word.

"Mr. Reardon spoke so positive-like—I am sure they expect you, ma'am; shall I put up your hair?"

The woman was scarcely prepared for the promptitude with which her usually self-willed young lady rose, and, gathering the abundant hair into loose, heavy folds, confined it with her comb and passed out from the room. When she entered the library, her cheeks glowed like carnations, and her eyes shone like twin stars. Mr. Reardon stepped forward to meet her, and led her directly under the chandelier.

"Did you ever see her so brilliant?" he asked, turning with a smile to Mrs. Cullen, and then letting his eyes rest on her again, with a bold admiration which could not have been tolerated by any woman but a coquette, in whom the pure and delicate instincts of her sex had lost their native sensitiveness.

"Elise," he continued, "your mother wishes to know whether you will consent to our marriage to-morrow. I have told her you would feel it was better than to be separated as we must otherwise be; but she wished to hear it from your own lips."

"Surely, my child, this is very hurried," said Mrs. Cullen, whose motherly heart was wounded for her daughter, she could scarcely tell why.

Elise hesitated; she raised her eyes to her mother, and her lips parted; she turned to Reardon, and they closed again.

"Speak, Elise," he said, as his brow darkened perceptibly, and he loosened the clasp in which he had held her hand; "tell your mother if you are willing to be mine."

"I am willing to be yours," she said, looking not at her mother, but at him.

"And to-morrow, Elise?"

"And to-morrow," she repeated.

"You will not now refuse us," he said to Mrs. Cullen,

with something of triumph in his tone, throwing his arm around Elise and drawing her close to him as he spoke.

"Oh, I never refuse Elise anything," was the answer.

"Then I will bid you good night, for I have something still to do before I sleep. Make your arrangements as early as you can to-morrow, Elise; I shall be off while it is yet night with you, and return as soon as possible with the license; suppose I leave a note for Mr. Mortimer, asking him to be here at noon?"

"Oh! the note for Mrs. Moray," cried Mrs. Cullen; "you must not forget that."

"Certainly not, here it is," handing it to her; "I think it would be most effective if it were received when Elise had the right to invite her to remain," he added, laughing lightly at what he called the feminine malice of Mrs. Cullen, as he withdrew from the room.

"Elise, he is a bold man," said Mrs. Cullen, doubtingly.

"I told you he was afraid of nothing," answered Elise, with a proud smile.

And so each saw the black spot in the soul of the other, yet shrank not from it.

One of the things that Mr. Reardon did before he slept that night, was to write the following letter, which he sent off by the mail of the next day. We insert it here, both as characteristic, and as giving the reader fuller insight into his motives of action.

St. Mary's Isle, *May 12th*, 18—.

My dear Peyton:

I wrote you, three weeks ago, begging you to sell the horse I left in your stables, and settle my hotel bill in Washington. I told you then that I had a special liking for the horse, and would not part with him, except to get rid of a teasing creditor, whom I must either satisfy or shoot.

This is to countermand that order if it be not too late, and to ask that you will see W——, and tell him that, as soon as I can go to Savannah, I will send him a draft for the amount of the debt. You will conclude I must have had a run of luck to talk of indulgence in such an unwonted luxury as drafts. A run of luck! Peyton, I am the luckiest dog alive. You were all envious last winter of the good fortune of Moray in stepping so unexpectedly into one of the finest fortunes in the country. Peyton, that fortune is mine! Don't start. I have not forged a will and poisoned him; I have departed from my principles, it is true, and played with my host, but the temptation was irresistible—no man who had blood in his veins could blame me. He is a good enough fellow, too, Charles Moray; I am really sorry for him, or rather I would be, if I could be sorry for anything to-night; but he ought to have known that he could not play with me; I knew it, and would not have made a stroke against him, if he had not made me half mad.

Do you remember that Elise Cullen, whose brilliant coquetries and sharp tongue made you all wild in Washington last winter? Think of Charles Moray wanting to marry her. She would have boxed his ears in a month. She is like a spirited young horse, that wants a strong will and a steady hand to guide him. I wish you could see how submissively she yields to my lightest touch—for she is mine, Peyton, mine, heart and soul—and to-morrow I shall be "Benedict, the married man," and even her mother cannot snatch her from my arms. Peyton, I told you I was the luckiest dog alive. But for the vantage ground of this fine estate I know Mrs. Cullen would never give me her daughter; and though Elise would have given herself at a word, that would hardly have suited me without her mother's sanction, as the old lady has all the fortune, and a very good fortune, too, I have learned lately. Charles Moray promises fair, and I believe will stick to his bargain, but he has gone off to New York, and that lawyer cousin of his may put some dishonorable notions in his head—there is always risk in such cases, since the law does not protect us; so I have obeyed both prudence and inclination in pushing on affairs here in a manner perfectly Napoleonic. After to-morrow I shall be sure of a tolerably comfortable living, if I should even lose St. Mary's, and with that living, my pretty, bright, spirited Elise, who, think what you will, is, just now, worth both the fortunes in my eyes. Pray do not imagine that any fortune would have made me marry her, if she had not interested me—piqued me. The passionate, self-willed thing, I can see, has been accustomed to rule her mother and every one around her; she has found her master now, and there is delight in mastery over such a will.

I am afraid I have said some foolish things here. I wanted you to know that I was safe as to the matter of fortune, and my head is so full of Elise to-night that she would mingle herself with all I had to say; good night. I shall stay here through June, perhaps through July; it is quite safe, they tell me, till August. Your friend,

H. REARDON.

CHAPTER XIV.

> "How would you be,
> If He which is the top of judgment, should
> But judge you as you are? Oh! think on that,
> And Mercy then will breathe within your lips,
> Like man new made."—SHAKSPEARE.

It was a pretty picture to see Mr. Mortimer and Augusta Moray seated at their early breakfast in the piazza, draped with flowering vines. The old man, with his flowing silvery locks, and his face, clad in kindly smiles, was as beautiful in his way as the graceful girl, whose dark, glossy tresses fell around a face wearing the rich hue of health and touched with a gentleness that was not its predominant expression in earlier life. Charity stood near, somewhat more full in person, but scarcely older in face, than when we first knew her, with large gold rings in her ears, and a white handkerchief, folded like a turban, round her head. Charity had concluded of late that "'twasn't 'spectable for any but young gals to wear them bright red an' yaller things," so her turbans were now all white. Mr. Mortimer, at the moment we choose to look in at them, is reading a note which Charity has just delivered to him.

"Well, well!" exclaimed the good old man, as he passed the note across the table to Augusta, "that does surprise me. I was quite sure when we saw them last that Miss

Cullen was engaged to your cousin Charles; did you not think so, my dear?"

"I am afraid you will think me very unkind if I give you the answer which was on my lip," said Augusta, after a moment's smiling hesitation.

"Then don't make it, my dear," said good Mr. Mortimer; "but tell me, instead, whether I shall say that you will comply with the lady's request and go with me to the wedding."

"I am afraid I should hardly be an acceptable guest in my deep mourning."

"But, Miss 'Gusty, aren't dare a white dress in de trunk Miss Moray send here for you?"

"I don't know, Charity, I have not opened it; she said it was filled with things I had left in Washington; I have no idea what they were."

"But I bin gone an' looked at dem, an' I seed the beautifullest dresses—"

"But I could not wear those now, Charity," said Augusta, shrinking from even seeing what was associated with her life of gayety in Washington; "if there were a simple, white morning dress among them, I might perhaps—"

"Well, jist give me the key, Miss 'Gusty, an' let me go see."

Charity got the keys and went off with a little consequential toss of the head to an examination which she had long desired to make, and Mr. Mortimer would have risen to reply to his note, but Augusta begged that he would permit her to write for him, which she did, promising for herself that she would come if possible.

In the mean time let us look in, at a somewhat later hour, at the breakfast table over which Mrs. Moray presides. Her duties are not very onerous this morning, for Mrs. Cullen is her only visible guest.

"Sambo, have you called Mr. Reardon to breakfast this morning?" she asks.

"Mr. Reardon done gone before daylight dis morning to the main," answered Sambo; "the main" being the usual mode of designation with the negroes for any place on the main land, whether town or country.

"I thought he would find it very tiresome here with none but ladies;" the observation was addressed to Mrs. Cullen, and Mrs. Moray added, as she handed her a cup of coffee, "I hope Elise is not altogether *désolée* for the same reason. It was cruel in Mr. Reardon to leave her."

"Not at all; Elise begs that you will excuse her this morning; she has so much to do before Mr. Reardon's return."

"Preparing, I suppose, to play off all her batteries upon him; tell her she must not be too overpowering; she must remember he is left here all alone to our mercy."

"It would be a waste of labor for her to get up any batteries for Mr. Reardon," said Mrs. Cullen, with a smile which Mrs. Moray did not quite understand.

"What? you despair of him? He does seem very insensible."

"Insensible! ha! ha! ha! You must excuse me, my dear, if I laugh a little at your blindness. Sambo, won't you bring me some hot water? or, stay, a glass of cold water, if you please, fresh from the well;" then, as Sambo darted from the room, pitcher in hand, she continued, "I only wanted to get rid of him, my dear, to tell you that Elise and Mr. Reardon are engaged, and that they will be married to-day, if he can get the license and return in time."

They looked at each other for a moment in silence, Mrs. Cullen nodding her head and smiling up in Mrs. Moray's face with a little air of triumph, and Mrs. Moray staring in blank amazement, which she vainly strove to hide; at length the words "Engaged to Mr. Reardon! To be married today!" fell from her lips; then, as the color suddenly flushed her face, seeming to recover herself, she added, "Excuse me, my dear Mrs. Cullen, if I am taking too great a liberty, but I do truly sympathize with you. Elise is still too young to throw herself away on one who could only be regarded as a *pis-aller*; my dear friend, you should not consent to it, even if she had been disappointed—"

"Disappointed, indeed!" cried Mrs. Cullen, with more violence of manner, though perhaps scarcely more bitterness of feeling, than Mrs. Moray's. "Disappointed! Mr. Reardon was always the first choice of Elise."

"Oh! indeed!" ejaculated Mrs. Moray, with a look and accent that made Mrs. Cullen long to box her ears.

"You may say oh! and indeed! as much as you like; I can tell you, I had to beg and entreat almost on my knees, to make Elise civil to your son when Mr. Reardon was by."

"You don't say so? What a good child she must be, that your wish should have made her so very, *very* civil to him."

"Not so civil but that he found it was of no use to try to cut Mr. Reardon out."

"My son try to cut Mr. Reardon out! Pardon me, my dear Mrs. Cullen, but the idea is so ridiculous that I cannot, for my life, help laughing; he! he! ho!"

Mrs. Moray lay back in her chair, and gave herself up apparently to the mirth-provoking thought, though it must be acknowledged that her laugh was a little hysterical.

Mrs. Cullen rose from her seat; at that moment she could hear nothing except the cry for revenge that sounded within her. The melodramatic scene she had arranged in her thoughts as the fitting conclusion to the marriage of her daughter, in which Elise should assume the position of the urbane and sympathizing hostess, and Mrs. Moray should be compelled to bow her haughty spirit in presence of those before whom she had so ostentatiously paraded her honors—all this faded from her mind in the burning desire to crush her there, even as she sat, with the mocking laugh upon her lip, and she believed she held that which would stab with deadlier result than sword or dagger. Her hand fumbled nervously in her pocket, scarcely able to draw out quickly enough the little instrument of her anger.

"There's a note that Mr. Reardon gave me for you; it came to him yesterday, but he hated to give it to you. It may convince you he is not such a very bad ——, Mrs. Moray!—Mrs. Moray!" in a loud, startled voice; "mercy on me! is the woman going to die, and Elise to be married and all!—here, take a swallow of this water." Sambo had just returned from the well, and stood gazing with stupid wonderment at the scene.

"What do you mean by standing there like an idiot?" cried Mrs. Cullen, glad of some one on whom to vent her dissatisfaction. "Go and call some one here, can't you? Call Miss Cullen, quick."

Meanwhile Mrs. Moray lay back in her chair, pallid and seemingly unconscious. One deep groan had been her only sign of life since reading the terrible note.

"Elise, what shall we do?" cried Mrs. Cullen, in a terrified voice, as her daughter entered; "I gave her the note, and she has been so ever since; you don't think she's dead?" the last word spoken in an awed whisper, with the feeling that if this were so, then was she a murderer before the bar of conscience and of God, whatever human tribunals might pronounce her.

"Oh no! she has only fainted," cried Elise Cullen; "throw some water in her face," suiting the action to the word, before Mrs. Cullen, who knew the danger of so violent a remedy, could check her. Drawing her breath with a quick, oud gasp, Mrs. Moray passed her hand in a bewildered way over her wet face, then sat up erect and looked around her, as if waking from a dream. Her eyes fell on the two ladies, then on the note, still held with a convulsive clutch.

"Don't be so distressed, Mrs. Moray," said Mrs. Cullen, in whose shallow soul the tempest of anger was already subsiding. Her voice seemed to call back the past in all its vividness to Mrs. Moray, the blood rushed to her pale face, she rose, and though at first compelled to grasp her chair for support, soon stood erect, and with the graceful courtesy for which she had been celebrated in former days, thanked them for their kindness, and regretted having given them so much trouble, then added, "Elise, your mother says I am to congratulate you on your approaching marriage; you have my best wishes, my dear, if, indeed, you are determined to marry Mr. Reardon; but, first, take my solemn assurance that Mr. Reardon is not, and never can be, the possessor of St. Mary's."

There was a depth in her voice and a gleam in her eye which none had ever heard or seen before. Mrs. Cullen was a little shaken; she looked toward Elise, whose own eyes fired, and whose voice trembled with suppressed passion, as she said, "Gentlemen understand these things better than we do, Mrs. Moray; I am quite willing to trust your son and Mr. Reardon."

"You shall not do it without warning; they know nothing about it; but I "—with great emphasis on the pronoun, which was twice repeated—"I tell you that Mr. Reardon can never make you mistress of St. Mary's, and whoever tells you he can, is deceiving you."

Elise saw that these repeated and emphatic asseverations were producing an influence on her mother's mind, and she determined to end them. With a haughtily repellant gesture, and a vain attempt at calmness, while her whole frame was quivering with intense irritation, she answered, "You must excuse me, Mrs. Moray, I have really no time to listen to such ravings; it is natural enough that you should be unwilling to admit the idea that this beautiful place is no longer yours."

"And you—you fancy it belongs to you!" cried Mrs. Moray, losing all her self-control, and speaking again in a tone of great excitement.

As she became demonstrative, Miss Cullen regained her quietude of manner and tone, so that it was with a firmer voice that she said, "Not mine yet, Mrs. Moray, but Mr. Reardon's, and mine when I become his wife; I know that I speak his wish when I say that it will give us both pleasure to have you remain as our guest as long as it may suit you."

"Your guest, insolent girl! never!" exclaimed Mrs. Moray, almost wild with rage at this attempt to push her from her seat of power; "I will make sure of that before another hour shall pass."

"Come, mamma, I really cannot stop here all day; and now that Mrs. Moray has got over her hysterics, I suppose you can come and help me," and with an air of studied nonchalance she drew her mother off, pausing, as they drew near a window, to make some trifling observation on a passing object.

Had they paused to mark the glance of concentrated hate, to hear the low laugh that followed them, even the daring spirit of Elise Cullen might have been quelled; but they hastened away, Mrs. Cullen glad to escape from the unequal war, and Elise triumphant in her success, bursting, ere she reached her room, into a gay, joyous carol, whose trills reached Mrs. Moray, even in her own room, to which she had hastened, preserving the intensity of her feelings, and giving stability to her purposes.

"She shall never stand in this house as its mistress, if I have to put everything at jeopardy, if I have even to lay my dead body across her path to bar her entrance; but there is no danger."

Even while this soliloquy was passing in her mind, Mrs. Moray had drawn her desk toward her, and prepared to write. More than once, when goaded almost to madness by Saville, she had contemplated a letter to Hugh—not a letter of confession, for hers was not a penitent spirit, seeking to make atonement, and ready to accept humiliation and grief as the just punishment of conscious crime. It was only that what she was no longer able to enjoy herself, she would fling back into the hands of those to whom it rightfully belonged, and this not from a sense of justice, but to snatch it from more hated possessors, and to punish one whom she had thought her tool, and found to be her tyrant. The *tact*—such was the name she gave it—which she had cultivated so carefully and invoked so often, did not desert her even in this hour of passionate emotion; there was a whirlwind within her, but her pen moved steadily and rapidly over the page and her expressions were clear and decided.

DEAR HUGH:

I have long *known* what I am going to communicate; mark, I say *known*, not suspected. How I learned it, it would be futile to ask; there are secrets in every life—this is mine. Why I have not revealed it before I will frankly tell you: to have done so would have been to strip my own child, the dearest thing to me on earth, of wealth which his luxurious habits made more needful to him than to you, or even to Augusta. You will tell me this was no reason for hesitation; perhaps not to your cold nature—to me it was enough. I should have been silent still, but the property is passing from Charles to those I hate, and now I tell you that it never belonged to Charles—that Mr. Hugh Moray's will—the only will which he intended to take effect, is in the possession of Saville. He has not destroyed it—he will not destroy it—for he thinks it an engine by which he may still wring wealth from my unwilling hands. So much does he value it that he carries it always on his person, and is always armed for its defence. Courage and caution—you will need both to win the prize; but the prize is St. Mary's Isle and wealth for Augusta. I trust all that is dear to me in your hands. ANNE MORAY.

"He will think I mean my honor, my reputation; he does not know that at this moment revenge on these harpies is dearer than all else," said Mrs. Moray to herself, as she glanced over her letter before folding and sealing it.

In less than an hour after leaving the breakfast room, this letter had been written and sent by a negro in a canoe, who promised that it should be at the post town on the mainland before the closing of the evening mail.

"And now I may be at ease—now I may rest," said Mrs. Moray, throwing herself, as she spoke, upon her couch; but she found rest impossible—there was a fever in her blood, her pulses throbbed, her eyes flashed, she walked rapidly about her room, exciting herself still farther by going over and over again the scenes of the morning, and painting the disappointment which the successful execution of her project would inflict on those whom she called her "enemies."

"I am glad they are to be married," she exclaimed, suddenly. "How silly I was to say anything that might throw an obstacle in their way! Let me see—ten days, a fortnight, perhaps,—Hugh will be prompt, I know;—their honeymoon will not be long. That old fool will just be queening it to the height, when down she will go, and find her Elise, who has been flung at the head of every single man of fortune they have met for the last two years, the wife of a dishonored gamester, whom 'she preferred to Charles Moray,'" mimicking the tones of Mrs. Cullen in the last words. As she did so, a sudden flash of pain made her press her hand to her head and sink back again upon her couch; but only for a minute, when she was again upon her feet, saying, hurriedly, "I must go to them; I would not have the marriage delayed on any account, and what I said may have frightened the mother. I'll tell her—I'll tell her,—oh! what *shall* I tell her?" pressing her hand again upon her head, with a bewildered look; then suddenly brightening again, she walked with a quick and somewhat unsteady step to the door of the room occupied by the mother and daughter. Her knock was answered by Elise opening the door herself. Her surprise at seeing Mrs. Moray was speechless; but it was merged in satisfaction as her visitor, entering, said, "My dear Elise, I begin to suspect that I must have treated you very badly this morning. Charlie's note shocked me so much, that I really do not know what I said; and, after all, I begin to think I may not have understood it; at any rate, I will not think of anything unpleasant to-day—your wedding day—let St. Mary's belong to whom it will, it shall look gayly to-day. Shall I arrange the library for your chapel, and give you Charles's rooms in the west wing?"

"Thank you, Mrs. Moray! thank you! that will do nicely, I think," said Elise Cullen, shamed into a return to at least the conventional forms of politeness, by this elaborate show of kindness, which had the further effect of at once hushing all her mother's doubts.

Mrs. Moray next despatched a message to Augusta, so

urgently demanding her help, that she came to her at once, and aided her with both head and hands, in giving something of a festal air to the library and the rooms she had devoted to Elise. More than once in their work, Augusta advised Mrs. Morny to rest, as she accidentally touched her fevered hand, or saw her burning cheeks; but every such suggestion was answered impatiently, almost angrily; and at length she forbore, though saying to Mr. Mortimer, when he arrived, that she feared Mrs. Moray was ill, or would be soon.

"I do not understand her at all," she added; "she says she is glad of this marriage; and yet I think she is very unhappy about something."

"Her son's absence, perhaps," suggested Mr. Mortimer.

"It may be; though she assures me she would not have him here for the world."

They were interrupted by Mrs. Moray herself.

"My dear Augusta, not dressed yet! Charity has your pretty morning dress ready for you in my dressing room; pray, be quick. Mr. Reardon has come, you know,—we must not keep them waiting."

At two o'clock the little company were assembled in the library; Mr. Reardon looking triumphant and joyous— Elise Cullen a little frightened, yet not the less attractive for that in the flowing silk with its lace draperies and the white orange wreath, which the taste and skill of her maid had arranged for her, and Mrs. Cullen dignified and a little sullen, for she had not quite forgotten the scene of the morning. Old memories and tender thoughts were giving a quicker movement to Augusta's pulses as she stood there in her simple white dress, seeming, as Mr. Mortimer fondly fancied, like something sacred with her face always so beautiful, and now so serene and gentle. We have said that Mr. Reardon looked triumphant—scarcely less marked was the triumph in Mrs. Moray's smile as she watched them with unwavering eyes during the ceremony, which bound them together through all the good and ill of their earthly course. As the prayer by which Mr. Mortimer sought to consecrate their union closed, she stepped forward with the hurried manner of one who had restrained herself to the last possible moment; "I wish you joy," she said, with a courtesy, to Mr. Reardon, seeming entirely to ignore Elise, "I wish you joy of your *good fortune*, Lord of the Isle—"

"Not so," said Mr. Reardon, reddening, yet bowing politely, "while Mrs. Moray is still here to play the part of its Lady."

"To play the part! How witty you are! ha! ha! ha! —play the part! that is just it. We are all players, Mr. Mortimer; and so you have been at a theatre; fie! fie on you, Mr. Mortimer."

She stood addressing Mr. Mortimer and Augusta, who had drawn near her, while Mrs. Cullen and the new married pair had moved a little aside, and were watching her movements with puzzled looks. There was an unnatural excitement in her looks and tones, for which they could not account; but, to Mr. Mortimer's more practised eyes, the cause was plain—she was in the height of an access of fever.

And so life and death were brought near together, and looked, as it were, into each other's eyes. Over in the west wing life revelled in young veins, and throbbed in young hearts, saying, with each throb, "To-day is ours—we live and love;"—in the east wing restless tossings, burning heat and parching thirst, with the incoherent mutterings of a delirious fancy, seemed to mark the approach of life's great enemy. For many days, for weeks, indeed, physicians from the mainland came and went, and Mr. Mortimer hovered around that east wing, less in sympathy with the stricken and deserted mother than with her who never left the fevered couch, except to speak to him. All the color had faded again from Augusta's face, and much of the brightness from her eyes; her movements were languid, her tones spiritless; yet she would not listen for a moment to Mr. Mortimer's entreaties that she should leave Mrs. Moray to the care of Charity and her own maid, long enough at least for rest.

The forgiveness which had seemed so difficult, so impossible to Augusta, was easy now. That helpless form, that face so death-like in its pallor, preached peace more persuasively than even Mr. Mortimer could do. It was herself that Augusta now found it hard to forgive. The keener pangs of contrition were felt through the gentle stirrings of pity, as she remembered how repellant had been her manner, how hard and unrelenting her heart, to that scarce breathing clay. For forty-eight hours, the muttered ravings of delirium had sunk into feebleness, which seemed the precursor of death. The physicians spoke of no hope, but that which leaves us only with the heart's last throb. The night was waning toward those chill, dreary hours, the most trying to the watcher, though they are the immediate precursors of dawn. Charity, who shared the vigils of Augusta on this night, had fallen asleep in a large rocking chair. Augusta bent over the sick-couch to moisten the parched lips, and almost suffered the cup to fall from her hands, as they unclosed, and in a voice which was scarcely more than a sigh, breathed forth, "Who is it?"

"Augusta Moray," she said, almost as softly, feeling in her self-condemnation that the name could give no pleasure. It seemed indeed that her apprehension was correct, for with a sigh the sufferer's lips closed, and her heavy lids drooped over her dim eyes. Half an hour passed away with no sound breaking the death-like stillness save the ticking of a watch, which was painfully audible to Augusta's excited nerves; and again, in pursuance of the physician's directions, Augusta held the cooling draught to the lips of her charge. Again the eyes unclosed and fastened themselves upon her with a strange intensity.

"Can I do anything for you?" she asked, in reply to the wistful look.

"Forgive me," was faintly whispered in return.

"Dear Mrs. Moray, forgive *me*—my pride, my coldness, my ingratitude," and Augusta clasped the thin hand that lay on the coverlet with a caressing touch, such as she never had given it, from the hour that her new-found relatives first trod the soil of St. Mary's to the present; then added, "But we must not talk of what would agitate you."

"I must talk—you do not know—all—Hugh's letter, you remember,—A. M. was Anna Melville—he loved you then—always—the draft he sent—there was a note—I took it—" and from the failing eyes there came an intenser gaze, which seemed to say, "Can you forgive me now?" And Augusta was surprised to feel how easy it was at this solemn hour to forgive even these wrongs—the deepest she had known or could know.

"Do not distress yourself needlessly," she said. "All is forgiven, and shall be, from this hour, forgotten."

"You do not know all yet—St. Mary's—" she closed her eyes and groaned.

"Pray, do not distress yourself, you cannot bear it," said Augusta, soothingly.

"I must—you must know—I wrote to Hugh, I believe—Saville has the will—St. Mary's belongs to—"

"Say nothing more about it, I entreat you; you will exhaust yourself."

"And you forgive me?"

"Fully, freely, as I hope that God will forgive me."

"God!" what an expression of awe there was in the whispered name, "will He forgive me?"

"He never refuses those who ask to be forgiven."

"Ask—I cannot—will you—pray—pray," and the feeble hand closed with all its little strength upon that which held it, and the eyes hung as if for life upon the face that bent above them.

Augusta thought herself in the presence of death—a presence so intensely real, that all which is factitious falls before it and leaves our naked spirits in contact with the truth. It was nothing to her at that moment that the language of prayer was unfamiliar to her lips, that she had only lately learned to pray for herself. She thought only of the passing spirit, the dread eternity it was approaching, the mercy which it craved, and sinking on her knees, in broken sentences, whose low but earnest utterance sounded like the importunate crying of one who pleaded for more than life, she asked pardon and peace for both; and with a tenderness, which seemed new-born in her spirit, she commended the feeble, helpless sufferer to the compassionate love of the Divine Redeemer. When her voice had sunk into silence, she still knelt, and her thoughts still rose in those short ejaculations which are the most frequent language of strong emotion.

"She sleeps," a voice at length whispered in her ear, and she started to see Mr. Mortimer beside her. "You had better sit there," pointing to an easy lounging chair and assisting her to rise, "I will watch your patient."

"When did you come?" said Augusta, softly, as she obeyed him, and resting her weary head upon the chair, suffered him to wrap her in a large shawl.

"I have been here half an hour," then, as if overpowered by all he had heard and seen, with a half sob in his voice, he added, "God bless you, my child, and grant you all your desires!"

All her desires! Had she not already received them? What could she ask more? As she lay there, too weary even for connected, voluntary thought, there floated before her passive mind an image of manly truth and unblemished honor, of "high thought seated in a heart of courtesy," in whose reflected beauty the world grew beautiful, in whose clear light every shade of misanthropy, of distrust, of scorn faded from her own soul, which,

> "Like the stained web i' the sun
> Grew pure by being purely shone upon."

If she did not fall down in worship before this image, it was because she had become conscious of a higher beauty, a more perfect purity, and we worship only that which is our highest and our best. After a while she slept the light sleep which care permits a watcher, but the same thoughts so inwove themselves with her dreams, that she did not seem to herself to have been asleep when Mr. Mortimer bent over, and whispered her name. Starting, she opened her eyes, and found the sunlight entering the room through the half-closed shutters. Her looks turned instantly toward the bed.

"She sleeps still," said Mr. Mortimer; "I have taken good care of her; and now Charity will watch by her till you can get some better rest than you have taken here."

"Oh! I have rested well. I will change my dress and come and breakfast with you in the library, if you think I may venture."

"I am sure you may—her sleep seems to me more natural than it was—she may recover yet."

A silent pressure of Mr. Mortimer's hand showed Augusta's heart touched by the hope thus given.

A cold bath gave her greater refreshment probably than such sleep as she could have obtained in her present excitement would have done—it quickened her languid circulation, and wishing to show Mr. Mortimer that she had not suffered from her vigils, she arranged her hair with even more than her usual care, fastening in its glossy braids a white rose with its rich green leaves, from which the dew was not yet dried, and put on, instead of the wrapper she had worn for several days, her close-fitting black dress somewhat open at the throat, to show the folds of soft illusion lying beneath it, which were caught together just above the bosom by a bunch of fragrant violets. So attired, she went tripping down the stairs, with a lighter step, because a lighter heart, than she had had for many, many months. As yet no thought of the difficulty, perhaps we should say the impossibility, of making those explanations to Hugh, which would be necessary to break down the barrier raised by her wounded pride, had mingled itself with the joy of knowing that he was all she had believed him. So her feet moved lightly to the music in her heart as she went on toward the library where she expected to meet Mr. Mortimer. Why was it that, as she laid her hand upon the lock, the sudden memory of that morning long ago, when, entering her uncle's library unconscious of his presence, she found Hugh awaiting her—why, we say, did this rise before her in such truth of form and vividness of coloring that it called a rich glow to her cheek? She threw open the door, and—did she dream, or was she under the influence of some weird enchantment?—there, before her, standing near a window, was Hugh himself. At her first glance, his face was turned away, but there was no mistaking that tall form, whose proportions promised both power and grace—there was no mistaking that noble head with its attitude of command. It was but one breathless instant. She had no time to withdraw, no time to think, when he turned and they were together, she knew not how and scarcely where—she only knew that her head swam, that her limbs trembled, and that she must have sunk to the ground, had not his strong arm supported her. He placed her in a chair, and turned, without a word, to the window again. Her head was bowed, her cheeks burned, her heart throbbed, as if it would have burst its prison bounds.

Overcome by a shyness, whose source it would have been hard for her to tell, it was long before she could lift her eyes to his face. When she did, his were fastened on her with an expression in which an angry cloud contended with gleams of passionate fondness. Her startled look roused him from his silent mood.

"Augusta!" he exclaimed,—the tone was low and deep, and again she gave him a quick, anxious glance, from which he turned away and walked twice across the room, ere he approached her again, saying in the same low, passionate tones, "You are feeble, ill, and ought to be spared all agitation; but I can no longer restrain myself—I am but man,—not ice, as you have probably thought me; but pardon me, that I am compelled to speak of myself—it shall be but a few words. You have wounded me where alone the wound could have aroused anger, or awakened remonstrance—that you had thrown back with scorn the passionate love which had become a part of my life—that you had rejected even my friendship as a presumption or an impertinence, I have borne in silence."

"Oh Hugh!" burst from her; but he seemed not to hear, and proceeded, passionately, "But there is one thing I cannot—I will not bear,—once before, you suspected me of an indelicacy, inconsistent with the instincts of a gentleman, and I forgave you; and now I find that you actually believed me capable of conduct that would have proved me not only dead to honor, but to common honesty; I stood beside you last night, and heard that broken confession which—God forgive me!—I have found it less easy to pardon than you did; and yet I can pardon *her* sooner than I can pardon *you*—she knew not the looks, the words which had said to you a thousand times 'I love you,'—she knew not, as you did, the depth of the falsehood she was fastening upon me, and which you accepted—no wonder you fled from all association with one you believed thus recreant to truth and honor."

She had covered her face with her hands, and seemed literally to cower before his passionate outburst, which was all the more terrible from its contrast with his usual calmness and self-possession. When he paused she uncovered a face from which every vestige of color had vanished, and lifted to him eyes which seemed glassy with despair. Her lips opened, but in vain—no sound issued from them. He turned away, for his heart was melting within him; yet he was too thoroughly angry to be willing to show himself so quickly appeased. He was moving to the door. Was he leaving her? leaving her forever? and thus?

Pride dies hard, but hers sank down and died at that thought.

"Hugh! Hugh!" Never had human voice shaped itself to a more passionate appeal, than was heard in that simple cry. It sank into his soul. He turned. She had risen from her chair, and stood, with white face and clasped hands and gasping breath, "Hugh, can you not forgive me?"

He came toward her with an eager step and looks of passionate emotion, saying, "No, Augusta! I cannot forgive you—I can only love you with the whole force of my being. Will you trust that love now, and let me prove its truth by the devotion of my life?"

He opened his arms, and with scarcely a conscious volition she passed within their circle pale, tottering; but, as they closed around her, and she felt herself drawn to that broad bosom and pressed against that beating heart, new life seemed to flow through her veins—life, pure and joyous as that of her early childhood, yet a thousandfold more intense.

Such moments can be but *moments* in human life; and it was, perhaps, well for both that Mr. Mortimer's step and " ahem "—both purposely loud, recalled them so soon to the existence of a world outside of themselves. What Mr. Mortimer had seen and heard on the preceding night, if not wholly understood, had been sufficiently so, to induce him to plan this surprise and *tête-à-tête*, which had begun so stormily, and ended by effecting all he desired for the two most dear to him of all the world.

We will leave the trio to take " with what appetite they may," the breakfast which seemed, we suspect, but a grand impertinence to two of the party, while we turn back the wheel of time a fortnight or thereabouts, and recount the circumstances that brought Hugh Moray so unexpectedly to St. Mary's.

CHAPTER XV.

*"What stronger breastplate than a heart untainted?
Thrice is he armed that hath his quarrel just;
And he but naked though locked up in steel,
Whose conscience with injustice is corrupted."—Henry VI.*

CHARLES MORAY had hastened at once to Hugh, in his distress; yet, when he found himself near him, the confession he had come to make, seemed impossible. The temptations, under which he had fallen, Hugh would have brushed like cobwebs from his path. He had lavished in one year on the momentary gratifications of sense, even before these debts of honor, what would have seemed to Hugh a fortune. How could he ask for his sympathy? And yet from whom, if not from Hugh, could he hope for sympathy and advice? Two days in succession, after his late breakfast at the Astor House, he walked to the house in Beckman street, on whose dingy stairs and wall stood conspicuously the names of Holton and Moray, Counsellors at Law, and walked away again without ascending to the little office, where he was almost sure of finding the person he had come to seek. The third day he might have done the same, but that, as he was turning away, he found himself face to face with the very man whom he sought, yet dared not meet.

"Why, Charlie! old fellow! so you've come at last? I began to think you were anchored at St. Mary's for life.

Come up with me—we'll find a few minutes for talk between the comers and goers."

Hugh seemed to Charles Moray to have grown younger in manner—less careworn, more expansive. It strengthened him to look into the calm, determined face, and the serene eyes; and he followed him up stairs with the weight already a little lifted from his heart. Still he was not prepared to tell all yet. Perhaps he would go to Elizabethtown to spend the night and then, when Hugh and he were together in the old den, he would talk. In the mean time, having passed through a large room where several young men were seated, some reading, some copying, they entered the smaller private office of Hugh. Charles Moray was not altogether displeased to find it occupied. He dreaded, while he desired this *tête-à-tête*. The occupant was one who was waiting to consult Hugh, and as Charles saw the respect with which his cousin was approached, and the confidence evinced in his judgment, his heart was stung by a new and poignant sense of shame and self-condemnation. It was impossible not to draw a contrast, little to his own advantage, between the positions they at present occupied. Hugh, with little aid from others, was fast winning all which, having received as a free gift, *he* had flung to the winds. Hugh had won far more indeed. Better than fortune, better even than the esteem and friendship of others, was the self-reliance, the calm strength, the disciplined powers which he had gained in the contest through which he had passed so successfully. They had left on him the stamp of a completed manhood, which the maturest age would fail to give to him who had not learned to conquer himself, and to postpone life's pleasures to its duties.

When his client was gone, Hugh took his letters from his desk and throwing himself into a large armed chair, began to question Charles of St. Mary's and of Mr. Mortlmer. If another name was in his heart, it did not escape his lips. As he talked, he opened, one by one, the letters he held, looked at the name subscribed, threw aside some unread and glanced carelessly over the contents of others. At length, one letter seemed to startle him into more earnest attention. As he looked at the address, a deeper color tinged his brow. He tore the letter open hastily, looked at the name of the writer, glanced at Charles, seemed about to speak, then turned again to the letter, ran his eye quickly over the contents, then read them more carefully, too deeply absorbed in them, apparently, to hear a question which Charles addressed to him. After this second perusal, his eyes remained for some time riveted on the paper, then, looking up, he said, with an abruptness that made Charles start, " You say you left your mother at St. Mary's —was she well?"

"Yes," said Charles, not without some slight uneasiness at the tone of the inquiry, "quite well."

"There was no apprehension of her having fever?"

"None whatever; but why do you ask? Is my mother ill?" and Charles Morny grew pale with vague apprehension, as the last words fell from his lips in an accent that seemed to belong to a more terrible word, a word he dared not use.

"No—at least not that I know of; but I have here a letter from her, a very strange letter, so strange that I doubted if it were not written in the delirium of fever."

Charles Moray would have given much to see that letter, yet he dared not ask for it, for he felt sure it contained the history of his own folly.

"Will you look at it?" asked Hugh, holding it toward him.

He received it mechanically and in silence; but the first few lines sent the blood back to his face, from which, in his agitation at the impending disclosure, it had retreated; and before he had finished the short letter, he sprang from his chair, exclaiming, "I would give my right hand, Hugh, to be sure that this was true—I mean that you could prove it."

"That is very generous in you, Charlie."

"Not so generous as it seems, Hugh; I am afraid you will think me, as I begin to think myself, a fool; but, Hugh, I have thrown away St. Mary's—all that fine property is now Harry Reardon's, unless you can prove that it never was mine, and so, having no title myself, I could give none."

"Are you jesting with me, Charles?"

The lightness had passed from Hugh's face; it looked grave even to sternness, as he added, "I cannot believe you would feel at liberty to part with a property, which you know Mr. Moray left to you, to the prejudice of his own niece, only that he might insure the perpetuation of his name in connection with it—I will not believe it of you."

"You may believe it or not; it is no less certain that Harry Reardon holds that property, and will continue to hold it, unless you can prove that I had no right to it. As to my being willing to part with it—there was no will in the case; though I suppose one ought to take nothing which he is not willing to part with, to a billiard table, with Reardon for his antagonist."

Charles Moray was now walking about the room; his restlessness betraying somewhat of the bitterness which he would not express in words. Hugh sat for some minutes with folded arms, compressed lips, and eyes determinately downcast. He did not look up even when he asked, in a voice which he forced to be calm, "Did the negroes go with the estate?"

"All—it was a clean sweep; but, Hugh, it's no use to look glum about it," Charlie drew near, and stood leaning on the mantelpiece opposite to Hugh. "If it's gone, that will not bring it back—and I really begin to hope that Reardon may be disappointed after all. By George! that will be grand! But now, what are you going to do? How are you going to get at this will? that, I suppose, is the first thing."

"If I could only be sure—"

Hugh ceased abruptly, looking down upon the open letter in his hand.

"That it was as my mother said," suggested Charlie; "I think you may depend on her. She would not be so foolish as to make such a charge without being sure of her ground. And now I think of it; doesn't she say something of Saville's wringing money from her?"

"Yes, there it is," and Hugh pointed to the passage, as he handed the letter to Charlie.

"The villain!" exclaimed Charlie, when he had read the passage again. "That accounts for the disappearance of the bank stock. He must have found this will among the papers I left for him to examine for me, and has kept it as a threat over my mother—and she—"

Charles paused suddenly. At that moment the thought that his mother had, by her silence, become an accomplice in Saville's villainy, had first suggested itself to him, occasioning a sharp spasm of pain, which sent the blood in a quick torrent to his brow.

"Hugh!" he exclaimed, in an altered voice, "you do not suspect me of having known anything of this?"

"Not for a moment, Charlie, not for a moment; and as to your mother, we must not press too hardly on a mother's feelings—it was doubtless a great temptation."

"You will spare her then, Hugh."

There was shame and grief in the tone, such as neither the loss of fortune, nor the consciousness of his own folly had caused in Charles Moray. Hugh hastened to reassure him.

"Be assured," he said, quickly and warmly, "that I will make any personal sacrifice rather than compromise her name. Were my own interest involved instead of Augusta's, I would not stir in the question; as it is—"

"You must, of course; but how will you begin? If you should write—"

"Oh, whatever is done must be done in person, and without warning; I shall go to Washington this evening."

The tone of the last words marked that whatever doubt or struggle had been in Hugh Moray's mind had passed away—the decision had been made. And yet, in making that decision, his mind had moved over an area covered by a network of delicate threads, the careless handling of any one of which might precipitate into ruin his own most important interests or those of others. Let it be understood here, as a reference to Mrs. Moray's letter will render clear, that Hugh did not suppose himself personally interested in the question of fortune. His action was for the sake of Augusta, to whom he supposed "St. Mary's and wealth" alike to belong. The object to be attained was the possession of the will held by Saville, and of proof that it was the true will of Mr. Hugh Moray, and to do this without compromising Mrs. Moray, of whose complicity with Saville he had little doubt; and last and least of all, in his estimation,—though certainly not least in difficulty—he was to deal with a felony, as he was firmly convinced, in such a manner as to prevent the exposure of the felon, yet not to subject himself to the charge of compounding it. It was to have time to think over these seemingly irreconcilable objects, and arrange a plan of action that would embrace them all, that Hugh advised that Charles should rather follow him than accompany him in his hurried night journey to Washington. Yet, before he reached that city, he had resolved to see Judge Mellen, and, if possible, induce him to accompany him to Washington. It is true this would lose him at least one day of time, which he could ill spare; but, after careful consideration, he judged that it was worth the sacrifice, and accordingly, having travelled all night from New York, and reached Washington in the early morning, he pressed forward and found himself, with six hours' further railroad travelling, about noon, at the plantation on the James river, where Judge Mellen was enjoying a life of calm repose and domestic peace. To return to Washington was, perhaps, the least agreeable proposition that could have been made to the Judge, but he was too kind and generous to hesitate in his compliance when, without communicating to him all his suspicions, or even all the facts on which he acted, Hugh told him that his business in Washington was to obtain, it might be to *compel* an act of justice to the niece of his old friend, Mr. Morny, and that his presence would make the task more possible, if not easy.

They arrived in Washington late in the evening, or, rather, night.

"Too late for business to-night, I suppose," said Judge Mellen, as Hugh seated himself beside him in the carriage which was to convey them to Willard's.

"Yes; I must rest to-night; I want a clear head and a strong arm to-morrow," answered Hugh.

"A strong arm! that sounds warlike. Am I to take part in the combat?"

"No; or, at least, only as a *corps de reserve*, in case I should fail; I fear it may seem hardly respectful in me, Judge, to ask the sanction of your presence without giving you my confidence more entirely; but, if you can trust me—"

"Fully; I put myself under your banner—no light thing,

let me say, for an opinionated old fellow like me, to a youngster with not half his years on his head."

"It is no light thing, my dear sir; I shall remember it ever with the deepest gratitude."

"What time will you breakfast, gentlemen?" asked the waiter at Willard's, as he preceded them up the dimly-lighted staircase to their sleeping rooms.

"Ask Mr. Moray, he's captain," said Judge Mellen, good-naturedly.

"At nine o'clock," answered Hugh, with a smile, naming the hour at which he knew the Judge was accustomed to breakfast at home.

"Whither now?" asked Judge Mellen, the next morning, as they rose from the breakfast table.

"To the Navy Department, if you please," Hugh replied.

"Hem—to Saville; well, I am ready."

"So I perceive, sir, with thought as well as action," said Hugh, laughingly.

"Excuse me. Not another word—*thought*, I mean—will I be guilty of, unless, indeed, you will permit me to suggest a carriage to take us to the department. A Washington sun is no trifle; a walk under it may cause our courage, or our strength, to exude, through more than the ends of our fingers."

The carriage caused some delay, and it was near eleven o'clock when they were set down at the department. The strange lightness which they had shown in the morning, and which so often comes to men on the eve of a great effort, had passed away, and the latter part of their drive had been performed in silence. Hugh sprang from the carriage, and waited quietly for his companion, who descended more slowly. Judge Mellen was startled by the paleness of his face as he glanced at him, but the iron firmness of the compressed lips, the sternness of the brow, the light which seemed literally to glow in the eyes, showed that it was the paleness rather of concentrated determination than of weakness or of fear. They entered the department in silence, and proceeded at once to the office of the chief clerk. Two or three officers in undress uniform stood chatting near the open door of this office, within which Saville sat at his desk, and beside him stood an officer, seemingly about to leave him, yet pausing to say some last words in a tone of eager remonstrance, as he pointed to a chart outspread before them. Judge Mellen paused to speak to one of the officers at the door. Hugh entered the office, and as the commander engaged with Saville turned away, took his place at his side, and in a voice low, but deep, said, "I must speak with you, sir; shall it be here?" glancing at the open door and the officers, who stood near enough to hear a raised tone from within.

"Must! you are imperative, sir," Saville said, sneeringly, glancing upward.

Their eyes met, and what else he meant to say, faltered and died on his lips, as he bent his eyes again upon the chart. Hugh stooped till his words were spoken in Saville's ear.

"It is of Mr. Moray's will I would speak; my information is so certain, I have no objection to make our interview public, unless you prefer it should be private."

Saville visibly shrank at the first words, and ere Hugh had concluded, turned to him, with white, gasping lips, and eyes like the tiger's when prepared to make his spring. Again Hugh's met the gaze steadily, and Saville's sank before them, while with a voice which strove in vain for firmness, he faltered out, "What do you mean, sir?"

"Again I ask you, shall I close the door before I tell you?" said Hugh.

"If you please." The tone was steadier, and the hand which had rested on the chart, moved a little nearer to the left side-pocket of the light summer coat—changes which Hugh's quick eye perceived.

"I have a word to say to Judge Mellen first," he said; "but do not be afraid, he knows nothing;"—then, raising his voice, he called, "Judge Mellen, will you do me the favor to step here for a moment?"

Saville glared upon the Judge as he approached, and the hand moved nervously again toward the left side, while he forgot to acknowledge the bow which Judge Mellen, never unmindful of the claims of courtesy, made him on his entrance.

"Will you be so kind, Judge Mellen," said Hugh, still speaking low, "as to tell Mr. Saville whether I have communicated to you the object of my interview with him?"

"No, indeed, Mr. Saville; I have followed him here without knowing whether it was a chase after a wild goose or a fox."

"What you know, sir, is of no consequence to me," said Saville, snappishly.

Hugh did not seem to hear him, but drawing a sealed packet from his bosom, held it to Judge Mellen, saying, "In this packet is a full account of the business which has brought me to Washington; I intrust it to your safe keeping; you will oblige me by handing it unopened to Mr. Saville when I leave this room; but should Mr. Saville attempt to leave the room without me, stop him, and in that packet you will find your warrant for doing so. Now, may I ask you, my kind friend, to leave us, and to close the door as you pass out?"

"Is that written in the bond?" asked Judge Mellen, with an almost playful reference to his promise of obedience, while yet there was an expression of uneasiness in his eyes as he glanced from Hugh to the pale and sullen face of Saville. A grave bow was Hugh's only answer, and Judge Mellen turned and left the room, closing the door after him.

"Now we may speak without reserve," said Hugh.

"Have a care, sir; I am not unarmed, and you may try my patience too far," and Saville's hand entered the pocket it had been approaching.

"I will trust Mr. Saville's knowledge of his own interests, if not his patience," said Hugh, with a contemptuous smile. "Any violence would bring this whole affair necessarily before the public; besides, you will find in me a more lenient prosecutor than in Judge Mellen, who would immediately take my place. This is irrelevant, however. My business is to receive from you Mr. Moray's will, which you —found, we will say—and have retained, from friendship, it may be, for those in possession of his fortune. The moment you deliver it, I will relieve you from my presence."

"And suppose I should acknowledge that I have it, yet refuse to deliver it; you know, if you know anything about it, that you cannot bring a charge against me without risking the disgrace of your own name," hissed forth Saville.

"There is no question of bringing a charge; this matter is to be finished between us, man to man; the will is on your person, I know."

"Touch me," said Saville, after a glance at the stalwart frame that stood in passive strength beside him; "touch me, and I will call for help and shoot you like a dog; it will be self-defence."

"Judge Mellen has a packet which will show you had good reason to desire my death; and he knows I came here unarmed."

"D——n you!" muttered Saville.

Hugh only smiled, and remained watchful, but motionless.

"What will you give for this will?" cried Saville, suddenly looking up.

"My promise that you shall be safe from any investigation into the circumstances by which it came into your hands, nothing more."

"I think your testimony would hardly go for much, since, if it be true that I have committed a felony, you are guilty of compounding it."

"Felony! that is an ugly word. There is no felony in finding a will among papers which you were authorized to examine. I do not know when you found it; you may not have been able to restore it before; now I am ready to receive it."

"Very well, I will send it to you—at least, I will send the packet which I think may be a will."

"You will give it to me here, and now, Mr. Saville, or I call in those gentlemen, and in their presence force it from you, and so prove your infamy." Hugh's words were low, but every one was uttered with a force which sent it straight into the coward heart before him. "Here, and now, sir," he repeated, stretching out his hand to receive it.

With a muttered imprecation, Saville dashed on the table a packet drawn from the breast pocket, in which his hand had been placed, adding, as Hugh lifted it, "Now leave my office, sir, and never dare to set foot within it again."

"I shall obey with pleasure when I am assured that I have what I came to seek," said Hugh; then, after reading the superscription of the packet and examining the seal, he stepped to the door and asked Judge Mellen to enter. The Judge having complied, and the door being again closed, Hugh said, "I will be obliged to you to witness Mr. Saville's acknowledgment that this packet contains the latest will and testament of Mr. Hugh Moray, which he witnessed, and which he has now delivered to me for the benefit of the heirs. You acknowledge this, Mr. Saville?"

The steady eyes were upon him—the inflexible tone in his ears—and after a moment's pause, he assented.

"I will now thank you, in fulfilment of my conditions, to hand Mr. Saville the packet I gave you."

Judge Mellen laid it on the table, and without another word, Hugh withdrew with him from the room.

"Whither now?" asked Judge Mellen, as he took his seat again in the carriage.

Hugh hesitated; it was only for a moment.

"To Willard's," he said to the coachman, adding, as he placed himself by Judge Mellen, "I think Charles must have arrived—lazy fellow. I have no doubt he stopped to sleep in Baltimore last night. If he is here, I think, as this is directed to you, we may, with your permission, open it."

"Had you not better wait till Miss Moray can be present?"

"Under ordinary circumstances I should say yes; but Miss Moray is in Georgia; it may be weeks before she can come here, and that document is too precious to be subjected to the hazards of those weeks; it must be recorded, and we must have certified copies of it."

"And am I still to ask no questions?"

"Ask, my dear Judge, and, as far as I can, I will answer—though, the truth is, I *know* very little."

"But suspect very much."

Hugh's face grew fixed.

"Which you don't mean to tell," added the Judge, with a slight laugh, as he glanced at that determined face.

"Well, I will try my powers at cross-examining. What put this business into your head? How did you know of this will?—for, of course, you would not have ventured to attack Saville on suspicion."

"Attack Mr. Saville! My dear sir, you labor under a mistake. I heard from Mrs. Charles Moray that she knew the last will and testament of Mr. Hugh Moray was still in the hands of Mr. Saville. My visit here was only to receive it from him. It was possible that Mr. Saville might dispute my right to receive the document, and I therefore requested your company, believing that he could not hesitate to deliver it to you."

"And you heard of this will first from Mrs. Charles Moray? That puzzles me."

"Here is Charles, and our puzzles will soon be at an end," cried Hugh, as he stopped the carriage, and putting his head out of the window, called to Charles Moray, who was sauntering along one of the avenues in a spiritless, discontented way. His countenance brightened as he saw Hugh, and he approached the carriage with a brisk step, shook hands cordially with Judge Mellen, and took a seat with them at Hugh's invitation. Hugh drew the packet from his bosom and showed it to him.

"You've got it then! By George, I could hug Saville for having found it," exclaimed Charles.

"You're a generous, noble-hearted fellow," said Judge Mellen, warmly; "such a heart is better than a fortune."

"Oh, don't give me too much credit, sir," cried Charlie, with that frankness which was his redeeming trait, adding, with a slightly embarrassed laugh, "Harry Reardon has more interest in that document than I."

"Harry Reardon! hem—there is no puzzle now," cried Judge Mellen, with a glance at Hugh.

When the will was read, Judge Mellen declared that he recollected it perfectly as the will which Mr. Moray had read to him. Hugh was silent and grave.

"I am truly glad, old fellow, since I could not keep it, that it is to be yours," exclaimed Charles Moray, trying to speak more brightly than, if the truth must be told, he felt just at that moment.

Hugh shook the hand extended to him without a word; then, suddenly turning to Judge Mellen, said, "Do you not think, sir, that there is some reason to doubt whether Mr. Moray's mind was to be trusted when this will was made?"

"Not the least. When he read that will to me, his judgment was perfectly clear."

"It is scarcely a proof of it that he should have left any other than his niece as his heir."

"Poor Moray! To leave St. Mary's to one who would perpetuate his family name, seemed almost a point of his religion; but his niece is well provided for by this will; the other was inhuman."

Charles Moray reddened; then, turning quickly to Hugh, said, "There is something I do not understand in this business. How did my mother know of this will?"

"I cannot tell; you saw your mother's letter," Hugh answered.

"Where did Saville find it?"

"I do not know; I did not ask him."

"Well, I shall," and Charles took his hat from the table, and walked to the door, then coming back, he said, warmly, "You understand, Hugh—I have no doubt of you; but it is necessary for my mother's sake that this affair should be better understood, especially that it should be known why this will was not introduced until I had lost the property. I shall wring the whole secret, if secret there be, from Saville's cowardly heart."

He spoke with passion, and was turning away again, but Hugh caught his arm and drew him forcibly back, while he said, "Charlie, you are no match for Saville; nay, do not be angry—I mean in cunning, the only strength of mean minds like his. Choose a good lawyer and place your case in his hands; he will unravel all the mystery and establish your rights."

"I have no rights—I want none. I tell you again, I am truly glad the property is yours; but I will know all about this will, which could not be found at Mr. Moray's death, and which comes so opportunely to light now, just in time to prevent his fortune being made ducks and drakes of."

"Your cousin gives you good advice, Mr. Charles; put yourself in the hands of a good lawyer—take Choate, who is here, attending to some business in the Federal Court— as joint executor with your cousin of this will, and guardian to Miss Moray, I will defend their side. If it be necessary, we will go into court—"

"Not for me," interrupted Charlie.

"Not for you, but for the right, and in order that whoever enjoys the property may do it without a doubt. I think I can throw some light upon the subject when I am again at home. I have been accustomed for twenty years to keep memoranda of each day's engagements, and I do not doubt I shall find notes and dates which will substantiate this," and he laid his hand upon the will.

"And we will go to New York and await the result," said Hugh; and, but half satisfied, Charles Moray assented.

The law, which under ordinary circumstances "drags its slow length along," moves swiftly enough when friendly parties meet with the one object of discovering truth. Judge Mellen sent home for his papers, found all the data he had anticipated, and established the fact that on the day on which this will was dated, Mr. Moray had made an arrangement with him to call and witness his signature to a will, the rough draft of which he had seen and corrected, and the several items of which he had noted and recorded. These items differed in no respect from those of the will now so strangely brought forward. Mr. Saville, too, did not withhold his testimony when asked for by one of the dignitaries of the law. Indeed, he gave it in such a manner as to be complimented for his clearness and conciseness, after he had been told that if any doubt was left on the minds of the parties interested, the case would be brought into court and thoroughly sifted. He established, *on oath*, the fact of having drawn up and witnessed two wills, of which this was the later. When the other will was produced after Mr. Moray's death, he had supposed that this had been destroyed, and finding it afterward among the papers left with him by Mr. Charles Moray, he had retained it only till he could deliver it into the hands of some one of those concerned—indeed, he had immediately informed Mrs. Charles Moray of the fact. Nothing could be clearer, and so Mr. Choate wrote to his client, telling him at the same time that the actual possession of the estate gave him a position from which his opponents might find it difficult to dislodge him, should he suffer the case to go into court, as the whole burden of proof would be left on them. "Nevertheless," he added, "there are circumstances in this affair which make me hesitate to advise your submitting it to the decision of a legal tribunal."

The truth was, clear and concise as Mr. Saville had been, there was not one acquainted with the circumstances, who did not feel that the next step from this clearness would be into the deep profound of sinful human hearts—into the very mystery of iniquity. All shrank from that step except—strange to say—Charles Moray, who, now that suspicion had been aroused, felt its grasp more strongly than any, dreaded more than any to exchange it for conviction, yet experienced something of that fascination which tempts a man to throw himself headlong down the gulf whose very sight has made his brain reel. It was the belief expressed by Mr. Choate that he might succeed in retaining the property, through some want of legal evidence, from the heirs by the present will, which at length decided him. His success would be the success of Harry Reardon, the alienation of the property from the name of Moray, the defrauding of Hugh and Augusta, the triumph of injustice. Better go to his grave with this unsatisfied doubt standing as a wall of ice between him and his mother.

Hugh had awaited his decision in pitying silence. When it was announced, he received it with such a clasp of the hand as a man gives to one who announces to him a great sorrow, and with the few earnest words, "We are brothers now, Charlie."

"You will go immediately to St. Mary's?" said Charles Moray, when they had sat a few minutes in silent musing. "I have written this morning to Harry Reardon and enclosed a few lines from Mr. Choate, to whom I had submitted the question whether he could give you any trouble in the matter. The opinion was so decided that I think you will scarcely find him at St. Mary's, if you give my letter twenty-four hours the start of you."

When Charles ceased, Hugh looked up and spoke, yet his words bore little reference to what had been said to him.

"How strange it is," he said, in the tone of one but half roused from a deep reverie, "how strange it is that this estate, the bestowal of which cost Mr. Moray so much anxious thought, should fall to those who value it so little;—first to you, who could throw it away on a game of chance, and then to me, who am not at all sure I shall accept it. So God pours contempt on human pride!"

"But, Hugh, what do you mean by not being sure you shall accept it?"

"I mean more than I can say in a few words, Charlie;

but I will play the Yankee and answer your question by another: What should I gain by accepting it?"

"What should you gain? Why, if well managed, I have no doubt it would yield a clear fifteen thousand a year."

"I do doubt it very much; but suppose it did; it would hardly be more than I may one day hope to realize from my practice here."

"Then you may have twice fifteen thousand."

"You mean that I may own the Southern property and draw its income without living upon it? but that is just what I could not do. No, no, Charlie; that might do if we could 'jump the life to come.' Conscience is terribly in the way sometimes, Charlie—is it not?" and Hugh looked up with a smile from the sketch he was drawing.

"I do not understand you; surely you are not one of those hypocritical abolitionists."

"Neither hypocritical nor abolitionist—terms which I do not like to hear you thus couple together; I have known few abolitionists, but among those few there were several who were certainly not hypocrites, though I thought them enthusiasts, it may even be, fanatics."

"That they certainly are; but let them pass, and tell me plainly where your difficulties lie in the acceptance of this property; I do not understand you any more than if you spoke in an unknown tongue."

"That would make a pretty object in a landscape, and a neat, convenient cottage for a poor man's family—would it not?" and Hugh pushed over to his cousin the sketch he had been making.

Charles Morny reddened. "You must think me a child indeed to be put off from a serious subject by pictures. If you have any secret motives, I do not wish to pry into them," and he rose and took up his hat from the floor.

"Sit down again, old fellow," said Hugh, catching him by the arm; "I will try to make you understand what is hardly yet plain to myself. I am the furthest man on earth from being an abolitionist. There are wrongs and evils in connection with American slavery which I would gladly see abolished—which, if I come in contact with it at all, I shall fight against with head, and heart, and hands, so help me God!—but so there are in all human institutions. In the essential features, the dependence of the slave, the rule and authority of the master, I believe it to be divinely appointed for the noblest ends. Woe be to him who makes it minister to his selfishness—to his degrading sensualities! Woe to him who is indifferent to its grand responsibilities! Ham was to be a servant of servants; but it was to be 'to his BRETHREN,' through whom he would still be united to their common Lord. Now you see that if I undertake this charge, with these views, I assume no light responsibility. Is it wonderful if I hesitate between competency here, won by the exercise of a profession I like, and say double or treble the income there, with such a burden on my life? I shall be a king on my own land, it is true; but, with my views, I must be priest as well as king. Instead of these people living for me, I must live for them. I hope I am no coward, Charlie, and yet I shrink from it, and if I only dared, I would cast it off; but am I at liberty to do this when, without my own seeking, these people are given to me? This is the question to be decided. I must decide it at St. Mary's, and there I shall go immediately. And now, how do you like my plan for the houses of those negroes who may merit advancement and reward?" and Hugh touched the sketch which Charlie had pushed away so indignantly.

"Hugh, you make me ashamed of myself," cried Charlie, clasping and pressing the hand thus outstretched.

"If I did, it would only be what you have often made

me feel while contrasting your cheerfulness lately with what I fear I should have felt under such a change; and now, Charlie, you will let me ask you, what are your plans?"

"I must first know on what terms you will let me off for my debts to you."

"Debts to me! For what?"

"For the sum received from St. Mary's."

"We will offset them with what you expended on it— no bad bargain for me either, according to Mr. Mortimer's account of your improvements—and now, what else?"

"I have tried everything except study; I have a great mind to ask Mr. Holton to take me as one of his students," said Charlie, with a laugh,—"or shall I write a book?"

"Do both; the book will be capital amusement for idle hours; if it succeed, come and I will build you a cottage at St. Mary's, which shall be the *beau ideal* of a literary retreat."

"Well! I'll think of it."

"In the mean time, till your mother comes, will you make your home with us, and let me be your banker, Charlie?"

And so they parted, the one to choose between two positions of honor and affluence, both gained by the honest discharge of duty—the other to seek some means of opening that yet closed oyster—the world. Truly, as we sow we shall reap.

CHAPTER XVI.

> "And so, from hour to hour we ripe and ripe,
> And then, from hour to hour we rot and rot,
> And thereby hangs a tale."—SHAKSPEARE.

THERE are hours in which the interests, the joys, the cares of long years seem to be compressed. Such were the early hours of the day after Hugh's arrival at St. Mary's. The great gulf which treachery had dug between him and Augusta had been passed, and once more they stood with hearts unveiled and hand linked in hand, as they had done long years before, under the same soft skies. Except in the house itself there was little change around them. Old Ocean tossed as restlessly on his sandy bed, and moaned as loudly as ever, when the wild winds were abroad; and when they were still, the wavelets danced as gayly and flashed back the sunlight from their diamond spray as merrily as they had done of old. The flowers still bloomed from which Augusta had woven wreaths to deck her childish beauty, and the old oaks still stretched out their giant arms, and waved abroad their gray drapery. But how different was all within them. That wondering look into the future which hopes all and fears nothing, that carelessness of the present which drops its brightest possession to grasp the unknown—these, the characteristics of opening life, were gone, and in their place were memories sweet and bitter, not one of which, even the bitterest, would have been willingly surrendered, and a solemn sense of the responsibilities of the present as the seedtime of the future.. In him experience had wrought calm self-reliance, not incompatible with the humblest sense of his dependence upon a Heavenly guide; to her it had given a deeper insight into the requirements of her nature; she knew that life would lose not only much of its grace and sweetness, but much also of its worth and dignity, if she could not draw from his stronger soul, stability for her purposes, confidence in her aims, and a quiet assurance of the ultimate triumph of truth and justice. He, the type to her of a guardian Providence, a union of strength, wisdom, and benevolence; she, to him, the brightest emanation of love, that principle which pervades and attracts all, which conquers even in yielding. Poet and novelist have striven in vain to paint that light tenderer than the moon, warmer than the sun, which kindles all nature,—all life, into a diviner glow when two hearts thus answer to each other. It matters little to them whether their path be overarched by the laurel and the rose, or shadowed by cypress boughs, they carry within them light music and ever-springing flowers.

"Have you written to Charles of his mother's illness?" asked Hugh, as Mr. Mortimer still lingered over the cup of coffee, which was his nearest approach to a sensual indulgence, and Augusta waited to supply him with another.

"I wrote a week ago, which was as soon as she would permit me; she seemed before that to dread his return—by the by, she told me something about a will, Hugh; could she have been delirious? It was something about Saville—"

"She told you probably that Saville had your uncle's

will—she wrote me on the same subject—her letter was written on the 13th of May, nearly a month ago."

"The very day she was taken ill—the day of Mr. Reardon's marriage."

"I have not been idle since," said Hugh; "it has been little more than three weeks since I received the letter, and here," taking out a pocketbook, and producing a folded paper as he spoke, "here is a copy of your uncle's will—the original is in Judge Mellen's hands, and the will has been recorded."

Augusta grew pale as she received the paper and held it still unfolded.

"Read it," said Hugh, with a smile, meant to inspire her with courage, "or shall I read it for you?"

"No! tell me; but first, how did Mr. Saville get it? how did Mrs. Moray know?"

"I know not—I do not wish to know; he says he found it—we will try to believe him."

"That is right, Hugh," said Mr. Mortimer; "charity believeth all things."

"For the sake of your uncle's memory, dear Augusta, you will be glad to know that he did not forget your claims upon him; keep this copy and read it by and by—it will please you to read the tender words in which you are named as his 'dearly loved and dutiful niece—his nurse and comforter.'"

Tears rushed to Augusta's eyes—her lips quivered, and covering her face with her clasped hands, she wept, soothed, but not restrained, by the silent sympathy of Hugh, who rose and stood near her with his hand resting on her chair. As her sobs grew fainter, he spoke again, in a tone which conveyed all of tenderness that the fondest epithets could have done.

"You were left with railroad and bank stocks, which it

was supposed would produce an income of two thousand dollars per annum—if it failed to do this, the property here was to be taxed to make up the deficiency; but your home, this dear St. Mary's, can only be yours, dear Augusta, by taking an incumbrance with it—it was left to me."

"Oh! I am so glad!" and a face full of emotion, smiles dancing on the lips and dimpling the cheek, while the long lashes were yet wet with tears, was lifted to him.

It was irresistible, and Hugh had kissed the glowing cheek before he remembered that Mr. Mortimer was present. Mr. Mortimer thought of some old poet's "love ever young," as he met a brighter smile than he remembered to have ever seen before on Hugh's face and heard his almost boyish, "Indeed, I could not help it, sir," in excuse. Then, ere Augusta had made up her mind whether to frown or smile, he continued, "I was not glad at first, dearest; indeed I came here doubtful whether I should accept it, anxious to find some way of avoiding that which involves the entire sacrifice of all my plans of life—"

"Hugh!" and "Oh Hugh!" in different tones, yet both expressive of painful surprise, burst from his auditors.

"Do not be frightened, dear love,—if I should drop the burden it would only fall on you, and so I must take it up again. Mr. Mortimer must help us to bear it; he must teach us what to do for these poor people, for whom we must henceforth live far more than for ourselves."

"God bless you, my children!" said Mr. Mortimer, in a voice husky with emotion, for he felt that the realization of his brightest dreams was near.

Augusta said nothing; indeed, her heart was too full for speech, full of reverent love for him, whom she felt to be nobler than even her ideal—full of generous sympathy by which she felt herself refined and lifted into a higher and more glorious life.

It was hard to turn from such converse to the still, darkened room, where one, who had done them deep wrong, lay, counting with feeble pulses what seemed her last waning minutes. Mr. Mortimer and Hugh had gone to the plantation, and the house seemed preternaturally quiet to Augusta as, having sent Charity away, she sat alone in the darkened chamber, moving only to moisten the parched lips or cool the throbbing temples of the sleeping patient, who, but for the slowly heaving chest, might have seemed dead, so motionless had she lain for hours. Yet, amid all this stillness, never had Augusta felt less lonely, for sweet memories nestled warm at her heart, and bright images of her future life flitted before and around her, while, with some of her childish superstition still lingering in her mind, she felt that angel visitants were near her, or rather in her heart, enfolding her with their white wings, and rejoicing in her consecration to a life so full of heavenly beauty. Let her dream out her sweet dreams, and call them not vain and idle; they shall soften for her many a stern reality, lift her feet over many a stone of stumbling, and so make her a more cheering helpmeet to the strong, yet sometimes, it may be, wearied laborer at her side.

Her dreams were interrupted by a whisper from Charity, who had entered and approached her noiselessly.

"Dey's all a going, Miss 'Gusty, de ole lady an' all—dere dey is now, you can just see 'em," and Charity peered through the half-closed shutter with a countenance by no means indicative of sorrow.

Augusta needed no explanation of the persons meant by "they all." She had seen Mrs. Cullen every day for a week past; that lady having expressed great anxiety respecting Mrs. Moray, and having suffered no day during that time to pass without sending for her to the library, to inquire, with much apparent interest, how her "poor old friend" was. To-day she had not seen her, but she knew that Hugh and Mr. Reardon had had an interview, and she doubted not that this departure was the result of it.

To us, who are *seers* by virtue of our office, a fuller revelation has been made, which we communicate unreservedly to our readers.

The letter of Charles Moray had been received by Mr. Reardon with anger and distrust.

"I do not believe a word of it—it is a pitiful evasion to save the property which he had no right to hazard, if it were not his—it is all the fabrication of that lawyer cousin."

This, varied by every form of expression possible to the English language, and adorned with every expletive common to dashing young gentlemen under the influence of disappointment and of that emotion which Horace assures us is a "*brevis furor,*" was the staple of Mr. Reardon's conversation for that day; and when, the next morning, he heard of Hugh's arrival, he sent a note to him requesting an interview, which took place by Hugh's appointment at 11 A. M.

"Pray, Harry, command yourself; a man who would do anything so desperate as attempt to palm off a false will upon you, must be dangerous," said the young wife, as she saw her husband look at his watch and take his hat from the table to cross the sunny piazza to the library, which had been appointed for the place of meeting.

"Little danger of anything but being cheated," replied Harry Reardon in a tone of contempt. "I suppose," he added, "I must make some compromise and surrender part of what is justly mine; but he will see he has no child to deal with; good-by;" he touched lightly with his lips the fair cheek of his bride and went to his appointment.

Scarcely half an hour had passed when he returned. Elise was watching for him.

"Well!" she exclaimed, as he entered, rising to meet him.

The reader is doubtless aware that there are many "wells." There is the "well" congratulatory, the "well" triumphant, the "well" surprised, the "well" despondent, and the "well" interrogatory. This last "well" was that of Elise Reardon, who could not discover from her husband's face, whether the occasion would admit of congratulation, triumph, or despondency.

"It is not well at all; this is quite another sort of Moray, I can tell you, and neither to be coaxed nor driven from his purpose."

"Why, I met him in Washington once, and I thought he seemed the most harmless, quiet sort of person imaginable; I should have thought you could do anything with him."

"Quiet enough; if there had been any bluster about him I should have hoped to gain my point; but it is no use to waste time in trying to intimidate or to blind one of your thoroughly quiet men, whose eye tells you that he reads your cards as plainly as you do yourself, and that he both can and will trump your trick."

"And do you believe this story of another will?"

He hesitated a moment; then, flinging his hat on the table and himself into the lounge from which Elise had just risen, he said, "Yes, it's a cursed stroke of fortune; but I am compelled to believe it—at least I am sure Hugh Moray believes it himself."

"And what are you going to do, Harry?"

"The first thing is to get away from here. I have only about fifty dollars left, so you must see what you can do with mamma."

"But, Harry, she will feel dreadfully."

"You must spare her feelings, my beauty," and he drew her to his knee and lavished caresses on her as he spoke; "tell her there will be some delay in getting possession here; nothing can be truer than that, *mia bella*, and that we must hurry away. Stay, don't you think this fever—it has put on a typhoid form, they say—may make her anxious to get away? You can tell her that I am very desirous on your account to be gone—that is true, too, my heart's darling; and that, though I am short of funds now, I will repay her, if she will advance what we need, as soon as we get to Saratoga, and I have time to communicate with my banker. Do you not think this will do?"

How could the lips that were burning with his kisses say him nay! or the heart which throbbed in his close embrace distrust him? To degrade the man to whom she has given herself by a doubt, is the last thing a woman will do; for is not his degradation her own? Elise Cullen did as her husband had directed, and performed her task so skilfully that her mother, terrified at the very name of typhus, would scarcely wait to have their trunks packed, and declared she was quite ready to pay the expenses of the whole party, if Harry would only consent to go at once. And they went, without even an inquiry after her whose prosperity they had come to share. Mr. Reardon, indeed, proposed that his wife should make a farewell visit to Miss Moray, and express their regrets at leaving their former hostess so ill; but Mrs. Cullen entreated that they would spare her nerves such a terrible trial.

"Why, that girl is in her room day and night. Elise might as well stand by Mrs. Moray herself as by her. Indeed, Harry, I am surprised at your proposing it. Think, if anything should happen to Elise."

Mrs. Cullen must be kept in good humor at present, and so Mr. Reardon withdrew his proposal as inconsiderate, and they passed in silence and in haste from the home they had coveted.

That word typhus, spoken by one of Mrs. Moray's physicians, that evening, when he joined the little family at tea, threw a shadow over the stronger soul of Hugh Moray, and sent his eyes to rest with a troubled glance on Augusta, beside whom he was seated.

"You are pale, dearest," he said, bending toward her, and speaking in a tone so low as to be unheard by any other.

She raised her eyes to his for a moment, and a soft yet rich color rose to her cheek. She felt the glow, and as her eyes fell, answered, "It was only for a moment."

"But the fear that caused it may return when I am no longer here, and I—oh! how can I leave you?"

Augusta tried in vain to steady her voice as she asked, "When must you go?"

"I ought to go to-morrow."

"Is that necessary *now?*" she asked, with a somewhat timid accent upon the "now."

"Oh yes!" was the quick answer. "Mr. Holton has been very indulgent to my frequent absences of late; but I must not leave him with a press of business and no help: yes, I must go; I had hoped that you, and perhaps Mr. Mortimer, would return with me, but now"—he paused.

"Now it would be impossible; I could not leave her as she is."

"And yet—stay, I must speak to the doctor."

He rose, but Augusta's hand, laid lightly on his arm, checked him for a moment.

"It can make no difference what he says, Hugh; I cannot leave her to strangers."

He looked down on her tenderly, admiringly, for a moment, then, with the tone of one who felt that the question must at last rest on his own decision, said, "We shall see —we shall see," and turning to the doctor, asked for a few minutes' private conversation with him.

The result of this conversation was to convince Hugh that whatever danger there was for Augusta had been already incurred. That there had been some danger in her constant attendance, by day and by night, on his patient, the doctor admitted. "He had told Miss Moray so, some days ago," he said, "but it had made no difference. She ought to have some one near her who would make her rest a part of every night and go in the open air every day."

"Mr. Mortimer will do that, if you tell him its importance," said Hugh.

"He may advise, but I doubt his being able to *make* her," said the old doctor, a shrewd observer; then added, with a laugh, "not that she does not do all he wishes, but only that she has the power of making him wish just what she pleases."

Hugh smiled, and the smile still lingered in his eyes, if it had left his lips, when he reëntered the room in which were Mr. Mortimer and Augusta. She had risen from her chair before Hugh came in, and he heard her say to Mr. Mortimer, as if in answer to some remonstrance from him, "Indeed, dear sir, I do not need sleep; I slept so much last night."

"Hugh, what shall we do with this dear child, she will kill herself; I wish we could send her away."

"That I fear we cannot do now; but I will stay to help you take care of her."

"Will you, Hugh? Can you stay?" she exclaimed, turning to him a face which said as plainly as any words could have done, "I am glad."

We know not exactly how Hugh accomplished it; but that night, and ever after during Mrs. Moray's illness, Augusta went to her own room at midnight, and Hugh and Charity took her place as watchers, and each day she was lured out and spent some hours wandering about under the shadow of the great oak, or by the sea shore, living over the sweet hours of the past, or anticipating the future, and learning, both in the retrospection and anticipation, better to understand herself and him who won from her, every hour, a more perfect esteem.

It was not long. Little more than a week had passed after Hugh's arrival, when Charles Moray entered again the house he could no longer call his own. His letters had all been addressed to Elizabethtown, whither he had promised Hugh to go, but, shrinking from the pain of explanations to his aunt and cousins, he had accepted an invitation to join a party of young men going on a fishing excursion. They were gone for ten days. Charles Moray had shaken off much of his dejection when he returned. With his old Epicurean philosophy, he had resolved to think no more of what was disagreeable in the past. "There is nothing to be done but to enjoy what is left," he said to himself, and in this spirit went to Elizabethtown, and found four or five letters awaiting him, each bearing tidings of his mother's illness more discouraging than the last. He was even then obliged to delay till he could see the person who acted for Mrs. Moray in the management of her property, that he might procure money from him for his travelling expenses. Impatient of these delays, thinking of his mother's danger with the more bitter regret, perchance, because of the coldness with which he had parted from her, and the suspicions which had lately darkened his thoughts of her, he allowed himself no rest, by day or night, till he was once more at St. Mary's.

It was ten o'clock at night. Augusta was in the sick-room, and Hugh had retired, to obtain, if possible, a few hours' sleep before he should take her place. Mr. Mortimer sat alone in the library, reading. A step approached the door; a tall form crossed the threshold. Mr. Mortimer rose, but his dim eyes had not yet told him who it was, when a cold and tremulous hand clasped his, and an agitated voice exclaimed, "My mother!"

"Mr. Charles Moray! My dear boy, sit down; you are trembling."

"Oh, Mr. Mortimer, tell me that she is not dead—that I may see her once more."

"You may—you may; though she is very low, she still lives."

"And may recover? Oh, Mr. Mortimer! do you think she may recover?"

He was answered only by a warm clasp of the old man's trembling hands; he knew well what that silence meant, and dropping on the chair beside him, he covered his face with his hands, and deep sobs heaved his bosom. Mr. Mortimer wiped the tears from his own eyes, as he stood looking down upon him. At length the sobs ceased, and laying his hand on his bowed head, Mr. Mortimer said, "Come, my son, I will show you to her room."

Their sudden entrance into the darkened room, hushed as it was, startled Augusta, who, having brought a light stronger than the shadowy night lamp that usually burned there, to the side of the sickbed, was bending over it, endeavoring to rouse Mrs. Moray sufficiently to swallow the strong stimulant, which was now administered every half hour by the physician's order. Rising suddenly and turning as she heard movements behind her, the light flashed upon the ghastly face and sunken eyes of the dying woman just as Charles Moray took his place beside her. The long-closed eyes opened suddenly, the long-silent lips stirred, and a feeble voice uttered, "My son! Charles!"

It was the last word, the last thought; the one pure affection of her life had outlived all her petty ambitions—all her selfish aims. The voice of prayer ascended from beside her, but it bore no conscious appeal from her faintly throbbing heart. The agonized cry of Charles, "Mother! speak to me! forgive me!" fell on ears seemingly as insensible as if death had already sealed them. A few hours of such unconscious sleep, a few slow, deep-drawn sighs, and then, that stillness which we need no voice to tell us is death.

Charles Moray's nature, amid all its levity, did not want tenderness, and he stood with all the abandonment of a first great bereavement beside his mother's grave—remorseful for every unloving thought—mindful only of her cherishing affection. She was laid to rest with the reverence due to that which had been the habitation of an immortal soul, while those whom she had striven most to injure, if they could not wholly forget the past, remembered it only to pity, and, where it was possible, to excuse. We say "*had striven* to injure them," for, in truth, they had received no injury, though they had suffered some sorrow. Sorrow had but given greater consistency, a mellower ripeness, to the noble qualities of Hugh Moray. Augusta had, indeed, grown, or seemed for a time to grow, colder and haughtier under its influence; but this evil was from within—not sorrow, but pride was its source—pride, the demon of her life. Sorrow had not withdrawn its shadow from her path, when Christian love first nestled in her heart, yet the coldness and misanthropy had vanished. She did not, perhaps, quite clearly perceive this yet, but she saw enough to make her more forgiving to others than to herself—enough to make her recognize the great principle that our true well-being can be permanently affected only through our own action; that it is *being*, not *having*, which makes our life. Perhaps just conclusions were scarcely to be expected from her in the days which immediately succeeded Mrs. Moray's death.

While there had been anything to do for Mrs. Moray, she had shown—she had felt—no fatigue; but this excitement to action removed, she sank down in inexpressible weariness, and her languid movements and pale face excited the keenest solicitude in Hugh and Mr. Mortimer. For herself, she was conscious only of a quietude which made the thought of change the most dreaded of all things.

"Oh, Hugh! I am resting so here!" was her answer to his first suggestion that it would be well that she should go immediately to Elizabethtown, where his mother and sisters were expecting her, and whither he hoped to induce Mr. Mortimer to go with her.

Resting, indeed, she was, as she had never rested before; the wandering bird had found its nest. Where was her pride, her independence now? All exchanged for the sweetness of entire trust in the large heart, the clear judgment, the firm will of him whom she had chosen as her earthly guide. She had exercised wisely her woman's right of choice, and the result was this ineffable peace. What could the poor, vain ranters about woman's independence have given her in exchange for it? Ah! they know not how sweet it is to "obey," when obedience has been preceded by "love and honor." Only see that he whose rule you accept bear the lineaments of the Divine Master, and be assured your highest happiness and truest dignity in this, as in every relation, will be found in obedience to God's arrangements. So felt Augusta Moray, and though she would gladly have lingered in that sweet quietude, even as the thirsty traveller in the desert pauses beside the green oasis with its gushing wells—she yielded to Hugh's wishes, and began, or rather suffered Charity to begin, the preparations for their departure. She did not know then how much Hugh shared her desire to remain undisturbed in that sweet home, which was so dear to them both, associated, as it was, with their memories of the past and their hopes of the future. But the voice of duty, ever powerful with him, called him away, and the assurance of the physician, whom he consulted, that change of scene and air would be Augusta's best restoratives, left him no wish to disobey, and in one week after the last duties had been performed for Mrs. Moray which human kindness could perform, the house at St. Mary's was again silent and deserted. The parsonage, too, was closed, for Mr. Mortimer could not resist Augusta's entreaties that he would go with her.

"You must come with us and grow strong this summer, dear sir, or you will never be able to do half that Hugh is planning for you to do the next winter; besides, how can I leave you?"

And Mr. Mortimer's heart grew warm with the thought that there was yet work for him to do for his Master in heaven, and that there was one on earth who could not leave him. It was an evening glow, bright and beautiful.

As for Charity, she rose in her own estimation, and that of her acquaintances, many degrees above her ordinary height, when she was known to be about to go to that distant "North," of which they had heard so much, with "Miss 'Gusty and Mr. Hugh and their own young master," as they continued to call Charles Moray, notwithstanding the mysterious innuendoes with which Charity had sought to enlighten their ignorance. Her own information was not sufficiently exact to enable her "to tell a plain, unvarnished tale," but she had, almost of necessity, heard some things, and she had guessed a great deal more; so that, through her, the idea became very prevalent on the plantation that some change was awaiting them, which Charity considered as greatly for their benefit. This idea was strengthened by Mr. Mortimer's farewell words to them, in which he told them that he was parting from them only for a little while, and that he hoped, when he came back, to be able, through the kindness of their good master, to do a great deal more for them than he had ever yet done. For Charles Moray's sake, each one felt indisposed to speak of the new state of affairs at present. To the manager of the estate, however, who came to him for orders, Charles Moray said, "You must go to Mr. Hugh Moray; he is master here now."

"Why, you don't tell me so," exclaimed the man in his surprise; "you've sold out to Mr. Hugh?"

Hugh was present at this interview, and the glance which Charles Moray cast upon him, seemed to ask help in the explanation which he was called upon to give.

"Before we answer your question, Mr. Carter, I must claim your congratulations on my approaching marriage with Miss Augusta Moray; it was her uncle's wish that on our marriage we should reside here."

"Indeed!" exclaimed Mr. Carter with a puzzled look, feeling that his question had not been answered; yet at the next moment subsiding into satisfaction with an arrangement which he accepted as natural and just, he added, "I'm very glad to hear it, sir, I'm sure; but I hope we sha'n't lose Mr. Charles—we all like Mr. Charles, sir."

"To be sure you do," said Hugh, laying his hand affectionately on the shoulder of his cousin, "everybody likes Mr. Charles; I wish you may like me half so well."

Charles clasped, with grateful warmth, the hand that rested on his shoulder.

"And now, Mr. Carter," continued Hugh, "as to these orders, I think I had better ride over and see you in the morning."

And Mr. Carter departed with vague impressions which grew into certainties as he thought, and were, according to a very common process, reported as information received from the young gentlemen themselves, that Mr. Moray had divided his property between his young relatives with the request that his niece should marry one of them, and that the one she married should have St. Mary's. It was an understanding which shielded the reputation of the dead and the feelings of the living, and as Hugh Moray was not one of whom many men would be disposed to ask impertinent questions, it was an understanding not likely to be disturbed. Once more Augusta Moray saw her home fade into dim distance, but with feelings far different from the passionate sorrow of her childhood. It was dear to her as ever; ay, dearer, for not only was it connected with all she valued in the past, but it was to be the theatre of her life-work.

"*Our* home," Hugh bent down and murmured as he watched her last lingering looks. And how much was compressed in that little "our." How her heart swelled beneath the sound! The gladness of the present—the hopes of the future were all there.

To one of the party, there was relief in leaving that lone island. The heavy gloom, which had rested of late on Charles Moray's brow, grew perceptibly lighter as the distance between him and St. Mary's increased. There he could not forget the wrong and the sorrow which it was useless torture to his light spirit to retain.

"I think I shall go abroad for two or three years," he said to Hugh.

"Better go to work," was Hugh's answer. "Believe me, Charlie, any happiness worth having, must come from what we are and what we do."

"Go to work!" and Charles Moray laughed the light laugh of his boyish days, "a strange receipt for happiness! I fear you will be very unhappy the rest of your life—a Southern planter with nothing to do; poor Hugh!" and again came the ready laugh.

"Nothing to do!" repeated Hugh.

"Why, what will you do? Carter will do all the business."

"Come and see what I shall do."

"Perhaps I will, ten years hence."

Words spoken in thoughtlessness, to be strangely fulfilled.

The motherly and sisterly love, which awaited Augusta at Elizabethtown, seemed to give a new sanction to her joy. It was a joy which lay too deep in her heart for smiles or words—a joy which made her humble toward God and tender toward her fellow creatures, by its contrast with what she felt she had deserved by her pride and her distrust. She had been in Elizabethtown about a fortnight when Lily came one morning early to Esther's room, and closing the door carefully behind her, said, "Esther, I am going to ask you a question; if you think it wrong, you will not answer it."

"Certainly not, Lily."

"I want to know if you think that Augusta really loves Hugh, as she ought to do; I mean, if you think she is so very happy?"

"If Augusta loves Hugh? if she is happy?" repeated Esther in surprise.

"Yes, she is so serious; I think she laughs less at the little pleasantries that pass before her than she did when she was here before; and it seems to me any one that Hugh loves, ought to be so very, very glad."

"And do you think, dear Lily, that the gladdest heart makes the merriest face? Can you not conceive of a happiness that shall so fill the heart that the little pleasantries which excite the merriment of others, shall be unobserved altogether, or observed only as intrusive impertinencies?" Just here, there was a knock at the door; and on its being opened, Augusta presented herself. Lily looked conscious, and would have stolen away, but Esther caught her as she passed, and said, "Stay, Lily! Augusta, Lily is afraid you cannot be happy; she says you are so grave."

"Grave! Not happy!" exclaimed Augusta, while the flush of a surprise, which was almost indignant, rose to her brow. "Hugh's promised wife, and not happy! Oh, Lily!"

"Pray, forgive me!" pleaded Lily, as she rested her head on Augusta's shoulder, ready to laugh or to cry at the next word, "I am such a little ignoramus—I don't know about such things; I shall learn better by and by, I hope."

"I hope you will," said Augusta, as she kissed her cheek.

Her tone seemed to Lily to express that such ignorance was scarcely pardonable, and she stole away like a culprit; and again and again, through the day, her thoughts reverted to the subject, and each time with a little protest on the judgment of herself. In all doubtful cases Hugh was her ultimate appeal; and, on his return from the city that evening, she found or made an opportunity of speaking to him alone, and, detailing the whole scene, words and looks, she wished to know if he thought she "was so very wrong." Hugh answered only with laughter and kisses, till Lily grew quite indignant, and declared he treated her "like a child."

"Like just what you are, then, Lily, my dear child-sister," said Hugh, holding her fast, "I wish I could keep you so; but it cannot be: you must pass the portal of womanhood, and then you will understand. In the mean time you need not tell Augusta that I have heard this," he added, as he released her.

"I dare say you will tell her yourself," said Lily, with a little pout in her voice, and that conjecture was so true as to show that she was not entirely ignorant of human nature.

Hugh found his kind friend, Mr. Holton, laboring under a pressure of business, and he devoted all his energies to him and his cases, till another was found to take the place which he could no longer fill.

"I am sorry to bid you farewell, Mr. Moray," said Mr. Holton, at parting, "sorry for my own sake, and, if you will pardon me for saying so, for yours. The life of a Southern planter seems to me to offer no sphere for talents such as you possess, and with your education and past associations, I should think there must be much in it which you would find distasteful."

"You are so far right, Mr. Holton, that it is certainly not the life of my own choice; but I accept it without reluctance, convinced that if its responsibilities be fulfilled, it will accomplish life's highest ends, the glory of God and the good of man."

"I have not looked upon it so—but, perhaps, you are right," said his friend, after a pause, "the world does not see this, however; you will have the best spirits in every land against you."

"The best!" exclaimed Hugh, "I think not; many good men, certainly—but, some, I will hope, will rise above even amiable prejudices, and see the true position of those to whom this hard service has been appointed."

Mr. Holton shook his head. Hugh lifted his higher, and a loftier expression glowed in his face, as he said, earnestly, "Be it so; human sympathy is dear, but it is not necessary."

It was in the last week of September that Hugh and Augusta were married. The ceremony was performed by Mr. Mortimer in that simple home in Elizabethtown, which she had herself described in the memorial of her early life. No gay company disturbed with sounds of revelry the echoes on which the tones of the loved and honored dead seemed still to linger. None, except Augusta herself, and Lily, who was her bridesmaid, laid aside, even for that evening, the dress which was their last visible link with that tenderly cherished memory. So there have been many gayer, but, we will venture to say, never a happier bridal. Even Charles Moray, the only groomsman, was touched by the solemn tenderness of Mr. Mortimer's tremulous tones as he uttered the words which bound their lives together, to be parted only by death; and, as Mrs. Moray, having first folded her new daughter to her heart, turned to Hugh's embrace, and he heard the murmured words, "The blessing of the mother whose life you have crowned with joy, be upon you, Hugh!" the white gravestone at St. Mary's rose before him, around which his own life seemed to stretch like a desert waste. Sweet might have been the uses of such wholesome pain, but his Epicurean nature quickly banished the vision.

The only guests on this occasion were Judge Mellen, his daughter, and Miss Drayton. The bridal present Annie Mellen made to Augusta, was the set of pearls which Miss Drayton had purchased from her in her hour of need, and which the tender-hearted Annie could never be induced to wear.

The next week, Charles Morny fulfilled his design of going abroad. His property in Elizabethtown had lately risen in value, so that it yielded him about fifteen hundred dollars per annum. Mrs. Moray, distrustful, as it seemed, of her son's prudence, had made such arrangements that Charles could only command the income. To the questions of his friends respecting the time of his return, he answered, "Probably, never. What is there to bring me back? I have no home and no occupation."

"You can have both whenever you please," said Hugh, with a smile, "and as for occupation, come and help us at St. Mary's."

"Help you do nothing!" was the mocking reply.

And here we might leave those whom we have accompanied so far on their life-journey, having fulfilled, as we believe, our pledge to the reader, and proved that to every picture on which we look, whether bright or dark, there is another side; that outward prosperity often carries storm and gloom in its bosom, while the clouds of sorrow as often show the "silver lining" of a peace which passeth understanding. Between the probable destinies of the two young Morays when they were first introduced to the reader, few, perhaps, would have chosen his who seemed doomed to work his toilsome way up the hill of life, unaided even by those natural gifts which are as a letter of credit, insuring us a friendly reception everywhere. But let us look upon the pictures of those two lives from the point of view at which we now stand, and we do not ask you, intelligent reader, whose present or whose future would you choose, but whose past? Shall it be Charles Moray's with its frivolous gaieties and luxurious self-indulgence, enervating and satiating without satisfying the soul; or, shall it be Hugh's with its privations and its toils—a sombre picture, but with a glory around it—the glory of a soul which has risen to the height of its being and treads down resolutely all which is only earthly and sensual?

Here, we say, we might leave them; but there is one picture to a new aspect of which we would especially ask your attention. We have shown you wealth held for ambitious purposes, to build up a name and family influence, and wealth held for purposes of self-indulgence; we have yet to show it held for the glory of God and the good of man.

This, we think, will be done most pleasantly by culling a few leaves from the journal of Augusta Moray, from which earlier passages of this family history were extracted. The first extract is dated a few days after her arrival at St. Mary's.

CHAPTER XVII

*"A settled virtue
Makes itself a judge, and, satisfied within,
Smiles at that common enemy, the world."*—DRYDEN.

October 23d.—This little book has not been unclasped for many a day. It was my solace, my friend, when my heart was sinking under a weight of woe, which I was too proud and too distrustful to confide to any being, human or divine. Oh! that terrible loneliness of soul. I stand appalled before its very memory—it chills me.

I am chill no longer—Hugh has just come in with Mr. Mortimer. I hear his voice as he is passing to the library. He will soon seek me, if I go not to them; but I must say to my little book how his very voice fills my heart with the sweet, warm consciousness of human love, and how, through this, I feel and adore the glory of the Divine goodness. He is coming.

October 24th.—I had no time to write yesterday after Hugh left me. To-day I have been with him to the plantation for the first time since my return. Both the delay and the visit were of his planning, and had their reason. He drove me in a little low pony-carriage, which he purchased for me in New York. Our first halt was beneath the old oaks, whose boughs form an arch above my uncle's grave. There, at the head of the grave, had been reared, on a broad pedestal, a massive granite column, on which is inscribed:

HERE REST THE MORTAL REMAINS

OF

HUGH MORAY:

A just man, a generous friend, a kind master; his life was cheered by the grateful affection of those who owed all worldly good to his liberality, and his last hours were made bright by the hope of a glorious immortality.

A Senator from Georgia to the Congress of the United States of America, he died in Washington, April 10th, 18—, aged 61.

In silent sadness we stood beside this place of rest—and yet not all sadness; it was consoling to feel that in consummating our own happiness, we had fulfilled his last and strongest earthly wish. It seemed, as we stood together there, that a new blessing had been breathed upon our union. Tears, not altogether of sorrow, were on my cheeks, as Hugh drew me away. "I promised to love you for him and for myself too," he said, as he kissed them away.

We went on toward the plantation, passed beyond it, and stopped at a little cove or bay, where the water lay as calm as if it had been a mountain lake instead of a part of that great sea which roared and dashed on the beach not much more than a mile away. From the water the land stretched away for nearly half a mile in a flowery savanna, broken only here and there by clumps of oaks. There was no road in this direction, but over the level surface of the savanna, the ponies drew the little carriage without a jolt. A new feature had been added to the scene since I looked upon it last. Two small, inexpensive, yet neat cottages had been built. They were only one story in height, and contained four small rooms, so arranged as to be well aired. Each cottage had a piazza, around which ran a bench, fastened to the floor. In an enclosed space, in the rear of each, vegetables and a few common flowers were already growing, while two or three hens and a pair of turkeys, clucking in two little poultry-yards, gave the animation of life to the scene. Within, the cottages were furnished very plainly, but with neatness. A table with folding leaves, a few chairs, and a cupboard with glazed doors, made of the red wood of the wild cherry, formed the furniture of the sitting room. The sleeping rooms had each a bedstead and bureau of the same wood. On the bedsteads, which were corded, lay, first, a thoroughly cured skin, with the glossy hair unshorn, and above that, a mattress made of coarse osnaburg, and stuffed with moss from our own trees.

Dear Hugh! I do not believe he ever enjoyed winning a case as he did showing me there, in those pretty white cottages, so neat and comfortable within and without, the embodiment of one of our earliest plans for the improvement of those committed to our care. Something was yet to be done before the fulfilment of our dream was complete. We had not to wait long for the cart, which was following us with two large boxes, into which Sambo's inquisitive eyes longed to peep; but we well knew that if they had done so the little surprise we had planned for our good Cato and Gib would have been no surprise at all, so Muster Sambo, notwithstanding all his offers of service, was forced to drive away before we opened them. What a pleasure it was to us to draw out the few plates and dishes and cups and saucers, and the bright tin coffee-pot, which we know will be the most valued of all, and arrange them on the shelves of the cupboard—to lay the cotton sheets and tablecloths, and the osnaburg towels, in one of the drawers of each bureau, and to spread a warm blanket and quilt upon each bed. I looked with a warm, glad heart upon all; but there came suddenly a little cloud over the brightness of my thoughts.

"Hugh! if they should disappoint us after all, and be lazy and slovenly, as that cross Mrs. Williams predicted the other day."

"Then we must try to be patient with them, remembering how often we have disappointed our Master in heaven, and thwarted His plans for us."

"Hugh, do you know, sometimes I think—but you know better, so I will not say it."

"Yes, you will," said Hugh, as he drew me to him and held me fast; "do you not know your very thoughts belong to me now, and that it is a robbery to keep one back? so now for the thought."

"It was only that sometimes it had occurred to me that at last it might have been easier just to give these people their freedom, send them to Africa, and live upon your law business."

"Easier! yes, a thousand times easier, and ten thousand times more noble in the world's eyes; but we are living, I hope, not for ease, not for the world's praise. I told you, my wife,"—how sweet that name is on Hugh's lips!—"I told you that this would be a heavy burden; but be not afraid, darling; He who lays on us the burden will give the strength."

And so to-morrow Cato, who was my father's playfellow in his boyhood, and Gib, my uncle's faithful attendant, both religiously conscientious men, are to take possession of these houses, the first of our colony of "Good Behavior." To become a member of this colony will, we hope, prove an incentive to all our people, not only to be honest and good, but to acquire habits of neatness and carefulness. The members of this colony will have land given them for cultivation, where they will work at their own free will, without any surveillance. They are to have their seed given them, and to draw their provisions as the others do, for the first year. They will afterward be expected to provide these for themselves, as well as to pay a portion of what they make for ground rent. Should unforeseen disasters occur, they will be taken care of; but should they fail entirely through indolence or carelessness, the punishment will be the forfeiture of their position, and a return to their old work and their old homes. I hope this will never be—it will grieve Hugh so much. It has been Hugh's desire to make his plans so rational and unromantic as to insure their practicability. The first step may not raise them very high, he says, but if it be planted surely, it will give us vantage ground for the next. We hope to build another cottage before the end of the year, perhaps two, by giving up the organ which Hugh contemplated purchasing for the library.

This was not the only pleasure of yesterday that I have to record. We stopped at the church, where dear Mr. Mortimer met us and rejoiced with us over its improved appearance. It has been thoroughly cleaned and painted inside and out, and the old pulpit has been taken out and a more comfortable one arranged for our dear pastor and friend. A little way from the church, under a clump of oaks, is another building, which we call the school, and our people call the *prayers-house*. It will serve for both. There they will assemble for evening prayer, sometimes with Mr. Mortimer, sometimes with Hugh himself; and there I hope to teach them to read God's holy word, and to awaken their minds to observation of much in His works which is yet hidden from them. What a new value does my life seem every day to acquire! Grant, Heavenly Father, that I may never forget the Giver in His gifts!

Five years later we have the following entry:

"*November 10th, 18—.*—How pleasant it is to come home! I think, if it had not been to show my treasures—my little Hugh and baby James—to their grandmamma, who loves them so tenderly, I should have tried to let Hugh go without me—and yet, to speak truth, I fear the trial would have been vain. They have not been idle here since we left them. Two more cottages have been built, and twenty families now compose our colony. Their crops have been injured by the heavy rains, and they will need help the next year, but everything around them looks neat and comfortable, and well cared for; and Mr. Mortimer has been quite satisfied with the attendance on the school, to which, he says, Sarah Carter was very attentive while I was absent. Hugh thinks my little gentlemen require so much of my time that I had better leave it in her hands, and give her a small salary, but I cannot consent to this yet; a year or two hence, perhaps, it may be necessary. Poor Joe! I was very sorry when we were obliged to send him back from the colony to the plantation, but Hugh was right. When was he otherwise? With the encouragement of good Mr. Mortimer, Joe has regained his lost ground, and to-morrow he will come back to the colony, while the example, I am sure, has done good to the others."

Two years after this date, we find this:

"*November 20th.*—Once more at home with our three children, all well, thanks to our Heavenly Father! Our little girl was so ill in the summer that I feared she would have been ere now with the angels. Perhaps it was wrong to write *feared*, but He who made a mother's heart, and

> Who knows each chord, its various tone,
> Each spring, its various bias,

will forgive me. She is a lovely flower—our May, Hugh's pet lamb. She grew so strong as the cold weather came on that we delayed our return on her account, and should hardly have been here now, except that we became a little alarmed for Mr. Mortimer's health, not so much from what he said of himself in his letters, as from what he did not say. We find him looking feeble and worn. What shall we do without him? He asked to see Hugh this morning, and he has gone to the parsonage."

"*November 22d.*—'Commit thy way unto the Lord, and He will direct thy steps.' Mr. Mortimer has been in correspondence this summer with a young clergyman who, he thinks, will be glad to come here, if Hugh will invite him. He is highly recommended as a devout, Christian man, and is, besides, a gentleman and scholar. His first letter to Mr. Mortimer was to inquire about Hugh's plans for his people, which, it seems, have begun to be noised abroad. He made these inquiries on his own account, having himself a small property mostly in slaves, for whose good, here and hereafter, he is anxious to do all in his power. His present home is in South Carolina, where he owns a plantation, which, he says, is not very productive. Mr. Mortimer has written, at Hugh's request, to ask him to make us a Christmas visit, and to bring with him his young wife."

Later we read: "*January 15th.*—Mr. Law and his wife left us to-day. Their visit has been a great enjoyment, and has brought us bright hopes for the future. They are coming to make their home with us on St. Mary's. They will sell their place in Carolina and remove their people here. Hugh does not feel at liberty to sell any part of this island, but he will make as long a lease as Mr. Law pleases of the land he needs, the payment of it being Mr. Law's services now as pastor to us and our people, and by and by as teacher to our boys. Mrs. Law is a cultivated, agreeable woman, and is quite an artist with the pencil. Little May, will you ever paint? Dear Mr. Mortimer looks better already for the prospect of a helper in his work. The carpenters are very busy building an addition to the parsonage, for Mr. and Mrs. Law are, by Mr. Mortimer's own request, to reside there."

In the ensuing autumn, under date of *October 12th*, we read: "We have returned earlier this year, that we might accompany Lily, whom her husband was impatient to show to his friends at home; and that we might be ready for our dear mother and Esther, who are coming to spend this winter, and, we hope, many other winters, with us. What a lovely bride our Lily made! And Hugh says, if he had had the world to choose from, he would have selected Mr. Forester for her husband—he is so thoroughly good. Such a son as he has been to his widowed stepmother, and such a brother to his little half-brothers, must make a good husband to our Lily. Hugh has been for years his confidential adviser in the management of his people, in whom he feels the interest of a Christian master, who does not forget that he, too, has a Master in heaven. I rejoice to say that this is not a rare instance of Christian faithfulness. Our hearts have been encouraged and our hands strengthened by unexpected sympathy. While there are many who, like my dear uncle, kind to their slaves and careful of their health and comfort, still reject all innovation on established usages, believing it impossible to raise them to a higher status, there are more who are anxiously striving to lift them up, to make them new creatures, freedmen in Christ Jesus. We know instances of self-denying devotedness in this class which can scarcely be paralleled in the annals even of missionary life. Hugh has lately been urged to become a candidate for the United States Senate. At first I wished him to consent, desiring to see him occupy a position which would give full scope to his abilities, and ambitious, I acknowledge with shame, that the world should honor him as he deserves.

He knew what was in my heart, though I did not speak it out so boldly to him as I am doing to you, my little book, and he answered it by opening the Bible on my table and pointing with a smile to the passage in which the Apostle remonstrates with those who 'seek honor one from another, rather than that honor which cometh from God only.' To my plea that I wanted to see him where his abilities would be more fully exercised, he replied: 'You know, dear wife, that the position in which they are now exercised was not of my own seeking; I did not accept its responsibilities without counting the cost; part of this cost was the relinquishment of worldly honor and all choice in the exercise of such mental power as God has given me; all is pledged to this work, and all is needed to prevent honest but narrow-minded, one-ideed men, from spreading through the land and through the world, a spurious philanthropy, the counterfeit presentment of Christian love, which must do incalculable injury to this unfortunate race. I have hitherto found my best way of opposing this to be through the press and by my work here; should I ever see reason to believe that it can be better done in Congress, I will go there.'"

Nearly a month later, we read: "*November 10th.*—The Storm King has been abroad—has it been in wrath or in mercy? In mercy, we will hope, for he has brought home our wanderer. My heart is still too full for words.

"*November 15th.*—The last five days I have been the constant witness of a strife to which that of wind and water, in their wildest rage, is tame—the strife of Life and Death in a human soul. Life, I trust, has won. Dear Charlie! How memory springs back to those early days when, through all our wilfulness, we yet loved each other. Will it be false to that love, if I leave here a record of the sad goal to which you have been led in your chase after pleasure? I have already left your impress here in your gay, innocent youth, and in your manhood, when drunk with the world's exciting flatteries: shall my hand tremble to trace those 'strange defeatures' which time has written on your once fair and open brow? If I conquer my reluctance to do this, it is because I, too, have a Charlie—a boy whose bright blue eyes and merry laugh have often brought you before me—and one day, when you and I, my cousin Charlie, have gone from earth, he may need some loving voice to warn him from ill, to cheer him on to good; and I would have this little book, begun in selfish abandonment, and continued as a thankful acknowledgment for life's choicest blessings—this little book, which may yet bring back some tone of the mother's voice, that now wins its way so easily to his heart—to contain lessons which may teach him when he is tempted as you have been, not to fall, as you have done.

"Even my little May, now five years old, will probably carry with her through life, some memory of the storm which, a week ago, gathered us all in the library, to look out upon the picture that had so often awed me in my childhood. The air was thick with spray, through which we could yet dimly discern the sheets of foam, driven far up upon the land by the hurricane, which snapped the branches of the stout oaks, and snatching their leaves and twigs, dashed them against the windows through which we gazed. I have never lost my childish awe of a storm, and as our good mother, ever thoughtful of others, cried, 'God pity the poor sailors!' a selfish joy arose in my heart that none of my circle of blessings was exposed to its fury. The howl of the tempest, and the dash of its dripping wings against my chamber windows, kept me awake till long after midnight, and I slept the next morning till the sun stood high in a clear sky. Hugh had risen earlier, and when I was dressed, and with my little Hugh and Charlie sought him in the breakfast room, I found that he had taken a cup

of coffee an hour before and mounted his horse to ride to
the colony, where, he feared, there might have been some
suffering.

"'Nuff tree blow down las' night," said Harry, as he
gave me this information. "I 'spec' Massa fin' he hab to
walk."

The suspicion was correct; and fastening his horse to
the branch of a fallen oak, Hugh tried to find, through the
changed scene, the footpath leading by the graveyard to
the colony. There were many obstructions in the way,
rendering it no easy task, so that the sun was shining very
warmly and brightly before he had arrived in sight of the
graveyard. A little beyond this toward the sea, there is an
open glade; and Hugh made his way thither to see how high
the sea had flowed in at this point, directly toward which
the wind had set. The line of sedge that marked the farthest limit of the flood was higher even than he had expected
to find it. As he stood looking at it, and beyond it, to the
glittering sea still tossing itself in but half-subdued agitation,
his dog, which had followed him from home, dashed forward,
and reaching the line of sedge, began to race with wild, frolic
glee to and fro. Suddenly he stopped, as if about to make
a point; then running round in a circle several times with
his nose low to the ground, stopped again, and throwing up
his head, uttered a long howl. Hugh whistled to him to
come in, and too well trained to disobey, he came; but
when Hugh would have gone on, he could not be induced to
follow. Turning again, he ran toward the shore; but halt-
ing about halfway, looked back wistfully at Hugh and gave
again that melancholy cry. Human speech could scarcely
have expressed more intelligibly the desire that Hugh should
follow. He so understood it and went, the dog bounding
before him till, halfway between the uppermost line of sedge
and the shore, he stood still beside what seemed a heap of

sedge, a little beyond which, were the broken fragments of a boat. Quickening his steps, Hugh soon stood beside that heap, and found the seemingly lifeless body of a man. A little examination gave him hope that life was not quite extinct. He even thought there was a slight movement in the muscles of the face, as, with a faint hope that the sufferer might hear and understand, he said, "I am going for help to carry you to my house; my dog will guard you while I am gone." An order to Don, the setter dog, and he seated himself, with his eyes fixed on the motionless body, while Hugh hurried back to his horse, and rode rapidly home.

"There is a man fainting, dying; give me brandy—a spoon,—he cannot drink from the bottle; have a warm room and bed ready for him, and send all the men after me to the graveyard—the coachman, gardener, Gib and Harry." He was already on his horse, and scarcely checked him to shout back to me, "Let them bring blankets and a handbarrow, if there is such a thing about; but no delay."

All was done as Hugh directed; and two hours after, a seemingly dying man was borne into our home, Hugh walking beside him, and occasionally moistening his lips from the flask, which he carried in his hand. He was taken to the room prepared for him, undressed, laid in a warm bed, and restoratives administered by Hugh himself, who never left him till our friend, Mr. Law, who is a physician for the body as well as for the soul, arrived. Trusting his patient with him, Hugh came to me.

"Augusta, do you know whom we have with us?" he asked.

My looks answered him; for there was something in his tones which almost took my breath away, and made it difficult for me to speak. He drew me close to him, and whispered "Charlie!"

"Oh, Hugh!" a moment's awed silence, and then came

the heart's protest, "Oh, Hugh! it cannot be; that furrowed brow—those sunken cheeks, of which I caught a glance—it is impossible!"

"It is he, love; somewhat of his ill looks you must ascribe to his present condition."

It was indeed he; and when he seemed almost restored to us, life was again imperilled by his excitement at discovering whither the storm-spirit had borne him. For two days past, however, our good Dr. D., for whom Hugh sent immediately, has pronounced his life out of danger, and has removed all restrictions from our intercourse with him.

"Augusta," he said to me, yesterday, "I told you I would come back to you in ten years; it is just ten years since. Is it not strange?"

"Is not what strange, Charlie? that you should keep your promise?"

"That it should be kept without, nay, *against* my will. St. Mary's is the last place on earth—pardon me for saying it—to which I should have come by my own desire. Do not look hurt—it was neither you nor Hugh; it was my own past self I could not bear to meet."

"Is the present self so much better and happier, Charlie? But it is your turn to pardon now—I had no right to ask that."

"Ask what you will," he replied, "and I will answer you, if I can. Better, you ask? no—happier? yes—well, perhaps not happier—I believe not—but "—he paused, and a deeper shadow fell on his pale, thin face, and his voice sank lower, as he added, "there are some things we would gladly forget forever. For that matter, I should have no objection to forget my whole life; a dreamless sleep is not an unpleasant thing in prospect for one whose life has disappointed all his wishes and destroyed all his faith in himself."

"Faith in ourselves, dear Charlie," I said, in a voice

which, if it was not tender, belied my heart, "faith in ourselves, we all find to be a very fragile thing, I fear; but there is a faith which never fails us"——

I had laid my hand on his, while speaking; he drew his away with a quick and impatient movement, and turning from me, closed his eyes as if to sleep. God help us to do him good!

So far we have quoted from the journal; but, that we may have time and space for details more interesting to the reader, we must touch the changes that followed in Charles Moray's life, more hastily than Augusta Moray's tenderness permitted her to do.

Though restored to life, Charles Morny continued to suffer from his exposure during that terrible night, in such a manner as to make it necessary that he should spend the winter in a warm climate. Resisting all persuasions to remain at St. Mary's—receiving them, indeed, with almost childish petulance,—he went off to Savannah; but a return of illness sent him back to Hugh and Augusta more conscious of his dependence on their care. It was a care exercised with such unobtrusiveness, that it rarely jarred even the morbid sensitiveness of an invalid. Most anxious for his soul's health, Augusta might, by imprudent urgency, have excited his resistance to the truth she desired to commend, had not Hugh restrained her.

"Let us *live* our principles—not *talk* them," he said. "Charlie may shut his ears against our voices, but he cannot close his heart against the influence of a consistent, Christian life."

Respect for his old friend, Mr. Mortimer, led Charles Morny to the church; and the truths he heard there, certainly acquired new force from the lives of those around him. When he had heard Hugh profess his desire to hold the property which God had given him only as His steward, and to make his position of master but a vantage ground, from which he could better teach and guide the slaves, whose guidance he accepted as his life-work, Charles Morny had listened to it as to the dream of an enthusiast, noble, beautiful, but impossible. Here he saw the dream fulfilled; and before the majesty of such a life he strove in vain to maintain his careless levity. The continued delicacy of his health made a mild winter climate necessary to him; and after the experience of the home life of St. Mary's, the life of foreign travel, with its loneliness of heart in the midst of gay and busy crowds, offered nothing tempting to the sated, weary invalid. He therefore returned winter after winter to Hugh and Augusta; and each year their hearts were gladdened by seeing his increasing interest in the success of their plans and the growing power of Christian truth as a restraining principle in his life. And so, with these good omens brightening the termination of a career, which has long ago left *pleasure* behind, and which had little *happiness* to leave, we part with him and return to Hugh and his plans.

Hugh Morny was cheered by seeing the influence of his example extend first to his neighbors, and then to others more remote. Men, who had satisfied themselves with making the bodies of their slaves comfortable, began to recognize the needs of their spirits. Men, who had been accustomed to talk in an apologetic tone of their relation to slavery; who had pleaded, in extenuation of that relation, that it was not their deed; that it was England which had forced it upon them; that it was the trading communities of the Northern United States which had brought these people from their homes in Africa, and landed them at their doors; that immediate emancipation was clearly impossible, and they must do the best *possible* with them since the best *absolute* was not in their power—these men, rising to a higher stand-point, began to see more truly,—to see that not England, not their Northern neighbors, but God, who rules on earth as in heaven, according to the counsel of His own righteous will, had brought to their doors these beings, so ignorant and degraded, yet none the less His children and their brethren, that they might lead them to that truth which should form them anew in the image of God. They began to repent, not of slaveholding, for in this they could not recognize a sin; it was but a condition in which they had been placed by the providential circumstances of their birth: their repentance was that they had failed to estimate the greatness of the trust committed to them, and that they had, therefore, failed to meet its high responsibilities. Consulting with Hugh, they brought to him many difficulties, some speculative, some practical.

"Do not your views," said one, "authorize a continuance of the slave-trade with Africa or, indeed, with any heathen nation?"

"By no means," was the decided answer. "In the darkness of the past, good men might engage in such a business, and 'the times of that ignorance God winked at,' overruling the mistakes as well as the wrath of man for the good of His creatures and the glory of His name. What was committed to us for such purposes, we may have used meanly and selfishly. If so, let us set ourselves vigorously to work to undo the evil we have done; but feeling already that our responsibilities are so heavy, we shall be the last to desire their increase."

Hugh Moray had chosen his life-work; and, as we have seen from the journal of his wife, he had refused to leave it at the call of ambition. There came a time, however, when he felt that at the centre of our national life,—the senate chamber at Washington,—he must meet and grapple with influences, fraught with deadly peril to his hopes. He accordingly consented to his nomination, was elected, and served out his term of six years. But he declined a reëlection, convinced that the calm voice of Truth could not be heard amid the discordant clamors of the selfish interests represented there. His last letter to his wife, from Washington, closed with the words, "Be brave and hopeful for me, my darling, for I have become a coward before the phantoms of the future."

And Augusta was strong, and brave, and hopeful, when Hugh returned to his home, relaxed and spiritless. There he soon grew strong again in the exercise of the Christian charities, to which he had devoted himself: "Work and wait," was his motto.

And now we will look once more upon St. Mary's, smiling in all the dewy freshness of the early spring. The Cherokee roses are again whitening the hedges, which a few weeks ago showed only the glossy green of their leaves; the jessamine is sending its flaunting tendrils into the window of that library which was once the scene of reunion between two hearts severed by treachery. There they sit —she in matronly beauty, undimmed as yet by advancing years, no thread of silver in the glossy black of her hair, no line of care upon her brow. Her lips have lost the haughty curve that sometimes marked them in earlier life. At this moment, however, the face is not quite serene.

Augusta is reading a newspaper which bears a foreign postmark. From this, and from the letters scattered on the table on which Hugh Moray writes, we augur that the semi-weekly mail has just come in. Suddenly Augusta lifts her eyes. They are sad, and some irrepressible emotion causes her lip to quiver and her voice to falter slightly as she exclaims, "Oh, Hugh! how unjust!"

"You are reading that review of 'Uncle Tom,' with its

unflattering portraiture of Southern planters," said Hugh, looking up with a smile.

"That they should think thus of you!" added Augusta, while her cheeks flushed and her eyes kindled as she contrasted the picture of the vulgar and beastly tyrant just presented to her, with the image enshrined so reverently in her heart.

"You know, love, there are two sides to every picture," said Hugh, still smiling, but with tender seriousness in his voice, as if he read her thoughts.

"True; and I thank God there are—that we are not obliged to see ourselves or each other as the false world sees us," answered Augusta, warmly.

"You are right, dear wife. The world's picture of us is seldom just; to look at it would either inflate us with vanity, or irritate us by a sense of wrong; we will turn from it, and try to see ourselves as God sees us; this will make us at once humble and hopeful."

In the quiet strength derived from this thought of a Divine Rectifier of all human judgments, we take leave of those whom we have followed thus far on the journey of life. There is little to fear for them while they thus draw their life from a heavenly source.

One parting word to the Reader. We have looked together on many pictures here, and have seen to each of them two aspects: the world's favorites have looked darkly to us when we viewed them on the reversed side, and some whom the world contemned have shown themselves to us as glorified by the light of truth, courage, and loyalty to their Master in heaven. What may be the world's portraiture of you, then, you may esteem as of little moment. It may be all fair and lovely, it may be all dark and hideous; it scarcely *can* be just. Look rather at that picture which conscience is making of you by successive touches, each day, each hour of your life. Let not self-love tone down its dark shadows, or delude you, by throwing her false and dazzling lights into the picture. Look on yourself truly, and it will help you to look on others charitably, and on God reverently.

THE END.

www.ingramcontent.com/pod-product-compliance
Lightning Source LLC
Chambersburg PA
CBHW051859300426
44117CB00006B/458